WORK BETTER LIVE BETTER

WORK BETTER LIVE BETTER

MOTIVATION, LABOR, AND MANAGEMENT IDEOLOGY

DAVID GRAY

University of Massachusetts Press
Amherst and Boston

Printed in the United States of America

ISBN 978-1-62534-534-9 (paper); 533-2 (hardcover)

Designed by Jen Jackowitz
Set in Minion Pro and Cache
Printed and bound by Books International, Inc.

Cover design by Frank Gutbrod
Cover art by Packer (poster artist), "*We're Ready for the Challenge Tomorrow, Let's do the Job Together!,*" ca. 1941–1945. Courtesy National Archives and Records Administration (NAID) 516115.

Library of Congress Cataloging-in-Publication Data

Names: Gray, David (Ph. D. in American Studies), author.
Title: Work better, live better : motivation, labor, and management ideology / David Gray.
Description: Amherst : University of Massachusetts Press, [2020] | Includes bibliographical references and index. |
Identifiers: LCCN 2020019274 | ISBN 9781625345332 (hardcover) | ISBN 9781625345349 (paperback) | ISBN 9781613767832 (ebook) | ISBN 9781613767849 (ebook)
Subjects: LCSH: Management—United States—Psychological aspects—History. States—Psychological aspects—History. | Psychology, Industrial—United States—History. | Success in business—United States—History.
Classification: LCC HD70.U5 G687 2020 | DDC 658.3/14—dc23
LC record available at https://lccn.loc.gov/2020019274

British Library Cataloguing-in-Publication Data
A catalog record for this book is available from the British Library.

A portion of chapter 2 was previously published as "Managing Motivation: The Seth Seiders Syndicate and the Motivational Publicity Business in the 1920s," *Winterthur Portfolio* 44, no. 1 (Spring 2010): 77–122. A portion of chapter 4 was previously published as "New Uses for Old Photos: Renovating FSA Photographs in World War II Posters," *American Studies* 47, no. 3 (2006): 5–34. Used by permission.

FOR SARAH

CONTENTS

PREFACE

Although this book centers on work and motivation in America, its inspiration reaches back to my preacademic life in northern England in the 1980s. At the core of the era's dominant political ideology—Thatcherism—was a relentless quest to transform how people thought about work and its rewards. Inspired by conservative free market theorists, Margaret Thatcher and her government focused much of their energy on dismantling the communitarian values that for years had underpinned attitudes about work. That goal was distilled in Thatcher's famous claim that "there is no such thing as society; there are only individuals and families." The Thatcher government's efforts to recast work in individualistic terms formed a major pillar of its larger mission to define market-based capitalism—or neoliberalism, as we now call this ideal—as the irrefutable core of modern life. Work, according to Thatcher, was a route to the entrepreneurial sense of self needed for the individual to flourish and succeed.

Years later, having embarked on an academic path in the United States, I began to research similar developments in American work ideology. The Reagan era, given its assault on the labor movement and endless assertions of work's individual rewards, seemed a logical entry point. Yet my interest in history drew me to the ideology's roots and longer-term trajectory. The massive propaganda campaigns of World War II, one of the twentieth century's most visible attempts to promote work's rewards, became a central focus in my research. What role did the U.S. government's wartime motivation efforts play in the larger ideological contestations around work and citizenship that took place between the Depression and the early Cold War era?

Once I began to dig into boxes in research archives across the country, however, a more layered history emerged. It revolved around not just propaganda but also the subjects that eventually became the focal points of this book—*motivation* and *motivational ideology*. Attempts to develop and use motivation involved not only designers and coordinators of propaganda but also a host of specialists in and on the fringes of the management community. Among them were industrial psychologists, economists, management theorists, business organizations, communications experts, human relations and employee relations professionals, independent vendors of motivational posters and films, and often managers and supervisors. Although these individuals did not necessarily know one another, they nonetheless participated in a collective enterprise, even a loosely knit motivational "movement" of sorts. While specialists' theories about workplace motivation were far from singular or unified, their goals invariably converged around the same impulse: to grease the wheels of management control in the factory by selling employees on work's rewards. The "motivational project," as I call this protracted quest, is this book's central focus.

As we will see, the motivational project has many strands, and tracing its emergence and development takes us into an array of histories—of work, management, propaganda, and communication techniques—and into various kinds of work ideology. Ultimately, this is a story about how managers and their ideological allies constructed managerial visions of work and its rewards and promoted them in efforts to extend their control over workers, diminish the labor movement, and further their own power. That quest, it turned out, was remarkably successful. Today, over a century after industrial psychologists and economists began to think seriously about how to exploit motivation in the workplace, and decades after the assaults on the labor movement ramped up in the 1980s, the managerial mission to sell work's promises and rewards is flourishing more than ever, albeit via techniques that are more extensive and sophisticated than those of the past.

The goal of this book is to provide an accounting of the emergence and historical development of motivational ideology in the workplace. But I hope that it can be just as useful in helping us understand the power of today's motivation ideologies. In an era when corporations and educational institutions continually cast work as a route to personal fulfillment, and when older rewards such as economic security and collective well-being have been eclipsed by managerial jargon about self-discovery through work, an assessment of motivational ideology and why it matters seems long overdue.

Tulsa, 2020

ACKNOWLEDGMENTS

I have incurred many debts while writing this book. My thanks to the hard-working archivists and curators at the Archives Center at the Smithsonian's National Museum of American History in Washington, D.C., who, during two summer-long research fellowships, were unflagging in their assistance. I am grateful to Harry Rubenstein, Larry Bird, and Peter Liebhold, who generously opened their research files to me, and to Craig Orr, who introduced me to the Sheldon-Claire Company Records and took me to one of the Smithsonian's off-site storage repositories for a daylong trawl through piles of posters under a suspended airplane. I also thank Kay Peterson, who fielded requests for image reproductions. My appreciation also goes out to Barbara Gilbert at the University of Chicago Special Collections for her assistance with my exploration of the Charles Rosenfeld Collection during several research visits and to Laura Alagna, who conducted additional searches of the collection.

Archivists at the Hagley Museum and Library in Wilmington, Delaware, aided my research into the National Association of Manufacturers collection during two residential fellowships. Thanks especially to Lucas Clawson and to Marge McNinch, as well as Roger Horowitz and Carol Lockman, who made my research and my monthlong stay at the Hagley's eighteenth-century blacksmith shop on the banks of the Brandywine Creek so rewarding. My gratitude to Patrizia Sione and Melissa Holland at the Kheel Center for Labor-Management Documentation and Archives at Cornell University who provided invaluable assistance during my research on General Motors. Thanks also to John Pollack and Eri Mizukane who offered equally vital help with my research into Lemuel Boulware and General Electric at the Kislak Center for Special Collections at the University of Pennsylvania. My appreciation to Chris Hunter at the Museum of Innovation and Science in Schenectady, New York, and Katie Levi at the Chicago History Museum for fielding requests for various documents, images, and permissions, and to the research librarians at the Library of Congress, Washington, D.C., who supplied images and fielded research queries. A big thank-you also to Rick Prelinger for generously obtaining frames of *From Dawn to Sunset* and to Jamie Edford for assistance managing some of the digitized images in chapter 4. I am grateful also to former motivational poster salesmen David Bernstein and the late Sheldon Shalett for supplying important insights into how Sheldon-Claire's poster campaigns were sold and implemented in the factory after World War II; the late Wanda Shalett for her recollections about her husband, Lew Shalett; and Sharon Rogers, who kindly shared memories about the work of her father, poster salesman Ralph Rogers.

I began this project in a highly supportive academic community—the American Studies Department at the University of Minnesota. The department provided a wonderful base from which to develop the research. I thank Thomas Augst, Paula Rabinowitz, Elaine Tyler May, and the late David Noble, all of whom were model mentors and unflagging supporters of my work. I am especially grateful to Lary May, whose mentorship was integral in getting the project off the ground and shaping its development. I hope I came through on his advice not to lose sight of the "big picture." Thanks also to Jennifer Pierce and Dave Roediger, whose teachings helped shape some of the core ideas in the early stages. Many friends provided critical readings of early versions of the chapters that follow. I thank Megan Feeney, Mary Rizzo, Jennifer Gowen, Scott Laderman, Melissa Williams, Sharon Leon, Stephen Young, Yuka Tsuchiya, Mary Strunk, Dave Monteyne, Jason Stahl, Jeff Manuel, and others who participated in the Mays' writing group during my years in Minnesota. My appreciation also to Amy Tyson, Jennifer Beckham, Adam Barrows, Marie-Therese Sulit, Julia Bleakney, Dave Wehner, Melanie Brown, Ebony Adams, David Slater, and Dorthe Trofen for their insightful feedback. I also thank Jonathan Munby for setting me on my early academic path at Lancaster University before I hauled my life off to Minnesota.

My sincere thanks go to Liam Kennedy and Catherine Carey at the Clinton Institute for American Studies at University College Dublin, both of whom provided fabulous support and friendship during a yearlong fellowship in 2007–8, and to the members of the institute's writing group that I and fellow scholars founded that year. Thanks especially to Madeleine Lyes, Marisa Ronan, Barry Shanahan, and Wendy Ward for their insightful critiques on my work and their camaraderie that year. While at the Clinton Institute, I had the opportunity to organize a conference that brought together academics from around the world to discuss their research on work and emotion. The conference supplied opportunities to develop some of the book's core ideas. My everlasting gratitude goes out to Jacqueline O'Reilly, Alan McCoy, and wee Maitiu for showing me the beauty of Irish hospitality that year. I also thank the American Studies Program at the University of California–Davis, which supplied employment in slightly warmer climes in 2008–9, as well as Laura Grindstaff, Ryken Grattet, and the delightful Chella for taking me into their home, lending me a bike, and allowing me to live in Davis on the cheap.

Feedback at talks at various conferences and workshops was helpful in shaping the book's arguments. Particularly useful were presentations at the Department of Work and Organization at the University of Minnesota's Carlson School of Management hosted by John Budd in 2006; the Business History Conference in Columbus, Ohio, in 2013; the Hagley Museum and Library's public lecture series hosted by Roger Horowitz in 2014; and Lancaster University's Management School hosted by Bogdan Costea in 2017, who, along with his colleagues Kostas Amiridis and Norman Crump, offered insightful critiques. I also thank Neil Wilson for his perceptive feedback at the latter event and for his insights in our subsequent conversations at the Storey Institute about managerial ideologies, work, and the happiness industry.

Two of the book's chapters include significantly revised material from academic journal articles. Part of chapter 2 appeared in longer form as "Managing Motivation: The Seth Seiders Syndicate and the Motivational Publicity Business in the 1920s," *Winterthur Portfolio* 44, no. 1 (Spring 2010), and a section of chapter 4 appeared as "New Uses for Old Photos: Renovating FSA Photographs in World War II Posters," *American Studies* 47, no. 3 (2006). Thanks to Amy Earls at *Winterthur Portfolio* and Sherrie Tucker at

American Studies for granting permission to include the respective article pieces in revised form here.

Over the last decade I have had the good fortune to work with wonderful colleagues in the American Studies Program at Oklahoma State University. I thank Laura Belmonte, Stacy Takacs, and John Kinder for their invaluable collegiality. Thank you John for being the best writing partner I could have hoped for and for never letting anything slide, and Stacy for your insightful critiques of several chapters and vital technological savvy with digital images at the eleventh hour. Thanks also to Andrew Rosa for your helpful feedback on several chapters. I am grateful as well for research funding from the American Studies Program, without which this book would have only three chapters. My appreciation goes out as well to the History Department, especially to Susan Oliver for her work on acquiring many of the book's images, and to the hardworking librarians at OSU-Tulsa for their diligent research assistance. Friends beyond OSU have also offered invaluable support. Thanks to Cheryl K (she knows why) and to Andrew Grant Wood for his friendship, his critiques in the latter stages of the project, and sharing his wonderful family with me. Friends in England have supplied much moral support during my lengthy absence. Thank you especially to my dear friends, Jon Carter and Jenny Atkinson, for your friendship from afar and during my visits home to Lancaster over the years and for helping me maintain my connections to the city of my youth.

My editor at University of Massachusetts Press, Matt Becker, and production editor Rachael DeShano made the publishing process a pleasure. Thanks to you both for shepherding the project from the manuscript to the book so supportively. I hope that I delivered on Matt's advice to avoid excessive endnotes. My eternal gratitude goes out to Nancy Raynor, whose copyediting skills improved the book immensely. Any mistakes are mine, of course. Thanks as well to Sally Nichols for her work on the book's production and design, not least its illustrations, and to Frank Gutbrod for the terrific cover design. My appreciation goes out also to UMP's director, Mary Dougherty, for backing the book's publication and to Courtney Andree for her work on marketing it. I also give my sincere thanks the two anonymous readers whose insightful critiques of the manuscript helped me sharpen the book's ideas and arguments.

My biggest debt of gratitude is reserved for Sarah McKemie, whose love and patience sustained me throughout the project. I'm no longer mad about you bursting in and interrupting all those times while I was trying to write my "little book report." I also appreciate that you figured out some sneaky ways to motivate me that did not feel like the manipulative techniques I discuss in the book (but that were no less effective in motivating me to get the work done). Your love, laughter, and wisdom continue to nourish me.

WORK BETTER LIVE BETTER

INTRODUCTION

In the United States, a motivated attitude is often characterized as a requirement for existence. Tributes to motivation are all around us. Posters exhorting motivational sentiments are ubiquitous on the walls of workplaces, billboards touting similar messages line our highways, and motivation-themed videos receive millions of hits online. Bookstores dedicate ever-expanding shelf space to motivational literature, while Get Motivated! seminars have enticed hundreds of thousands of Americans to listen to speakers sermonize about how to achieve financial success and happiness. Fueled by a self-improvement industry that is projected to grow to nearly $14 billion by 2023, motivational aphorisms—"determination," "perseverance," "achievement," and so on—have become an unofficial national language. Such sentiments pervade the spiel of daytime talk show hosts and internet self-help gurus who posit motivation as a solution to everything from family disputes to low self-image, career failure to cancer and infectious diseases.[1]

Motivation has always been linked especially to *work*. Exponents of moral authority in America have long touted the virtues of cultivating a motivated attitude toward productive labor. The belief that the United States possesses an exceptional capacity for motivated work has been upheld as decisive in the nation's triumph over adversity in the Great Depression and World War II. Likewise, the nation's rapid economic growth and rise to global dominance during the Cold War era were interwoven with bold assertions about the supremacy of the American work ethic.[2] This faith in Americans' aptitude for motivation is embodied in many of the iconic images that shape collective memory. Photographs portraying gritty common men and women striving for a better life during the Depression; Rosie the Riveter's (now endlessly mimicked) "We Can Do It" pose from a World War II poster; and advertisements and films depicting workers reaping the rewards of the "American way of life" in the postwar era: these and other images have helped sustain a seductive story about a people united in their belief in the virtues of a motivated attitude toward work.

Although a strong work ethic has long been central to perceptions of American life, in reality, the idea that motivation is virtuous and that we should devote ourselves to it is the result of a lengthy and determined crusade to sell us on work's rewards. The roots of this effort took shape in the "gospel of work" literature of the nineteenth century. Such bestsellers as Samuel Smiles's *Self-Help* (1860) and Andrew Carnegie's *The Gospel of Wealth* (1899) asserted an idea that later became the unifying principle in the concept of motivation: by believing in the character-building properties of diligent labor and adhering to a strong work ethic, one could achieve a more fulfilling life. Throughout the Gilded Age, exponents of the gospel of work espoused the virtues of competitiveness, an ideal drawn from the Darwinist theories ascendant during the era. Their rhetoric laid foundations for the assertions about work's rewards that proliferated in the twentieth century. From Elbert Hubbard's 1899 inspirational essay "A Message to Garcia," which was issued to millions of workers over the next two decades, to the propaganda disseminated during the world wars and the Cold War era, and to today's self-help books, disciples of the work ethic have long preached that a motivated attitude will yield economic and psychological benefits.[3]

Despite these claims, the goal of motivation's devotees has always been to render workers more acquiescent to management control and, in turn, to allow management greater leverage to impose its will. Whether couching their assertions in patriotic sentiment, calls for teamwork, or promises of economic or psychological rewards for workers, their goal has been to grease the wheels of the organization by encouraging workers to adopt a managerial perspective. The concept of motivation, steeped in assertions about to the meritocratic nature of the industrial system and the freedom-granting qualities of capitalism, offered managers a powerful instrument through which to craft their visions of the ideals to which workers should ascribe (figure 0.1).

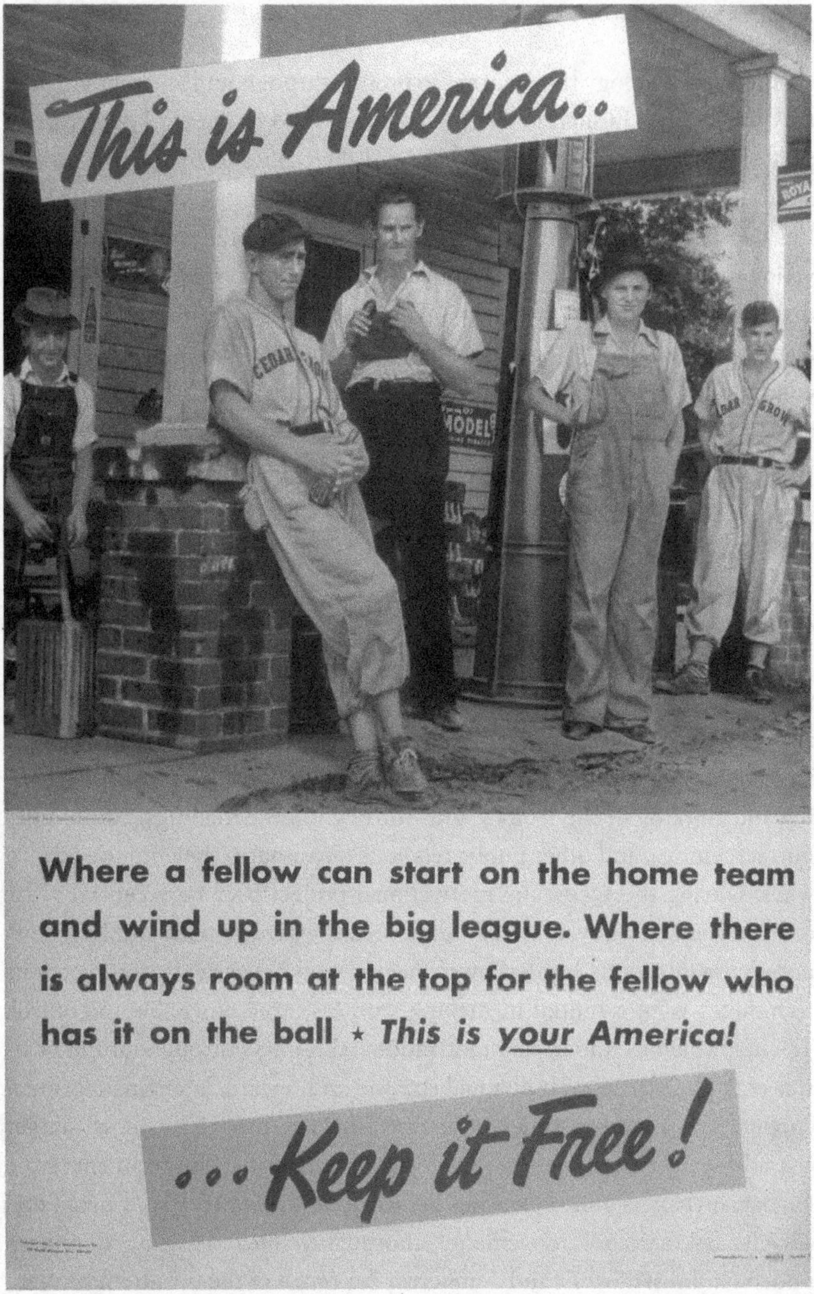

FIGURE 0.1. Posters like this one, created by the Sheldon-Claire Company during World War II, played on a long-held parable in which Americans, by believing in the work ethic and adopting a motivated disposition, could gain entrée to the rewards of meritocratic capitalism. Sheldon-Claire Company Records, 1942. Archives Center, National Museum of American History, Smithsonian Institution, Washington, D.C.

The work ideology that became so prolific throughout the twentieth century was neither limited to rhetoric nor restricted to the workplace. It was part of a broader effort by managers and their allies to realize the powers associated with the concept of motivation. The *motivational project*, as I call this quest, serves as the focus of this book. Although the roots of the motivational project reach back to the gospel of work, it began to cohere as a distinct undertaking in management around 1910. From this point forward, a growing cadre of specialists—industrial social scientists, economists, communications experts, and management theorists, among others—came to regard the then-emerging concept of "motives" as a valuable tool in management's perpetual quest to make workers more productive and acquiescent. These specialists pushed back against the prevailing belief that workers' attitudes and behaviors were determined by economic incentives, emphasizing instead the role of instincts (whether innate or learned) and emotions, arguments that drew in part on Freud's writings.[4]

Galvanized by World War I, specialists honed modern communications techniques, including booklets, poster campaigns, film screenings, and speeches. For decades to come, these and other media provided a wide-ranging apparatus for advancing managerial visions of work's meaning and rewards in the factory and—through home mailings, community film screenings, and other public relations techniques—beyond the factory walls. During the 1950s, the motivational project became a central pillar of management, buoyed by the human relations movement and large corporate organizations headed by managers who believed communications techniques were essential in making workers more amenable to control. The main themes underlying motivational discourse throughout the postwar era—the virtues of individual striving and reward, labor-management cooperation, and consumer-capitalism—helped propel business's larger crusade against labor and the New Deal. In infusing such sentiment in the factory, managers and their allies helped pave the way for later neoliberal assaults on the labor movement.[5] Thoroughly integrated into dominant understandings of work and democracy for much of the twentieth century, motivational rhetoric formed part of the foundation of American capitalism's ideology of individual striving.

This book charts the motivational project from the early twentieth century to its apex in the early Cold War era before tracing its development into our own day. The discussion centers mainly on the factory but also moves beyond its walls as we explore specialists' efforts to advance work ideology in the public sphere. The first part of the book's title, *Work Better, Live Better*, taken from the name of a 1955 workplace poster (figure 6.7), reflects the central idea associated with motivation during the twentieth century: by embracing work's promises as defined by employers (or the specialists who developed the messaging), workers would enjoy a more rewarding life. Motivational propaganda is today largely associated with wartime. Yet, from World War I onward, it was a constant presence in the workplace during war *and* peace. As we shall see, it was shaped by numerous individuals and organizations, many of whom had different aims, and it therefore took on various forms. In its array of expressions, motivation became an indispensable weapon through which management asserted control over workers and shored up their own power.

MOTIVATION AND MANAGEMENT POWER

Throughout the period examined in this book, managers modified their approach to disciplining workers as new theories about motivation emerged. Until World War I, managers generally believed that the worker's productivity was determined by economic incentives, a view that informed scientific management. Its proponents believed that calibrating workers' bodies and their physical actions with the machinery of production would incentivize them to work faster because of the prospect of earning higher wages. However, as psychologists' theories about human agency gained influence, managers gradually came to believe that the worker's mind, not the body, was a more direct route for establishing control. This belief was pivotal in galvanizing managerial interest in psychological-based motivation for decades to come.[6]

One of the major developments to emerge in the wake of this shift was that managers began to deploy images far more extensively in their communications techniques. Like many businessmen, managers had traditionally shunned images, believing that appeals to viewers' emotions embodied "irrational" impulses. However, encouraged by the influence of advertising and the visual education movement, each of which flourished in the early twentieth century, managers eventually came to see practical value in images. Posters, films, image-laden booklets, and other visual communication forms, they realized, could help promote "good" attitudes and behaviors via either reason- or emotion-based appeals. Low literacy rates among the largely immigrant industrial workforce, coupled with the elitist perceptions among many businessmen and managers that immigrant workers were captivated by visual images, opened the door for an influx of visual communications into the factory.[7]

As this book shows, motivational rhetoric proved to be a powerful apparatus for advancing the ideological ambitions of managers, businessmen, and their allies during their lengthy campaigns for authority. After World War II, communications specialists in industry couched their workplace motivational messaging within the creeds of the "consensus" ideology that permeated American life throughout the postwar era. As well as promoting consumption and anticommunism, consensus ideology was, at its core, concerned with expunging class from American life. As journalist Godfrey Hodgson notes, "No tenet of the consensus was more widely held than the idea that revolutionary American capitalism had abolished the working class or . . . that everybody in America was middle class now or that American society was rapidly approaching economic equality."[8] Directly and indirectly, this effort to erase the specter of class became the central logic of management's efforts to exploit motivation after the war. Management specialists at such large corporations as General Motors and General Electric arrived at a slick synthesis of psychological and economic motivation. Their employee communications campaigns blended the emotionally manipulative capacities of images with a finely tuned use of rhetoric extolling the virtues of the free market and the dangers of government and labor union influence. By infusing the factory with such sentiment, corporate managers found a means to counter the more class- and communitarian-based motivational sentiment voiced by labor unions and to weaken the effects of the New Deal liberalism in industry. Aided by communications specialists, managers also extended their motivational rhetoric into the culture at large, blending it with sophisticated public relations (PR) and advertising techniques that portrayed a rising consumer-based standard of living as the reward for workers who embraced managerial ideals.

While motivational rhetoric was invoked primarily in efforts to prevail over class tensions in industry, it was from the outset steeped in assumptions about race and gender. Many of the management specialists who first brought attention to motivation in the 1910s characterized immigrant workers and workers of color as "maladjusted." They claimed that "foreign" and nonwhite workers were prone to acting on instinct rather than reason and sought out the camaraderie of the irrational "herd" instead of aspiring to individualism. Specialists believed that motivation, rooted as it was in prized Anglo-Saxon virtues of self-discipline and personal ambition, could be a powerful salve for these perceived problems. This linkage between motivation and the civilizing effects of Anglo-Saxonism reinforced assumptions that the white worker was the natural embodiment of motivated labor. Such beliefs endured in motivational rhetoric for decades to come. Even as racial segregation in the factory was outlawed through legislation during World War II, managers continued to assume that motivation could most effectively be conveyed through images of white—and usually male—labor. Such thinking explains why such a large proportion of work motivation publicity produced throughout the twentieth century deployed such depictions, including the poster on the cover of this book, which was distributed by the federal government's Office for Emergency Management during World War II. This tendency endured well into the postwar era in employee communications campaigns waged by industrial corporations that emphasized work's consumer-based rewards. While framing motivated work as white and male, the specialists who designed these campaigns habitually depicted women as homemakers and consumers despite the fact that many women were engaged in paid labor. This practice reflected the demographic makeup of the field of industrial communications, which was largely male.[9]

For many managers, the concept of motivation was advantageous because it provided a means to disassociate themselves from the coercive connotations of propaganda. After World War I, "propaganda" became a byword for manipulative misinformation and outright lies as many Americans came to view the war as a "racket" spurred by greedy munitions makers and power-hungry politicians.[10] Interest in motivation gathered steam in the 1930s in the wake of the influential human relations research in industry by Elton Mayo and his Harvard colleagues. Steeped in the therapeutic language of social psychology and espousing a commitment to improving workers' mental health and morale, motivation helped managers define themselves as agents of workers' well-being even as in reality they became more dogged in their efforts to perfect discipline and control in the factory.

Although motivational rhetoric has not been examined extensively, several historians have addressed business leaders' efforts to advance their agendas through communication techniques during the period explored in this book. Motivational rhetoric paralleled corporate public relations, which, by promoting images of businesses as benevolent, helped big business acquire a sense of what historian Roland Marchand calls "corporate soul" during the early twentieth century. Elizabeth Fones-Wolf's book *Selling Free Enterprise* demonstrates that in the post–World War II era, corporations and business organizations like the National Association of Manufacturers used communications techniques to powerful effect in their mission to weaken the labor movement and the New Deal. More recently, Kim Phillips-Fein has extended this line of analysis by linking businessmen's crusade against the New Deal to the revival of conservatism. *Work Better, Live Better* explores similar terrain to these studies but brings to the table a different set of insights, revealing that the struggles for power by managers and businessmen relied not only on partisan political campaigns but also a protracted use of motivation in the workplace aimed at anchoring work's meanings and rewards in a classless ideal. Moreover, it shows that propaganda campaigns were but one part of a larger ideological apparatus used by management beyond the workplace: the motivational project. Spilling into industrial social science, economic and labor policy, positive-thinking literature, and corporate public relations, motivation was an amorphous idea with surprisingly wide influence.[11]

As the preceding discussion suggests, this book operates from the stance that management's investments in motivation are purely concerned with controlling the prevailing definitions of work and its rewards so that it can extend its dominion over workers and subject them to its desired production regimens with greater agility. Sometimes these objectives involved speeding up production for the nation's military victory, as during the world wars, or to boost the firm's competitiveness. Yet while motivation is always presented as being in the worker's own interest, it was and still is an instrument designed to help management achieve its principal goals—higher productivity and profit. Born at the dawn of the industrial revolution as a way to "manage men," management practice focused increasingly on making workers more acquiescent. The motivational project became a powerful means for advancing this goal, a reality that today is largely obscured by claims about the personal rewards and sense of empowerment that work provides. As Miya Tokumitsu has detailed, such ideals have recently been given new life through the "do what you love" mantra that many employers tout when urging us to pursue "meaningful" (and often poorly compensated) work.[12] In tracing the rise and development of the motivational project in industry, this book shows how management consolidated its authority through image and word and how the motivational idioms that saturate the workplace and much of public life today came into being. The motivational project provides, in other words, a roadmap for understanding the roots of the motivation-infused culture that continues to bombard us with illusory promises about work.

ACCOUNTING FOR MOTIVATIONAL RHETORIC

My goal in using the term "motivational rhetoric" throughout this book is twofold. First, it serves as a catchall for the many ways in which managers and various specialists in industry used communications techniques in efforts to make workers more amenable to their objectives within the broader scope of the motivational project. Second, I invoke the term to emphasize that the many forms of publicity disseminated in the workplace were components of a larger apparatus. While the rhetoric was not singular and its forms and sentiments fluctuated over time, its core ideas and goals remained quite consistent. Its devotees were principally interested in helping management instill work discipline, boost productivity, and firm up its control. They always hoped that motivation would result in workers' identification with the ideals promoted, but controlling the official definitions of work's rewards usually took precedence.

Although this is a cultural history, my discussion is informed partly by theories about how power relations are influenced by the control of language or discourse. I draw inspiration especially from historian Michel Foucault's writings. Foucault argues that discourse plays a decisive role in how such organizations as prisons, schools, hospitals, the military, and government agencies govern their subjects and, in turn, how power relations are constituted in those organizations. Foucault was not himself especially focused on the workplace, but analysts of organizations have since extended his arguments to the workplace and to management, though usually with a contemporary rather than historical focus. In tracing the decades-long efforts by managers and their allies to better govern workers through motivational discourse, this book contributes fresh insights into power relations in the factory. A key insight offered by Foucault and those who draw on his theories is that, in Western liberal democracies like the United States, subjects are disciplined and controlled not by restraining their freedoms, as was once believed, but by defining them and addressing them as autonomous individuals. Motivational discourse, I argue, acted precisely in this manner. Couching communications with workers in a language of empowerment—for example, in posters and films that expressed an investment in workers' emotional needs, psychological well-being, and standard of living—allowed managers to obscure their efforts to instill discipline and shore up their own power. Because the concept of motivation was steeped in democratic-sounding sentiments about the virtuousness of work, managers could claim that their messages were in keeping with traditional American work ideals. The task of governing workers could be achieved more easily, they believed, if they emphasized the freedom-granting properties of motivated labor.[13]

Motivation has always been a means to regulate the emotional dimensions of work and, in particular, workers' *affects*—their outward displays of emotions. Industrial social scientists initially became interested in emotional conditioning because they thought it to be a useful tool for combating group solidarity. They believed that the "group mind" was dangerous, being rooted in the irrational instincts and emotions of the masses. Such concerns paradoxically prompted managers to deploy emotion-laden messaging in efforts to channel workers' affects in what they regarded as more "constructive" ways. Drawing from the techniques of advertising, managers and their allies could use motivational publicity to frame ideas in emotional terms, emphasizing the psychological and material rewards available if employees adhered to the visions of work presented.[14]

Posters, films, pamphlets, speeches and other forms of management communications are usually associated with wartime propaganda. The field of propaganda emerged during World War I. The Creel Committee, the government agency chiefly responsible for disseminating such information, waged a massive campaign aimed at selling Americans on the merits of U.S.

involvement in the war and urging them to throw their support behind industrial production.[15] My analysis of motivation involves discussions of wartime propaganda, but I employ a broader lens than is available when we employ the now familiar emphasis on propaganda's powers of "persuasion." Instead, I draw on propaganda theorist Jacques Ellul's concept of "sociological propaganda." Ellul argues that, whereas political propaganda aims to instill in the service of a specific goal, often by attempting to convince its audience, sociological propaganda taps dominant societal myths and trains individuals to adopt not only beliefs but also new behaviors, largely through an unconscious process. In this way, sociological propaganda acts as a form of social conditioning and paves the way for conformity on a large scale. Sociological propaganda, Ellul adds, is espoused continuously through channels that are not typically perceived as propaganda, such as advertising, public relations, and human relations, and via such methods acclimatizes us to new perceptions and circumstances indirectly regardless of the degree to which we identify consciously with the ideas presented.[16]

Motivational rhetoric was informed not only by the field of propaganda, but also by advertising and salesmanship, each of which absorbed Freudian ideas in the 1910s and 1920s. Vendors of motivational posters and other publicity, most of whom were centered in Chicago, a major hub of the advertising industry, presented their product as a form of advertising for the factory. The owners of these firms and many of their copywriters, artists, and sales managers had formerly worked in advertising and drew heavily on its conventions. Similarly, managers, when administering motivational poster campaigns or film screenings in the factory, approached these tasks in the manner of advertisers, pitching and merchandising their ideas to their "customers"—workers. Like advertisers, producers of motivation drew on the concept of *visualization*, which was premised on the belief that images, being steeped in emotion, influenced viewers' behaviors subconsciously via a process of suggestion regardless of what they "thought" about them. From World War I onward, propaganda experts and vendors of employee educational films used this principle to promote their claims about work's rewards to factory employees.[17]

Ironically, after World War II, as management specialists developed more systematic techniques for regulating emotions, scholars who studied work and organizations—mainly social scientists at this time—became *less* attentive to emotion in the workplace. As Helena Flamm notes, at the center of postwar social science was a belief that emotions were nebulous and thus not amenable to rational scientific study. This declining attention to emotions is ironic given that some of the era's major studies of organizational life—including C. Wright Mills's *White Collar*, David Riesman's *The Lonely Crowd*, and William H. Whyte's *The Organization Man*—emphasized that regulating emotions was central to management techniques. Paradoxically, then, social scientists who wrote about work soured on studying emotions at the very moment when managers were beginning to more fully exploit and master the art of emotional conditioning in industry.[18] Until quite recently, historians of work and the workplace have been just as disinclined to examine management efforts to manipulate emotion in the workplace. According to the empirical tenets that traditionally informed labor history, emotions were considered too amorphous to be subjected to scholarly scrutiny, which also applied to discourse. Due to these views, as well as a longstanding respect for workers' agency, labor historians have dwelled little on management efforts to shape workers' minds through propaganda and other communication forms.[19]

Since the 1980s, social scientists have shown that emotional conditioning is a core part of management's strategy for achieving discipline and control. In the wake of the publication of Arlie Hochschild's 1983 book, *The Managed Heart: Commercialization of Human Feeling*, social scientists brought emotions to the center of studies of work. Today, little doubt exists that what Hochschild famously termed, "emotional labor" is a core component of work.[20] Moreover, emotional conditioning, touted by industrial psychologists since World War I, is widely recognized by managers as a basic function of management. Aided by a growing array of consultants, managers today deploy an abundance of emotion-based techniques aimed at inducing habits and conduct that make workers more acquiescent to management control. Increasingly, these techniques focus on shaping behaviors via modifications of the workplace's aesthetic and sensory dimensions. Gamification—the use of digital and Web-based games to increase employees' productivity—is just the latest manifestation of management's quest to hone motivational tools that center on emotional conditioning.[21]

In this book, I argue that management's use of motivational discourse in the twentieth-century factory, though not as sophisticated as it is today, was no less consequential. Tracing the motivational project—bringing to bare on the history of work what the sociologist Simon Williams calls the "secret history" of emotions—is an important task if historians are to account for how managerial ideologies shaped the course of industrial modernity.[22] This task is all the more pressing given that, for years, management specialists in business and academia, as well as management consultants, have been working ceaselessly to advance employers' holy grail—to make motivation more effective and thus render workers more acquiescent to management's goals.

As should be clear, the main characters in this story are managers and their allies (industrial social scientists, management theorists, and suppliers of motivational posters and other communications). Although the goal of motivational communications was in part to indoctrinate workers, managers and management specialists made relatively few efforts to assess workers' perceptions of or reactions to them, and such efforts were usually fleeting and inconclusive. The absence of such assessments may appear strange, but it reflected practices used in many other communications fields. Much like advertising and PR specialists, devotees of motivation did not believe it necessary to *prove* that posters, films, literature, and other communication mediums had their intended effects on workers. Taking cues from the well-established influence of advertising in the culture at large, they believed that exposing workers to modern communications techniques was a self-evidently useful enterprise. Like human resources specialists in large organizations today, they mostly assumed that workers' habits and dispositions could be improved without conscious acceptance of messages.[23] After World War II, large corporations like General Motors and General Electric *did* begin to solicit workers' feelings about their jobs in a more methodical way, often using the resulting surveys as evidence of the company's goodwill toward workers and vice versa. Where available, I discuss these materials, but I read them not as insights into how workers truly felt or how they reacted to management messaging but for what they are—components of management's communications arsenal.

In exploring the managerial quest to exploit motivation, we must put aside any assumption that workers were impervious to the emotion-laden messaging used in the factory. As Ellul observed pointedly in 1965, American social scientists were resistant to believing "that the individual—that cornerstone of democracy—can be so fragile" as to be influenced by propaganda, a view that led them to disregard propaganda as a subject of analysis.[24] This book rubs against the grain of the tendency that Ellul pointed to. By detailing the role of the motivational project in managers' efforts to control workers and shore up their own power, it aims to stir further consideration of managerial uses of motivation past and present.

ORGANIZATION AND GOALS

The book's discussion proceeds chronologically, tracking the development of the motivational project and motivational rhetoric throughout their key stages of formation. Most chapters trace changing understandings of motivation among management specialists, businessmen, and managers before turning attention to the use of messaging in the workplace. To minimize repetition, I sometimes use the term "motivational discourse," "motivational sentiment" or just "motivation," but I always have in mind the ideology described above.

The first two chapters examine the rise of motivation as an influential idea in management thought and the industrial arena from the turn of the nineteenth century through the 1920s. Three developments were integral to the growing interest in motivation among managers: the ideas of such businessmen as Elbert Hubbard that emphasized the value of employee communications publicity; the influence of industrial social science, which, via its growing interest in psychology and the "mind" of the worker, stressed the link between instinctive drives and productivity; and the increasing use of motivational films, posters, and other visual media in the factory. Although their efforts to deploy such media were initially stymied by their elitist assumptions about workers, communications specialists and managers learned to deploy emotion-based messaging and thus laid groundwork for later efforts to craft motivational ideology.

Changes in motivational discourse during the Depression and World War II comprise the focus of chapters 3 and 4. Amid the mass unemployment of the Depression, politicians, businessmen, and management specialists turned to motivation as a way to promote faith in the system. Elton Mayo and other human relations specialists advanced the insight that emotion was central to motivation in the workplace. The New Deal brought motivational sentiment to the center of public life in the form of political oratory and photographs of rural Americans striving to survive the dust bowl. The realities of the Depression prompted industrial leaders to abandon the appeals to individualism that dominated in the 1920s in favor of emotion-based appeals to groups, a tendency reflected in the culture at large, not least in popular films. The challenges of the Depression and the war allowed designers of motivational media to define their messages as vital to the attainment of higher productivity and American victory. The mobilization of millions of industrial workers during the war prompted motivational propagandists to pioneer more sophisticated approaches to design. Most consequentially, they used advertising techniques to link the rewards of war work to postwar consumption, an approach that helped management promote its image as an agent of workers' economic progress.

In chapters 5 and 6 I chart the deepening influence of the motivational project in the postwar era, a process that culminated in the early 1960s. During this period, motivation outgrew its earlier functions as a tool for increasing discipline. While it continued those functions, it also expanded to encompass a larger framework for translating the ideas of postwar consensus policies that emphasized consumption as a salve to class conflict. In the workplace—and increasingly beyond the workplace via corporate PR campaigns and Cold War discourse—motivational sentiment became fused with the rhetoric about the superior virtues of the "American way of life" familiar to mainstream advertising. Motivation also emerged as a thriving field of research at large corporations where management specialists promoted Cold War ideologies emphasizing labor-management cooperation and consumer-based rewards. Many smaller employers, meanwhile, turned to the expertise of motivational publicity firms, which supplied them with posters and literature. At large and small firms alike, the result was a new regimen of highly orchestrated, image-driven campaigns that touted the rewards that workers and their families would receive if embracing the ideal of labor-management cooperation. The Cold War's antilabor and anti–New Deal credos, meanwhile, lent the disciples of motivation further leverage in their crusade to define America as a "classless" nation.

In tracking the development and uses of the amorphous discourse of motivation from the turn of the nineteenth century through the early Cold War era, this book provides a historical framework for analyzing one of the most ubiquitous yet underanalyzed ideologies of industrial modernity. I argue that motivation became entrenched not because it is a natural outgrowth of work but because motivational sentiment in its array of forms was designed, sold, and proselytized with determination and, at times, evangelical zeal.

As I detail in the epilogue, the motivational ideology that was used to sell work's rewards in the twentieth-century factory laid foundations for management's more recent motivational efforts. The motivational rhetoric familiar to the workplace today has mostly abandoned the emphasis on work's long-term economic and material rewards that characterized its twentieth-century iterations. Since the 1980s and 1990s, motivational sentiment has been more apt to espouse ideals such as personal empowerment and self-discovery, which help shore up neoliberal management ideals. Tributes to inspirational living and work's capacity to deliver individual fulfillment have thus replaced economic rewards in work motivation. Even so, today's rhetoric bears the indelible stamp of the twentieth-century motivational project. The long-touted managerial promise that this book examines—"work better, live better"—remains as powerful as ever.

This book examines motivation as a broad field of endeavor whose development has been shaped by numerous individuals and organizations. Understanding its development sometimes requires us to take what may at first blush feel like a detour but that is, in fact, an essential part of the task at hand. Motivation cannot be understood sufficiently if we look only to its raw materials—posters, films, speeches, and other propaganda forms. As we shall see, it was and still is the product of a great deal of activity by specialists both in and outside the workplace. For this reason, the forthcoming chapters often center on the work of industrial social scientists, management experts, and other specialists who left their mark on the motivational project. Also at the heart of the story in two chapters are the owners of poster companies and the "foot soldiers" of motivation—the salesmen who sold their products across the country. These men (their employers only employed men, echoing the traditionally male-dominated nature of traveling sales work) pitched poster campaigns to managers in their territories across the country. I examine their activities, including their sales techniques and their interactions with managers and supervisors, because their work was pivotal to the proliferation of motivational campaigns at industrial firms and thus to the deepening reach of the motivational project.

For some, the fact that employers try to make us work harder in exchange for rewards might not seem especially troubling. After all, what's so wrong about feeling good, even enthusiastic, about our work? This may seem reasonable enough, especially when we consider that one of the most pressing problems throughout the history of work is that people have too frequently been compelled by circumstances beyond their control to perform jobs that leave them feeling unappreciated or exploited. Yet while workers generally desire meaningful and rewarding work, motivation always has strings attached. Motivation is transactional, and what workers have received from the transaction has historically been far less than what management has reaped. This was as true for workers in the industrial workplace of the twentieth century as it is for those in the service, healthcare, or educational workplace today.

Motivational ideology is amorphous. Its power derives from its similarities to other widely espoused ideals associated with American capitalism, such as individualism, consumer-based prosperity, and personal fulfillment, each of which have at particular times provided fodder for management's motivational techniques in the workplace. To grasp the ideology's implications, we must abandon the belief that we already know what there is to know about motivation. This book shows that, far from being limited to wartime or the workplace, the motivational project was a powerful force throughout the course of industrial modernity, inside the factory and beyond the factory walls. Only by tracing its roots and development over time can we understand how managers and others who sought to grease the wheels of organizational life reframed work's meanings and rewards and, in the process, advanced their quests for control.

CHAPTER 1

Motivation, Management, and Industrial Modernity

> Emotions may be conditions of stimulation or interference, and no one ought to underestimate the importance of higher motives, intellectual, aesthetic, and moral motives, in their bearing on the psychological impulses of the laborer.
>
> —Hugo Münsterberg, *Psychology and Industrial Efficiency*, 1913

In 1899, Elbert Hubbard, the business writer and founder of the Roycroft arts and crafts society in East Aurora, New York, penned a brief inspirational essay that, to his surprise, would become an overnight sensation and go on to be a model for much of the publicity that employers used in efforts to motivate workers during the next two decades. Although the word "motivation" was little used at this juncture, the essay's wide circulation and enthusiastic reception among businessmen suggested that communications media could play a powerful role in promoting work discipline.

The essay appeared in the March issue of Hubbard's "little magazine" of business, the *Philistine*, which had around one hundred thousand readers, most of whom were businessmen and admirers of Hubbard's tributes to bootstrap individualism. It took the form of a tribute to Lieutenant Rowan, the soldier whose actions in the Spanish-American War the previous year were widely reported to have been decisive to the war's outcome. In the much-celebrated incident, Rowan was tasked with delivering a message from President McKinley to General Calixto García, the leader of the Cuban insurrection against Spain, a mission that he performed dutifully, securing the alliance that McKinley desired and aiding the American victory over Spain in the process.

Hubbard contrasted Rowan's dedication to the job at hand with the attitude of the era's workers, who, he scoffed, were sorely lacking in such qualities. Rowan "took the letter and did not ask, 'Where is he at?'" Instead, after being dropped off the coast of Cuba, he "strapped it over his heart" and "traversed a hostile country on foot" for three weeks before delivering the letter. "By the Eternal!" Hubbard exclaimed in admiration, "there is a man whose form should be cast in deathless bronze and the statue placed in every college of the land. It is not book-learning young men need, nor instruction about this and that, but a stiffening of the vertebrae which will cause them to be loyal to a trust, to act promptly, concentrate their energies: do the thing—'Carry a message to Garcia!' Hubbard added ruefully, however, that Rowan's single-minded commitment to the job was all too rare in the nation's workplaces where "slipshod assistance, foolish inattention, dowdy indifference, and half-hearted work seem the rule." These unmotivated work habits were, he added, regrettably familiar to the nation's employers, the unsung "other Garcias," who spent their days struggling to get their workers in line but were "well-nigh appalled at times by the imbecility of the average man—the inability or unwillingness to concentrate on a thing and do it."[1]

The essay's stark contrast between the resourceful Rowan—a clear analogy for the ideal employee—and the "slipshod" workers who Hubbard described so disparagingly was embraced by employers far and wide, bringing him and the *Philistine* widespread acclaim. Hubbard was inundated with requests for copies of the essay from employers across the country and around the world. The New York Central Railroad ordered one hundred thousand copies in pamphlet form for its workers under the new title, "A Message to Garcia." Many other employers followed the example, and in turn, most workers at large or midsize firms in America received a copy or read it in company publications over the next few years. In 1900 it was translated for all employees of the Imperial Russian Railways, and during the Russo-Japanese War of 1904–5, Russian military leaders supplied copies for all Russian soldiers. For two decades after its publication, schoolteachers assigned the essay to their students as a moral lesson about the importance of self-discipline, and it was eventually translated into all major languages and adapted for the stage and screen. By 1925, over forty million copies had been printed worldwide, making it the third-most-reproduced piece of literature after the Bible and the dictionary.[2]

"A Message to Garcia" was far from the first inspirational tract that employers circulated to workers—this had occurred since the early days of industrialization—but it made clear to managers as never before that such communiqués presented valuable tools for promoting employee discipline. Hubbard's sneering admonishments of employees for failing to live up to managers' idealized visions of work gradually gave way to more positive-toned messaging. However, the dichotomy between the motivated and the unmotivated worker that his essay popularized was to become increasingly prominent in management's efforts to influence attitudes and behaviors in industry. Indeed, many of the propaganda posters, booklets, and films used to motivate workers in the factory in the decades ahead channeled Hubbard's comparison between the productive and the unproductive worker and adapted his rhetoric about the virtues of diligent work.

Although Hubbard and his writings faded from view in the 1910s—he was aboard the *Lusitania* when sunk by a German submarine in 1915—the motivational genre that he helped establish remained highly influential among businessmen.[3] Throughout the Gilded Age, the industrial system had been steeped in intermittent conflict as workers asserted their collective hopes for industrial democracy through labor unions and industrialists suppressed labor strife with coercion and violence. Inside the factory, managers maintained control by disciplining workers' bodies on the production line, but in the early twentieth century they gradually discovered that the mind could be a no less useful route of regulation. This realization opened the door for an idea that was to become central to management quests for control and power in the decades to come: motivation (or, as it was more commonly called at this early stage, *motives*, meaning the range of factors that impelled an individual to action). Conveniently for industrialists, this insight coincided with the advent of modern communication techniques. Specialists of many stripes—reformers, industrial psychologists, educators, propaganda designers, among others—believed that pamphlets, posters, films, and other media could be an effective means for dispensing motivational sentiments to workers and thereby shaping their minds in "positive" ways.[4]

This chapter tracks the emergence of motivation as a management idea and charts the spread of motivational rhetoric from the turn of the century to the end of World War I. According to many historians, motivation began to gain influence in industry only in the wake of the high-profile experiments into employee productivity conducted by human relations specialists in the 1920s and 1930s, especially the Hawthorne studies, which revealed that modifications of the working environment, along with workers' awareness of being observed, led to changes in behavior. Yet managers' interest in motivation emerged well before these influential studies, albeit in less formal and structured ways. This was the case especially in the discourse that they invoked, both among themselves and in employee communications techniques. Motivational discourse was useful to management in part because it was so wide-ranging and adaptable. Along with closely related concepts such as motive, incentive, and morale, it allowed managers to address a multitude of workplace concerns. The ideal of employee motivation proved useful to them when emphasizing work's economic and psychological rewards alike, or when trying to impress on workers the benefits they would receive if they embraced company mindedness or adopted a cooperative attitude toward management. In reality, managers intensified their efforts to extract more labor from workers and to suppress labor unions, and work became even more grueling throughout the early twentieth century due to managers' speedup of the production line. Yet through the concept of motivation they could reframe their calls for increased productivity within oratories about the need to satisfy workers' needs and aspirations, a tactic that deemphasized the inherent power hierarchies between themselves and the workers who toiled in their factories.

MOTIVATION'S PROGRESSIVE ERA ROOTS

At the beginning of the twentieth century, efforts to motivate workers, when pursued, were mostly ad hoc. During this time, managers generally regarded workers as a component of the production process—as "labor" or "human capital," in the terminology of the day. This characterization was informed by the rapid expansion of an industrial system that, as business historian Alfred Chandler explains, prioritized large-scale planning, production, transportation, communication, and bureaucracy.[5] Operating from this standpoint, managers thought little about influencing workers' dispositions. Any worker deemed not productive enough could simply be replaced in the same manner as a machine part. Nor did managers see much point in trying to persuade less productive workers to modify their ways. According to the dominant theories of the day, behavior was determined by one's instincts or inborn traits, which were believed to be unchangeable.[6] These views also informed employers' responses to industrial conflict. Throughout the late nineteenth century, they met strikes with violent putdowns and coercion.[7]

Beginning in the late nineteenth century, however, businessmen began to search for new ways to prevail over the "labor problem." Many of them believed that industrialization, with its large and impersonal factory system, had severed the close connections that had existed between employers and workers in the preindustrial age. Factory work brought both a deepening sense of alienation in the workforce and ongoing labor conflict as workers asserted their demands for a more humane existence. In the wake of these tensions, many businessmen began to adopt a more benevolent tone in their deliberations about employees. They hoped that by talking about workers as individuals with feelings and aspirations, they could counter criticisms of harsh industrial conditions, diminish labor conflict, and, as Roland Marchand argues, infuse the corporation with "soul."[8] Throughout the first quarter of the twentieth century, managers' assumption that workers' dispositions were unchangeable waned. Gradually, the door opened for "incentives" and what would later be called "motivation" to enter their thinking.

The emerging notion that workers' dispositions were malleable was derived from the progressive reform movement, whose influence was felt throughout all areas of American life from the 1890s through World War I. Progressivism embodied a broad-ranging effort to reform politics, industry, and other major areas of society, with the goal of improving Americans' lives, especially those of the largely industrial working class who lived in the nation's swelling urban centers. Progressives generally rejected the "survival of the fittest" ethos of social Darwinism that, since the Gilded Age, had insisted that biology and inherited traits were the major determinants to shape the individual's life. Instead, they emphasized the role of education and social and environmental conditions in shaping experience. These views were a cornerstone of the work of reformers from Jacob Riis to Jane

Addams, and they became tenets of industrial psychology, which flourished from the 1910s onward.[9]

Progressivism had a complex relationship to modern industrial work. At a time when generations of workers were condemned to lives of grueling and repetitive labor, progressives, including many businessmen, worried whether America could remain true to republicanism—the nineteenth-century ideal emphasizing virtuous, independent work—and sustain its claim to be different from the "old world" of Europe with its dehumanizing factory systems. These concerns prompted many progressives to push for workplace reforms. But while progressives wished to make work safer and more enriching, the ideas that they promoted dovetailed with managers' efforts to discipline workers and increase their productivity. This tendency, as Daniel Rodgers argues, stemmed from progressives' hopes about the democratizing possibilities of technology and industrial education.[10] By championing work enrichment, progressives helped lay the foundations of the motivational ideology that managers used to extend their control over workers, often in highly exploitative ways, for years to come.

The importance of motivation in progressivism is seen in the ideas of some of its leading figures. Jane Addams, one of the foremost proponents of "industrial betterment," saw factory work as acceptable as long as workers were taught to see their work as part of a collective enterprise.[11] While Addams's beliefs stemmed from a humanistic sensibility, they contained antecedents of the "teamwork" ethos that became central to motivational techniques aimed at disciplining workers and weakening unions. The writings of John Dewey, the most influential educational reformer in America in the first half of the twentieth century, embodied a similarly accommodating stance toward industrial work. Dewey opposed "instrumental" forms of industrial education because they acted to "subsidize industrial capitalists in their need for labor." Work, he believed, should instead be a vocation that provided workers with access to "self-development and personal growth."[12] As generations of managers discovered, however, this progressive ideal proved useful in encouraging workers to see themselves as members of the "team," a goal that, in turn, helped managers to impose more stringent forms of control in the factory.

Progressives' efforts to sustain faith in work's rewards were not entirely new. In the nineteenth century, American business writers published countless books and pamphlets espousing the virtues of the work ethic, many of them inspired by business writers in England. This literature extolled the "gospel of work," the nineteenth-century philosophy asserting an inviolable link between hard work and morality. In the first half of the nineteenth century, the gospel's chief evangelist was Benjamin Franklin, whose best-selling *Poor Richard's Almanack* was considered the bible of "good" work values. By the century's end, Franklin's writings had been eclipsed by a more unabashed insistence on the necessity of hard work by such authors as Samuel Smiles and the industrial tycoon Andrew Carnegie. Eager to fuse the gospel of work with social Darwinism, these authors couched labor's rewards in moral terms, proclaiming that self-discipline and initiative would lead to success, a formula exploited to powerful effect by Elbert Hubbard in "A Message to Garcia."[13] After the turn of the century, however, employers perceived the gospel's "survival of the fittest" reasoning as a hindrance to their efforts to instill "cooperative" attitudes among workers. Progressive ideals like work betterment seemed a more viable means to incorporate the worker into the rhythms of industrial life.

Although they sought to enrich workers' lives, progressives, like many earlier thinkers, helped businessmen make the brutalizing demands of industrial work more palatable to Americans. Their calls for industrial betterment comprised a sort of proto-motivational ideology that connected the image of virtuous work in nineteenth-century republicanism with work in the new factory system. Industrial labor, in this formulation, was as rewarding as preindustrial work, but managers would need to remind workers of it continually to sustain this belief.

MOTIVATION AND THE "HUMAN FACE" OF INDUSTRY

At the same time that progressive reformers were helping pave the way for motivational ideology in industry, managers were beginning to implement ideas that later formed the basis of a motivational apparatus in the workplace. Managers became aware of motivation owing to the rise of the "human factor." Invoked by employers increasingly in the first two decades of the century, the human factor was part of an effort to recast industry's image in more humane terms and to build familial bonds between workers and their managers. As Bruce Kaufman argues, it became a byword for a variety of reforms in the workplace during the first quarter of the twentieth century, including increased safety regulations, improvements in working conditions, insurance plans, and employee counseling.[14]

The human factor appealed to mangers because its emphasis on workers' needs and desires offered a useful counterbalance to the harsh demands associated with their main method for instilling discipline in the factory—scientific management. The most influential advocate of scientific management, Frederick Taylor, as well as the efficiency engineers inspired by him, used stopwatches, production flow charts, and time and motion studies to determine the "correct" amount of time that each task should take on the production line. Using this method, they set the pace at which each employee was expected to work on a particular task. The "piece-rate system," as this practice was known, gave managers a benchmark from which to set bonus rates for higher output and to determine when production was too slow. Its advocates argued that it would alleviate "soldiering," whereby workers collectively adopted a comfortable pace of work, impeding managers' desired productivity levels. Taylor and his followers touted scientific management as mutually beneficial all parties. For managers, it increased efficiency, whereas for workers, its proponents asserted, it would result in higher wages, a claim that was much disputed by workers who found themselves working harder for the same or even less pay as management sped up production.[15]

The worker incentive or motivation efforts that proliferated through scientific management did not aim only to increase efficiency. They were part of a larger managerial quest for control. At their center was an attempt to institute a highly individualized ideal of motivation that would weaken workers' social bonds and collective sense of workmanship. The goals included the appropriation of the knowledge and skills that underpinned the craft labor traditions built by workers for generations; the specialization of production (the breaking down of the production process into discrete, individual tasks that required less and less craft knowledge); and the implementation of a management-orchestrated system of production that made clear that managers, as the holders of rational expertise, should organize and administer production. In reality, scientific management had pernicious effects on workers. Not only did it intensify an already harsh work regimen by tethering workers' bodies to the ever-faster machinery of production, but the much touted promises of higher earnings also proved illusory as managers sped up the line. For managers, these outcomes were of limited concern because workers, they reasoned, were as replaceable as were machine parts. However, scientific management had some clear limitations for managers, not least that it reinforced their image as harsh disciplinarians who had little regard for workers' welfare.[16]

The human factor, in advancing the perception that management had a stake in workers' feelings, helped counter this image. An amorphous, catch-all phrase for an array of management ideas, it was vague enough to mean anything its advocates desired. Espousing the Progressive Era ideal that individuals' behaviors could be improved by modifying their environment, a reversal from nineteenth-century management precepts, the human factor helped imbue management with a more forward-thinking image. It also paved the way for motivational ideals of our own day—witness the ceaseless proliferation of "employee wellness" initiatives in corporations, universities, and the health care sector—that help obscure the power hierarchy between management and workers through lingo about the rewards of self-discovery, personal fulfillment, and similar managerial ideals.[17]

Among the most prolific expressions of the human factor was welfare work, the philosophy that shaped the policies of many large and midsize firms from the late nineteenth century through to the early 1910s. Welfare work encompassed an array of activities and schemes aimed at encouraging emotional bonds between workers and the firm. Large companies, such as Ford, International Harvester, and National Cash Register, created departments that administered employee welfare activities. Typically, these initiatives focused on education, health services, transportation, entertainment, and sometimes profit-sharing schemes.[18] As historian Sanford Jacoby notes, welfare work focused mainly on workers' lives away from the factory floor and was "frequently condescending and manipulative," attempting to "recast the intemperate, slothful worker or the ignorant immigrant in a middle-class mold."[19] Even so, in defining the firm as a "good" employer and asserting that the rewards of working there were "worth it," welfare work provided a powerful motivational tool. The Ford Motor Company's Sociological Department, founded in 1912, comprised the most far-reaching of these initiatives. Ostensibly an effort to improve workers' quality of life by deepening connections between their home lives and the factory, the department amounted to an apparatus for monitoring workers and promoting company mindedness. Although it ceased operation in 1915 amid workers' criticisms that it was a front for managerial "snooping" and anti-union activity, the experiment nonetheless served as inspiration for motivational efforts at other firms and was itself later revived.[20]

Motivation and Visual Communication

Innovations in workplace communications and management theory further elevated motivation's importance in the modern factory. Motivation depended increasingly on visual communication. Most managers were skeptical about images because, according to the rationalist values of their profession, they embodied the irrational sensibilities of the lower classes.[21] Even so, managers' skepticism began to soften as the value of images grew more apparent, especially in the face of advertising's growing influence on consumption, which was noted increasingly in the press. From the 1880s onward, employers, anxious to mitigate labor conflict and the problems of scale associated with industrial expansion, used photographs to define the firm as a human community and a "family."[22] Photographs in employee magazines depicting workers participating in baseball, dances, picnics, and other company-sponsored leisure activities helped firms counter perceptions that they were indifferent to their employees' needs (figure 1.1). Indeed, as historian Andrea Tone emphasizes, in the early twentieth century, "company photographs encouraged employees to shift their locus of self-worth from the increasingly monotonous rhythms of labor to the unpredictable, 'exciting' world of company-controlled leisure."[23]

Most of the large corporations that practiced welfare work used images to visualize their humanistic policies toward workers. Images enabled firms to portray themselves as agents of the human factor—benevolent organizations committed to improving the emotional well-being of their employees.[24] Photographs published in employee magazines and public relations (PR) materials helped produce what historian Larry Peterson calls "traditions of seeing," whereby workers were trained to see the firm as it wished to be seen.[25] In encouraging workers to perceive the firm as an organization built on emotional bonds—as a "family" and a community—welfare work photographs embodied an early form of motivational communications,

FIGURE 1.1. In the early twentieth century, many firms used photographs portraying aspects of welfare work. Such images embodied a belief that, by modifying environments, employers could improve workers' dispositions toward their work and the firm, an increasingly common tactic in early motivational techniques. This 1906 photograph, created for the Brooklyn Rapid Transit Company, depicts the firm's recreational facilities. Workers play snooker and checkers, and one plays the piano, while the kitchen at the rear supplies beverages. Harvard Art Museums/Fogg Museum, transfer from the Carpenter Center for the Visual Arts, Social Museum Collection, 3.2002.2309, Cambridge, MA. Photo: Imaging Department © President and Fellows of Harvard College.

emphasizing the rewards that workers would supposedly receive if they adopted the company's values. At the center of this use of photography was an implicit realization that workers' attitudes and behaviors could be changed through a strategic modification of environments, activities, and aesthetics. The value of images was reflected in the progressive-minded *Pittsburgh Survey*, a multivolume study of industrial life in Pittsburgh from 1907 through 1914, which used photography and illustration to promote reform. Included in the study were photographs by Lewis Hine and illustrations by Joseph Stella, which presented dignified portrayals of workers and immigrant communities. The genre of images that came out of the *Pittsburgh Survey* embodied a type of motivational representation in that their portrayals of dignified workers engaged in specific work types invoked the virtue and integrity of work. These qualities led to many of the images being used throughout the interwar period in the *Survey* (a periodical produced for social workers) and economic textbooks for a general audience, a development that foreshadowed a more widespread usage of motivational photography and other images during the New Deal.[26]

Although welfare work fell out of favor as workers came to associate it with management surveillance and antiunionism, its emphasis on benevolence lived on in literature read by managers themselves. Management magazines advised that the best way to counter the tensions arising from workers' alienation was for managers to become better listeners and to hone their morale-boosting skills. These ideals were emphasized regularly in *System, the Magazine of Business*. When launched in 1900, *System* was firmly focused on increasing efficiency by using the economic incentives of scientific management. By 1910, however, it had begun to embrace the idea that managers should "inspire" and "enthuse" workers. A common trope in *System*'s illustrated articles was the scenario of the "heart-to-heart talk" between a manager and worker. Typically in these stories, a manager takes a worker under his wing and teaches him the value of determination, diligence, or some other motivational trait.[27] *System* also carried regular pieces urging managers to be attentive to workers' "feelings," accompanied often by illustrations of managers in contemplative poses, ruminating in dreamlike scenarios over what their workers were "thinking about" (figure 1.2).[28] Like the heart-to-heart talk stories, these articles reminded managers that the route to cooperation and better productivity lay in boosting workers' morale so that they would perform their work more efficiently—motivating them, in other words. As the illustration emphasizes, however, the lesson of motivation was not only for workers; managers too had to change.

The proliferation of motivational rhetoric and imagery in the 1910s reflected a subtle change in managerial discussions about workers. To be sure, this rhetorical shift was aimed at advancing familiar management objectives—efficiency, discipline, and control—not at improving work or giving workers more autonomy. Moreover, industrial work was no less grueling, and workers regarded rhetoric about management benevolence as lip

FIGURE 1.2. Throughout the Progressive Era, discussions about the importance of the human factor in industry encouraged managerial interest in motivation. The above illustration from *System* conveys a popular theme in early deliberations over motivation: the assertion that managers should be more mindful of workers' "thoughts" and "feelings." This tactic, the accompanying article claimed, would increase cooperation and efficiency. *System, the Magazine of Business*, September 1915.

service or plain propaganda. Yet gradually the belief that increased productivity was linked to boosting morale and satisfying workers' needs and motives gained traction.

INDUSTRIAL PSYCHOLOGY, MOTIVATION, AND EMOTIONAL CONDITIONING

Managers' interest in motivation grew stronger throughout the 1910s owing to the rise of behavioral psychology. Rooted in the work of late nineteenth-century German psychologists, behaviorism upheld two ideas that were highly compatible with management efforts to harness motivation: first, that human behavior was determined by environmental conditions, and second, that humans had the capacity for adaptation. These theories left few areas of American life untouched in the 1910s, influencing everything from medicine to education, urban planning to prison reform. However, they were especially consequential in the industrial arena where psychologists were developing techniques for conditioning workers to the demands of mass production and for harmonizing worker-management relations in large impersonal organizations.

As Elspeth Brown argues, behaviorism was attractive to managers in part because it challenged the still-lingering Darwinian view of some industrial psychologists that conduct was determined by inborn traits, a belief that was at odds with managers' efforts to condition workers to factory life.[29] Like the human factor, behaviorism also encouraged managers to consider how workers' attitudes and behaviors were influenced by emotions. Behavioral psychologists themselves had little interest in emotions, which they deemed nonobjective and thus not deserving of empirical study. However, for many management specialists, behavioral arguments about the positive effects of environmental conditioning and human adaption in the factory seemed to go hand in hand with the emerging idea that the worker's motivation was bound up with his or her emotions.

Managerial interest in environmental conditioning rubbed against the view of scientific managers that economic incentives were the most important component of motivation at work. That said, despite its emphasis on economic-based motivation, scientific management did not altogether dismiss the influence of emotions on workers' job performance and productivity.[30] Indeed, Taylor argued that to succeed, scientific management must include "the accurate study of the motives which influence men" and produce "a complete revolution in the mental attitude and the habits of all of those engaged in the management, as well of the workmen." Many researchers who conducted studies on workers after World War I were even more attentive to the role of emotions in shaping workers' performance than was Taylor.[31]

Environmental conditioning and emotional regulation increasingly converged during the 1910s. Each gained traction as the writings of psychologists, influenced by the pioneer of American psychology, William James, found their way into management discourse. The work of Walter Dill Scott, a professor of psychology and advertising at Northwestern University in Chicago, is illustrative. In his 1911 book, *Increasing Human Efficiency in Business* (much of which was serialized in articles in *System*), Scott argued that workers' behaviors could be positively affected by the use of "suggestion," a tactic used in advertising to influence consumers. By adjusting the mood of the workplace, he argued, managers could improve workers' attitudes and enhance teamwork, boosting productivity. With this insight, Scott furthered the idea that motives could be used to instill cooperative attitudes and behaviors among workers. Motivation, Scott argued, was rooted in "competition" (which could be established by implementing contests and games); "concentration" (which could be increased by modifying the physical and sensory environment); and "wages" (which would induce greater productivity if work was made more satisfying). The employer, meanwhile, should "transmit his enthusiasm to his managers and subordinates" and maintain workers' "interest in work" via "the injection of new motives to action."[32]

What distinguished Scott from many of his contemporaries was his interest in the practical application of psychology in business, a step that most psychologists, favoring theoretical-based research, rejected. His claim that workers' motives were integral to efficiency and productivity also diverged from the views of most management specialists, many of whom, despite growing interest in emotions, believed that workers were incentivized chiefly by pay. In advancing the idea that applied psychology could induce motivated attitudes and behaviors, Scott encouraged managers to conceive the factory as an emotional arena.[33] In the decades that followed, this perspective would become pivotal in motivational techniques. From this thinking emerged the game- or ludic-based motivation later common to the factory and the office.

Emotional and environmental conditioning through motivation gained further prominence through the research of Hugo Münsterberg, a German émigré and pioneer of American industrial psychology. Münsterberg's studies were focused not on motivation per se but—like Taylor, whose work inspired his own—on increasing efficiency and productivity.[34] Münsterberg placed greater importance on the psychological dimensions of industry than did Taylor, including fatigue and the physical and social aspects of work, ideas already emphasized by the industrial betterment movement. In his 1913 book *Psychology and Industrial Efficiency* Münsterberg sought to bring applied psychology's insights out of the laboratory and to the center of "practical life" in industry. Increasing productivity, he argued, was no mere rational affair; it would require managers to attend to the "higher motives, intellectual, aesthetic, and moral motives, in their bearing on the psychophysical impulses of the laborer."[35] Working from this view, Münsterberg brought attention to the influence of motivation on job placement and productivity.

Münsterberg's research was pivotal in establishing the idea that aesthetics, in conjunction with emotions, helped to shape workers' dispositions. The harmonization of industrial life, he argued, was closely related to the "instincts," "impulses" and "sensations" that prevailed in the society at large. In the workplace, such aesthetic matters as color, music, and even the adoption of cats in the factory had favorable effects on workers. Likewise, the provision of educational and recreational amenities and entertainment satisfied the worker's "reservoir of psychophysical energies."[36] Management textbooks today often note that Münsterberg and other industrial psychologists performed little research on motivation and emotion, each of which only became subjects of study in the field decades later.[37] Yet while Münsterberg did not develop his arguments into a procedure for motivating workers, his ideas, like Scott's, encouraged managers to approach the workplace as a human environment where workers' dispositions could be influenced by images, language, sounds and other sensory factors. In encouraging managers to see workers as adaptable to changing conditions, Münsterberg laid groundwork for the motivational techniques that managers and their hired consultants use to this day to induce cooperation and increase productivity.

Attempts to condition workers became systematized through the establishment of personnel departments at large corporations in the 1910s. Founded to organize hiring, job placement, and production, these departments proliferated rapidly, especially after the United States entered World War I. While they were designed to meet bureaucratic demands, personnel departments also served to bring discussions of workers' motives to the forefront at many firms because they were informed by the motivation-oriented theories associated with the human factor, welfare work, and industrial psychology. Among the companies that founded personnel departments were Ford Motors, AT&T, Westinghouse, National Cash Register, International Harvester, and Standard Oil. For leaders at these firms, the solution to the "labor problem" lay in emphasizing the human factor and addressing workers' grievances on an individual level. This approach spurred the use of employee counseling and prompted a greater emphasis on "mental health." Although managers characterized such measures as evidence of their commitment to employee well-being, their individualizing tactics were largely aimed at undercutting the collectivist approach of unions to grievances. The proliferation of personnel departments encouraged interest in motivation in industry, even as many companies scaled back these departments after the war.[38]

Claims about the value of motivation also gained traction due to management efforts to redefine the role of foremen. Since the late nineteenth century, foremen had been responsible for hiring and firing, and their role on the production line had typically been to "crack the whip" to impose discipline. The factory, as management historian Daniel Nelson argues, was the "foreman's empire," and the foreman was often a feared figure among workers. To allay criticisms about the dictatorial foreman, many firms began to transfer hiring and firing duties to personnel departments and to cast foremen in a more humane light by referring to them as "team leaders," "facilitators," and similarly munificent sounding designations.[39] In reality, authoritarian supervision methods changed little.[40] Yet this recasting of the foreman's image, illusory as it was, became central to the development of the motivational project. Toward the end of the decade, the view that foremen should be trained to adopt a more motivational, personality-driven approach to workers was upheld routinely in management magazines (figure 1.3).[41]

FIGURE 1.3. This illustration in *Industrial Management* asserts that management's failure to attend to workers' human needs through supervision practices undermined their morale, a core element of motivation. At the top we see what the magazine deemed the positive results achieved by the idealized supervisor who uses an emotionally supportive approach to motivation, and below we see the negative effects of the supervisor who uses "senseless" authoritarian methods. *Industrial Management*, November 1918.

Industrial psychology's emphasis on workers' adaptability and emotional needs did little to improve workers' experiences on the shop floor. The "foreman's empire" remained intact throughout the interwar period, and work remained as brutalizing as ever as management continued to rationalize production. Managers' esteem for "humane" foremanship reflected their efforts to reassure foremen that their authority was secure at a time when managers were continually trying to bring planning and decision-making on the production line (responsibilities typically overseen by foremen) further under their own control. Regardless of its illusory nature and its true goals, however, the advocacy for a "gentler" approach to foremanship provided managers with a powerful rhetorical tool through which to invoke a more humane image of industrial work. In this version of industry, the foreman—the pivotal link between managers and the rank and file—was defined as a motivator rather than a tyrant (a figure who was supposedly disappearing amid the spread of a more enlightened model of management).

The idea that motivation could play a significant role in influencing workers' attitudes and behaviors gained traction in the wake of the federal government's backing of industrial reforms. In 1912, Congress established the Commission on Industrial Relations, a body that investigated industrial problems and promoted reforms aimed at improving working conditions. After coming to office in 1913, Woodrow Wilson's administration took a forceful approach to industrial reform. Wilson continued a Cabinet-level Department of Labor (instated by his predecessor, William Taft, on his last day in office), which formed a warm relationship with labor leaders. Wilson also enacted workers' compensation, health and safety regulations, and restrictions on child labor. As the labor historian Joseph McCartin shows, at the heart of Wilson's first term was an emphasis on the virtues of "industrial democracy." Since the 1890s, industrial democracy had been a rallying cry among workers, embodying their collective hopes that unions would gain greater influence over industrial planning and thus curtail the brutalities of rationalized production. Wilson's stance stoked belief that industrial democracy might become a reality. Although Wilson's support for labor was a tactical measure aimed at securing power (and reelection in 1916), his administration, in championing workers' rights and lending support to unions, boosted anticipation of radical change. In the process, the state emerged an agent of motivational discourse in industry.[42]

By the time the United States was fully embroiled in World War I, the idea that emotions were integral in shaping workers' productivity had been taken up widely in management discourse. Years before emotions received widespread study, the need to shape and control them was invoked habitually by management specialists. In the process, motivation, which figured only vaguely in managers' minds at the start of the decade, became central in their efforts to condition workers and to make them more acquiescent to desired goals.

"SELLING THE WAR TO THE WORKING MAN": WORLD WAR I AND MOTIVATIONAL PROPAGANDA

The United States' entry into World War I turned motivation into a national cause célèbre and an expedient mechanism through which the federal government and industrial leaders could advance wartime objectives. Industrial workers were deeply skeptical toward American involvement in the war, worrying that business leaders would use it as an excuse to undermine union activity, a concern that was borne out in the wartime crackdowns on strikes. In the face of such widespread skepticism, government and business leaders mounted a massive propaganda campaign to rally support for the war effort among workers and the broader citizenry. The largest in the nation's history until then, this campaign was waged with particular intensity in the factory, where emotionalized appeals to cooperation and teamwork became all-pervasive.[43]

The nation's participation in a war widely touted as one to "make the world safe for democracy" gave employers and business organizations unparalleled opportunities to define themselves as devotees of a fairer industrial order who were committed to advancing industrial democracy. The organization tasked with orchestrating the government's propaganda following the U.S. entry to the war, the Committee on Public Information (CPI), waged a relentless crusade to drum up public support for the war effort. Under the leadership of its director, George Creel, the CPI produced an immense communication apparatus. The CPI's campaign used a multitude of media, including posters, radio, films, newsreels, advertisements, billboards, wage packet inserts, and home mailings, as well as speeches, comprising what Creel later described as a "vast enterprise in salesmanship." During the year and a half that the nation was at war, the CPI disseminated around seventy-five million items of propaganda, infusing public and private spaces with motivational sentiment. The challenge of selling workers on what the CPI called a "people's war" was especially acute given that many workers dismissed the conflict as "capital's war."[44] Believing that industry was "part of the intricate mechanism of war" and anxious to avert a slowdown in production, the CPI threw massive resources into the crusade to induce support for the war among workers and labor unions.[45] To gain support for this "people's war," the CPI, along with many other government agencies, tapped the rhetoric of industrial democracy, casting workers as "partners" (along with the troops) in a war to preserve freedom (figure 1.4).[46]

While the CPI's propaganda crusade helped sell Americans on a war that was later viewed by large swathes of the public as one drummed up by profit-hungry munitions makers, it had another, less noted effect: it helped make motivation—an idea that was only hazily conceived before the war—a broadly accepted aspiration in industry. During the war, morale became a national obsession, touted by military planners, government propagandists, and industrial leaders alike as vital to the nation's success. The fervor for morale boosting also had more lasting effects on the ways that business leaders and managers framed discussions of work. From this time on, publicity aimed at workers defined loyalty, cooperation, and other motivational traits not only as obligatory but also as symbols of a higher sense of purpose among workers (an objective upheld by disciples of motivation from Elbert Hubbard to Hugo Münsterberg and Walter Dill Scott). This higher purpose was a mutable concept and could, depending on the needs of the moment, include the nation's victory in the war, a commitment to a company's goals, the success of capitalism, or some other ideal that managers or businessmen defined as necessary for workers. Simply put, the war made motivation a standard weapon in industrial leaders' arsenal and established the state as an agent of motivation, a role that it would reprise in the Depression and World War II.

Throughout the war, the federal government, continuing its prewar stance, pursued policies that were broadly supportive of workers, giving rise to state-sanctioned motivational rhetoric linking freedom and industrial work. The final report of the Commission on Industrial Relations, released in 1916, set the tone, concluding, "The question of industrial relations assigned by Congress . . . is more fundamental and of greater importance to

FIGURE 1.4. This poster, produced by James Montgomery Flagg for the United States Shipping Board Emergency Fleet Corporation in 1917 and displayed widely throughout the war, typifies the emotion-laden calls for teamwork and cooperation that characterized wartime propaganda. Linked in a spirit of patriotic unity, his fists clenched, the worker at center is portrayed as a hero whose participation in war work is vital to the United States' victory. Library of Congress, Prints and Photographs Division, Reproduction no. LC-USZ62–19926, Washington, D.C.

the welfare of the Nation than any other question except the form of government."[47] President Wilson also expanded his earlier support for labor by establishing the National War Labor Board (NWLB) in April 1918. The NWLB protected workers' right to join a union and participate in collective bargaining, undermined antiunion tactics by employers, and gave workers at firms with antiunion stances new leverage to challenge management in the form of shop committees. State-orchestrated labor reforms set the stage for a significant expansion of workers' power. More than a million workers joined unions during the eighteen months that the nation was at war, swelling union membership to around 3.5 million, more than the number serving in the American Expeditionary Force in Europe.[48]

Yet while the government's broadly supportive wartime position toward labor stirred workers' hopes for industrial democracy, its campaigns to mobilize the armed services and the industrial workforce were ultimately more accommodating to management. The CPI's campaigns castigated as "slackers" those workers perceived as insufficiently committed to the cause, and though it mostly depicted them honorifically, its insistence on labor-management cooperation was at odds with workers' class-conscious aspirations. In bringing psychologically manipulative communication techniques to the factory, propaganda campaigns helped unify the various strands of management's motivational efforts in industry that had been forming for years before the war, including the Progressive Era belief that labor should be connected to a higher purpose; the human factor's insistence on the need for meaningful connections between workers and their employers; and industrial psychologists' calls for managers to use emotional conditioning to influence motives. Each of these ideas came together in an avalanche of emotion-laden appeals to workers in wartime propaganda. The change occurred not only because motivation was now espoused continually and loudly from all directions but also because it was inextricably fused with the idea that an individual's commitment to the organization—the firm or, as much propaganda insisted, the nation—was nonnegotiable for "good" workers.

In 1917, in efforts to rally workers' support for the war, CPI director George Creel and American Federation of Labor president Samuel Gompers founded the American Alliance for Labor and Democracy (AALD). Operating under the auspices of the CPI and headed by Gompers, a vocal

FIGURE 1.5. Workers at the Bethlehem Shipbuilding Corporation pose for a photograph around a Liberty Loan display in April 1918. During World War I, employers used slogans, posters, flags, and other patriotic imagery to invoke emotion-laden motivational sentiment in and around the factory. Displays of this kind, including, in this case, a slogan atop the factory facade, became focal points in employers' motivational efforts. They also allowed managers to exploit the factory's aesthetic and sensory features for motivational purposes, tactics advocated by industrial psychologists. Library of Congress, Prints and Photographs Division, lot 5351, Reproduction no. LC-DIG-ds-12366, Washington, D.C.

supporter of the war, the AALD became a powerful force in suppressing antiwar sentiment among workers and the broader public. From the CPI's perspective, the AALD was imperative in winning the battle for workers' hearts and minds, a view that prompted Creel to describe it as the CPI's "most important body." In its first six months, the AALD established a hundred and fifty branches across the country, disseminated nearly two million pamphlets, held two hundred mass meetings, and published ten thousand newspaper columns. The AALD's campaign helped strengthen calls by industrialists for a wartime suspension of the right to strike and for labor unions to set aside their own interests and throw their full support behind the war effort. Typifying these calls was Henry A. Wise Wood, chairman of the Conference Committee on National Preparedness, who insisted, "Labor must be shown the necessity of rising above its *technical rights*, and that instead of doing its duty in a merely perfunctory manner, it must put all of its might into the work of producing."[49] Along with the CPI's other propaganda initiatives, the AALD helped undercut the power of labor opposition to the war.[50] Moreover, the creation of the AALD established a tactic that the state and business would use at many times in the decades to come, namely, the enlistment of labor leaders and labor rhetoric for motivational purposes in industry.

Equally dedicated in advancing wartime motivational ideology were powerful business organizations such as the National Association of Manufacturers (NAM). A staunch defender of business and a fierce opponent of labor unions, NAM became a potent ally to employers. In 1917 NAM established the National Industrial Conservation Movement (NICM), an anti-union body that espoused the mantra of labor-management cooperation. In a February 1918 article entitled "Selling the War to the Working Man," the trade magazine *Printers' Ink* enthused that NICM had disseminated over 1.5 million wage envelope fliers via fourteen hundred employers across the country, aiming "to refocus the public's industrial perspective." The envelopes likened workers to soldiers, extolling them as "Industrial Patriots" who were bravely manning "Fort Factory." The campaign also targeted the general public, securing over sixty thousand columns of publicity in newspapers and magazines.[51] Puff pieces authored by NICM's representatives and published in newspapers countrywide formed a continual wave of motivation-infused rhetoric linking patriotism with business leadership and condemning those (by implication, unions) who did not adhere unquestioningly to labor-business cooperation. As one proponent of NICM's campaign asserted, "Most of the evils inside of industry are the by-products of the class feeling that has been created and stimulated by the false public attitude on the outside."[52] Displayed in thousands of factories throughout the war, NAM's posters extended this theme visually, depicting workers as partners of employers and the nation in the war for industrial freedom (figure 1.6).

Motivation gained further traction through government efforts to instill morale in the armed services. In August 1917 the government established

FIGURE 1.6. The National Association of Manufacturers adapted wartime rhetoric about industrial democracy in pro-business communication media. Via speeches, newspaper articles, wage packet inserts, and posters like this one, NAM schooled workers and the general public in the virtues of "industrial cooperation" in the name of victory, an ideal represented here by an alliance between Uncle Sam, an employer, and a worker. Library of Congress, Prints and Photographs Division, Reproduction no. LC-USZC4-7848, Washington, D.C.

the Committee of Classification and Personnel (CCP), a body that conducted psychological tests on enlistees, and appointed as its director Walter Dill Scott, a leading proponent of motivation for a decade by this time. Under Scott's leadership, the CCP tested over three million men by the end of the war.[53] While the CCP's work was focused on servicemen, its methods, which included aptitude tests, counseling, and employee interviews and attitude surveys, were soon deployed by managers in efforts to boost workers' morale. The growing status of psychological testing owing to research by Scott and other devotees helped make motivation a centerpiece of "personnel management" at large industrial firms.[54]

The influence of propaganda hardly ended once the war was over. Although posters and literature disseminated by the CPI disappeared from factories at war's end, the wartime propaganda crusade had made clear that visual media was a powerful form of motivational communication. It confirmed the view that had been developing among managers over the previous two decades: the worker's mind was amenable to emotional conditioning and, therefore, emotion-based messaging about work's rewards could aid discipline and managerial control. In advancing such objectives, wartime propaganda laid the foundations for the techniques that many managers would adopt in the factory for years to come.

MOTIVATION AND VISUAL EDUCATION: INDUSTRIAL FILMS IN THE FACTORY

During the five-year period following the war, managers discovered another motivational tool: industrial films. These films were produced by a cluster of companies centered mainly in Chicago, including the Industrial Film Company, the Independent Motion Picture Company, the Universal Manufacturing Film Company, and the DeVry Corporation, all of which employed salesmen to sell their films across the country. Industrial films focused on subjects ranging from production line techniques to workplace safety and Americanization to moral guidance. For managers, these films offered many benefits. In addition to their practical utility in the realm of employee induction and training, they helped communicate the familiar claim that workers' livelihoods were linked inextricably to the economic performance of the firms for which they were employed. As a medium that influenced the viewer by way of the *senses*—vision, often with the accompaniment of sound in the form of instruction by managers during screenings—industrial films, advocates believed, could influence workers' emotions in positive ways and thus help managers to mitigate labor tensions and increase productivity.

The rise of industrial films was an outgrowth of the Visual Education movement, which became prominent in the 1900s. Its advocates, who included educational reformers and teachers, believed that visual-based communication forms could play a valuable role in educating Americans. Companies specializing in collections of educational photographs and slides and, from around 1905, films, sent their agents into the nation's schools to sell their products. After 1910, schoolteachers used images to teach history and science, and instructors at vocational schools and YMCAs used them when teaching about industrial production and workplace safety. After the war, visual education became a full-fledged movement with a growing number of devotees and several trade magazines, including *Reel and Slide* (established in 1918), *Moving Picture Age* (1919), and *Visual Education* (1920). Through these magazines, advocates encouraged managers to use films and other visual communication forms to enhance employee training and education.[55]

Proponents of visual education argued that visual communications worked through a process called *visualization*. A well-known concept in advertising and selling, visualization embodied the idea that people could infer deeper or associated meanings more readily through images than they could through the written word. Advertisers exploited this technique, as they do today, to impress upon customers the meanings associated with, say, a brand of soap or a make of car. According to advocates, industrial films worked in the same way: films emphasizing the importance of teamwork helped workers to "visualize" how their work served the larger objectives of the firm. Holding industrial film screenings in the factory could, they claimed, help managers train workers to be more cooperative and company minded or identify with capitalist ideals, a goal that complemented business's endeavors to weaken workers' attraction to unions.[56] Such sentiments were common in advertisements by DeVry and other suppliers of industrial films and screening equipment (figure 1.7).[57]

Organizations like the Bureau of Commercial Economics performed an influential role in the dissemination of industrial films. After its 1913

FIGURE 1.7. After World War I, suppliers of industrial slide and moving image films and screening equipment generated a thriving trade to employers. This DeVry advertisement emphasized the utility of industrial films by portraying a film screening in the factory. *Reel and Slide*, January 1919. Library of Congress, Moving Image Research Center, Washington, D.C.

founding, the bureau worked in conjunction with the Universal Film Manufacturing Company to loan its films to organizations across the country. By 1919 it owned eight motion picture theaters that were built into motor trucks that traveled the nation screening industrial (and other types of educational) films in factories and communities at large. The organization supplied questionnaires to managers and other authorities asking them to state their preferences for film content. As described in an article in the trade magazine *Furniture Manufacturer and Artisan*, the trucks carried a projector, an electricity generator, and a portable screen, allowing the bureau to show films in workplaces in "an isolated western ranch center as well as in a city."[58] The magazine emphasized the bureau's value in combating communism, a growing concern among employers in the wake of the Russian Revolution and amid the era's simmering labor-capital conflict. It informed readers, "If the masses of Russia had been as educated as the American people, Bolshevism never would have raised its head." It also praised the bureau director, Francis Holley, who, it claimed, "knows that there are thousands of workmen in this country who really believe that the shortest cut to a fatter pay envelope is through the destruction of the present employers." In the face of "professional agitators," it concluded, the bureau's "21,000,000 million feet of educational film are at the ready . . . Sitting in the silence of an improvised theater in a workshop, the employes [*sic*] can take their pick—the American plan or the Soviet Plan."[59]

As Heide Solbrig argues, while industrial films were, at this stage, mainly of an instructional nature, they were informed by social science theories that were concerned with training the individual—schoolchildren, vocational school students and workers being core audiences—in the attitudes and behaviors that industrialists deemed necessary for citizenship. Although it was not until the 1930s that managers used industrial films in more programmatic fashion when seeking to motivate workers, their earlier use was thus inseparable from quests to instill managerial values among workers (and future workers in the case of schoolchildren and vocational students).[60] Such goals were emphasized frequently by visual education proponents, many of whom, in their enthusiasm to spread the word to managers, left little room for doubt about the value of motivational films. One such advocate, H. L. Clarke, wrote in 1920, "The best education in industry is that which stimulates a workman to produce more for both himself and his employer. The ideal way to impart such an education is by means of the screen. It is a thoroughly tactful way. It does its work without creating antagonisms. Whether schoolboy or schoolgirl or factory worker, few will pick a quarrel with the motion picture's story, provided only it is the truth." Echoing a claim made by film producers, Clarke added, "It is obvious that visual methods—especially where there is only limited knowledge of English, as in the case of the foreign labor so largely employed in our factories and mines—will materially increase the rate of return on the money invested in industrial education."[61] Such confident claims about visual communication's effectiveness reflected the assumptions of advocates more than reality, but their frequent reiteration after the war raised the status of images as a form of conditioning in the factory among managers.

Chicago's role in the proliferation of industrial film was no coincidence. Not only were the leading educational film companies centered there, so too were the major visual education magazines and organizations. The growing interest in the movement turned Chicago into what film historian Anthony Slide calls "the non-theatrical film capital of the world."[62] The city's pivotal role in the effort to market visual education in industry also emerged, in part, because of its influence on salesmanship. Chicago's hosting of the 1893 World's Fair, followed by its rapid emergence as a hub of midwestern and national commerce, helped make it a marketing mecca. No less important, Chicago was home to the field of American sociology. After the war, the Chicago school of sociology became the epicenter for the sociological study of industrial life.[63] In turn, the city became a fertile ground for entrepreneurs who hoped to profit from industrial films and other workplace motivation media.

Industrial films were appealing to managers in part because workers were already familiar with them. When managers screened films in the factory, they did so in the knowledge that many of their workers had seen such films while at school or at vocational colleges or clubs. Among the institutions that exposed working-class men to industrial films, none was more active than the YMCA. As part of its mission to expand its influence in industrial areas, the organization's staff worked with DeVry, Universal, and other film suppliers to host screenings, not only at the YMCA but also in factories and other venues patronized by industrial workers. Writing in *Reel and Slide*, George Zehrung, secretary of the YMCA's Industrial Department, noted that its films were "rapidly becoming a regular part of the modern factory," with nearly eighty thousand workers having seen its programs to date. The successful integration of its films in the workplace, he added, was due to "the whole-hearted support of our captains of industry and factory superintendents who have learned the value of keeping their employes entertained and therefore satisfied and efficient." Among the goals of the films, he added, was "to bring capital and labor into greater sympathy with each other" and to inform "the workman in one branch of an industry concerning another branch by means of *visualization*, a language all can understand." The YMCA employed "industrial secretaries" who collaborated with employers to coordinate film screenings in factories, and staff also worked with city associations to schedule screenings and accompanying lectures. Zehrung listed over fifty such associations whose representatives regularly attended film screenings. *Reel and Slide*'s editors echoed his enthusiasm, announcing in the article's byline, "YMCA's Industrial Secretaries Work with Capitalists to Reach Employes. Educational Programs Exhibited Between Shifts in Big Plants, Day and Night."[64]

By the early 1920s, businessmen at large corporations were ebullient about visual communication. Capturing this mood, Stewart Ewen notes, was AT&T's public relations director, William J. Banning, who, rejecting the reason-based sensibility used in employee communications previously, called for "a more pictorial and impressionistic notion of persuasion." From now on, Banning stated, "emotionally directed vernacular" and "calculated optical seduction" would comprise the corporation's major PR approach.[65] The zeal for images was echoed at the National Cash Register Company, whose publicity managers proclaimed, "Sight is far the most important of the senses. It has been proved that 87 percent of what we know is learned through the sense of seeing. Only 7 percent of our knowledge is gained through the sense of hearing."[66] These exaggerated claims reflected managers' eagerness to discipline workers more than anything else. Nonetheless, managers would turn increasingly to visual-based motivation in the years ahead, finding it a potent tool through which to promote work's rewards and encourage workers' cooperation with management.

As the war receded and they set their sights on cementing control in industry during the New Era, managers and business leaders increasingly relied on the motivational discourse that had taken root during the previous two decades. Unlike their turn-of-the-century predecessors, they had at their disposal an array of motivational media through which to promote their visions of industrial work and a vocabulary through which to communicate motivational messaging to workers. The main factors driving this change—progressive industrial reform, the human factor, industrial psychology, propaganda, and visual communications—comprised a new framework for management's drive to shape workers' minds. Two decades earlier, businessmen's main responses to industrial problems were to use force and bemoan inefficient and undisciplined workers (a tactic embodied in Elbert Hubbard's "A Message to Garcia"). But now a different conversation about workers had emerged, one framed by oratories about workers' needs and aspirations and assertions about the value of emotional conditioning and visual communications. These ideas soon became pivotal in managers' efforts to counter what human relations specialists deemed workers' "maladjusted" attitudes and behaviors.

The rise of motivational discourse in no way blunted managers' endeavors to instill discipline and extract more labor from workers. Nor did all managers embrace motivational ideas, which prompted industrial psychologists and sociologists to continue promoting them for years to come. Yet managers and their allies were increasingly cognizant that motivational rhetoric could play a powerful role in advancing their ambitions. Motivation would gain even deeper influence in industry as psychological approaches to motivation gained traction in management and in the culture at large in the years ahead.

CHAPTER 2

Quests to Shape the Worker's Mind

THE RISE OF PSYCHOLOGICAL MOTIVATION

> **Human conduct tends to become not only more intelligible but more amenable to control as we view it in the light of an understanding of the instinctive mainsprings of action.**
>
> **—Ordway Tead, *Instincts in Industry: A Study of Working-Class Psychology*, 1918**

> **[Our posters must] create favorable action in [the worker's] mind, whether he be conscious or unconscious of this action taking place.**
>
> **—Poster design manager, Mather & Co., 1927**

From the end of World War I until the onset of the Great Depression, many experts in industry came to see psychological-based approaches to motivation as a useful instrument for encouraging workers to adopt a cooperative attitude toward management. As a number of experts saw it, the assumption among many managers that workers were motivated by wages alone and their failure to recognize the role of psychological needs in shaping motivation only served to weaken workers' morale and compound industrial tensions. Building on the ideas of industrial psychologists and others who advocated motivation in the preceding decade, postwar industrial social scientists rejected economic models of motivation and argued that workers' attitudes and behaviors were rooted in a complex web of psychological motives.[1]

Although such arguments had circulated since around 1908, the behavioral psychology initiatives of World War I prompted a new wave of research into the connections between psychological motives and work. At the center of the research was a belief that workers' motivation was based on their instinctive drives, a view that took its cue from the writings of behavioral theorists such as Hugo Münsterberg and Thorstein Veblen. The industrial social scientists who advocated this view not only challenged arguments about economic motivation but, in a modification of the Darwinian theory that instincts were fixed at birth, also insisted that workers' instincts and motives were malleable and could thus be directed in "positive" ways, aiding management objectives.[2] Interest in molding workers' motives was not confined to industrial social science. It was also taken up by opportunistic entrepreneurs who recognized that the idea could be adapted into communications devices for the workplace. Inspired by the swelling influence of consumer advertising, the visual education movement, and the new field of public relations (PR), these entrepreneurs developed posters and booklets containing emotionally stimulating messages designed to encourage "positive" attitudes and behaviors among workers. In channeling PR's use of visual, emotion-based messaging to the factory, entrepreneurs in the emerging motivational business took cues from PR's founder, Freud's nephew Edward Bernays. Drawing on his uncle's theories about humans' hidden emotional desires, Bernays used imagery and the written word to sell everything from cigarettes to political opinions and insisted that "the conscious and intelligent manipulation of the organized habits and opinions of the masses" was necessary to the well-being of democracy.[3]

This chapter charts this deepening interest in psychological motivation in two ways. First, I briefly trace its rise in industrial social science and management. Many researchers believed that the worker's instincts were an important factor in motivation. By influencing workers' instinctive impulses and drives, they argued, managers could habituate them to new attitudes and behaviors. Second, I discuss a corporation that attained considerable success supplying motivational posters and literature for workplace use—the Seth Seiders Syndicate. Although little known today, the syndicate enjoyed significant success supplying employers across the country throughout the decade, helped by its network of salesmen who sold the products coast to coast. The syndicate's arresting posters and emotional-based messaging drew on ideas about motivation originating from industrial social science and PR to encourage workers and foremen to adhere to what managers of the period considered to be "good" work values. Although social scientists and businessmen like Seth Seiders had different goals, they embodied the deepening realization during the period that motivation, to be effective, must focus on workers' psychological needs and aspirations.

As prolific as managerial interest in motivation was, industrialists would address it in halting and uncertain fashion throughout the decade. Employers remained fearful of the possible resurgence of labor unions and renewed class conflict, and some were torn over whether to respond to labor's challenges with force or appeasement. Their uncertainty caused them to embrace conflicting approaches to motivation. On the one hand, they continued to channel elitist visions of workers as a conflict-prone "rabble," a view that encouraged a continuation of bodily discipline and Taylorist "carrot and stick" incentives in industry. On the other hand, emerging theories about workers' psychological needs prompted managers to enlist mental manipulation in the form of motivational discourse steeped in emotional sentiment and images. However, although managers remained ambivalent in their approaches to motivation, mental manipulation gradually gained traction.[4]

Managerial interest in motivation reflected a more general societal uncertainty over the effects of modernization after World War I. In the wake of the most destructive war in human history, many prominent critics believed that industrial modernity, with its emphasis on standardization and conformity, had fueled alienation and discontent. From F. Scott Fitzgerald, Ernest Hemingway, and other writers associated with the Lost Generation to Robert S. and Helen Merrell Lynd's influential study of middle-class life, *Middletown*, ambivalence toward industrial modernity was widespread.[5] This anxious mood was hardly lost on managers and management specialists. In the wake of massive strike waves that engulfed the country in the aftermath of the war and widespread criticism about the dehumanizing effects of industrial labor, many came to regard psychological-based approaches to employee motivation favorably. Such ideas, they recognized, might not only help quell industrial tensions but, given their emphasis on workers' hopes and aspirations, also infuse management with a more benevolent image, a tactic that they considered no less useful in management's larger mission to control workers and shore up their own legitimacy and power.

MANAGING INSTINCTS: MOTIVATION AND INDUSTRIAL SOCIAL SCIENCE AFTER WORLD WAR I

During the early postwar years, little consensus existed among industrial social scientists, management specialists, and employers about what motivation should entail. The word "motivation" had still not entered wide usage, and specialists continued to debate how best to boost the worker's *incentive*, a term that was associated mainly with Taylorism. Monetary reward was still understood to play a significant role in incentivizing workers, but Taylorism had lost ground as a model for employee incentive during the preceding decade. Even so, researchers who believed that psychology was central to effective motivation were of many minds concerning how it worked. In the wake of widespread labor-capital conflict in the immediate postwar period and given the absence of an authoritative view about how to mitigate industrial tensions and cultivate employee goodwill toward employers, the emerging idea of motivation remained in flux.[6]

However, if no consensus existed about motivation, one thing was to remain consistent throughout the decade: the worker's psychology would be increasingly understood as the major terrain on which motivation operated. While specialists continued to believe that monetary incentives were significant, the view that management must take into consideration workers' larger hopes and aspirations and their sense of self in order to motivate them gradually gained traction. This view prompted much soothsaying about management's professed investments in the worker's emotional needs and general well-being. Although such claims were illusory—managers remained committed to squeezing out as much productivity as possible from their "human capital"—this stance nonetheless prompted a significant shift in management discourse about motivation. This strategic managerial interest in psychological motivation was to continue for decades to come.[7] Thus, a brief discussion of some of the core ideas that informed this shift will be helpful.

From the end of the war until the early 1920s, researchers who believed that workers' instincts were decisive in shaping their behavior gained considerable influence in debates about motivation. "Instinct theorists," as they were called, included psychologists, sociologists, labor economists, among other specialists. Like industrial social scientists more generally, their research was focused on advancing ideas that would aid workers' integration into industry and help management to maximize their productivity. They also shared the elite view common to management specialists that workers were prone to dangerous impulses and hostility. Where they differed from other industrial social scientists and most management specialists was their stance that instincts were malleable. If the worker's instincts, impulses, and urges were actively molded, they could be made more compliant and cooperative, instinct theorists believed.[8]

The writings of one of the era's most noted instinct theorists, labor economist Carleton Parker, are illustrative of the duality that informed theories of motivation after the war. In his influential 1918 article, "Motives in Economic Life," Parker levied a blistering critique of industrialists' failure to grapple with workers' "psychological motives." He declared, "The first quarter of this century is breaking up in a riot of economic irrationalism." "Why," in the face of such conflict, he asked, "does an agitated officialdom search today in vain among our writings for scientific advice [about] labor inefficiency or industrial disloyalty, for prophecies and plans about the rise in our industrialism of economic classes unharmonious and hostile?" The answer, Parker believed, was clear: economists and other industrial specialists were disinterested in human motives and behavioral psychology's insights into "the instinct stimulus."[9]

Although Parker condemned industrialists' failure to recognize the importance of workers' human motives, he did not reject biological explanations of behavior wholesale. Similarly to other instinct theorists, he also borrowed from turn-of-the-century ideas about biological determinism. The result was a blend of social Darwinism and progressive reform aimed at improving industrial conditions while also sustaining elitist management views of workers as maladjusted and of labor unions as a menace that should be subdued. Even as Parker lambasted industrialists for failing to recognize the importance of psychological motives, he claimed that during strikes, workers resorted to an instinctive capacity for "hysteria" and "violence." Calling labor conflict "psychopath-logical," he concluded, "Instinct perversion rather than freely selected habits of instinct expression" were rife in "modern labor-class life."[10]

Among the specialists whose ideas encouraged the spread of psychological-based motivation in the early postwar period, none was more influential than organizational theorist Ordway Tead. At the center of Tead's writing was the assertion that the worker's irrational motives and impulses could be productively influenced by management. In his 1918 book *Instincts in Industry: A Study of Working-Class Psychology*, he argued that workers possessed an instinctive attraction to the group, or the "herd," a view drawn from crowd psychologists, who, since the turn of the century, had warned about the destructive effects of the crowd's primal urges. The herd instinct, Tead asserted, caused workers to seek the protection of labor unions, which were "more intense, fickle, and primitive than are their constituent members as individuals."[11]

Tead nonetheless warned against suppressing negative instincts, which, he argued, would "smother" workers' aspirations and fuel their antagonism toward managers. Instead, managers needed to grasp more fully "the content of [workers'] mental life and the impulses by which they are moved" and thus channel workers' instinctive behaviors in productive directions while inhibiting "destructive" ones, a process he called *sublimation*. Tead noted that the task of sublimating employee instincts was made easier because they possessed instincts that made them amenable to constructive suggestions. These included "self-interest," which caused workers to seek economic security, distinguish themselves from peers, and emulate behaviors they believed would aid their success; the "parental instinct," which encouraged them to seek security and status for their families; and the instinct of "possession" (especially of one's own home), which "satisfies family pride and connotes prosperity and distinction." Tead claimed that workers also had an instinctive "desire to be led and to have aims and ends imposed upon them or at least defined for them." Because "independence" was "wearing on the common man," he added, the worker "longs for peace and protection in the shadow of a trust-inspiring leader. To submit under the right conditions is not only physically pleasant, but much of the time to be leaderless is definitely distressing." Managers, Tead advised, use "personality" to secure workers' "acquiescent submissiveness."[12]

The 1920 publication of Whiting Williams's book, *What's on the Worker's Mind: By One Who Put on Overalls to Find Out*, brought the psychology of motivation to greater prominence among businessmen and managers. After working for a year as a personnel director of a Cleveland steel company, Williams decided to embark on an experiment aimed at deepening his insights into worker aspirations. For the first seven months of 1919, he went undercover and "became" a hobo, traveling the country in search of unskilled work so that he could observe workers' experiences and feelings firsthand. He worked as a laborer in mines, steel and iron mills, shipyards, and oil refineries and wrote his field notes at night. The resulting book was a kind of undercover exposé that, in humanizing the industrial masses and their struggle for a better life, sought to arouse the empathy of middle-class readers.[13]

What's on the Worker's Mind argued that managers must realize that workers were not antagonists of capitalism but human beings with hopes and aspirations who, like middle-class readers, acted largely from an instinctive desire to advance security for themselves and their families. In emphasizing workers' strivings for psychological and economic well-being, Williams found a way to elicit readers' empathy for a group that many middle-class Americans regarded as a maladjusted and conflict-prone "herd." Williams encouraged managers to reject their "universal assumption that putting men into the group called Labor or Management or Capital changes them even down to the bottom of their souls where life's motors are set upon the piers of their foundation desires."[14]

The writings of Parker, Tead, and Williams typify the blend of elitism and progressivism that characterized management assessments of workers and the emerging ideal of motivation after World War I. The duality in their assessments would continue to frame management approaches to motivation for years to come.

Although instinct theorists' arguments about the role of psychology in motivation were not universally embraced, they had a wide influence in industry.[15] They formed a pillar of institutionalism, which became a major school of thought about organizations in the 1920s. Institutionalism emphasized that the firm and the workplace, not abstract economic forces, were the most influential factors in shaping labor relations. This view in turn provided a social-scientific rationale for the view that workers' motivation derived from psychology and could thus be "improved" if managers modified the social aspects of the factory.[16] Efforts to motivate workers via psychological means also informed welfare capitalism, the mechanism used by many employers to instill company loyalty throughout the decade. As well as workers' insurance, healthcare, and other provisions, welfare capitalism involved the use of practices that were broadly motivational, including employee literature, films, PR campaigns, picnics, sports, musical bands, employee contests, and open days and hobby shows during which workers' families and the public were invited into the factory. Such corporations as International Harvester, National Cash Register, Western Electric, and U.S. Steel made ample use of such practices throughout the decade.[17]

The view that workers' sense of motivation was rooted in psychology also informed many of the experiments into workers' productivity conducted by human relations specialists beginning in the middle of the decade. The most influential of these studies were those run by researchers from the Harvard Business School (HBS), especially the Hawthorne studies, a protracted research project run by several HBS specialists at Western Electric's Cicero Plant near Chicago between 1924 and 1933. The Hawthorne studies were not focused especially on motivation, but the researchers' findings would have a profound effect on management approaches to motivation. In 1927, in what was to become one of the most consequential experiments—the relay assembly test room—researchers experimented with changes in lighting in the factory, hypothesizing that workers' productivity would increase or decrease according to the level of lighting in their work area. Workers' productivity did increase, but it did so whether lighting was increased or decreased. Better productivity, the researchers concluded, was therefore due not to fluctuations in lighting but to the heightened attention workers' received as participants in the study. This realization gave birth to the view that productivity was intrinsically linked to the degree to which managers paid attention to workers' feelings. The "Hawthorne effect," as this insight came to be known, later became a cornerstone of motivation research, paving the way for the proliferation of employee counseling and other techniques aimed at instilling positive affect among workers.[18] Although claims that the Hawthorne researchers discovered the importance of emotions in the workplace are exaggerated, the studies had considerable influence in management after their findings became known in the 1930s.[19] Regardless, by the mid-1920s, psychological-based motivation had gained significant currency in management.

While industrial researchers emphasized the psychological dimensions of motivation, one of the era's leading political figures took a more traditional approach to motivation—boosting morale. As secretary of commerce from 1921 through 1928, Herbert Hoover, deployed motivational rhetoric as a weapon in the crusade to resolve labor-business disputes and impose industrial order. He also strove to cultivate widespread voluntary cooperation between businesses, private institutions, and experts with the goal of generating prosperity through a consumer-driven economy. Often regarded as an antiunion ideologue today, Hoover in fact believed that unions and shop committees could play an important role in engendering cooperation. He insisted that the industrial conflict be addressed "from the bottom, not the top," with unions installed as full partners with management in resolving disputes.[20] Yet while Hoover was no antiunion crusader, his approach to labor-business relations represented mixed fortunes for workers. His proposals for works councils failed to materialize owing to the suspicions of industrialists and union leaders alike that they would undermine their respective interests.[21] Hoover's strategy offered workers little in the way of substantive gains and mostly amounted to a form of "harmonious coercion."[22] The tributes to growing prosperity that Hooverites liked to tout also belied increasing unemployment throughout the decade as employers responded to greater efficiency by engaging in indiscriminate hiring and firing.[23]

Yet while Hoover's larger vision failed to materialize, his promotion of labor-management cooperation nonetheless left an indelible mark on motivational discourse and ideology for the next two decades. Hooverite rhetoric established a framework through which politicians, businessmen, and sometimes labor leaders would talk about work's rewards in the years ahead. Morale-boosting tributes to "prosperity"—an ideal that became prominent in national discourse from the Depression through the post–World War II era—first received broad airing through Hoover's campaign to promote labor-management negotiations. Unsurprisingly, the rhetoric about the rewards of a highly individualistic work ethic and consumer-based citizenship that Hoover helped popularize also formed a core strand of the motivational propaganda then being sold across the country by a new wave of specialists based in the nation's capital of salesmanship, Chicago.

MODERNIZING MOTIVATION: THE RISE OF THE MOTIVATIONAL PUBLICITY BUSINESS

Management preoccupations with shaping workers' minds established a fertile environment for turning motivation into profit in the 1920s. Sensing opportunity, a cluster of enterprising salesmen began to develop a new market in motivational posters and literature for the factory. Exploiting the visual-based emotional appeal that informed advertising and PR, these entrepreneurs adapted the core theories of motivation ascendant in management to the purposes of workplace communications.

Unsurprisingly, Chicago—the center of the visual education movement and a hub of industrial social science, instinct theory, and institutionalism—became the base of this new venture. Since the 1910s, Chicago had been home to several small firms that sold incentivizing publicity aimed at salesmen. In 1923, the Seth Seiders Syndicate began adapting these materials for motivational posters and booklets aimed at workers. Founder Seth Seiders, an ambitious salesman from Ohio, was himself the product of motivational ideals. After a decade selling everything from soap to advertising space, followed by a stint designing workplace safety campaigns for DuPont during the war, Seiders had earned enough money to take control of two small Chicago firms that specialized in motivational publicity. His first acquisition, Mather & Co., sold wage envelope inserts carrying motivational illustrations and mottoes that managers could place in workers' wage packets, as well as "pep" booklets for motivating salesmen. The second firm, C. J. Howard, Inc., sold illustrated pamphlets called "pivot man letters" that advised the foreman—the "pivotal man" in the workplace—how to promote good attitudes and behavior among workers. Working with a small team of designers and copywriters, Seiders reworked the assorted products of both firms into a series of posters and pivot man letters that the firm marketed to employers as aids for character building, an ideal venerated by businessmen since the nineteenth century as a means to uplift "uncivilized" workers and immigrants.[24]

Operating independently, but coordinating their products and sales closely, Mather and Howard established the first operation to sell workplace motivational publicity from coast to coast (figure 2.1).[25] Each firm's publicity emphasized the rewards that workers would supposedly receive if they adopted the "positive" traits modeled in the posters and pivot man letters. Among these traits were loyalty, discipline, efficiency, ambition, and teamwork. Attributes that workers should avoid included laziness, lack of initiative, failure to work well with others, and similar "destructive work practices," as defined in each firm's marketing materials. In delineating

FIGURE 2.1. Seth Seiders Syndicate photograph album, Receiving and Shipping Department, 1924 or 1925. The syndicate's two concerns, Mather & Co. and C. J. Howard, Inc., disseminated hundreds of thousands of posters and pivot man letters from here between 1923 and 1930. Special Collections Research Center, University of Chicago Library, Chicago, IL.

these traits and their likely outcomes, the posters and pivot man letters presented a dichotomy between the motivated (and therefore disciplined and cooperative) worker and his undisciplined counterpart who failed to adopt a motivated attitude. By producing publicity that used modern advertising techniques to address familiar workplace problems, the syndicate discovered a winning formula that had significant appeal for many managers.

Only a partial record of the firm's sales exists, but available documentation underscores its success in selling publicity to a wide variety of businesses, especially in the second half of the decade. Larger companies whom it supplied sometimes purchased scores of copies of the posters and pivot man letters so as to install them company-wide. Smaller firms, on the other hand, often purchased double- or single-digit orders. A sampling of notable orders filled by Mather in 1927 included 900 copies of that year's poster campaign to the Employers' Liability Assurance Corporation in Boston; 500 to the Gillette Safety Razor Company in Boston; 400 to the Mutual Trust Life Insurance Company in Chicago; and 150 to the Seiderling Rubber Company in Barberton, Ohio, and scores of double-digit orders to companies in the industrial and commerce sectors in New York, Chicago, Seattle, and Georgia.[26]

A money-making venture run by opportunistic salesmen, the syndicate made no efforts to undertake research to ascertain the effectiveness of its products, even as it made such claims in its marketing materials to boost sales. For these reasons, my focus here is the firm's approaches to designing and selling motivational propaganda.

Much of the syndicate's publicity revolved around the dichotomy between the productive and unproductive worker that Elbert Hubbard had popularized at the turn of the century in "A Message to Garcia." The firm's adaptation of Hubbard's ideas was no coincidence. Seth Seiders appointed as the syndicate's sales manager none other than Felix Shay, who had been Hubbard's second-in-command and sometime ghostwriter at Roycroft from 1911 until Hubbard's death in 1915, then manager of Roycroft until 1918. In hiring Hubbard's protégé as one of his right-hand men, Seiders adapted Hubbard's rhetoric for the modern age. Shay remarked on the adaptation of Hubbard's ideas in a 1926 biography of his former boss, written during his employ at the syndicate. No doubt with the syndicate in mind, he observed that in the years since the sensational reception of "A Message to Garcia," "American business discovered [the] Roycroft booklets and appropriated them" with the goal of instilling discipline among workers.[27]

Materializing at a moment when interest in psychological approaches to motivation was gaining traction in industry, the syndicate enjoyed significant success. By 1925 it employed a sales staff of eighty-eight that sold its products across the country. In the second half of the decade, its sales exploded, reaching projected sales of around $12 million in 1928, its most successful year, bringing motivational publicity to thousands of firms in the process.[28] The syndicate nonetheless faced challenges, not least the fact that many managers were skeptical of posters on account of their emotion-based messages, which were at odds with the rational values associated with management. In efforts to overcome this obstacle, Seiders and his associates designed visual messaging that emphasized "practical" solutions to workplace problems.

The syndicate's efforts to hone design did not occur in a vacuum. The firm borrowed heavily from the tactics of modern advertising. As Stuart Ewen argues, the rapid proliferation of advertising throughout American life during this time was fundamentally aimed at pacifying the public and quelling class conflict by instilling the desire for consumption.[29] The syndicate borrowed from these tactics and, indirectly, from ideas associated with instinct theory, providing managers with tools through which to direct workers' attitudes and behaviors in "constructive" directions. It also tapped into broader discourse about the power of modern communication forms to address societal problems, a goal touted widely, albeit in different ways, by leading intellectuals such as Walter Lippmann and John Dewey. Although the syndicate was motivated by profit rather than a desire to improve democracy, the widespread assertions about the educational function of communications made its marketing job much easier.[30]

By the 1920s, many large companies had begun to use films, posters, and other modern communication forms in the workplace, but thousands of smaller firms and even many larger ones had not. As Seth Seiders and his associates recognized, there was a ripe market for workplace motivational publicity. However, they faced a dual challenge—how to create publicity that, for managers, successfully distilled the values that they hoped to instill among workers and that could be presented to managers as credible educational tools. In tackling these challenges, the syndicate brought the era's motivational theories squarely into workplace communications.

Honing Motivational Posters

The design efforts of the syndicate's poster wing, Mather & Co., illustrate the difficulties involved in surmounting these challenges. At the center of this new style was a strategic use of "suggestion," a concept heralded since the 1910s by Walter Dill Scott and other advertising specialists as a tactic for inducing consumption. Because its influence was widely recognized among businessmen, suggestion provided Seiders and his associates with a useful rationale for how the posters "worked." Mather's posters also echoed the views of Hooverite politicians and businessmen of the day who called for a practical application of resources to boost production and combat the scourge of "waste." Such sentiments were upheld not least by Herbert Hoover, who proclaimed that advertising was the "hand-maiden of mass production." Seiders expressed a similar view in a number of articles in business magazines in the middle of the decade. The solution to "waste" and "loafing," he informed readers, was to "sell" the worker by appealing to his "self-interest."[31] Employers, he argued, should identify the firm's "strongest talking points" and convey them "as simply, as convincingly, as *constantly* as you know how. *Advertise to your men*."[32]

As alive as Mather was to managers' needs, its designs involved considerable trial and error. At a time when there was little consensus among managers concerning how they should influence workers' attitudes and behaviors, Mather found itself adjusting its posters constantly in hopes of distilling what was believed to be the ascendant vision of motivation and thus arriving at the most marketable product.[33] Mather's first series after incorporation into the syndicate in 1923 had a unified design that included a horizontal format (just over three feet by two feet), three-color illustrations and a conveyance of the character-building theme through pithy captions. The posters in the series treated a wide array of subjects that included affirmations of "positive" behaviors such as "teamwork," "loyalty," and "employee suggestions," as well as warnings against "negative" ones as "waste," "tardiness," "loafing," and "spreading rumors."[34] These subjects collectively echoed many of the concerns of industrial social scientists and managers during this time.

Even so, Mather's early posters had significant limitations. Most notably, they were steeped in an elitist vision of work that was frequently out of step with the perspectives of the industrial workers who comprised their audience. This limitation is evident in "There's Only One Way To Become Manager" (figure 2.2). The scenario that it depicts—a manager reclining in his chair examining technical documents—revolves around the fanciful claim that any worker who adopted a managerial disposition and a strong sense of individualism could rise through the ranks and attain a management position, aided by the meritocratic nature of industry. For most of the immigrant workers toiling in American factories at this time, this and similar messages were far-fetched. Mather's posters warning workers against

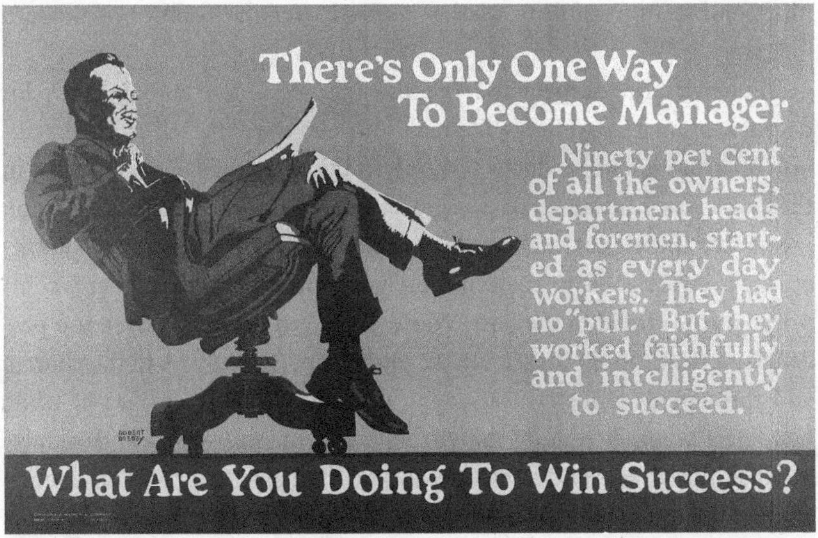

FIGURE 2.2. Mather and Co., "There's Only One Way To Become Manager." Mather and Co., 1923. Emanuel Gerard Collection, Archives Center, National Museum of American History, Smithsonian Institution, Washington, D.C.

"negative" behaviors were steeped in similar limitations, as is seen in "What Are Loafers Paid?," a veiled condemnation of union organizers. The poster depicts a suspicious-looking man lurking at the factory gates and states in its caption that such "loafers" received "harsh looks from their fellow workers who are on to them."[35] With their moralizing warnings against involvement with groups—a major obsession of instinct theorists—such posters revived a World War I–style rhetoric regarded by many workers as condescending propaganda.

Mather's high-minded messaging was largely owing to the values of Seiders and his team, who together came up with the posters' messages.[36] For them, a disciplined and success-oriented outlook was essential for career advancement. Like many white professional men, they assumed that working-class immigrants would benefit by being exposed to these same values. Guided by this assumption, Mather invoked images of work more reminiscent of the nineteenth-century small workshop and the office than of the factory. At the center of the firm's output was a nostalgic vision of the affectionate bonds that supposedly characterized relations between workers and managers in the past. In anchoring its posters in an idealized nineteenth-century milieu, Mather glossed over the realities of modern industry.

The firm also perpetuated the practice, common among elites for decades, of assuming that white male workers were the self-evident symbols of virtuous and productive labor.[37] At the center of elites' worldview in the 1920s was a sustained disparagement of "foreigners" (based in part on race-based theories of intelligence) and unions, which elites deemed antagonistic to Americanism. These antiforeigner and antilabor sentiments comprised a core strand of the post–World War I crusade to preserve 100 percent Americanism. From schools to youth clubs, the YMCA to the church, and throughout industry, leaders of all stripes invoked images of white manliness when esteeming the virtues of productive work, while implying that immigrants and nonwhites lacked the capacity for self-disciplined labor. For the era's elites, rhetoric about discipline and national vitality thus went hand in hand with the kind of motivational discourse espoused by industrial social scientists and firms like Mather.

The firm also channeled the era's success-laden business rhetoric. Many of its posters asserted that workers could climb the company ranks by cultivating managerial traits. One stated that a worker had "no future" at his firm unless he "inspires and deserves Confidence." Another proclaimed, "If you owned this business you would promote the serious, honest minded man who was filling his job, who knew his job and the job higher up."[38] That personality-fueled motivation would yield success was a powerful middle-class ideal in the 1920s, one that businessmen touted regularly. This ideal was a core theme in the era's popular literature, no more so than in Sinclair Lewis's 1922 novel *Babbitt*. As well as savaging standardized middle-class lifestyles and values, Lewis lampoons the era's motivational discourse. Throughout the novel, the pompous businessman George F. Babbitt espouses the virtues of "pep," "right thinking," and other motivational precepts in hopes of acquiring an aura of manly success. His oratories, steeped in the canned language of salesmanship, would be at home in Mather's posters. At one point, he cautions an employee that he "ain't the kind of upstanding, energetic young man, with a future—and with Vision!—that we want here. How about it? What's your Ideal, anyway? Do you want to make money and be a responsible member of the community, or do you want to be a loafer, with no Inspiration or Pep?"[39] Like real-life disciples of motivation, George F. Babbitt regards personality as a powerful form of motivation, which, if channeled effectively, can lead to distinction and success at work, a middle-class fantasy that the syndicate and its ilk were busy marketing to those further down in the class hierarchy.

While Mather's motivational messages were informed by elitist visions of work, their tone shifted during the middle of the decade. From 1924 through 1926, its designers deployed advertising techniques more strategically, adopting a tabloid format along with eye-catching images and urgent captions that allowed for a more immediate conveyance of message. A series included seventy-eight posters, each of which Mather marketed as a solution to a specific workplace "problem" when displayed for one week. The posters channeled the mantras of salesmanship. They included "Say it with Snap!" (which depicted a domineering salesman-like figure to encourage workers to aspire to a managerial demeanor); "Leaders Get There" (which used a disciplined group of rowers winning a race to remind workers that "Laggards Never Lead"); and "Say it and Smile" (one of a small number of posters that depicted women, in this case, using a smiling female worker to underscore the importance of adopting a positive attitude). Emphasizing the rewards of self-interest and the power of "personality," the posters offered ways to redirect workers' emotions in a more "constructive" fashion, an ideal embodied in Tead's theory of sublimation.[40]

In the second half of the decade, Mather, inspired by advertising principles, adopted an increasingly uniform design. Its posters included an ornate wallpaper-like border, allowing for a unified aesthetic throughout the series. This invocation of the soothing tones of home life paralleled employers' efforts at this time to draw connections between the home and the factory, a tactic aimed at emphasizing the rewards of consumption.[41] This wallpaper-like motif is typified in "I Am Responsible" (figure 2.3), which depicts a worker visiting his boss's office to own up to damaging a company vehicle (visible through the window behind the boss with a smashed windscreen and twisted fender). With cap in hand and bowed head, the worker adopts a respectful demeanor toward his boss and, by admitting culpability for his "mistake," acquires an aura of integrity. The scene evokes the virtues of close worker-manager relations, even as it reminded the worker who viewed the poster of his boss's authority. The scenario echoes a device used in Elbert Hubbard's "A Message to Garcia" whereby the individual prioritizes the

FIGURE 2.3. Mather and Co., "I Am Responsible." Poster Photo Archives, Rennert's Gallery, New York, NY.

needs of the organization above his own, thereby placing himself in his boss's good graces. Mather channeled Hubbard's ideals in other posters, including "Drifters Never Harvest" (which rebuked workers who drifted from job to job, a practice criticized frequently by Hubbard).[42]

Seeking to appease doubts about the value of the posters among rational-minded managers, Mather developed scientific-sounding justifications for its products. Marketing copy declared that its posters were scientifically proven to affect workers positively, asserting, "80 per cent of a person's intellect comes through the sense of sight. SEEING IS BELIEVING. Science tells us that there are 23 optical nerves registering on the brain through the eyes against one registering through the ears, so a piece of advertising matter through the printed word, has an opportunity 23 times greater to sell thoughts than the spoken word." Mather claimed that its posters, with their colorful and arresting designs, held particular appeal for industrial workers, an approach that echoed elite assumptions that the era's largely immigrant workforce, having a weak command of the written word, had a special fascination with images.[43]

In reality, Mather's assertions that its publicity could alter workers' attitudes and behaviors embodied savvy marketing rather than scientific evidence. Like many businessmen who touted the powers of visual communication, the firm possessed little understanding of the capacity of images to induce "positive" behavior. And yet its claims did capture the general consensus of the research on motivation—albeit one understood only abstractly by its devotees—that motivation was rooted more in emotional desires and environmental conditions than in rational incentives. Although Mather's claims about the effectiveness of its posters were weakly substantiated, the firm was able to point to the dramatic proliferation of advertising and PR as testimony of the power of visual communications.

During its final two years of poster production in 1928 and 1929, evidently recognizing the limitations of the high-minded approach used to date, Mather embraced "popular" imagery. The posters' themes once again lauded individualism and success but now offered a riot of brightly colored designs and an even more eye-catching, action-packed feel. This livelier tone was reinforced in the use of characters that included clowns, wild animals, hunters, lion tamers, and speedboat drivers, figures associated with popular entertainment. In place of the earnest messages of the mid-decade posters were bright yellows and pinks and simpler images that filled the entire surface area of the poster. This approach evoked aspects of French poster design and the influential German *Plakatstil*, or "poster style," as well as mainstream entertainment and adventure-type stories popular at this time.[44]

In using "exciting" subject matter to couch its motivational messages, Mather tapped sensibilities that had been expressed in adventure stories since the nineteenth century and, more recently, popular movies. Posters depicting animals offered ways to allegorize the specific "destructive work practices" listed in Mather's catalog. A brooding rhinoceros emphasized the need to face troubles, asserting that of having "half your mind on worry and half on work gets you only 'half' results"; an annoyed bear symbolized the negative effects of "growling," which "keeps at a distance those who could help you along"; and a vulture embodied "waste," which should be "starved." Less ostensibly, these posters depicting wild beasts echoed the assumption of many businessmen that workers were driven by animalistic impulses that needed to be managed, a view encouraged by instinct theorists.[45]

A similarly strategic effort to encourage self-discipline informed posters depicting climbers, speedboat drivers, airplane pilots and other adventurers who were extolled as models of success in the 1920s. This approach was echoed in Mather's sports-related posters. From the determined football team that won through solid teamwork to the boxer whose disciplined work led to a knockout, its sports-based posters suggested that a manly sense of motivation would boost the worker's success. "Over the Plate!" typifies this formula, invoking baseball's connotations of individual achievement (figure 2.4). The pitcher's performance, it informed workers, was crucial to the team's success. The middle caption, "Winners never have to say they're good—their work proves it," implies that the good worker was one who adopted a managerial disposition.

Mather's embrace of a more popular poster style reflected a belated realization that the high-minded approach of its earlier output was out of sync with workers' values and that a more unrestrained approach to emotion-based communications was in the ascendance. Although the new posters were no less rooted in pep-infused success rhetoric, their breezy designs and condensed captions allowed for a less didactic approach to motivational messaging. This design shift mirrored a growing recognition among industrialists that the task of influencing workers would require a more robust use of emotion-based techniques. Mather's quest to hone its posters, despite lingering elitism, had gone some way to achieving that end and had established principles that later motivational poster designers would continue to adapt.

FIGURE 2.4. Mather & Co., "Over the Plate!" Internationalposter.com, Boston, MA.

Indoctrinating Foremen: The Pivot Man Letters

The syndicate's other main concern, C. J. Howard, Inc., strove for a similar sense of aesthetic unity in its second main product: the pivot man letters. The letters comprised four-page, eight-inch-by-eleven-inch booklets that offered the "pivotal man" in the workplace, the foreman, a moral lesson that could be digested in one sitting. The letters were sold to managers by Howard salesmen and espoused the notion that business efficiency depended on foremen seeing their interests and those of their employer as the same.[46] For managers who purchased them, the letters were a highly didactic communications tool that could aid their efforts to indoctrinate foremen in management values, a major preoccupation at this time.[47] Those managers who also purchased a Mather poster campaign (as did most who bought the letter) had the benefit of a synchronized campaign, as foremen and rank-and-file workers were exposed to similar motivational messaging.

Early versions of the letters consisted mostly of text and were sold in conjunction with data-driven publications offering foremen "the best thoughts and quotations, and the valuable Economic and Human Element facts that appear from month to month in the Magazines, Newspapers and books of this country."[48] By 1926, Howard was including images in the letters, a change that reflected the syndicate's interest in visual communications. Each letter offered a moral tale highlighting the rewards of good conduct, loyalty, or some behavior associated with the "good" pivot man. Like Mather's posters, the letters revolved around a good/bad employee (in this case, a foreman) dichotomy, usually depicting him encountering a challenge that threatened to undermine belief in the company or "the American system of business." By the end of the didactic tale, the pivot man always overcame this challenge by internalizing a management disposition, thus restoring order.[49]

Typical stories in the letters include that of the initiate pivot man who makes a mistake that undermines productivity or damages the employer's reputation; the foreman who uses poor judgment and makes a "mountain out of a molehill"; the cavalier foreman whose blasé attitude sours worker-manager relations; and the foreman who undermines morale by unduly criticizing or failing to praise the worker who tries his best. Other letters illustrated foreman foibles through adventure-theme stories. Each letter utilized a standard format and displayed on its cover a large color illustration that symbolized the lesson of the story. With their uniform appearance and serialized format, the letters exposed foremen to a regular stream of motivational messaging aimed at encouraging them to adopt managerial values.

One letter, "Yourself, Incorporated," exemplifies the subtle managerial ideology at the heart of the pivot man letter genre. It narrates the story of Charlie Young, a troubled young foreman who voices envy for the independence of his friend, a local storekeeper. An older foreman, a mentor figure, helps Charlie see that that he already has independence as well as the support of a larger community, which the storekeeper does not have. The mentor explains: "Every Pivot Man's department is a *business* in its own right . . . its real name is: 'Yourself, Incorporated.' To make that business a genuine success, you need invest no capital; you need worry about no competition springing up in the next block; you have, instead, the co-operation of the management ahead of you, and with the right handling of your workers, can count on having their own co-operation back of you."[50] By the end of the story, Charlie comes round to the elder's way of thinking, referring to himself as "Myself, Incorporated." Charlie's internalization of the letter's refrain embodies one of the major tactics of motivational communications: management's efforts to get foremen to view themselves as members of the "team."

The thematic similarities between the letters and Mather's posters provided consistency between the two products and meant that foreman and rank-and-file workers were exposed to the same kinds of messages. The serialized nature of the letters, like Mather's posters, allowed managers to expose foremen to a highly rationalized form of social conditioning that de-emphasized class-based bonds. By the mid-1920s, workers had been exposed to serialized literature and entertainment in movie theaters and newspaper comic strips for at least a decade. In this sense, the pivot man letters put into practice formulas already used in the culture at large.

The rationalized nature of the letters extended also to their integration into the workplace. Howard provided instructional literature to managers explaining how to effectively blend the letters with their training and communication practices. This literature included the "Secretary's Record Book," which managers issued to the secretary appointed to distribute the letters to foremen. The booklet hailed the secretary as a vital player in the administration of the "Pivot Man Service," stating, "You, as Secretary to the Official in your Firm supervising this Service, play a most important part in the success it will attain. While your work may seem merely a bit of detailed routine, it is highly influential." This motivational rhetoric was followed by detailed instructions, reminding the secretary to send foremen the special binders and the various publications explaining the objectives of the service. By following these and other instructions, the secretary would help "reduce costs, increase profits and make better managers of the Pivot Men of your firm."[51] This systematized distribution method extended the ideological reach of the letters beyond their primary audience—foremen—and into the work of secretaries.

The serialization of pivot man letters and their harmonization with Mather's posters reflected a more generalized endeavor to hone the communicative capacities of imagery and rhetoric in the workplace. Throughout the era, topical magazines encouraged managers to come up with their own motivational rhetoric. Typical was a 1927 article in *Industrial Psychology Monthly* that advised, "Get a slogan for your factory! If workers lack morale, give them a catchy phrase which will focus their interests in the right direction, or present them with an idea simple enough and general enough for everyone to grasp with a sympathetic grip."[52]

The ideological import of the pivot man letters, like that of the motivational genre more generally, lay less in the extent to which foremen consciously accepted the letters' messages than in shaping the routines and norms in the environments in which they worked. Regardless of how individual foremen perceived the letters, they were exposed to a regular stream of copy that positioned them as members of a management community, reminding them that they must adopt a managerial demeanor if they were to be seen in a positive light by their managers and employers.

Selling Motivation to Factory Managers

While the syndicate's products were well-suited to prevailing managerial notions of motivation, its success depended on an effective sales strategy. Its marketing operation was based on the pyramid structure familiar to sales firms since the advent of scientific selling. At head of the operation was the syndicate's sales manager, Felix Shay, who oversaw the Mather and Howard sales forces. Each firm consisted of two divisions, which covered the east and west of the country, respectively, both under the direction of its own division manager. All four division managers directed a sales team of twenty-two men, comprising two field managers and twenty salesmen. Hence, although the sales force fluctuated to a higher or lower number owing to newly added territories and turnover, Shay strove to maintain a force of eighty-eight salesmen, each of whom was responsible for his own region.[53]

FIGURE 2.5. A salesman training session at the syndicate's Chicago offices. At these sessions the firm's sales specialists drilled Mather and Howard salesmen in the scripted sale talks and motivation-infused sales pitches that they would use when selling posters and pivot man letters to factory managers across the country. Charles Rosenfeld, the architect of the syndicate's sales techniques, stands at the back of the room to the right of the column. Special Collections Research Center, University of Chicago Library, Chicago, IL.

This hierarchical organization offered the syndicate a powerful motivational metaphor that emphasized the idea that salesmen could advance up the ranks as they made higher sales and impressed their managers.

The firm's selling techniques were based on meticulously scripted talks that salesmen had to deliver using personality-driven pitches. Written by Charles Rosenfeld, architect of the syndicate's sales strategy, the talks were designed to dominate the customer, in this case, the manager or whoever was responsible for buying outside products. At the same time, sales managers encouraged a highly competitive sales culture in which salesmen were under continual pressure to increase sales and outperform one another. The combination of rationalized and emotion-based techniques that the syndicate used to motivate salesmen echoed the formula used in the posters and pivot man letters sold out on the road. Thus, the products and the techniques used to sell them revolved around a similar preoccupation with motivation.

To encourage competitiveness, the syndicate paid salesmen on a commission-only basis of 25 percent on sales.[54] Seiders set a high sales bar, defining the "three-in-one" (three sales per day) as the salesman's target, and deemed one salesman's attainment of three sales in a week "mediocre."[55] The syndicate incentivized salesmen through bonuses, including a prize of $500 to the man who sold the most contracts each month. Mather and Howard also offered their own bonuses. In 1924 Mather promised to award any salesman who sold triple his annual quota a Packard automobile and sent letters to salesmen's wives asking them to encourage their husbands to work harder to increase sales. No one achieved this improbable target, and like other bonuses, its primary purpose was to stoke competition among salesmen.[56] The syndicate also deployed motivational rhetoric at induction and training sessions, where salesmen were drilled in Seth Seiders's "Big Vision" of "Financial Independence." This "Big Vision" comprised Seiders's own longtime dream of making a million dollars and retiring early with economic security and acted as a motivational mantra at the firm.[57] Although no salesmen achieved such lofty ambitions, some made high bonuses or even became field managers, aiding the syndicate's claim that a motivated attitude would bring salesmen financial and personal rewards.

When out selling, salesmen were expected to use a highly scripted sales talk written by Rosenfeld. The sales talk typified those used at other scientific selling organizations at this time. Consisting of several stages—subopener, opener, pitch, and closer—and running at several pages, it provided the entire spiel for the salesman in meticulous detail. Built into the sales talk were numerous contingencies so that in the event a prospect challenged any of the salesman's claims about the product or tried to shrug him off, salesmen had a canned response that, if used effectively, could nullify the objection and get the talk back on track. Designed to guarantee the salesman's total domination of the prospect and get him to buy, the sales talk embodied a subtle blend of scientific and emotional selling techniques.

By far the most important tool that salesmen had at his disposal was the "Verbal Proof Story." The V.P.S. was a testimonial letter or quote from a customer that attested to the effectiveness of the posters or pivot man letters. The syndicate supplied salesmen with reams of V.P.S.s that detailed a multitude of benefits offered by its products: if a prospect raised a specific objection, the competent salesman could pull out his binder and read aloud a few statements from satisfied customers that invalidated the prospect's case, quashing his resistance.[58] In reality, V.P.S.s were a bricolage of old and current customer responses, anecdotes, and salesman hearsay. In response to some salesmen's concerns about the questionable nature of V.P.S.s, sales managers reassured them that the practice was "not new as it has been in religious books for hundreds of years. It has been used by prominent writers, newspapers, and by your very own preacher, minister, priest or rabbi." Thus, salesmen should realize that at "church on Sunday" was heard "V.P.S.s, all through the services . . . The mere fact that you change the name of the Prospect and the name of the salesman makes no material difference, because after all, you are talking about what someone said about our service."[59] This rationale comprised a subtle form of arm-twisting whose goal was to secure the salesman's belief in his work and in the product.

Objections to the products took on many forms. Managers at firms undergoing economic troubles often stated that they could not afford the posters. Likewise, some at heavily unionized firms rebuffed salesmen on the basis that unionized workers would condemn the posters as propaganda, whereas others objected that their firm was too small to warrant the posters or that the specific type of work carried out at the firm was not portrayed in the posters or letters. If a salesman had mastered his V.P.S. file, he could read aloud statements from clients that verified the product's positive effects in any of these circumstances.[60] One of the most commonly raised objections by managers was that the posters would not be effective because "foreign-born" workers lacked basic literacy skills.[61] Upon encountering such objections, salesmen informed the prospect that immigrant workers were attracted to the posters due to their "brilliant colors" and the "action of the illustrations." Moreover, they added, on seeing allegorical posters depicting a football player, flaming airplane, or leaping tiger, the "foreign born worker" "asks someone who knows, generally his boss or straw-boss. The picture is explained—the text of the Poster is read to him. His inquiry gives a better opportunity to drive home the message through personal explanation."[62] Howard's salesmen used similar tactics, telling hesitant prospects that foreign-born foremen's "desire to learn" led them to implement the ideas of the pivot man letters far more readily than English-speaking workers.[63]

Managers at firms that employed a high number of black workers often rebuffed Mather salesmen based on similar concerns about low literacy. In such instances, salesmen were instructed to "put across to [the prospect] the thought that the human brain works about the same in a black skull as in a white skull and is just as responsive to constructive ideas and positive suggestions."[64] Sales managers supplied salesmen with a canned response based on this reasoning, which were added to the sales talk binder. The salesman was advised to "sit down with this Section of your Binder. Absorb all the information thoroughly. Tomorrow morning you will be hoping your first Prospect's payroll is loaded with the names of Negroes . . . Black or white, it makes no difference, when you know how to meet this Objection—except the difference in the size of your commission checks."[65] Like the syndicate's designers, its sales specialists appear not to have seriously considered incorporating representations of nonwhite workers.[66] Only in later decades—beginning during World War II—would designers begin to depict workers of color, and even then, their attempts were meager.

The syndicate kept the pressure up on salesmen through a weekly "pep" letter. Each letter was one to two pages long and concerned a specific theme challenging the salesman to improve his performance. Letters often revolved around contrasts between the effective salesman who cultivated self-discipline and confidence and the ineffective salesman who failed to adopt these traits. The syndicate reinforced this theme via cartoons that contrasted the "go-getter" salesman who studied his sales talks meticulously with his ineffective alter ego who was depicted as a failure, both as a salesman and a man.[67]

The syndicate's fixation with the line between success and failure as touted in its sales-boosting techniques helps explain why it embraced similar rhetoric in its products. The success-driven ideals espoused in its posters and pivot man letters were an extension of the obsessions of salesmen—Seiders and his associates—who reflexively assumed that their own ideals would be fitting for publicity aimed at workers. The links between salesmanship-type values, manliness, discipline, and what would later be called "impression management" are evident in the posters reproduced above.

The parallels between the syndicate's approaches to design and selling made for a highly unified culture of motivational messaging. The worker who saw a poster in the factory, the foreman who read a pivot man letter, and the salesman who sold the product were exposed to a singular ideology. This ideology, revolving around assertions of the virtues and rewards of hard work, repackaged sentiments that had been invoked by businessmen for workers' edification since the nineteenth century. In blending work ethic rhetoric with Elbert Hubbard's pithy contrasts between self-disciplined and undisciplined workers and the sensibilities of modern advertising, the syndicate synthesized the main strands of post–World War I motivational discourse. As the first firm to market modern motivational publicity nationwide, it also established a model that later firms would emulate and refine.

Ultimately, the Seth Seiders Syndicate's brand of motivation was unable to survive beyond the 1920s. Amid the economic belt-tightening that followed the onset of the Depression, managers had less money to spend on communication products sold by outside specialists. The firm's decline was also compounded by internal conflict between Seiders and some of his associates due to a tax avoidance scheme that resulted in Seiders being sued.[68] The company eventually broke up, and its remaining stocks of posters and pivot man letters ended up in the hands of a few of its diehard salesmen, who struggled on for a while after the Depression hit, eking out a meager living by selling them to schools as character-building aids for seventy-five cents each.[69] Seth Seiders himself wound up with a rosier future, retiring to a ranch in New Mexico, where, according to local legend, he sometimes entertained Al Caponc.[70]

The syndicate's failure symbolized the decline of the much-idealized managerial hope, inherited from the turn-of-the-century writings of Elbert Hubbard and his ilk that employees could be made to work harder by exposing them to continual reminders that doing so would lead to personal success. Seiders and his associates were too enthralled by the hope of realizing their fortunes to see that their brand of success-infused rhetoric spoke little to the workers who comprised their audience. Nonetheless, the syndicate's impressive sales indicate that many managers were becoming more accepting of psychological- and emotion-based motivation as well as the use of motivational images, and its success helped open the door wider for the continued spread of motivational propaganda in industry in years to come. Although independent sellers of motivational publicity would not reemerge on the national scene until World War II, the syndicate had paved the way for the spread of motivational propaganda in the industrial arena.

The 1920s brought mixed fortunes for the businessmen, economists, politicians, and entrepreneurs who were drawn to the promise of psychological motivation. On the one hand, the idea that united them—that workers' pathological instinctive drives and emotions could be "improved"—had serious limitations. Despite challenging Darwinist models of human behavior, this view was rooted in the assumption that emotions could be modified by scientific methods, a claim that reflected the overconfident mood of social science more than reality. On the other hand, those who believed that emotions were integral to workers' behaviors helped reframe motivation in more psychological terms, advancing ideas that first bloomed in the writings of Thorstein Veblen, Hugo Münsterberg, Walter Dill Scott, and instinct theorists.

The Wall Street crash in October 1929 and its devastating effects made clear that work's rewards were fragile, even if one could find work. Yet as the Depression began to add millions to the unemployment lines, devotees of motivation grew even more convinced that psychological-based approaches to motivation could help stifle class antagonisms and sustain faith in the promises of work and American capitalism.

CHAPTER 3

Visions of Striving

DEBATING WORK'S PROMISES IN THE GREAT DEPRESSION

> Better methods for the discovery of an administrative élite, better methods of maintaining working morale. The country that first solves these problems will ineffably outstrip the others in the race for stability, security, and development.
>
> —Elton Mayo, *Human Problems of an Industrial Civilization*, 1933

> Men are out of work. Our men. Our neighbors. Our citizens. Honest, hard-working folk. They want jobs. They're eager to work. But there aren't jobs enough to go round. Somebody's got to tide them over . . . We're going to share our luck with the folks out of work, aren't we? Remember—there's no National fund they can turn to for relief. It's up to us!
>
> —Poster published by the President's Organization on Unemployment Relief, 1931

> We're the people that live. They can't wipe us out; they can't lick us. We'll go on forever, Pa, 'cause we're the people.
>
> —John Steinbeck, *The Grapes of Wrath*, 1939

The Great Depression is not usually regarded as an era of motivation. In collective memory, the period often brings to mind mass unemployment, breadlines, and poverty-stricken farmers and rural migrants living hand to mouth, images that invoke struggles for survival and the decline of hope and suggest that all sense of motivation had eroded. However, amid the era's spiraling unemployment and mass suffering, motivational ideology took on new form. As the Depression destroyed jobs and, with it, hopes that work could deliver on its promises, interest in motivation deepened among industrial social scientists, management specialists, politicians, businessmen, and public relations specialists. Tributes to motivation of varying kinds also abounded in business culture, New Deal publicity, and Hollywood films depicting the strivings of the downtrodden. In a wide array of visual and written forms, motivational sentiment touting work's rewards became a pillar of national life.

While motivational discourse was multifaceted, it revolved largely around two distinct strands, a trend that was encouraged in part by the stark economic realities of the Depression. The first strand was rooted in elite conceptions of workers and the "labor problem" and was chiefly associated with industrial social scientists and businessmen. Elton Mayo, the most influential management theorist of the era, argued that workers were irrational and prone to conflict. By deploying an "elite" corps of human relations experts skilled in interviewing and counseling, he claimed, management could shape the worker's emotional life and induce cooperative attitudes. A similar view of motivation informed the policies of the era's first president. Herbert Hoover crafted a distinct kind of motivational discourse, one overlapping with that of management specialists but relying on tributes to bootstrap individualism. Believing that self-sufficiency was the basis of prosperity, Hoover rejected government intervention in the economy in favor of voluntary, state-level efforts to motivate the unemployed and institute cooperation between business and labor, measures he believed would help stave off class conflict.

The second strand of motivational discourse emerged outside the workplace and was grounded in the populist language that characterized the New Deal and much Depression-era culture, each of which emphasized the transcendent power of communal bonds. At its heart, the New Deal upheld the virtues of workers and labor. This stance informed New Deal policy, not least the Wagner Act of 1935, which granted workers the right to establish unions and required employers to recognize them. The New Deal's support for labor was reflected in Roosevelt's oratories to the "forgotten man" and New Deal photographs of the rural poor struggling for a better life amid the Depression.[1] In endeavoring to put the nation back to work, New Dealers positioned the state as a powerful agent of motivation, a stance that businessmen found objectionable because, they believed, it undermined self-sufficiency, bred dependency on government, and empowered unions.

This chapter traces the shifting discourse about motivation throughout the Depression, charting its role in shaping ideas about work and democracy. In an era when work became a major preoccupation in national life, discussions about motivation rapidly spilled over from industry into other arenas. Although debates over motivation had always cross-pollinated between the workplace and other spheres, this process intensified during the Depression as work became a central concern in politics and mass culture. Given that the populist strand of motivation proved the most enduring as the New Deal gathered steam, one might expect that the era ultimately embodied a triumph for workers and others who rallied around a more democratic vision of work and industry. After all, as Michael Denning argues, the era produced a new "laboring of American culture" whereby American life became infused with working-class imagery and rhetoric.[2] However, while motivation acquired a more populist tone, industrialists and their allies were quick to adapt its tributes to "the people" and their struggles to more conservative goals in their communications techniques. The appropriation of populist motivation also helped lay groundwork for businessmen's campaigns to weaken the New Deal and labor in the postwar era.

HUMAN RELATIONS AND THE RISE OF "THERAPEUTIC" MOTIVATION IN INDUSTRY

In the shadows of the Depression's more visible events, ideas about work and motivation underwent a far-reaching shift as management specialists continued to abandon economic models of motivation in favor of those that deployed psychology. Although Taylorism remained central to strategizing production, its claim that workers were motivated chiefly by earnings continued to lose authority. Psychological-based theories of motivation, in emphasizing workers' "needs" and "desires," helped management to cast itself as an agent of democratization, which in turn veiled its core goals—to assuage labor conflict, marginalize unions, and secure its dominion over workers.

These changes gathered steam partly because of the proliferation of corporate-sponsored research studies into industry as well as the rising status of human relations in academe. The era's most influential industrial research initiative was the Hawthorne studies, conducted by researchers from Harvard Business School (HBS) over a period of nine years at Western Electric's Hawthorne plant outside Chicago. For its first five years, the project focused on issues relating to productivity and remained largely unknown beyond management circles. In the late 1920s, however, the prominence and influence of the studies grew as HBS received financial support from a powerful new sponsor: the Rockefeller Foundation. The foundation had deep roots in antiunionism and motivational ideology. During a 1914 strike at a Rockefeller-owned mine in Ludlow, Colorado, the mine's management sent in police and state militia. The brutal put-down that followed left eleven children and two women dead. The Ludlow Massacre and the massive public outrage that followed prompted the Rockefellers to look for more subtle approaches to suppressing unions, including employee representation plans (company "unions" that offered little real protection for workers). These plans, which barred collective bargaining, were implemented throughout Rockefeller-owned companies and were taken up by many other companies during the 1920s.[3]

The foundation's escalating financial support for HBS extended the Rockefellers' antilabor ambitions into academe. Beginning with a $155,000 grant to launch an industrial psychology program in 1927, the foundation made additional annual grants to Harvard of up to $125,000 and multiyear grants of $875,000 and $360,000 in 1930 and 1937, respectively. Amounting to over $1.5 million between 1923 and 1943—the most extensive corporate effort to advance research into motivation and other workplace issues until that time—these monies funded HBS's research well beyond the conclusion of the Hawthorne studies.[4]

At the center of HBS's contributions to motivational research was the highly influential work of Elton Mayo. An Australian émigré, Mayo gained recognition as the figurehead of the field of human relations after joining the faculty of HBS in 1926. Over the next fifteen years, Mayo's reputation swelled owing to his association with the Hawthorne studies. His achievements were not all that they seemed, however. Not only did he smooth his career path by passing himself off as a physician, but his involvement in the Hawthorne studies was also more limited than he implied. It was not until spring 1928—several years into the studies—that Mayo first visited the Hawthorne plant, and even then, his role was mainly to interpret the findings for Western Electric's executives, not to conduct research.[5]

Despite his exaggerated claims, however, Mayo's writings had a lasting influence on motivation. Most important, he popularized within management the idea that "undesirable" attitudes and behaviors (labor conflict, for example) were the result of the worker's individual and irrational maladjustments. In turn, these maladjustments could be remedied only by the "therapeutic" approaches of psychopathologists and other medical experts. Given Mayo's far-reaching influence on managerial conceptions of motivation in the 1930s, a discussion of the formation of his theories is essential here.

Mayo's perceptions of workers and industry were shaped by his upbringing in Adelaide's highbrow culture. Adelaide was the hub of the educated and professional classes who disdained the industrial working class, which regularly engaged in strikes in Australia in the late nineteenth and early twentieth centuries. Like many of Adelaide's upper echelon, Mayo regarded the industrial class as pathologically prone to conflict and in need of civilizing. No less influential in shaping his outlook was his family, several of who were noted physicians. His parents had high hopes that he would continue that tradition, and with their support, he embarked on medical degrees three times between 1899 and 1903 in Adelaide, Edinburgh, and London but failed each time. Mayo nonetheless continued to regard himself as a medical specialist, and he couched his theories about motivation largely through the lens of psychopathology. Returning to Australia, he began to find his niche by taking a degree in psychology and philosophy. He graduated in 1911 with a thesis that emphasized the irrelevance of socialism and unions, arguing that only an elite of experts could resolve industry's problems.[6]

Mayo refined his theories about motivation over the next decade during lecturing positions in philosophy at the University of Queensland in Brisbane. There he adapted Freud's theories on neurosis to argue that industrial problems were due to the worker's individual maladjustment. No less influential for Mayo was the work of the Polish anthropologist Bronisław Malinowski, whom he met in 1914 and whose research among the Trobriand Islanders on "primitive" kinship networks Mayo drew inspiration from in his arguments about workers' pathologies.[7] A second theme to emerge in

Mayo's early writings—one emphasized in his 1919 book, *Democracy and Freedom*—was his critique of the state. He argued that democracy, by rousing the hopes and desires of the masses, had given rise to "irrational" forces, not least labor unions, which threatened civilization. Because the individual was irrational and prone to self-interest, neither the state nor political parties, he asserted, could manage democracy. Only experts trained in psychopathology could resolve these problems. Mayo developed these arguments in several articles on Australian industrial relations, in which he drew on Pierre Janet's theories about "hysteria" as well as his own research on soldiers suffering from shell shock after World War I.[8] Like Janet's patients and shell-shocked soldiers, he posited, workers were neurotic and dissociated from reality. Extending his earlier critiques of the state, he argued that classical economics was incapable of resolving industrial conflict because it assumed incorrectly that "human motives are based upon clear reasoning and logic."[9]

Mayo was far from the first to make such arguments about motivation—as we have seen, instinct theorists made similar ones after World War I—but it was he who would popularize them in America. In 1922, Mayo took academic leave and embarked for London, hoping to launch his career there. The journey included a layover in San Francisco, where he planned to give paid lectures to fund the rest of his trip. The lectures failed to materialize, however, and penniless and stranded, Mayo resigned himself to returning to Australia. One lead proved fruitful, however—an invitation to speak to the National Research Council (NRC) in Washington, D.C. Mayo impressed the NRC's leaders with his insights into industrial psychiatry and, with their support, was hired a few months later by the Industrial Relations Research Department of the University of Pennsylvania's Wharton School to conduct studies into Philadelphia factories. By 1924, with support from the NRC, Mayo was receiving funding from the Rockefeller Foundation. In his research on fatigue and monotony in Philadelphia, Mayo continued to make the case that labor problems were rooted not in work itself but in the worker's individual maladjustment to it. Alienated from his work, the worker was prone to "reveries"—daydreams—that encouraged his hostility toward management and fueled radicalism. These problems could be resolved only via a therapeutic treatment of these "abnormalities." The institution most capable of this task, he added, was the corporation. This conclusion, unsurprisingly, was well received by the Rockefeller Foundation, which granted three additional years of funding, allowing him to resign from his position in Brisbane.[10]

The timing of Mayo's arrival at Harvard Business School in 1926 was fortuitous. The school's dean, Wallace Donham, was at this point attempting to shift its focus from applied economics to human relations in industry. An admirer of Oswald Spengler's *Decline of the West*, Donham had a deep affinity with the sense of civilizing mission that swept through conservative academic circles after World War I, one that Mayo's theories complemented. Mayo brought to Harvard a Rockefeller grant of $12,000—the first of many over the next decade. These monies allowed the school to cast itself as a hub of scientific research into industrial problems, not least by setting up experimental labs and large research studies, which proved invaluable in inoculating it from criticism.[11]

In 1933, Mayo published what would become one of the most influential management books of the mid-twentieth century: *The Human Problems of an Industrial Civilization*. The book offered little that was new, mainly distilling his previous ideas, but three of its arguments would have long-lasting influence on management conceptions of motivation. First, Mayo claimed that industrial fatigue and monotony, which depleted workers' morale, were not caused by industrial work itself as many management specialists believed. Rather, they were rooted in the pathologies of an industrial society that weakened the individual worker's ability to cooperate. Second, scientific management, by offering workers economic incentives, addressed only the symptoms of poor morale, not its causes, and merely encouraged them to seek the solidarity of coworkers and unions. What was needed, he claimed, were therapeutic techniques like employee counseling and interviews. Pointing to the results of the Hawthorne studies (and slyly implying a more central role for himself in the research than was the case), he held that such methods were vital because they neutralized workers' antagonisms toward management by allowing them to air grievances about work. Finally, Mayo argued that the state was incapable of creating cooperation in industry because it was too "centralized politically and geographically" and thus "too remote morally and spatially." Therefore, it was necessary to create an "elite" of administrators skilled in therapeutic techniques. Of unions, Mayo said barely anything, believing that they were completely unnecessary and undeserving of management's attention.[12]

Although such arguments had been made by industrial social scientists for over two decades by this juncture, they had failed to break the hold of economic-based theories of motivation. But with such influential organizations as the Rockefeller Foundation and the Harvard Business School throwing financial support behind human relations research, the door was effectively opened for psychological-based theories about motivation to receive a warmer reception. By implying that he was the "leader" of the Hawthorne studies (and a medical doctor to boot), Mayo found himself in the right place at the right time.

Generations of management theorists have described Mayo's work as a major departure from Taylorism because it was rooted in a more holistic understanding of the worker and defined the worker's psychological and emotional needs as the core focus of management. The shift from Taylor to Mayo is still invoked in many management textbooks and popular business books as a democratizing one. Yet the two theorists were aligned in their belief that workers were pathological and that management had a divine right to "cure" them. The difference, as Gerard Hanlon argues, was that Mayo insisted that the mind was the route to this objective, not bodily discipline as Taylor believed. Mayo was also in agreement with Taylor's belief that labor unions were an irrelevancy.[13] Although Mayo obscured his antiunion views in his writings to make his theories more palatable to his Rockefeller Foundation sponsors (who wished to disassociate the Rockefellers from harsh antiunionism in the public mind), he was clear in his earlier articles in Australia that labor agitation was irrational. As he wrote in one such article, "Socialism, Guild Socialism, Anarchism and the like are very largely the phantasy constructions of the neurotic."[14]

The theories of motivation advanced by Mayo and other human relations specialists were gradually adapted in the factory by managers from the 1930s onward.[15] At many large firms, personnel departments became a means to formalize human relations techniques like employee interviews and counseling. By blending these motivational techniques with older welfare capitalism methods (such as company unions, pensions, and social events), many managers found ways to assuage workers' grievances and create a buffer against the era's increasingly powerful labor unions. As Loren Baritz argues, "By 'capitalizing' and 'integrating' [workers'] wants 'into the life of the business,' managers could funnel human behavior into the most profitable channels." Between 1932 and 1935, the proportion of companies employing over five thousand workers that had a personnel department rose from around a third to over three quarters.[16] Firms that created such departments or continued them after the onset of the Depression experienced relatively little labor-management conflict.[17]

Managers' interest in psychological-based motivation did not originate solely in the industrial arena or from theorists like Mayo, however. It emerged also through the era's politics and culture. Moreover, when the federal government, along with management and its allies, developed their motivational arsenal during World War II, it was from the imagery and language of Depression-era culture that they drew inspiration. Before continuing to explore workplace motivation, we must therefore trace the era's core developments in motivational discourse.

THE LAST HURRAH OF "BOOTSTRAP" MOTIVATION: MORALE BOOSTING IN HOOVER'S AMERICA

The crisis of the Depression prompted widespread discussion about work and motivation in the political sphere. While motivation took on many meanings when invoked in politics, it became central to debates over national recovery and political policy throughout the decade. The significance of these deliberations becomes clear when we consider the responses of the era's two most prominent political figures, Herbert Hoover and Franklin Delano Roosevelt, to the Depression, as well as the era's most important political event—the New Deal.

Herbert Hoover's presidency is widely regarded as a failure, not least due to his ineffectual response to the suffering caused by the Depression. His refusal to offer unemployment relief—which he dismissed as a "socialistic dole"—betrayed a disregard for the human devastation wreaked by the crisis.[18] Recognized less, however, is that under Hoover, the federal government began to adopt a more active role in orchestrating motivation. Although few would consider Hoover a "motivational" president—that mantle would be claimed by Roosevelt during the New Deal—history shows that he was nonetheless a transitional figure who, ironically, helped pave the way for the state's robust deployment of motivation. Hoover's stiff-upper-lip oratories marked the last gasp of the high-minded motivational rhetoric invoked by elites since the nineteenth century. Yet his main tactics for combating the Depression—he asked businessmen to support stabilization measures and encouraged the public to contribute to local unemployment relief initiatives voluntarily—signaled a grudging acceptance that the federal government could be used as an instrument for orchestrating motivation. While Hoover's influence on motivational discourse became evident only with the passage of time, he turns out to have been one of its most influential architects.

Hoover's rhetoric invoked the tributes to individualism and self-sufficiency invoked customarily by "successful" men in the early twentieth century. These beliefs reflected his unusual path to prominence. Orphaned at age nine, he surpassed expectations by becoming the most celebrated engineer of his day. In the 1900s he worked all over the world and built a $4 million fortune, gaining widespread acclaim as "the Great Engineer." During World War I, he headed the U.S. relief effort in Belgium and, after the armistice, became U.S. food administrator and director general of the American Relief Administration in Europe. His experiences instilled in him a belief that success was a matter of individual determination.

As president, with unemployment swelling and millions living meagerly, Hoover upheld self-sufficiency as an article of faith. Even as he lent support for the banks, he refused to provide government relief for the unemployed, adhering to his presidential campaign stance that relief would "stifle initiative and invention" and "cramp and cripple the mental and spiritual energies of our people."[19] When the bottom fell out of the market shortly before the Wall Street crash, his response was to dismiss it. "The fundamental business of the country," he stated blithely, "is on a sound and prosperous basis."[20] He continued to dismiss concerns about the unemployed, remarking, "No one is actually starving" and scoffed that "the Hoboes are better fed now than they've ever been."[21] Indeed, he claimed, "many persons left their jobs for the more profitable one of selling apples."[22] Hoover's efforts to minimize rather than tackle suffering were reflected in his use of the term "depression," a word chosen because it sounded less frightening than "panic" or "crisis" and implied that recovery would follow.[23]

While Hoover shrank from offering aid to ordinary Americans, he was glad to play the role of motivator when seeking businessmen's help in stabilizing industry. He urged employers to do their part to shore up industry by maintaining wages and implementing job sharing instead of firing workers. He also encouraged railway and utilities owners to continue with expansion plans while pledging that the federal government would fund construction, advising state governors to do the same.[24] Because these measures depended on voluntarism and were implemented unevenly, they did little to improve the livelihoods of workers or the unemployed. Many firms eventually cut wages and engaged in erratic hiring, worsening workers' situations. Hoover's morale boosting amounted mostly to impression management. As journalist Caroline Bird notes caustically, "Optimism was deliberate policy. The wisest and most learned believed that the country would become rich if businessmen could be made to believe that every day in every way they were getting closer and closer to prosperity."[25] And yet, though Hoover's attempts to rally businessmen did nothing to arrest the Depression, they marked a significant development: for the first time since World War I, the state was becoming an agent of motivation.

This shift became clear in 1931. With millions living in desperate conditions amid the deepening Depression, Hoover reluctantly began to advocate aid for the unemployed. Still staunch in his distaste for federal relief, he instead endorsed local- and state-level voluntary relief initiatives. The most prominent of these efforts was the President's Organization on Unemployment Relief (POUR), a program established by Hoover in late summer 1931. The organization echoed earlier Hooverite ideals of voluntarism but also involved a robust media campaign using billboards, radio, and magazine ads. While encouraging relief at lower levels, POUR publicity was careful to stress that the federal government was not itself funding relief. Hoover reaffirmed this position in radio addresses in the following months. As he told the nation in October, "No governmental action, no economic doctrine, no economic plan or project can replace that God-imposed responsibility of the individual man and woman to their neighbors." A better course, he noted, was "a spirit of mutual self-help through voluntary giving, through the responsibility of local government."[26]

The high-minded language of POUR, like Hoover's, championed the moral imperative of middle-class aid and was at pains to suppress the specter of federal intervention. This tactic is typified in an ad published in *Good Housekeeping* on New Year's Day, 1932 (figure 3.1). The text explains that, though unemployed, the man depicted is "combating adversity with

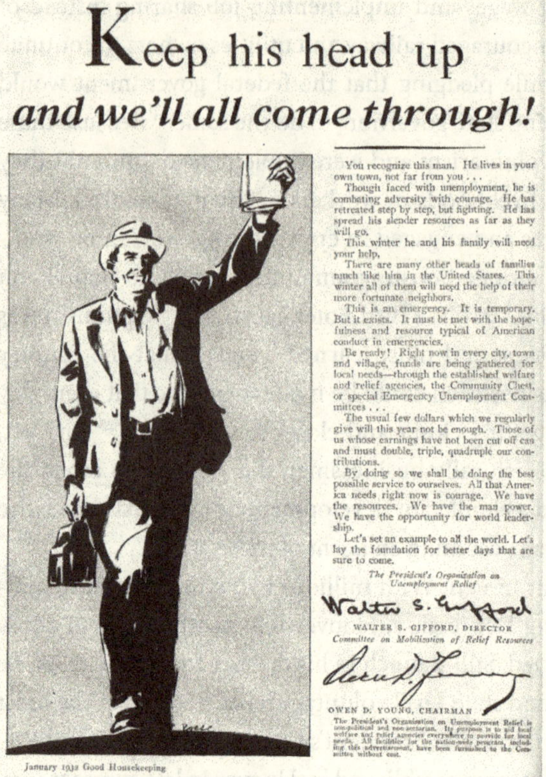

FIGURE 3.1. This POUR ad embodies the Hooverite principle that voluntary state-level aid, coupled with an individualistic sense of striving, was sufficient for the unemployed to "come through" the Depression. Managers would adapt this rhetoric after World War II in quests to counter the communitarian motivational discourse associated with the New Deal and labor unions. *Good Housekeeping*, January 1, 1932.

courage" and "has retreated step by step but fighting." These sentiments evoke an image of the embattled, heroic soldier of World War I, a tactic that deftly linked the man's resilience to national resolve during wartime, neatly avoiding suggestions of working-class agency. The ad's title, "Keep his head up and we'll all come through!" underscores POUR's core tactic: to placate calls for government relief and stave off anger toward government. Depicting a worker cheerfully waving his newspaper (suggesting perhaps that he was chasing up job ads?), he embodies an elite fantasy of the respectable and amenable worker who strives to improve his lot without complaint. Despite the hardships he faces, he symbolizes the essence of the upstanding striver whose qualities—not least his unthreatening demeanor—businessmen had extolled since the nineteenth century.[27]

Other POUR ads sought to enlist the support of middle-class readers by invoking a gutsier tone that recalled that of World War I propaganda.

Typical was "Of Course We Can Do It!," which was published in *Literary Digest* in November 1931. It depicted a middle-class man, with rolled-up sleeves and tightening his belt, who urged readers to do their part to help the unemployed. The text appealed to readers' patriotism, again touting the nation's past glories: "We dug the Panama Canal didn't we? And they said we couldn't do that. We put an army in France four months after we entered the World War didn't we? And surprised the world. Now we've got a tough one to crack right here in our own yard. Men are out of work. Our men. Our neighbors. Our citizens. Honest, hard-working folk. They want jobs. They're eager to work. But there aren't jobs enough to go 'round. Somebody's got to tide them over. Who's going to do it? The people who dug that ditch. The people who went to France, or bought Liberty Bonds, or went without sugar—Mr. and Mrs. John K. American. That means you–and *you* and Y O U—every one of us who is lucky enough to have a job. We're going to share our luck with the folks out of work, aren't we?"[28]

Despite its more robust motivational language compared with that of the first ad, workers are once again rendered passive recipients of aid, and any hint of their grievance is smothered by tributes to national perseverance. And to ensure that readers understood that the state was merely encouraging *voluntary* action, not federal relief, it added, "Remember—there's no National fund they can turn to for relief. It's up to us!"[29]

With its calls for voluntary cooperation and its resistance to unemployment relief, POUR brought the elite-minded motivational sentiment familiar to industrial social science in the 1920s to the center of government discourse. Minor adjustments of attitude, not fundamental change, were the order of the day. Hooverites, like many social scientists and economists of the previous decade, believed that the system would endure as long as people believed in it. POUR amounted to a slick advertising campaign, aimed at pushing responsibility for relief onto the states, one inspired largely by Hoover's desire to avoid "a socialistic dole," the effects of which, he claimed, would be "to lower wages toward the bare subsistence level and to endow the slackers."[30] These sentiments laid bare the logic that underwrote the campaign and, indeed, the Hooverite stance on labor relations and the role of government.

While affirming that the federal government would not provide relief, Hoover's acceptance that government should play a role in aiding economic recovery—albeit a limited one—cracked the door open a little wider for government to become an agent of motivation. No less consequential was his faith that the "science of advertising" (which had helped secure his 1928 election victory) was vital for instilling confidence and stimulating recovery. Yet Hoover's brand of motivation found few admirers beyond businessmen and elites. By summer 1932, POUR had run its course. It had become the source of ridicule, lampooned by the press as a grossly inadequate and callous response to the nation's suffering.[31] The ideals of individual self-interest and voluntary cooperation between labor and business that Hoover promoted did not disappear. Much of the publicity unleashed by FDR's New Deal in efforts to boost morale during the Depression contained echoes of his pep-driven vernacular, as did the consumer-driven motivational ideology that proliferated after World War II.[32] Although a political failure, Hoover thus turns out to have been one of the architects of twentieth-century motivational ideology, one whose visions of industrial progress would echo in the motivational discourse invoked by management and its allies in the decades ahead.[33]

POPULIST MOTIVATION IN THE NEW DEAL AND DEPRESSION

The 1932 election of Franklin Delano Roosevelt and the coming of the New Deal signaled not only a political sea change but also the rise of a very different kind of motivational discourse. Whereas Hoover's morale boosting was badly out of step with the realities of the Depression, the soaring motivational sentiment that issued forth through the New Deal's communications channels spoke meaningfully to them. At the center of the New Deal was a sustained tribute (one invoked regularly by politicians, artists, and visionaries) of the heroic struggles of "the people." While the era's spiraling unemployment meant that motivational messages touting material rewards receded, rhetoric about *striving*—an ideal related closely to motivation—was invoked widely. Such accolades formed the nucleus of New Deal art programs and much of the era's popular culture, supplying a sharp contrast to Hooverite rhetoric. Even so, New Dealers did not altogether discard the accolades to individualism common in the past. Instead, the older individualism was absorbed into them, supplying reminders that traditional routes to success remained open.[34]

The New Deal made ample use of motivational language linking collective striving to national recovery. This language was central to the National Industrial Recovery Act and such programs as the Public Works Administration, the Civil Works Administration, and the Civilian Conservation Corps, each of which framed recovery in visions of communitarian work, a stance that informed the New Deal's support for labor unions.[35] For Roosevelt, motivational oratory was a political weapon, one that he deployed to powerful effect in his inaugural address, whereupon he famously assured Americans, "All we have to fear is fear itself."[36] He honed it also in the intimate space of radio, especially during his "fireside chats," where he addressed listeners as "my friends" and spoke to them as members of a community whose destinies were bound together.[37] Pivotal to his command of motivational vernacular was his own struggle to overcome polio. For many Americans, Roosevelt's recovery provided a motivational metaphor about the power of resolve in overcoming seemingly insurmountable odds.

Portrayals of Americans as virtuous strivers circulated widely in mass culture throughout the Depression. Everywhere—in journalism, radio programs, novels, plays, music, and photography—images of Americans struggling against economic and social forces beyond their control formed the core of popular narratives. Such stories were especially prominent in the era's popular films, many of which concerned the struggle to find or keep work. The most successful films valorized the difficulties of ordinary Americans in the face of the Depression and mocked elites. In backstage dramas, paeans to the "common man," as well as stories about dust bowl migration, the formula remained consistent: the emotional crux revolved around survival through work.

These tendencies were typified by the popular backstage drama *Gold Diggers of 1933*. When a group of showgirls becomes unemployed after their show is shut down owing to lack of funds, its producer conceives of a musical that blends spectacular dance scenes with Depression-era commentary. Its rousing finale, "Remember My Forgotten Man," an homage to the "forgotten man" of World War I, with its cavalcade of injured soldiers and out-of-work men on the breadlines, made an impassioned plea for a collective response to the Depression's suffering. Charles Chaplin's 1936 film, *Modern Times*, offered a different take on work and motivation, dramatizing the dehumanizing effects of technological modernization on the worker's mind and body. The film follows Chaplin's Tramp as he endures the Depression's realities: the alienating effects of rationalized labor, unemployment, poverty, and hunger. Work's brutalities are captured viscerally in the factory scenes where he suffers mental and physical exhaustion and in the iconic moment in which he is literally sucked into the giant cogs of the machine (figure 3.2). John Ford's 1940 adaptation of John Steinbeck's novel *Grapes of Wrath*, published a year earlier, offered a more ostensibly critical take on work and striving. Like the novel, the film emphasizes the brutalities visited on tenant farmers by the agriculture business and the dustbowl. When researching the novel, Steinbeck visited migrant labor camps in California and talked with a Farm Security Administration (FSA) camp manager, Tom Collins, whose notes he consulted. Steinbeck also drew on "group man

FIGURE 3.2. Charles Chaplin, *Modern Times*. Modern Times Copyright © Roy Export S.A.S.

theory," an ideal adapted from philosophy that emphasized the superior collective power of the group as opposed to the individual.[38]

Despite dramatizing the Depression's human costs, however, the solutions to economic troubles that mainstream films offered mostly revolved around individualistic quests for prosperity, not collective defiance of an unfair system.[39] In *Gold Diggers of 1933*, working-class dignity and critique of elites is subsumed by the girls' hopes for traditional yearnings, including consumer goods (clothes and fancy dinners) and marriage. The broader message of the film was thus conservative: the crisis of joblessness can be overcome by remaining motivated and teaming up with elites. *Modern Times*, although a damning indictment of modern work, offers an optimistic if ambiguous conclusion. Its finale, in which the Tramp and his female companion walk toward the sunrise accompanied by the rousing tones of "Smile though Your Heart Is Aching," while underscoring the profound uncertainties of the moment, suggested that individual pluck and conjugal arrangements would see them and, it implied, the film's viewers through hard times.

The Grapes of Wrath invokes a similarly individualistic response to the Depression and, given its strong imprint on the era's iconography of virtuous striving (not least in FSA photography), is worth dwelling on briefly. The film's individualizing tactic is signaled in the opening text, which states, "This is the story of one farmer's family driven from their fields by natural disasters and economic changes beyond anyone's control," before describing the forthcoming story as a "great journey in search of peace, security and another home."[40] Despite its austere-looking shots, barren environments, and references to the unfairness of the system, the film reminds viewers that a gritty sense of determination will carry the family through. Whereas the novel closes bleakly with the Joads marooned in a railroad boxcar after Rose of Sharon has delivered a stillborn baby, at the end of the film she is still pregnant as the family heads into the horizon and, it is implied, a brighter future, symbolized by the impending birth. This feeling is reinforced by Ma's rousing speech that affirms, "We're the people that live. They can't wipe us out; they can't lick us. We'll go on forever, Pa, 'cause we're the people." Like the novel, the film reinforces another familiar tendency in Depression-era motivational narratives—it limits the effects of rural labor exploitation to whites. As Michael Denning argues, the novel and the film position a white Protestant family as the symbolic victims of rural labor exploitation, obscuring the fact that the majority of agricultural workers swept up in that system were Mexican, Filipino, Chinese, and Japanese.[41] Although Steinbeck and Ford were far from the first to invoke romanticized visions of white motivation—such assumptions had been common for years in economists' studies of labor—*The Grapes of Wrath* reinforced to its viewers the notion that white workers were the natural standard-bearers of virtuous motivation.

The fact that Hollywood films exhorted romanticized forms of individualism and deemphasized the racial complexities of Depression-era suffering and striving does not invalidate their explorations of alienation arising from work and its absence. The era's popular films exposed millions of Americans to examinations of economic disparities that they may not have otherwise encountered. Yet they also resolved such problems by reinforcing one of the most troubling claims of motivational ideology: they encouraged audiences to believe that work would pay off if they summoned up enough determination and got on with it. The very absence of work, in fact, allowed romantic visions of motivation to flourish because people could be depicted as noble strivers tenaciously seeking a means of existence. In crafting such narratives, Hollywood dramatized grievances about work in ways that preserved existing modes of authority and reinforced the legitimacy of capitalism. Although Hollywood tributes to motivation upheld the virtues of New Deal liberalism rather than the top-down visions of businessmen, in the years to come management specialists would prove highly capable in adapting the era's paeans to common struggle to sophisticated motivational propaganda designed to sell employees on work's rewards. The populist morale boosting that proliferated through the New Deal and Depression-era films thus provided raw materials out of which management later reinvigorated its propaganda apparatus.[42]

"People with a Little Spirit": Visualizing Virtuous Striving in FSA Photography

New Deal tributes to virtuous striving found their strongest expression through visual images, not least the widely circulated photographs created by the Historical Section of the New Deal's Resettlement Agency (RA, later the FSA). Established in 1935 and directed by economist Roy Stryker, the section was tasked with documenting the Depression's effects on the land, though its focus soon shifted to the rural poor. Photographs of struggling farmers and migrant workers and, later, resilient small-town communities conveyed the New Deal principle of collective determination in the face of catastrophe. During its nine-year existence, the section's dozen or so photographers produced over a quarter of a million photographs, comprising the largest collection of images of American life then created. Printed in newspaper and magazine articles on the Depression's effects, these portrayals of endurance during hard times became a powerful means for enlisting public support for New Deal programs aimed at alleviating rural poverty. Photographs, Stryker believed, could *induce action*—the literal definition of motivation.[43]

The FSA's efforts to leverage the emotional power of photographs were an outgrowth of the post–World war I endeavor to infuse economics with rhetoric about workers' needs and aspirations. Stryker became interested in photography's communicative potential while studying economics at Columbia University during that time. There, he was hired as a research assistant by his mentor, Rexford Tugwell, mainly to gather images for inclusion in a textbook. Published in 1925, *American Economic Life and the Means of Its Improvement* made the case that enhancing the living standards of the working class was not just an economic matter; to succeed, this goal would require a synthesized understanding of the array of economic and social factors that shaped people's lives. Containing scores of images of industrial and rural work gathered by Stryker, the book typified the view of a growing number of economists and social scientists that images could enrich understanding of labor economics.[44]

As director of the Historical Section—in 1935 he was again hired by Tugwell, who had been tapped to head the RA—Stryker adapted his belief in the power of photographs for a new purpose: to encourage Americans to support the New Deal's rural reform agenda. Photographs of struggling farmers and migrant workers, he believed, could humanize economic problems and, in so doing, enlist public support for programs that tackled rural blight. While Stryker believed that such goals could be served by images of men and women alike, he invoked men's struggles in particular. Especially potent, he believed, were the "faces" of the subjects. As he explained, "When a man is down and they have taken from him his job and his land and his home—everything he spent his life working for—he's going to have the expression of tragedy permanently on his face. But I have always believed that the American people have the ability to endure . . . You see something in those faces that transcends misery."[45] Just as Lewis Hine's photographs urged support for industrial reforms by giving a "human face" to the harsh realities of factory work, images of the rural poor striving nobly in the face of the Depression could advance the cause of federal rural reform.

The section's early photographs depicting those who bore the brunt of the Depression's effects were marked by two recurring tropes, which together formed the thrust of its portrayals of honorable striving. First, the suffering caused by the Depression was represented largely through images of the white rural poor. This tendency stemmed from prevailing assumptions among New Dealers like Stryker that images of poverty-stricken whites would be the best means to induce the sympathies of the photographs' predominantly white and middle-class viewers.[46] Second, the photographers represented suffering and resilience mainly through portrayals of individuals and families. This practice reflected Stryker's view (and that of many of the photographers) that such images, in conveying the Depression's human costs, could help enlist public support for New Deal rural relief programs.[47]

An emphasis on the enduring capacity to struggle on in the face of overwhelming circumstances was an underlying strand of some of the FSA's most well-known photographs. This feeling informs the photograph that has gone down in history as *the* symbol of the American people's suffering during the Depression, Dorothea Lange's *Migrant Mother*.[48] While the photograph's portrayal of the mother and her children gives visual testimony to suffering, her protective embrace of her children and her poignant stare also suggest an aura of resilience amid overwhelming challenges. Idealizations of striving amid crisis informed photographs of families, whether walking along the roadside searching for work; making their way to California on ramshackle trucks; or eking out a living on infertile land amid the dust bowl. Idealized striving was an underlying trope in another widely viewed photograph, Arthur Rothstein's *Fleeing a Dust Storm* (figure 3.3). Depicting a father and his two sons making their way to a cabin as a dust storm appears to swirl around them, the image, like much of the section's early output, portrays family members (in this case a homosocial representation)

FIGURE 3.3. Arthur Rothstein, *Fleeing a Dust Storm*, 1936. Library of Congress, Prints and Photographs Division, FSA/OWI Collection, Reproduction no. LC-USZ62–11491, Washington, D.C.

struggling on amid threats. As several historians have noted, the section's images reinforced idealized notions of whites as the "deserving poor," a characterization that was rooted in assumptions that whites were more capable of becoming "self-sustaining" and that deemphasized the racial dimensions of rural poverty.[49] In turn, the section's photographs offered visual corroboration of the idea that whites were more naturally predisposed to motivation, a belief ingrained in social science.

From 1937 onward, the section's portrayals of rural suffering receded as Stryker, seeking to emphasize the positive effects of the FSA, encouraged photographers to show the hope and resilience of the people.[50] Increasingly common in the section's output for the next few years were images depicting FSA migrant camps that helped displaced farm families get back on their feet; farm families who had begun to turn their struggling farms around owing to FSA loans; small-town life rooted in community and commerce; and families enjoying the rewards of home. Inspired by suggestions by sociologist Robert Lynd at a meeting in 1936, Stryker began to supply photographers with "shooting scripts" for their assignments. Conceived as a way to bring the sociological approach of the Lynds' *Middletown* to the FSA project, the scripts provided broad guidelines that encouraged the photographers to document everyday life and traditions. The first script that Stryker circulated following his meeting with Lynd called for pictures of "home in the evening." His suggestions included "photographs showing the various ways that different income groups spend their evenings, for example: Informal clothes; Listening to the radio; Bridge; More precise dress; Guests." The script also called for pictures of "the effect of the depression in the smaller towns of the United States [which should] include such things as the growth of small independent shops, stores, and businesses in the small towns; for example, the store opened up on the sun porch, the beauty shop in the living room."[51]

The guidelines that Stryker issued to photographers from 1940 onward underscore the shift to an even more upbeat portrayal of striving. In fall 1940, Stryker wrote to ask Jack Delano for some "autumn pictures" and to "emphasize the idea of abundance—the 'horn of plenty'—and pour maple syrup over it—you know mix well with white clouds and put on a sky blue platter. I know your damned photographer's soul writhes, but to hell with it. Do you think I give a damn about a photographer's soul with Hitler at our doorstep? You are nothing but camera fodder to me."[52] These optimistic qualities became increasingly common, not least in images of productive farmwork. Arthur Rothstein, the youngest of the section's photographers, who was known to be the most amenable to Stryker's requests, excelled in creating the more positive, motivation-laden images that Stryker favored. His photographs depicted farm families relaxing in their homes and wives posing with jars or cans of produce (figure 3.4). Rothstein was hardly alone in taking hopeful, bouyant photographs. Russell Lee, for example, produced a much celebrated series entitled *Pie Town* that depicted the cultural

FIGURE 3.4. By 1939, the FSA's images had adopted a more hopeful tone, emphasizing the fruits of family-based striving, a theme that would later be invoked in home front motivational propaganda during World War II. Arthur Rothstein excelled in this genre. Above, Arthur Rothstein, 1939. "Mrs. Alfred Peterson, wife of tenant purchaser borrower, with preserved food. Mesa County, Colorado." Library of Congress, Prints and Photographs Division, FSA/OWI Collection, Reproduction no. LC-USF34-028632-D, Washington, D.C.

life of a small New Mexico town, emphasizing the resilient and industrious ways of its residents and the prosperity arising from their collective striving.[53] Yet while optimistic photographs became the stock-in-trade at the section, it was Rothstein who adopted this mode most readily. Along with Lange's photographs, many of which emphasized the struggles of migrant workers, Rothstein's portrayals of domestic small-town resilience formed the core of federal government–produced motivational imagery in the late Depression.

After the United States entered the war in December 1941, the section, like other New Deal agencies, was placed on war footing as the government assigned it to publicize the mobilization of war production. In early 1942, Stryker asked Russell Lee and Arthur Rothstein for "pictures of men, women and children who appear as if they really believed in the U.S. Get people with a little spirit."[54] From this point forward the section's photographers trained their lenses on war production workers in the nation's factories and shipyards. Supplied to magazines and newspapers for inclusion in articles, their photographs served wartime motivational goals by encouraging Americans to back the war effort and take war jobs. By this time, Stryker had been urging the section's photographers to accentuate the positive effects of the New Deal for several years, and the shift from depicting late-Depression optimism to wartime determination through images of work was a relatively smooth one. As propaganda designers soon discovered, FSA photographs of resolve and hope from the late 1930s could often be reworked into powerful wartime motivational messaging.

POPULIST MOTIVATION IN THE FACTORY: FUN, GAMES, AND EMOTIONAL CONDITIONING

In the second half of the decade, managers' efforts to hone motivation in the factory absorbed many of the dominant themes of the era. The idea that emotional needs were pivotal to motivation, as suggested in the Hawthorne studies and emphasized in the New Deal and Hollywood films, became ingrained in the workplace. Motivation took an abundance of forms and was implemented unevenly. Economic belt-tightening led many firms to scale back motivation and to double down on the use of brutalizing speed-ups of production and a return of the authoritarian foreman. However, many managers continued to experiment with psychological-based techniques and emotional conditioning.

Whereas many large employers could dedicate resources to structured and protracted employee motivation initiatives with the aid of personnel departments, smaller firms, lacking resources, had to rely on more improvised methods. Their methods veered toward a use of the emotionalized sentiment common to Depression-era popular culture. This shift is illustrated in management journals of the day. Traditionally a source of technical subject matter, including lengthy articles on engineering, productivity flows, and other "rational" management matters, these magazines shifted tack, incorporating more accessible content about workplace activities, not least motivation gimmicks used in factories around the country. *Factory Management and Maintenance* (*FMM*), the most widely read of these journals, provides a useful case study. Founded in 1933 after absorbing several competitor journals, *FMM* abandoned the rationalist orientation of its predecessors in favor of a "newsy" style involving short articles and an abundant use of photographs and other images. It reported on such motivational ideas as slogan and poster contests, attention-grabbing safety campaigns, morale boosting games and entertainments, and lunchtime performances used to energize the workforce. These techniques were not new in the factory, but the stated purpose had changed. Whereas previously management magazines linked motivation to the worker's edification in "good" values (a tendency seen in the Mather's posters), *FMM* touted it as a tool for stimulating cooperation and, importantly, boosting productivity. Emotional conditioning, an idea questioned by many industrial social scientists who pushed back against instinct theory in the 1920s, was presented in *FMM* as a vital management goal.

As discussions about the human factor in industry grew more prolific during the second half of the decade, *FMM* encouraged managers to think about the factory as a human environment where attitudes and behaviors could be improved through the use of motivation.[55] Authors frequently emphasized the benefits of regulating the emotional dimensions of the factory. As one article stated, "Plants Are Like People . . . Individuals have personalities. Communities have personalities. Decidedly do industrial plants have personalities."[56] Articles of this sort suggested that both workers' emotions and the workplace's human dimensions were a new discovery, a theme that lent urgency to their claims. Different now was that managers were more open than in the past to adopting rhetoric from the culture at large to aid motivation. In replicating in modified form the pleasures associated with Depression-era games and entertainments, managers discovered ways to deemphasize the harsh disciplinary nature of factory work—at least until workers' returned to their workbenches.

Factory Management and Maintenance reported that some managers played records and broadcast radio shows, including music and sporting events, over the plant speakers. Others hired piano players to entertain workers. At the New York Brassiere Company, workers were entertained with "songs, music, and one-act plays, presented weekly during part of the lunch hour by various members of the company glee club and dramatic groups."[57] Slogan contests, one author noted, were useful devices for exploiting workers' "creative instincts" and "enlist[ing] their cooperation."[58] Another article enthused that the slogans themselves made workers feel like "a partner in the business" when viewed repeatedly and gave them "an increased appreciation of a satisfied customer." He added, "No political campaign results were ever argued any more than were the results of this contest. Many thought their choice of slogans was better and proceeded to tell why they thought so. All of this was extra thought that employees gave to the thing of which we wanted to make them conscious."[59] While such articles gave the wholly misleading impression that management was perpetually involved in boosting employee engagement, they nonetheless conveyed to readers that motivation was an indispensable tool for the modern manager.

Managers' efforts to channel "populist" ideas in their motivational techniques sometimes produced bizarre results. In 1936, *FMM* reported a popular technique among employers known as the "safety police" system, a device that used levity to promote safety regulations. In this practice, workers were elected to serve as safety police by popular vote and were required to report safety violations to a "safety committee" after which the offenders were tried by a "kangaroo court." Those found guilty were required to perform a humiliating stunt, which might include standing in a "rogues gallery" or being "arrested" with "their pictures . . . hung up at a prominent location, along with those of other violators." The magazine reported that at a cement company in Missouri, the firm's safety director "was himself caught in the meshes of this plan when he drove into the plant one morning a little faster than the speed rule permitted. His punishment was to spend half an hour of serious meditation before the big safety trophy which adorns the plant yards, while the gang taunted him in the usual fashion."[60] With their jocularity and simulated punishments, practices such as this allowed managers to tap some of the engaging techniques associated with popular entertainment and thereby smooth relations between themselves and workers.

In an era when attempts to sell workers on longer-term economic or personal rewards were unlikely to pass muster, dramatic safety campaigns provided managers with ways to exploit the powers of motivational rhetoric. With their mascots and booby prizes for work gangs with the lowest and highest accident rates, these campaigns, in manipulating feelings of camaraderie and morale, could help smooth management's objectives. The Reynolds Wire Company in Dixon, Illinois, was one of many companies that presented a booby mascot (in this case, a bedraggled effigy named "Dirty Andy") to the "dirtiest" department.[61] Managers at the Owens-Illinois Glass Company used a massive "safety calendar" to record accidents, a "safety derby" over which workers and managers posed during an award presentation, and a safety "honor roll" listing accidents and "doctor's cases." Safety campaigns operated largely through visual means and metaphors. An article about eye care described workers as "human seeing-machines" who were "emotional. Lighting and seeing conditions influence their feelings, attitude, and enthusiasm, upon which the quantity and quality of the useful work which they can do eventually depend."[62] Managers' interest in the capacity of visual images to motivate workers prompted greater use of films, posters, murals, and other forms of visual communications in the factory (figure 3.5).[63] As one author observed in 1936 when discussing safety education, "The trend towards visual dramatization is very pronounced. The dramatization of facts and figures through charts, the use of film strips, motion pictures, etc., is very common today . . . More for the eye—less for the ear: that seems to be the new trend. The visual lesson is more easily remembered—and of course the medicine is always more pleasant to take."[64]

Such emphasis on the power of dramatic, visual appeal was drawn from the era's advertising methods and portended a more general shift in management communications from information to entertainment and

To give zest to its safety work the Alton plant used "flash programs." Large displays in the yard, placed where all could see them as they entered and left the plant, kept the safety idea alive. At top is a display made up of calendar and safety poster. If an accident occurs, a card describing it is hung in the panel for that date, and the light over the panel is changed from white to red or blue. Center, the safety chain. Link of a department having an accident is detached and allowed to hang down, showing a break in the chain. Rest of the chain does not drop because it is supported from behind. Bottom picture shows head of department winning the safety derby as he receives congratulations

Name of person having an accident is added to the lists on this safety clock in the Central Mold Shop of the Fairmont plant. Lost-time cases are listed at left, doctor's cases at right, while the center space above the dial is reserved for "today's new member"

FIGURE 3.5. These images from an article on safety campaigns illustrate how some managers channeled Depression-era games and entertainments into motivational techniques in the factory. *Factory Management and Maintenance*, August 1939, 38.

therapeutic language. This rubric saw workers' submission to management goals not so much as a form of coercion but as a means of *curing*, a notion that deemphasized the disciplinary function of motivation. One article advised managers that "the cheer and cleanliness and life of color create an improved mental and psychological condition that means much in worker morale." Another noted that the "big firms spend hundreds of thousands of dollars a year in outdoor advertising" and that "it pays because the advertisers make it attractive through dramatization—by using special lighting effects, changing color, motion." Managers, it concluded, should use "the same psychology."[65]

In framing the workplace as an arena of emotional conditioning, *FMM* presented its manager readers with a different vision of the factory than the one that workers endured daily. In reality, factory work remained as brutalizing as ever and often more so, given that many firms imposed cost cutting to remain competitive. Yet as factory life became more punishing for workers due to speedups on the line, episodic hiring, and reduced wages, *FMM* encouraged managers to adopt the role of motivators. Until the Depression, discussions of motivation had mainly been limited to management specialists. But now many managers themselves—traditionally adherents of a rationalist worldview—were beginning to regard emotionally stimulating motivation as a valuable tool for pacifying class tensions and smoothing relations between themselves and workers.

ADAPTING POPULIST RHETORIC: NAM'S MOTIVATIONAL PROPAGANDA CRUSADE

As the Depression wore on, powerful business organizations waged their own motivational campaigns inside and beyond the factory walls, often by adapting the populist rhetoric about work and economic security invoked by the New Deal.[66] At the center of businessmen's motivational discourse was a strategic reworking of New Deal–era tributes to ordinary Americans. As disciples of business leadership saw it, the rhetoric of virtuous striving associated with the New Deal during the 1930s could be adapted to suit more conservative purposes by casting workers in common cause with business rather than the state and labor unions. Business's efforts to appropriate labor rhetoric was evinced in industrialist Nelson Rockefeller's 1932 commissioning of Mexican artist (and former Communist Party member) Diego Rivera to create a mural in Rockefeller Center depicting "Man at the Crossroads" between capitalism and socialism. Rockefeller had hoped for a mural that would invite viewers to contemplate the choice between these possible futures, but Rivera produced a vista that contrasted the self-interest and barbarism of the rich with a socialist workers' utopia led by Lenin. In response to April 1933 newspaper reports condemning the mural's anticapitalist message and Rivera's refusal to remove the depiction of Lenin, Rockefeller ordered an end to the project and, in February 1934, had the mural destroyed. However, although the destruction of the mural illustrated the tenuous nature of business's flirtation with labor populism, the episode also revealed the potential of such appropriations to help business portray itself as an agent of industrial democracy.[67]

At the forefront of business's appropriation of populist labor rhetoric was the National Association of Manufacturers (NAM). During the second half of the decade, NAM initiated a massive propaganda campaign promoting free enterprise as the American way of life. Since its founding in 1895, NAM's pro-business and antiunion crusade had consisted mainly of speeches to business organizations and church groups and the use of the written word, not least articles disseminated to newspapers. Only during World War I, with its use of posters, did NAM begin to venture into emotion-based messaging. In the mid-1930s, recognizing the deepening influence of visual and emotion-based communications, it doubled down on such techniques. Through billboards and other propaganda, NAM extolled the rewards of an individualistic, consumer-based "American way of life," an ideal through which it hoped to advance business's authority over the economy and undermine the New Deal.[68]

The association's shift in tactics gathered steam from the mid-1930s when it founded the National Industrial Information Council (NIIC) to orchestrate a public relations campaign encouraging employers to "build goodwill for your local industry"—a euphemism for weakening labor unions. The council's output included 2 million cartoons, 4.5 million newspaper columns written by pro-business economists, 2.4 million foreign language news pieces, and 11 million employee leaflets. It installed 45,000 billboard posters, which were viewed by an estimated 65 million Americans daily, and its films were seen by approximately 15 million viewers. It also supplied employers with "Service for Plant Publications," which included ready-made inserts consisting of NAM puff pieces that employers could integrate into their own publications.[69]

In 1936 NIIC began circulating to around two million monthly readers its "Uncle Abner Says" cartoons, which offered folksy tributes to free enterprise. In a typical cartoon, Uncle Abner sat reading a newspaper, lamenting "politicians [who] are bent on finin' th' taxpayer for reckless thrivin.'"[70] Such cartoons were thinly veiled warnings against what NAM regarded as the excesses of New Deal regulations on business. The organization's outdoor advertising campaign, meanwhile, brought its free enterprise rhetoric to public spaces. Designed by Campbell-Ewald Company, one of the nation's leading advertising firms, the billboards asserted pro-business sentiments like "What is good for industry is good for you" and "You prosper when factories prosper" and depicted highly idealized visions of family-based consumption that, they implied, was dependent on the worker's integration into a harmonious industrial system led by business (figure 3.6).[71]

The adoption by NAM of a more populist tone is seen further in NIIC's films of the late 1930s, which asserted that business was a more effective

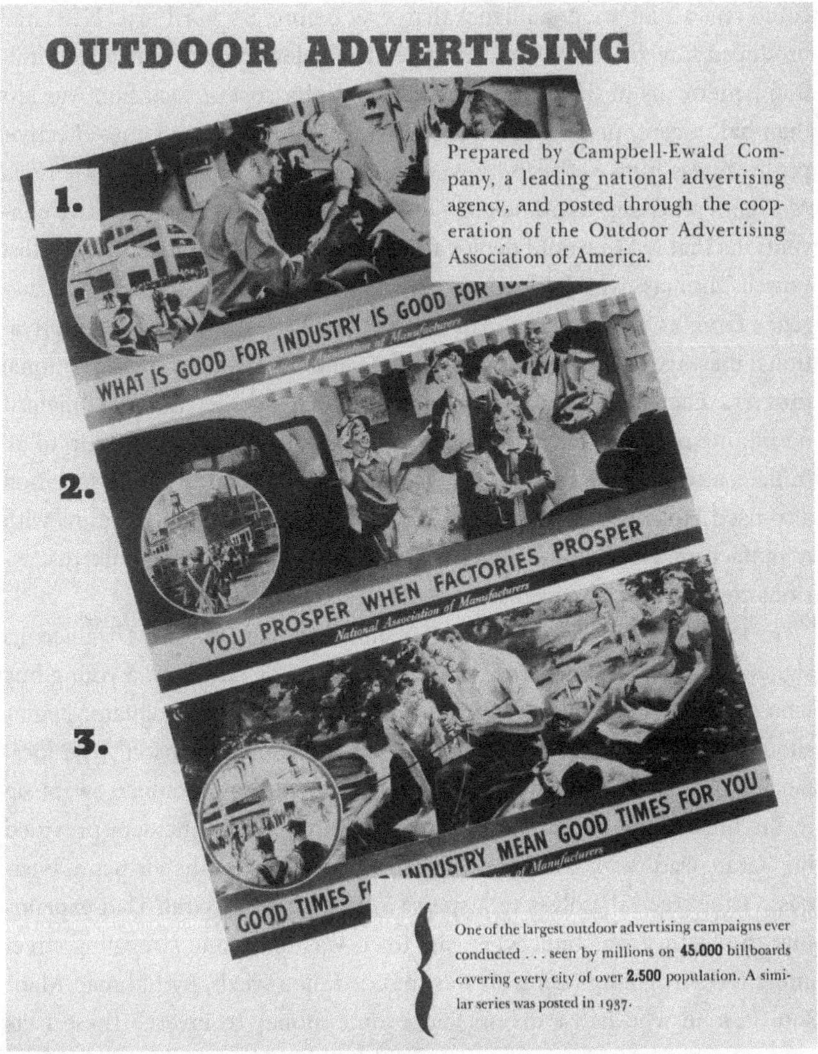

FIGURE 3.6. This page from a 1938 NIIC promotion booklet showcased NAM's sophisticated visual communications to managers. The association displayed thousands of billboard posters in industrial communities in the 1930s. National Association of Manufacturers Collection (Acc. 1411), Hagley Museum and Library, Wilmington, Delaware.

steward of the economy than government and thus better positioned to advance the interests of employees. While efforts to indoctrinate Americans through such pro-business messages were not new, NAM's extensive economic resources and distribution capabilities meant that its propaganda could reach a far wider audience than ever before. By April 1938, NIIC had produced four films, which were collectively viewed by over eighteen million Americans in the late 1930s. The per capita cost of each film was less than half a cent, making them the most widely viewed and cost-effective, pro-business films yet seen by American audiences.[72] Films like *Men and Machines* and *America Marching On* established formal and narrative conventions that NAM would deploy for years to come. Narrated by journalist Lowell Thomas, who had helped to bring British army officer T. E. Lawrence fame as "Lawrence of Arabia," NIIC's films offered rousing motivational messages about the vital role of free enterprise in advancing national progress. Each film offered a moral tale in which an older and wiser mentor figure imparted, in folksy idioms, the virtues of business leadership to an initiate, a convention used already in employee literature.[73] The association also used Hollywood-style promotional techniques, including tie-ins with manufacturers and film screenings for students followed by guided discussions convened by engineers.[74]

In its film *Your Town—A Story of America* of 1940, NAM trained its sights on critics of business. The film tells the story of Jerry, a young boy who gets embroiled in a fight that erupts in town when an agitator begins shouting, "Down with . . . capitalism [and] old man Manson" (the local factory owner). Jerry, it transpires, was an unwitting bystander, swept up in the melee only because it seemed like "fun," but the incident provided his "Gran-Dad" with an opportunity to educate him on the virtues of business. The screen dissolves to a sparse village street as Gran-Dad explains that the factory was built when the town was only "one straggling street and a few struggling farms." It was founded, he reveals, by old man Manson, "a man who had a dream [and] some money to invest." These facts are accompanied by images of a youthful-looking Manson dressed in 1890s attire, examining blueprints. When Manson beckons someone to help him build the factory, it turns out to be Gran-Dad himself in his younger days. The audience next sees the positive effects of the factory—a montage of homes, telephone poles, new stores, and schools. Toward the end, the film cuts back to the church steps in the present day, where Gran-Dad tells Jerry that he is "part of all this too" because he was born in the hospital, which exists only because the factory workers needed doctors. Enlightened about the positive effects of big business, Jerry undergoes a conversion. Yet

Gran-Dad reminds him not to take the fruits of business for granted, noting that the growth of the town happened only because the factory generated investment. Against a montage of prosperous small farms and hardworking locals, Gran-Dad laments, "a lot of folks think it would be fun to destroy all that the factory stands for," when in reality, "that factory made your town, and when you're working against the factory—you're working against your own best interests." The film concludes as Gran-Dad places his arm around Jerry's shoulder and walks him toward the church door as a double exposure of the church and the Stars and Stripes envelopes the screen.[75]

Your Town, like NAM's other well-honed publicity, signaled a growing adeptness among businessmen and their allies in channeling motivational sentiment in their communications techniques. The shifting propaganda tactics used by NAM reflected businessmen's recognition that their struggle for authority would henceforth require an embrace of the emotion-based populism that flourished through the New Deal and Depression-era culture, and that the task of promoting business's claims to leadership would be best accomplished via motivational images.

VISUALIZING INDUSTRIAL DEMOCRACY IN CORPORATE MOTIVATION FILMS

Unsurprisingly, the growing interest in the motivational capacities of visual images led some larger employers to try to deploy images strategically to promote loyalty and cooperation among workers. For many such companies, film became an especially important motivational tool. Industrial film producers made new inroads as employers enlisted their expertise in hopes of countering the power of the labor movement. Among the most influential producers of industrial films during the era was Jamison "Jam" Handy. As the film historian Rick Prelinger argues, Handy's films and other training publicity introduced a new level of sophistication in business-sponsored film and had a lasting influence on corporate communications. From its Detroit base, the Jam Handy Organization employed around six hundred people to produce and market its films, which were screened in the workplace, theaters, and classrooms around the country. The organization's earlier films were of a straightforward instructional nature, but after 1935, it developed a more dramatic, emotionally stimulating approach that blended aspects of documentary and Hollywood-style filmmaking with the goal of motivating employee and public goodwill toward the company.[76]

These qualities are embodied in the films commissioned by Handy's biggest client, the Chevrolet Corporation. Deploying story-driven plots, bracing music, and rousing voice-overs, the films embodied a powerful form of motivational storytelling. Handy's short film *From Dawn to Sunset* of 1937 established conventions that would become central in motivational films over the next two decades. Among these conventions were a slick story about the virtues of the firm and the rewards that workers received by identifying with it and with industrial capitalism more generally, along with a synthesis of the economic- and emotion-based aspects of motivation.

The film portrays a day in the life of Chevrolet and its workers, situating the company as a capable agent of the national interest and defining its aspirations and those of workers as one and the same (figures 3.7–3.10). It begins with a dawn shot of a town skyline onto which rolling text appears. A narrator, reading the text, espouses the "mighty army of builders who go forth accompanied by the whistles of America's greatest factories," a situation which "promises a new prosperity." To the sound of choral music reminiscent of another of the era's paeans to work motivation, *Snow White and the Seven Dwarfs*, we see a montage of homes, alarm clocks, and workers getting up and eating breakfast, accompanied by invigorating music. Workers are waved off by their families before heading to the factory as the narrator announces, "The clans gather in a score of cities. In thousands of homes, vigorous workmen rise to meet a new day and a new opportunity." These images and the narration establish a seemingly incontrovertible claim: that workers are satisfied and motivated. Scenes of lines of workers entering factories then follow, before segueing to scenes of production at twelve plants across the country, imagery that emphasizes the interdependence of Chevrolet's workforce. After footage of employees receiving their wage packets, accompanied by a zesty rendition of "We're in the Money," the narrator reminds viewers, "Tens of thousands of men on one single payroll have money for themselves and for their families to spend . . . money to spend on wholesome foods . . . for good clothes . . . money for comforts and conveniences." Over a montage of shopping scenes, he explains that this spending has led to "prosperity greater than history has ever known." In the final sequences, workers and their families enjoy dinner and recreation

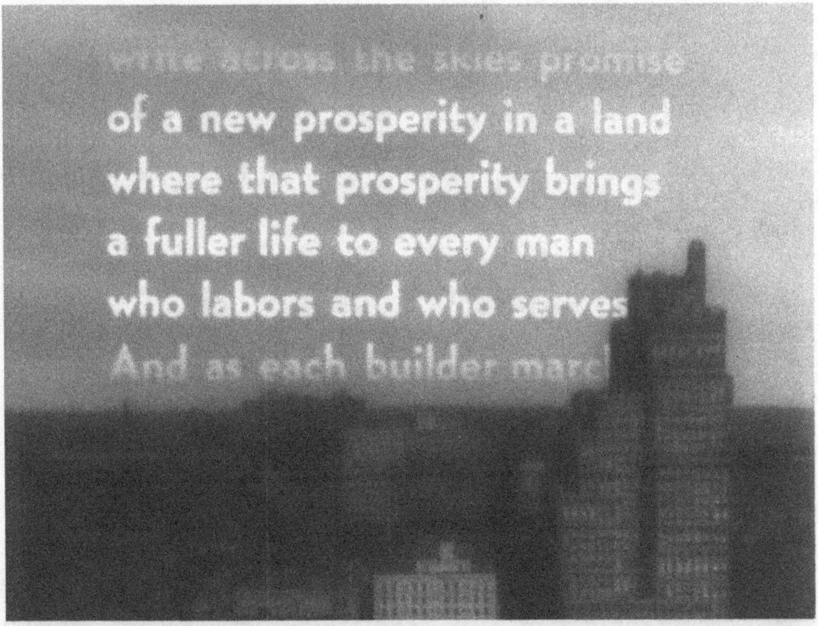

FIGURES 3.7 (TOP) AND 3.8 (BOTTOM): Jam Handy's *From Dawn to Sunset* took motivational storytelling to a new level, connecting Chevrolet, its employees, and the nation through a dramatic tribute to corporate-led industrial progress. Prelinger Archives, San Francisco, CA.

FIGURES 3.9 (TOP) AND 3.10 (BOTTOM): Jam Handy's *From Dawn to Sunset* took motivational storytelling to a new level, connecting Chevrolet, its employees, and the nation through a dramatic tribute to corporate-led industrial progress. Prelinger Archives, San Francisco, CA.

before readying for bed, while the narrator intones, "And so across America the thousands have worked today and done their tasks well. And as the lights blink out, a day of work, a day of fulfillment, of happiness, and of peace merges into the assurance of a fuller life . . . in the great American way." Complete with shots of lights dimming in the living rooms and bedrooms of Chevrolet workers, the fairytale-like ending exposed viewers to an emotionally stirring narrative steeped in motivational sentiment.[77]

The emotional power of *From Dawn to Sunset* lies in its portrayal of workers as a living force ("Along the roads to the factories, tens of thousands begin to mass. They swell the rising tide. Into the silent buildings goes the life stream") and its portrayal of Chevrolet as a benevolent corporate family. No less powerful are the connections that Handy emphasizes between workers and communities in different locations across the country. Viewers could potentially identify their own communities and workplaces and, presumably, feel connected to those at other Chevrolet factories. The repeated scenes of men lining up to collect their pay offer a symbolic retort to then-prevalent images of "forgotten men" shuffling along on the breadlines in newsreels and FSA photographs. In keeping with the film's larger schema, Handy's adaptations of Depression-era aesthetics helped deemphasize and disavow the hierarchical nature of the labor-management relationship. *From Dawn to Sunset*, like celebrated New Deal documentaries such as *The Plow That Broke the Plains*, offered up a narrative in which all aspects of the system were integrated and where regional specificities were connected to the aspirations of workers and the nation alike.

Filmmakers such as Handy offered businesses a major boost in their efforts to contain challenges to their authority. By appropriating labor and New Deal sentiment and adapting them for the purposes of corporate communications, large auto companies like Chevrolet could cast themselves as engines of industrial democracy. This process amounted to a wholesale plundering of images and language from labor whereby corporations borrowed from the democratic visions of work generated under the auspices of the New Deal and labor unions. Such appropriations and modifications would continue to inform employers' motivational tactics for years to come.

Motivation underwent significant changes during the Depression, both as a form of rhetoric and as a management practice. The high-minded tributes to an individualistic worth ethic and to character building that had infused motivation previously were eclipsed as a more emotion-based model of motivation moved to the center of discussions about work and its rewards. The rising esteem for the ideas of Elton Mayo and other human relations specialists helped propel this shift. Managers' embrace of emotional messaging indicated that, while scientific management remained central to production, Taylorist theories of motivation were rapidly losing authority. The democratic-intoned tributes to the strivings of "the people" during the Depression advanced a similar shift in motivation on a broader societal plane. Idealized images and rhetoric about the virtuous strivings of ordinary Americans quickly migrated from mass culture to the propaganda that business pumped out in efforts to sell the public on capitalist free enterprise. Despite being driven by different and often opposing ideals, New Dealers, filmmakers, and businessmen encouraged Americans to keep believing that work under capitalism provided a route to a better life regardless of economic hard times. The policies and sentiments of the New Deal, when all is said and done, sought to sustain Americans' faith that their country could still deliver on its promises of material and psychological reward—to motivate them to keep aspiring to work's promises.

Despite the New Deal's visions of a nation united in common striving, management and its allies made significant advancements in their efforts to frame the prevailing conversation about work. By the time the United States entered World War II, the high-minded motivational appeals to individual success used by businessmen, managers, and poster vendors a decade earlier seemed hopelessly outdated. As the nation once again threw itself into war, producers of motivational propaganda in business and government became even more cognizant of the advantages of appealing to Americans through messaging that adapted the language of industrial democracy. This rhetoric, they understood, was not only a means for mobilizing production but also for waging powerful visions of work's meanings and rewards.

CHAPTER 4

The War over Motivation

PROSPERITY RHETORIC AND THE REMAKING OF WORK'S REWARDS DURING WORLD WAR II

> Many Reich factories that are turning out guns meant for the enslavement of other people are themselves run by slaves. And workers of countries overrun by the Axis have been wrenched from their homes and shipped into the Reich as forced labor. In this country, we have placed our reliance on what President Wilson called "the highest and best form of efficiency . . . the spontaneous cooperation of a free people." We are fighting a battle of production confident that free labor will outproduce slave labor.
>
> —Archibald MacLeish, director of the Office of Facts and Figures, January 1942

> Repetition, repetition, repetition, repetition. The greatest rogue in history, Mr. Hitler, was shrewd enough to use that idea. He said: "You can take a story—even a lie—and if you repeat it often enough you can make people believe it." He was no paper hanger!
>
> —Lew Shalett, owner of the Sheldon-Claire Company, reflecting on his firm's high sales of motivational posters to factory managers during World War II

During World War II the United States orchestrated the largest work motivation campaign in its history. In the weeks following the Japanese attack on Pearl Harbor in December 1941, the federal government, employers, and business organizations urged Americans to support the war production effort through an avalanche of propaganda. While motivational rhetoric saturated American life, it was disseminated with particular vigor in the workplace. Employers used posters, banners, morale-boosting speeches, radio spots, films, and literature to encourage workers to produce more and faster. Labor-management committees called on employees to work overtime and unite with managers in beating production targets. For their part, workers supported the war effort by investing in war bonds that they would use to pay for consumer goods after the war. Many labor unions agreed to a "no strike" pledge, effectively putting aside grievances against management for the duration of the war.[1]

The mobilization of the American home front during World War II has long served as the basis of a powerful myth. As told in countless movies and as reinforced through the ongoing valorization of what Studs Terkel critically termed the "good war," this was a moment when the nation rallied itself spontaneously, motivated by a reflexive desire to defeat fascism.[2] Historians have shown that this interpretation of events is highly romanticized, and that Americans participated in the war effort for a wide array of reasons that were often more personal than idealistic.[3] This was also the case for industrial leaders and motivational specialists. In the decades before the war, despite significant advancements, they had struggled to create effective motivational messaging because they lacked a unifying idea. The war resolved this limitation. Not only did it end mass unemployment, but promises of future prosperity for workers in the impending postwar period also helped pave the way for motivational propaganda that depicted the United States as a classless nation. No less advantageous from business's perspective was that, amid the emergency conditions of wartime, the worker's spontaneous cooperation with management's objectives in the factory could be defined as obligatory.[4]

This chapter tracks the development of motivational discourse during World War II, arguing that it became a powerful part of the apparatus through which businessmen and managers advanced their quests for power and authority. In contrast to perceptions today that wartime propaganda revolved around rallying workers to defeat the Axis powers, it focused to a significant degree on preparing the citizenry for a postwar order rooted in consumer abundance and free market ideals. At a time when businessmen were supposed to be dedicating their resources unreservedly to the fight against Hitler, they were pouring their energies into defeating what they perceived as more dangerous threats—the New Deal and labor unions. Despite echoing assertions that the Axis powers must be defeated, businessmen and the advertising specialists who honed motivational propaganda were fixated on their private postwar goals: to neuter the New Deal and the labor movement and establish their authority in the coming postwar era.[5]

The wartime motivational crusade emphasized the concrete rewards that workers would receive following the war, including job security, a modern home, consumer goods, and a rising standard of living.[6] "Prosperity motivation," as I call this new strand of the discourse, paved the way for management to infuse the factory with rhetoric about consumer rewards for two decades after the war. Businessmen were not alone in invoking this rhetoric. The federal government's main propaganda agency, the Office of War Information, initially focused on providing information about the war but soon embraced the idea that promises of future prosperity were the best way to motivate workers. For the orchestrators of wartime propaganda, prosperity motivation was a powerful ideal through which to instill cooperation in the factory and advance longer-term quests for management control and authority.

MOTIVATION AND INDUSTRIAL MOBILIZATION

The contests over war mobilization were to have a direct influence on the motivational propaganda disseminated in the factory. For this reason, a discussion of the debates around mobilization is essential. At the core of the rhetoric circulated by the state, business organizations, and other producers of wartime propaganda were differing ideas about industrial mobilization and economic planning: How should mobilization be orchestrated? Should it be led by the federal government, labor, business, or an alliance of two or all three? Beyond these debates was another question: What incentives and rewards should be used to motivate American workers to support the war effort?

Many New Dealers hoped that the war would help consolidate the New Deal and secure its continuation. Industrial expansion, they believed, would boost the alliance between the state and the working class and solidify government influence over economic planning. However, efforts to instill support for wartime production ultimately revolved around prosperity-based motivation, not an expansion of New Deal liberalism or industrial democracy. The growing status of prosperity motivation was evident in New Dealers' shift away from the platform based on class embraced in the 1930s. As historian Alan Brinkley argues, in the face of totalitarianism in Europe, liberals grew increasingly cautious about state power and accepted that limits should be placed on the federal government's influence over economic affairs. Amid a war that pitted freedom against tyranny, liberals gradually discarded their commitment to class-based politics and embraced the credos of individual liberty and consumer-based freedom. Their acquiescence to these ideals, coupled with their growing wariness toward expanded state power in the face of totalitarianism in Europe, caused them to adopt a conciliatory stance toward the arguments of free market economists like Friedrich Hayek, which they had dismissed a few years earlier.

The motivational sentiment upheld through the auspices of the New Deal ultimately revolved around promises of a higher standard of living. By the end of 1943, many of the New Deal's flagship initiatives, including the Works Progress Administration and the Civilian Conservation Corps, had been eliminated. Instead, New Dealers rallied around calls for full employment and a rising standard of living. This change was reflected in the actions of the New Deal's Office of Price Administration, which mobilized citizens in a campaign to regulate prices of consumer goods and published numerous "consumer manifestos" that positioned the federal government as an advocate of consumer rights.[7] The connection between motivation and prosperity was reinforced by the New Deal's National Resources Planning Board, whose campaign for full employment and a rising standard of living sought to incentivize workers through consumption rather than an expansion of labor rights.[8]

Union leaders anticipated that industrial mobilization, in bringing millions of new workers into the labor fold, would strengthen labor's influence and advance the cause of industrial democracy. As industry mobilized for war in 1940 and 1941, Congress of Industrial Organizations (CIO) president Phillip Murray and United Automobile Workers president Walter Reuther continued to champion industrial democracy, insisting that labor must play a leading role in planning and orchestrating production. This gambit was a partial success. Union membership climbed from 10.5 million in 1941 to 14.75 million in 1945, and many workers experienced significant gains as unemployment dried up and overtime became abundant. However, if many workers did well during the war, hopes for industrial democracy receded as labor leaders embraced the wartime mood of obligatory cooperation.[9]

At the forefront of this stance of cooperation was Sidney Hillman, head of the CIO's Amalgamated Clothing Workers of America and associate director of the government's Office of Production Management. A devotee of industrial democracy since World War I, Hillman shifted right during the war. Rejecting the radical approaches of Murray and Reuther, he argued that increased purchasing power and a rising standard of living for workers were the best platform for labor. He also founded the CIO's Political Action Committee (PAC), whose goal was to help Roosevelt and other Democrats sympathetic to labor in the 1944 elections. For Hillman, the PAC was not just a means to advance labor's interests in general but also specifically to align the CIO with consumer-based liberalism. Hillman and other labor leaders' accommodation of prosperity rhetoric ultimately weakened the long-term aspirations of the industrial working class. Workers' hopes about the formation of a Labor Party and of a full-throated challenge to corporate monopoly dissolved as union leaders promoted all-out production with promises of postwar prosperity.[10]

For employers, the war marked an unprecedented opportunity to realize their decades-long efforts to improve motivational techniques. Despite puffed-up claims that businessmen "won the war" for America, the government's early attempts to get industry on board with war production proved difficult, as many large firms resisted converting plants to war production. Although industrialists eventually embraced the war effort, as Michael Adams notes, the notion that they were motivated by a commitment to democratic values or the national interest is a product of "mythmaking." Many businesses initially "dragged their heels." Automakers, for example, resisted transitioning to war production because of fears of losing position in the domestic market.[11] Moreover, industrial leaders' later self-congratulation for their role in winning the war contrasted sharply with their chilly response to Walter Reuther's December 1940 proposal to convert the nation's auto factories to aircraft production. Despite their claims, industrial leaders were motivated principally by the private aspirations of profit and power over labor unions more than a reflexive sense of patriotic duty.[12]

For management theorists, the motivation-laden atmosphere of wartime offered fresh openings in the quest to control workers. At the center of human relations research during the war was an effort to boost morale by approaching the factory as a "social system." Management textbooks today mostly offer only brief commentary on World War II, perhaps because formal research on motivation slowed owing to management's wartime exigencies.[13] However, efforts to boost production presented managers with unprecedented opportunities to experiment with motivation. The war also saw an increase in personnel departments and, with them, renewed efforts to train foremen to use "sophisticated behavioral techniques" focused on motivation.[14]

Among the most influential studies of the era was *Management and the Worker*, the much-celebrated 1939 book by Harvard Business School human relations specialist Fritz Roethlisberger that documented the results of the Hawthorne studies. Roethlisberger argued that one of the core challenges for management was that of "maintaining the equilibrium of the social organization so that individuals through contributing their services to this common purpose obtain personal satisfactions that make them willing to co-operate." This process, he argued, was dependent on the worker's "adjustment" to the system, which could be achieved through employee interviews and counseling, methods used in the Hawthorne experiments.[15] Although human relations specialists ostensibly sought solutions to the alienating effects of work in large organizations, their long-held management belief that workers needed to "adjust" to the system reinforced the dehumanizing notion that they were pathologically prone to maladjusted behaviors and thus in need of management's guiding hand. These views proliferated widely among managers during the war, even as large-scale studies into motivation tapered off and Harvard's core group of human relations researchers dissolved.

The idea that organizations could benefit from a strategic use of motivation became further entrenched through the writings of management theorists such as Peter Drucker. A Jewish Austrian émigré who fled to England in 1933 amid the rise of Nazism, then to the United States in 1937, Drucker emerged as the most influential management theorist of the twentieth century after the publication of his 1946 book, *Concept of the Corporation*.

Often overlooked, however, is Drucker's *Future of Industrial Man of 1942*, in which he posits that the only entity capable of reviving the worker's lost feelings of autonomy was the corporation, which, along with the "mass-production plant," was "the representative social phenomena of the industrial system of our time."[16] Drucker's arguments echoed those made for years by industrial psychologists. Yet in contrast to many other theorists, Drucker insisted that workers should be afforded an active role in creating a workplace culture that was conducive to the cooperation that managers desired. Workers, he maintained, should participate in labor-management committees that planned production and be given responsibility for organizing safety, educational, and social activities. In advancing these arguments, Drucker established an idea that has preoccupied management into our own day: that the corporation had "social" functions, not least, that of producing organizational cultures that assuaged class conflict.[17]

During the war, the theories of human relations specialists, social psychologists, and management theorists gained traction in the factory as managers honed motivational techniques. Although workers participated in the wartime production push for a diverse array of reasons, the patriotic discourse that proliferated during the war helped managers reinforce a culture of obligatory motivation in the daily life of the factory. Whether motivated by patriotism, short- or long-term economic gains, or the morale-boosting efforts of their employers, American workers encountered environments steeped in motivational sentiment. Factories were festooned with motivation-infused installations, banners, and posters that supplied daily reminders that labor-management cooperation was essential to victory (figure 4.1).

While ostensibly concerned with mobilizing the industrial workforce and winning the production battle, employers' motivational rhetoric was inseparable from their efforts to weaken labor unions, counter the New Deal's pro-labor policies, and secure management's authority in industry. The wartime honing of motivation also achieved something absent in the past: a compelling rationale that linked workers' futures to those of their employers and the nation. For the duration of the war, motivational messages urging labor-management cooperation and teamwork in the name of future prosperity became a lingua franca in the nation's factories.

FIGURE 4.1. Workplace photographs and posters were powerful tools for promoting war jobs and motivating workers to back the war effort. The U.S. government's main propaganda agency, the Office of War Information, sometimes deployed creative methods when pursuing these goals. The photograph was taken in February 1942 during an OWI-organized event in which a steel worker (front, center) gives a tour of the Allegheny Ludlum Steel factory to an army corporal and a navy radioman, who walk behind him. In October 1941, the OWI had included images of each of the men in a widely circulated poster entitled "Men Working Together!" (a copy of which is displayed above the door on the right). In arranging for the men to meet for a factory tour and photo shoot, the OWI found a novel way to promote unity of purpose between industrial workers and those in the armed services. Such images also channeled human relations theories that emphasized the managerial benefits available when exploiting the factory's social and human dimensions. Library of Congress, Prints and Photographs Division, FSA/OWI Collection, Reproduction no. LC-USE6-D-005645, Washington, D.C.

PROSPERITY MOTIVATION IN GOVERNMENT PROPAGANDA: THE OFFICE OF WAR INFORMATION

The task of refining motivational discourse was waged no more vigorously than by the federal government's main propaganda agency, the Office of War Information (OWI). Formed in June 1942 from the ashes of the Office of Facts and Figures (OFF), the OWI distributed a flood of motivational propaganda that included radio spots, billboards, literature, films, and posters. While the OWI was prolific, it was fraught with bitter struggle over how it should motivate Americans to support the war effort. Many of its staffers were New Dealers who believed passionately that the OWI should focus on providing information to the American people about the nature of the enemy and the role that citizens must play in defending democracy and freedom in the face of totalitarian regimes. In January 1942, OFF director Archibald MacLeish informed reporters that the "difference" in American and enemy propaganda was one "between the strategy of terror and the strategy of truth."[18] As MacLeish would write in OFF's "Report to the Nation" that month, the factories in the Third Reich were "run by slaves." Not only had the Nazis enslaved their own people for war production, they had subjected those they had overrun to "forced labor." American workers, on the other hand, adhered to the ideal that had helped the United States prevail in World War I: what President Wilson had called the "spontaneous cooperation of a free people."[19]

While "spontaneous cooperation" was more an idealization than a reality, the OWI's attempts to increase war production in the first half of 1942 focused on communicating to workers the threats posed by Nazism and the need to defend freedom and democracy. Just as vital, government officials believed, was the need to instill among workers a clear understanding of the importance of their work to the nation's war goals. Government officials frequently lamented opinion poll findings that Americans had little understanding about what they were fighting for.[20] Sam Lubell, a staffer at the Office for Emergency Management (OEM) wrote to a colleague in January, "A great many workers . . . have little feeling that the particular products they are working upon are vital to our war effort. They . . . may not visualize the long chain of production which brings that product into a gun or tank or plane. Plant by plant, it should be made clear to every worker how their particular job fits in with the war scheme, how important their work is." One useful tactic for achieving this goal, he argued, was to organize tours of the factory by soldiers, an idea practiced already by the War Department. Lubell noted that while "labor, traditionally, has regarded the Army with suspicion, as a strikebreaking organization, as working with Wall Street and Big Business," soldier tours of the factory helped "to break down this hostility" by allowing workers to hear from soldiers how the munitions they were producing were used on the front lines. Such discussions, he added, gave workers a newfound sense of significance in their work, and many plants saw increased morale, with workers and union officials offering ideas for boosting production.[21]

The struggle between "honest information" and "selling the war" came to a head in spring 1943 in the OWI's Graphics Division, the body responsible for guiding poster design and distribution.[22] Led by former *Fortune* art director Francis Brennan and staffed mainly by New Dealers, the division initially worked from the belief that propaganda should convey factual information and avoid the kind of hyperbolic messages espoused during World War I. Brennan hoped that the division could find a middle way between advertising specialists' desire to "sell" the war to the public, which, if unchecked, would produce "an insincerity repugnant to Americans at war," and an uncoordinated solicitation of contributions by artists, which would result in "confusion and dashed hopes for the artists" if not properly administered. The Graphics Division, Brennan believed, could develop relationships with artists and make "intelligent and efficient use of the talents available."[23] Informed by these ideals, early OWI posters emphasized the role that Americans must play in defeating the evils of Axis tyranny and defending the freedoms associated with American democracy.

Brennan's vision failed to materialize, however. Since the agency's early days as the OFF, some staffers had argued that its posters were too abstract and lacked a design strategy. As one had written in December 1941, its efforts amounted to "a hodge-podge of good, mediocre and bad design [with] no semblance of balance as to subject matter, and no coordination as to timing."[24] Although government propaganda in the factory would continue to espouse the rhetoric of democracy in the face of Nazi and Axis evils, by mid-1942, it had begun to promote the war effort through advertising-based techniques that touted postwar rewards. Formative in shaping the new strategy was the War Advertising Council. Founded by the nation's leading advertising agencies in early 1942 following federal government requests for help in developing industrial mobilization campaigns, the council "positioned itself as a private adjunct to the government's war information efforts."[25] Throughout that year, the council gained the upper hand in the planning and design of government propaganda. From its perspective, propaganda should connect victory to Americans' personal aspirations, especially those based on consumption. As Inger Stole points out, the council had the advertising industry's interests fully in mind. Its president, Chester LaRoche, was eager that its public relations initiatives would promote "a positive view of the industry behind the ads [while] giving advertising credit for 'an important war job well done.'"[26]

As the council's strategy gained dominance, OWI propaganda gradually sidelined its earlier focus on fighting fascism in favor of advertising-based messaging emphasizing the prosperity that workers would enjoy once victory was achieved. Telling was the OWI's responses to posters and proposals for posters submitted by independent artists and members of the public, many of whose messages encouraged Americans to join the fight against fascism. The OWI rebuffed these proposals with rejection letters that stressed the agency's obligations to consistent messaging. As a typical rejection letter stated, although it received "many such suggestions from similarly patriotically-inspired Americans," it had to turn them down "because our program involves long-range planning."[27] From the perspective of the OWI, propaganda created by ordinary citizens and artists had no place in a motivational campaign driven by the techniques of advertising specialists.

Amid the intense discord over propaganda strategy, Brennan resigned in April 1943, asserting that the posters produced by "the Ad boys" assumed that the "American people average twelve years old." While "American soldiers rotted in the desert heat," he wrote, "the Graphics Division was designing posters about ordering coal early." And, with the "African campaign at its height we are instructed to produce posters that would smile cheerfully from the billboards, saying: 'I'm happy with my new war job' and 'We'll have lots to eat this winter, won't we Mother?'" This approach had, he added, "done more toward dimming perception, suspending critical values, and spreading the sickly syrup of complacency over the people than almost any other factor in the complex pattern of our supercharged lives."[28] Brennan's departure was swiftly followed by the mass resignation of over twenty OWI staffers. A resignation letter signed by fifteen of them asserted that "the activities of the OWI on the home front are now dominated by high-pressure promoters who prefer slick salesmanship to honest information" and who believed that the only effective appeal to the public was "the selfish one of 'What's in it for me?'"[29] The resignations, along with the rancor over poster policy, were widely reported in the nation's newspapers, many of which expressed trepidation at the new direction of the OWI's propaganda.[30]

This spate of resignations cleared the way for the War Advertising Council to impose its ideas more fully on OWI poster policy. From this point forward, the OWI's posters revolved largely around visions of the prosperity that Americans would enjoy once the war was won. As George H. Lyon, the chief of the OWI News Bureau, wrote the day following Brennan's resignation, "The self-interest of the individual is identified with the larger interests of the Nation in a post-war world. For millions of 'nest eggs' will cushion the jars of changing from war to peace. They will furnish fuel for energizing our peace-time economic machinery."[31] To promote these future rewards, the advertising specialists who steered poster design at the OWI deployed the visual tropes of prosperity, economic self-interest, labor-management cooperation, and a consumer-oriented American way of life anchored in idealized images of the archetypal white family common in advertising campaigns. These tropes aligned with the consensus about prosperity motivation then emerging between the state, business, and labor leaders. Posters produced by the federal government's Office for Emergency Management, which was folded into the OWI in 1943, illustrate these developments in motivational poster design (figures 4.2 and 4.3).[32]

The OWI's commissioning of advertising specialists to design posters brought something to motivational discourse absent in previous decades: a coherent "story" that defined work's economic and psychological rewards as both tangible and imminent. Although motivational discourse had always touted promises of reward in exchange for hard work, such promises were rarely linked to a convincing vision of workers' lives as markedly better in the future. The war changed this equation. In anticipation of a coming postwar boom, designers were emboldened to assert that wartime sacrifices would be followed by prosperity. This change in tactics symbolized the state's deepening role in crafting accord between labor and business.

The OWI's espousal of prosperity motivation shored up an idea that became prolific on the American home front: that American workers were free because, unlike those who toiled under the bootheel of fascism, they did not need to be forced to work. Comparisons between the brutalizing slave labor conditions experienced by workers under totalitarian regimes and the freedom of American workers who threw themselves into defense work without coercion served as a recurrent theme in propaganda produced not

FIGURE 4.2. Posters such as these, produced by the federal government's Office for Emergency Management, underscore the government's use of idealized images of white family–based prosperity and obligatory labor-management cooperation during the war. National Archives, College Park, MD. Local Identifier 44-PA-2387.

FIGURE 4.3. Posters such as these, produced by the federal government's Office for Emergency Management, underscore the government's use of idealized images of white family–based prosperity and obligatory labor-management cooperation during the war. National Archives, College Park, MD. Local Identifier 44-PA-1384.

only by the OWI but also by organizations dedicated to advancing business's authority. This discourse laid groundwork for later motivational rhetoric contrasting American "free labor" and Soviet "slave labor," which became a powerful trope in early Cold War rhetoric asserting that American workers were the freest in the world and received more abundant rewards than their counterparts toiling under communism.[33]

Despite the OWI's tributes to the freedom of American workers, its propaganda depicted work and its rewards in highly gendered and racialized terms. Office of War Information posters encouraging women to take war jobs did not depict women of color and made clear that women would be expected to resume their roles as homemakers after the war.[34] Moreover, while the OWI condemned the race-based ideologies of Nazism, the agency's attempts to speak to the hopes and aspirations of black workers were meager. Although it distributed a handful of posters depicting noted African American servicemen, including Joe Louis, Dorie Miller, and a Tuskegee Airman, its output of posters portraying black workers on the home front was minimal. One of the rare exceptions is a 1943 poster entitled *United We Win*, which depicts a black worker and a white worker riveting an airplane turret. Another government-sponsored poster (produced by the War Production Board), depicts an African American welder named Obie Bartlett who had lost an arm at Pearl Harbor and was now working at a West Coast shipyard.[35]

The OWI was more robust in using films to motivate African Americans. It also produced a large number of photographs of black workers and other workers of color, which it published in pamphlets and distributed to the press.[36] However, the OWI's attempts to encourage African American participation in the war effort faced impediments from the start. Such problems were typified by reactions to *Negroes and the War*, an OWI seventy-two-page illustrated booklet authored by Chandler Owen, a former radical who veered rightward during the interwar period. Like many black intellectuals, Owen advocated that blacks throw their support behind the war effort. *Negroes and the War* warned about the threats that Hitler posed to blacks' freedoms, a tactic that was employed by many civil rights leaders.[37] Some prominent black leaders argued that such messaging was hypocritical, given the continued denial of civil rights in the United States. Among these critics was William H. Hastie, a civilian aide to the secretary of war who would later resign in protest over racial segregation in the U.S.

Army Air Forces. In a strongly worded letter in May 1942, Hastie criticized Owen for minimizing the realities of lynching and racial discrimination and rescinded his earlier support for the booklet during its drafting. Hastie declared, "Men and women with personal experiences of racial discrimination as bitter as those of most Negroes are in no mood to be told how well off they are. We need to direct our propaganda at indifferent or prejudiced whites, not at resentful Negroes." Signing off, he noted, "Morale will not be improved by such a project."[38]

Even stronger in its denunciations of *Negroes and the War* were conservatives in Congress, especially in the South. Many of them argued that the booklet was an underhanded tactic to generate favor for the New Deal among blacks or, alternatively, that its exclusive appeals to blacks threatened to sow racial disunity, a complaint that ignored the fact that the vast majority of propaganda portrayed white workers. One Louisiana congressman maintained that the booklet "undertook to glorify one race in the war." In turn, he warned, "such propaganda raises a race issue, which ought to be kept down." In the wake of such criticism, Congress cut funding for the OWI's Domestic Branch to a bare minimum, shelving its plans for further literature aimed exclusively at African Americans.[39] Although the OWI distributed 2.5 million copies of *Negroes in the War*, its attempts to avoid controversy and its concerns over how to square its appeals to blacks with the realities of racism undermined further propaganda efforts targeted at blacks. This stance led the OWI to rely even more so on its practice of portraying motivation via images of white workers. In turn, this tactic reinforced the decades-long assumption that white workers could stand in as archetypes for the "typical" worker in motivational communications. The OWI's failure to significantly address the hopes and aspirations of workers of color in its posters mirrored the entrenched racial discrimination in industry during the war. Indeed, despite New Deal legislation barring employers from discriminatory practices, black workers were routinely hired in lower-paying positions, denied promotion, and subject to informal discrimination throughout the war. The buoyant espousals of forthcoming prosperity thus offered little hope to black, Latino, and other workers of color who experienced scant economic and social gains during the war compared with white workers.[40]

Despite the ubiquity of motivational sentiment in the wartime workplace, workers hardly responded to it in lockstep.[41] On the one hand, as one worker reported, "After Pearl Harbor there was an immediate change in people's attitude toward their work—their sense of urgency, their dedication, their team work. When the chips were down, people dealt with it like survival. Things that might have taken days longer were done to meet a target so you didn't hold somebody else up—even if it meant putting in extra hours and extra effort."[42] On the other hand, visions of Americans unified in the fight to defeat fascism and advance democracy were highly romanticized. As a number of historians have demonstrated, workers and the broader citizenry participated in the war effort with varying degrees of enthusiasm and, for an array of reasons, not least the prospect of making personal gains.[43] In this regard, they were much like those in the theater of war, only 13 percent of whom, according to a study of three thousand soldiers by the U.S. Army's Research Branch, could name more than two of the Four Freedoms that comprised the nation's official war aims.[44]

In deploying prosperity motivation, the state and advertising specialists established a more unambiguous explanation of what workers were fighting for than was the case in early OFF and OWI propaganda. Yet, this strategy also came at the cost of stifling earlier efforts to rally workers to the production battle through warnings about fascism's threats to democracy. The orchestrators of wartime propaganda reasoned that individual consumer freedoms, not popular opposition to fascism, should be the overarching theme of motivational messaging. In the face of fascist coercion, rhetoric about Americans stepping up to support the nation's war objectives voluntarily added emotional weight to the notion that work was a route to individual freedom. Contrived as it was, wartime assertions that Americans were self-motivated came to embody a powerful ideological claim that would help the state define American workers as the most free in the world, an idea that employers would later use to counter labor unions' efforts to extract greater concessions for workers from management.

Although the wartime embrace of prosperity motivation and tributes to cooperation received broad acceptance, it was ultimately more favorable to business than to labor. The OWI's motivational discourse, steeped as it was in the language of labor-management cooperation and business leadership, lent weight to antilabor and anti–New Deal ideologues. Union leaders' abandonment of industrial democracy in favor of postwar consumer-based rewards served similar ends. Together, these developments weakened the militant stance that had served labor so well during the 1930s and helped pave the way for unions to become absorbed into the labor-business consensus of the postwar era, which framed work's rewards around individualism and classless ideals.[45]

VISUALIZING THE REWARDS OF WORK AND CAPITALISM: SHELDON-CLAIRE'S *THIS IS AMERICA*

The specialists enlisted by the federal government to produce workplace propaganda included not only Madison Avenue advertising firms but also independent poster suppliers. Early during the Depression, independent suppliers of motivational publicity like the Seth Seiders Syndicate collapsed as sales dried up in the face of employers' economic belt-tightening. However, the intense emphasis on the need for maximum production during the war prompted employers to take a more positive stance toward the use of motivational messaging. This development opened the way for one of the nation's few surviving independent motivational firms—the Sheldon-Claire Company of Chicago—to become an ally in the government's motivational efforts. As the most prominent independent poster firm to be commissioned by the government during the war, a discussion of Sheldon-Claire and its contribution to motivational design is useful in illustrating wartime quests to hone propaganda for the factory.

Sheldon-Claire was owned and led by Lew Shalett, a businessman who had worked as a poster salesman in the 1920s before launching the firm in 1936. Until the war the company specialized in motivational placards aimed at salesmen, but in 1940, as American participation in the war grew more likely, it abandoned these products and began producing slick motivational posters for use in the factory. Aided by Ben Schenker, a communications design specialist, and Charles Rosenfeld, the brains behind sales operations for Seth Seiders Syndicate, Sheldon-Claire's posters embodied the streamlined design sensibility and promises of prosperity that would become hallmarks of wartime motivational propaganda.

Sheldon-Claire's work for the federal government began in 1942 when the government's War Production Board commissioned it to produce a poster campaign that, with its help, would be sent out to thousands of factories across the country. The campaign, *This is America*, symbolized the growing sophistication of motivational propaganda.[46] It included thirty posters, each of which came in two sizes (four and one-half feet by two and one-half feet and three feet by two feet), complete with frames and spotlights to showcase the "poster of the week." Individual posters depicted Americans in an array of settings enjoying the rewards of American life, which the campaign attributed to free enterprise. Sold by Sheldon-Claire's salesmen, who traveled the country calling on employers, and promoted by government agencies, the campaign received wide usage. Large and small firms alike purchased it, and some corporations bought several hundred sets for their plants across the country.[47]

Thematically, *This is America* resembled Norman Rockwell's *Four Freedoms* paintings that were issued as posters several months later. However, through its thirty-week display schedule, the campaign established a more strategic approach to messaging than was achieved in early OWI posters—a coherent and emotionally stimulating story that tied the personal aspirations of ordinary Americans to the nation's future. The four posters shown below typify Sheldon-Claire's proficient use of streamlined campaign design (figures 4.4–4.7). Displayed in the workplace in weeks five, fifteen, nineteen, and twenty-seven of the campaign, these posters portray the virtues of pluralism ("the melting pot of liberty-loving people"); small-town life ("Main Street" as a product of "free enterprise"); American freedoms (to "speak," "worship," "work," and "live in your own way"); and the "free" American worker (who "Hitler hates" because he is "a man, not a slave"). The slogans "This is America" and "Keep it free!" that announce and conclude each poster conveyed an indeterminate yet powerful injunction equating belief in the nation with being a good worker and citizen.

As this sample of posters illustrates, *This is America*'s messaging was rooted in a strategic use of rhetoric about American democracy and an adept use of emotionally stimulating images. The campaign, by including other posters reminding workers of the freedoms they enjoyed in the workplace, the home, and civic life, provided managers with a powerful story about the rewards of work in a nation where class barriers were implied to be nonexistent. The appeal of this story was based in part in the contrast that it made between the autonomy experienced by workers (and citizens more generally) in the United States and the oppressions of Nazism. Such contrast was implicit in figures 4.4 and 4.6, which extol, respectively, America's embrace of immigrants and citizens' freedoms to "speak," "worship,"

FIGURE 4.4 (LEFT) AND 4.5 (RIGHT). The integration of altered FSA photographs into *This is America* underscores the subtle process of image manipulation in the service of a seamless motivational narrative. Two of the posters (figures 4.5 and 4.6) include altered versions of FSA photographs created by Walker Evans and John Vachon, respectively. Sheldon-Claire Company Records, 1942. Archives Center, National Museum of American History, Smithsonian Institution, Washington, D.C.

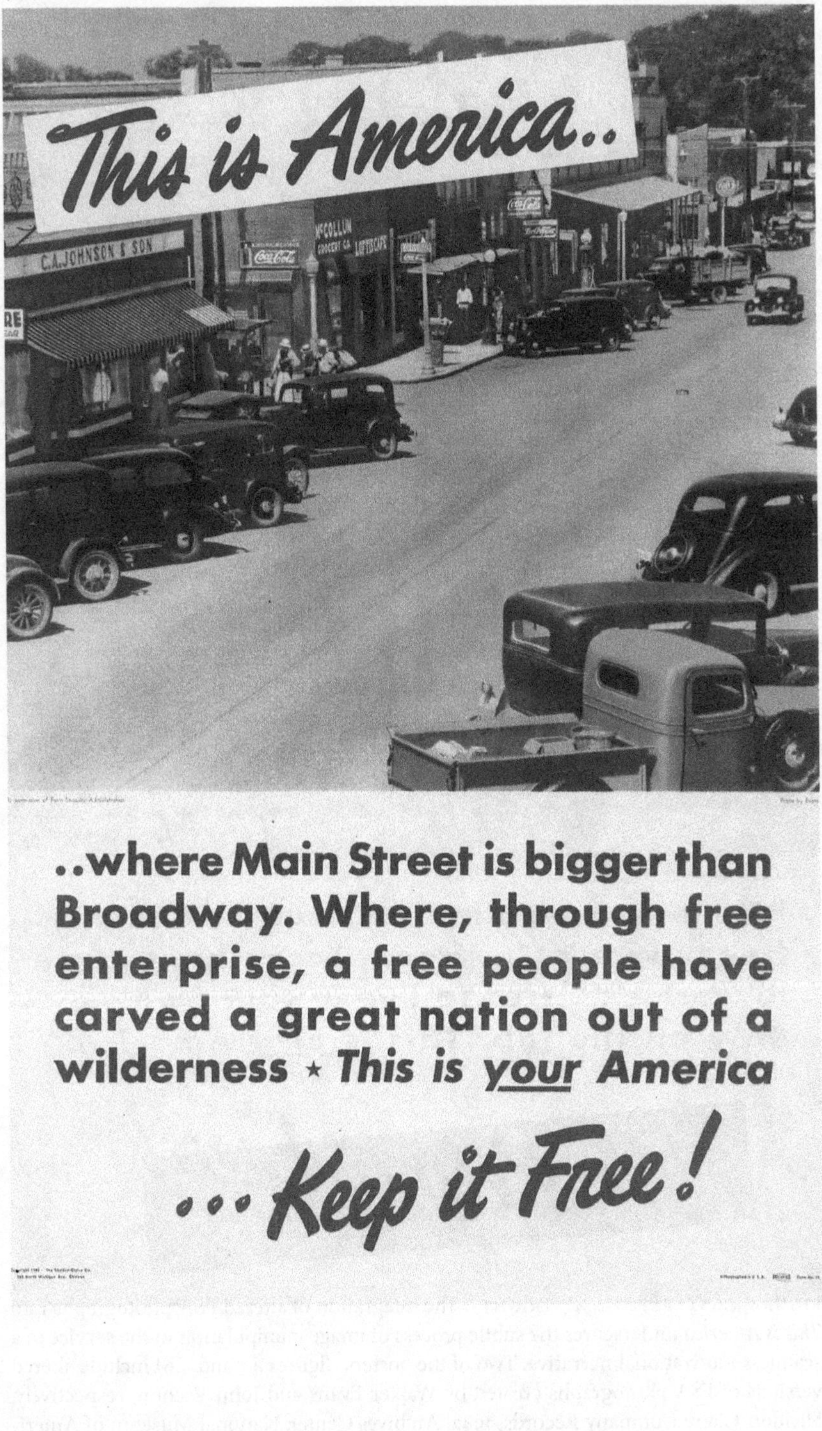
This is America..
C.A. JOHNSON & SON
McCOLLUM GROCERY CO.
Coca-Cola
..where Main Street is bigger than Broadway. Where, through free enterprise, a free people have carved a great nation out of a wilderness ★ This is your America
...Keep it Free!

FIGURE 4.6 (LEFT) AND 4.7 (RIGHT). The integration of altered FSA photographs into *This is America* underscores the subtle process of image manipulation in the service of a seamless motivational narrative. Two of the posters (figures 4.5 and 4.6) include altered versions of FSA photographs created by Walker Evans and John Vachon, respectively. Sheldon-Claire Company Records, 1942. Archives Center, National Museum of American History, Smithsonian Institution, Washington, D.C.

This is America..
...this is you--the man Hitler hates. He hates you because you are an American...because you are free--because you are a man, not a slave. This is your America.
...Keep it Free!

and "work." In other posters this contrast was more explicit (as is seen in figure 4.7, which portrays the "free" American worker as the object of Hitler's "hate"). The serialized display of these messages and the blending of older and newer images collectively suggested that America was and always had been a bastion of freedom for workers and the broader citizenry. This sentiment is established in figure 4.4, which includes a cropped and colorized 1909 photograph by Lewis Hine of immigrants arriving at Ellis Island.

The campaign offered tributes to ethnic diversity in the form of copy that emphasized melting pot idealism, and some posters included portrayals of workers of differing ethnic appearances. It thus depicted motivation in more inclusive terms than in the past when designers, assuming that immigrants had a low propensity for disciplined work, favored images of prototypically white workers. Such changes mirrored the declining authority of such views in a period when immigrants were gaining acceptance as whites and as "real" Americans.[48] While underscoring ethnic diversity, however, *This is America* did not depict workers of color, a practice largely mirrored at the OWI. This omission echoed visually the fraught racial tensions of the wartime industrial arena. During the war, white workers engaged in numerous wildcat strikes in which they walked out of the factory in the wake of new federal policies aimed at reducing racial discrimination in hiring. In excluding workers of color, *This is America* offered daily reminders in the factory that white and ethnic workers were the true embodiments of American labor.[49]

This is America was rooted in a highly ideological reworking of the meanings and rewards of work, one that linked workers' freedom and prosperity to free enterprise and involved a literal adaptation of New Deal motivational images. Seven posters in the series are based on photographs of rural and small-town life created by the New Deal's Farm Security Administration during the Depression. Photographs by Dorothea Lange, Walker Evans, Ben Shahn, Russell Lee, and John Vachon were cropped, colorized, and recaptioned, producing a tribute to the *individual* rewards that workers enjoyed because of free enterprise and cooperation. Created and used to promote the FSA's positive effects on rural farmers and their families, the FSA's photographs were already infused with motivational qualities, albeit of a more subtle nature than in their adapted state in the posters. Modified and integrated into *This is America*, these images of hope amid hard times served just as well, Sheldon-Claire believed, for wartime motivational propaganda. This adaptation of New Deal images, under way since the 1930s, as we have seen, marked an increasing sophistication in motivational poster design that would continue in the years ahead.

A brief discussion of this repurposing of New Deal images illustrates the ideological process at work in the campaign. The adaptation of a photograph by Dorothea Lange typifies this process. The poster included in this book's introduction (figure 0.1) depicts five men from a hometown baseball team. The group's demeanor—hands on hips and steely stares—suggests an aura of preparedness. The men's close proximity to one another and the unifying theme of baseball suggests a tightly knit group—a team mentality. Above, the large caption stating, "This is America," frames the men as representatives of the nation. The honorific depiction of the group is complemented by the caption at the bottom, which reads, "Where a fellow can start on the home team and wind up in the big league. Where there is always room at the top for the fellow who has it on the ball * This is <u>your</u> America . . . *Keep it Free!*" This caption links the "team" in the image to the free enterprise system, which is cast as an indubitable national ideal. The poster's vivid colors complement its message. The bright red gas pump that dominates the building frontage at the center of the image, the blue overalls and baseball caps, and the men's white baseball uniforms and shirts—the colors of the nation's flag—reinforce the poster's patriotic sentiments and add urgency to its appeal. The poster's image and text combine to uphold the virtues of teamwork and individuality: by working together as a team, workers would attain *individual* rewards.

Lange's 1939 black-and-white photograph on which the poster is based has a more mundane and austere tone than its reworked version in the poster (figure 4.8). Lange's caption reads, "Fourth of July, near Chapel Hill, North Carolina. Rural filling stations become community centers and general loafing grounds. The men in the baseball suits are on a local team which will play a game nearby. They are called the Cedargrove Team." The photograph includes four men who are cropped out of the image in the poster. In contrast to the poster's unified, team-like aura, the nine men in the photograph lack a unified sense of purpose. The photograph's laid-back feeling compared with the more urgent feeling implied by the poster is enhanced by the inclusion of a large area of sky and foreground. The cutting, colorizing,

FIGURE 4.8. Dorothea Lange's photograph on which Sheldon-Claire's baseball-themed poster (figure 0.1) is based. Library of Congress, Prints and Photographs Division, FSA/OWI Collection, Washington, D.C. Reproduction no. LC-DIG-fsa-8b34021.

and recaptioning of the photograph, along with its integration into the poster, dissolve the men's loafing demeanor and transform the image into a bold declaration of individual advancement. This feeling is reinforced by the caption's assertion that success is attainable for those who are "on the ball" enough to "wind up in the big league." This parable of upward mobility embodies the essence of American conceptions of meritocracy: the claim that regardless of status at birth, one can achieve economic independence through determination and enterprise. Altered and integrated into the poster, the photograph morphs into a rousing declaration that average workers can attain success and security by their own determination.[50]

FIGURE 4.9. John Vachon's 1941 photograph of a Minnesota farming couple. Library of Congress, Prints and Photographs Division, FSA/OWI Collection, Washington, D.C. Reproduction no. LC-USF3427-063342-D.

The campaign's reworking of New Deal images continued in a poster that includes a modified 1941 photograph of a Minnesota farming couple by John Vachon, in which the woman has been removed and the image reversed and, again, colorized and recaptioned (figure 4.6). In Vachon's photograph, the farmer's clothes appear well worn, suggesting the realities of farm labor, and a building is visible to the right (figure 4.9). In the poster, the now colorized image is cropped, removing the man's lower torso and diminishing the photograph's "rougher" qualities. This cropping gives the man a more elevated position in relation to the viewer, creating a more honorific pose. His ruddy complexion, made possible by colorizing, suggests a more healthful appearance than in the black-and-white photograph. The phrase, "This is America," positioned above over the man's head against the bright blue sky like a salute connects his seemingly motivated attitude to the campaign's patriotic sentiment. This theme is elaborated in the text below the image that reminded workers who viewed the poster of the freedoms the man enjoys as an American and that, by extension, they too enjoyed. The alterations also reinforce the campaign's theme of individual rewards. Whereas Vachon's photograph emphasizes the value of collaboration (implied by the emphasis on the positive effects of the New Deal's social programs and the hard work of the man and woman), the poster presents the man as an individualistic yet team-minded worker and thus the epitome of management's ideal employee.

A similar process of modification is used in the poster portraying "Main Street" (figure 4.5), which is based on an altered version of Walker Evans's 1937 photograph of Main Street in Moundville, Alabama, to symbolize small-town America as a wellspring of free enterprise. Whereas the black-and-white photograph by Evans suggests an uneventful scene, with just a few people ambling on the sidewalk, the colorized image invokes a bustling commercial hub replete with stores, cars, and trucks. The vivid blue, red, and yellow of the stores and cars, along with the cropping and colorizing of the photograph, the addition of text, and its integration into the vertical format, suggest a sense of urgency reminiscent of a tabloid newspaper. The poster's final caption further amplifies the theme of small-town vigor, stating that "Main Street" is a place "where, through free enterprise, a free people have carved a great nation out of a wilderness." Ripped from the context of Depression-era atrophy and integrated into *This is America*, the reworked photograph brings Main Street to life as a foundation of American striving.[51]

When employers purchased *This is America*, they received another powerful communications device, one that extended the campaign's messages to workers in their homes—its "employee mail-o-grams." An adaptation of the pivot man letters of the 1920s, each mail-o-gram consisted of a one-page précis of the forthcoming poster and was mailed by employers to workers' homes a week before the new poster appeared in the factory to elaborate its core message. Steeped in patriotic sentiment, the letters allowed employers to detail the poster's main ideas to workers in advance, with the goal of making them more receptive when viewing the posters on the factory wall. Many of the mail-o-grams espoused the individualistic rhetoric about prosperity disseminated in the culture at large throughout the war. Typical is the mail-o-gram in figure 4.10, which proclaims the rewards of free enterprise for workers. Tapping the appeals to prosperity motivation used throughout the series, it states in part, "[Hitler] hates you because you have things; because as an American, you have more than any man on earth. No other people have such freedom—such comforts as you. No other people have so many radios, motor cars, telephones, refrigerators, washing machines, bathtubs and other goods in life. Because of this, Hitler calls

POSTER OF THE WEEK!

. . . a nation with more homes, more motor cars, more telephones–more comforts than any nation on earth. Where free workers and free enterprise are building a better world for all people • *This is your America*

. . . Keep it Free!

This is America . . . and this is *you*, the man Hitler hates.

He hates you because you have things; because as an American, you have more than any man on earth. No other people have such freedom — such comforts as *you*. No other people have so many radios, motor cars, telephones, refrigerators, washing machines, bathtubs and other good things in life.

Because of this, Hitler calls you "soft". He believed you had grown too fat, too lazy, too self-satisfied. He thought you weren't tough enough or man enough to fight, to work, to sacrifice in defense of your rights.

Hitler has stolen the wealth and resources of other peoples, looted their warehouses, seized their factories, enslaved their workers, depressed their living standards to build up his "master race." The biggest and richest prize of all would be America — if he could only get his greedy hands at *your* throat.

That is Hitler's plan. That is Hirohito's plan. Make no mistake about it. *This war is for keeps*. To lose it would mean to lose all — your rights as a free worker, your privileges as a free citizen, your comforts — your individual liberties would vanish.

Keep that in mind — every minute you are fighting on the production front. This is your personal war — and your personal freedom is at stake.

Throw the lie back at Hitler — show him just how cockeyed he was when he figured that you were too soft, too lazy, too stupid to fight and to work for *your way of life*. Keep working — make every minute count.

STAY ON THE JOB! . . . KEEP AMERICA FREE

FIGURE 4.10. One of the employee mail-o-grams that Sheldon-Claire's clients sent to workers' homes to inform them of the forthcoming "poster of the week." Using these mail-o-grams, employers extended the reach of motivational propaganda to workers' homes. Sheldon-Claire Company Records, 1942. Archives Center, National Museum of American History, Smithsonian Institution, Washington, D.C.

you 'soft.' He believed you had grown too fat, too lazy, too self-satisfied. He thought you weren't tough enough or man enough to fight, to work, to sacrifice in defense of your rights." The text expands this theme, asserting that Hitler was driven by a desire to destroy workers' individual freedoms. Thus, he had plundered "warehouses" and "factories," "enslaved their workers," and "depressed their living standards to build up his 'master race.'" Now, it warned, he wanted to seize the "richest prize of all . . . America—if he could only get his greedy hands at *your* throat." Losing the war, it explained, "would mean to lose all—your rights as a free worker, your privileges as a free citizen, your comforts—your individual liberties would vanish." Workers, it asserted, should "keep that in mind—every minute you are fighting on the production front. This is your personal war—and your personal freedom is at stake."[52]

While the claim that Hitler "hated" Americans because they had more consumer freedoms grossly oversimplified his goals, it served as a powerful ideological tactic in a wartime motivational campaign that American leaders framed largely around the individual prosperity that workers stood to gain or lose. Such sentiments worked in tandem with those of other mail-o-grams delivered to workers' mailboxes emphasizing the rewards they enjoyed owing to the freedoms of speech, worship, and education. Woven through the mail-o-grams was a recurrent reminder to workers that their belief in the values celebrated throughout the campaign was imperative to victory. As one mail-o-gram stated, "Your job is <u>your opportunity</u> to fight the enemy. Your job is <u>your way</u> of keeping faith with America—yourself—your children. Your job is your fox-hole—your hand grenade to score for victory."[53]

The wartime success of Sheldon-Claire and the slick design principles of *This is America* reflect developments in longer-term efforts to advance motivational discourse in the industrial arena. First, the war had revived the privately owned motivational business that had been down on its heels since the onset of the Depression. With motivation once again a national prerogative, Sheldon-Claire, the most capable firm of its kind, was now poised to revive the poster market in the postwar era. Second, the repurposing of New Deal photographs in *This is America* shored up an emerging claim that the United States was a classless nation where workers would enjoy capitalism's abundant rewards if they embraced its values of cooperation, teamwork, and individual reward. This ideal was amplified throughout the war and into the postwar era as declarations about an imminent consumer utopia free of class conflict gained traction in an increasingly advertising-driven culture.

This is America also signaled the rise of a more robust approach to emotional conditioning in the workplace that would only grow more ingrained. From here on out, streamlined campaigns involving a strategic coordination of images and words, image manipulation, and the integration of home mailings and other tie-in materials would become hallmarks of modern motivational communications. Central to this new approach was a calculated use of that most revered tool of salesmanship: repetition. As Lew Shalett later remarked in the statement that heads this chapter, the key to Sheldon-Claire's wartime success was "repetition, repetition, repetition, repetition." He informed his salesmen, "the greatest rogue in history, Mr. Hitler, was shrewd enough to use that idea. He said: 'You can take a story—even a lie—and if you repeat it often enough you can make people believe it.'"[54] Although as a Jew and a passionate devotee of free enterprise Shalett had no love for the sentiments of Nazi propaganda, he nonetheless admired its slick manipulation of images and words in the service of mass indoctrination and would continue to exploit such practices to the hilt after the war.

BUSINESS PROPAGANDA IN THE FACTORY: NAM'S WORK INCENTIVES RHETORIC

The rise of prosperity motivation provided new opportunities for business organizations to hone their motivational propaganda and deploy it in the factory. Among the most active and influential of these organizations was the National Association of Manufacturers (NAM). Having developed an ample motivational propaganda apparatus in the 1930s, NAM now sought to calibrate its pro-business messaging with the wartime campaign for industrial mobilization. While NAM's propaganda consequently invoked patriotic sentiment about boosting productivity and winning the war, its main priority was to advance business's long-term power and authority in economic life. Victory over fascism was characterized as an afterthought at best. At a time when American troops were dying in the battlefields of Europe and the South Pacific, NAM's motivational specialists were excitedly anticipating a postwar order in which the power of the New Deal and labor unions had been eradicated and in which business leaders managed an economy based on free market principles.

During the war, the National Industrial Information Council (NIIC), the public relations agency for NAM, stepped up its use of newspaper advertisements, radio spots, films, and posters aimed at workers. At the core of its propaganda was the argument that business was better equipped than government to boost productivity, secure jobs, and achieve a higher standard of living. In January 1944, Herbert Hosking, an NIIC publicity director, decreed that the council's advertising campaign should try to "convince the public of industry's social consciousness by dramatizing the identity of our postwar objectives with those of the public." The campaign, he added, should emphasize that "full production" was the route to postwar prosperity and that management was a proponent of "cooperation," as opposed to "the class warfare that has been promoted for the past decade."[55]

Over the course of the war, NIIC enlisted managers to champion NAM's messages in the factory. By deploying speeches, literature, and films in the factory, managers could, NIIC officials believed, serve as powerful agents for NAM's pro-business and anti–New Deal agenda.[56] This approach gradually took precedence over that of the 1930s, in which NAM tried to take its messages to workers directly via billboards and other propaganda. Its new strategem rejected the notion that NAM's messages could be "reduced" to the level of the "common man." As Hosking wrote, NAM must "till the soil of public opinion so that management's recommendations will fall on fertile soil when the appropriate time comes to make them."[57] The new approach also favored the terms "incentives" and the "incentive system" over "free enterprise," which NIIC believed lacked "an intensely personal meaning to the average citizen."[58] The strategy of NIIC signaled a significant shift in business's broader quest to turn the workplace into a motivational arena. Now the largest and most influential business organization in the country was using managers as agents in its crusade to advance its ideological war against labor and the New Deal.

In its attempts to delegitimize labor unions and the New Deal, NIIC focused its attention on honing NAM's "incentives" rhetoric. One typical NAM newspaper ad proclaimed that "centralized government planning and bureaucratic domination of our economy" were inadequate "because FREE MEN ACCOMPLISH MORE BY INCENTIVES, NOT COMMANDS." These "incentives" included "New Products and Better Values for consumers," the chance to make "A Fair Return on Capital for investors," "Wages that Recognize Efficient Production for workers," and "Keen, Vigorous and Fair Competition for management"—in short, the ideals then defined by business leaders as central to a postwar consumption-oriented economy based on free market principles.[59] By couching its motivational discourse in the language of consumer needs, NIIC helped elide NAM's antilabor goals, veiling them behind publicity about the benefits of "business management," a term that NAM believed would invite less criticism than "private ownership," which it felt placed unhelpful emphasis on business's self-interest.[60]

In developing its vocabulary of incentivization, NIIC borrowed tactics from the labor movement. An NIIC study of the CIO's public information program noted enviously the impressive messaging of the organization's "39 international unions [and] 14,000 locals," which served as "an active distribution center through which CIO material reaches directly to millions of workers and additional millions of housewives, preachers, non-industrial workers, etc." The report also noted the accessibility and adept use of emotional communications in CIO publicity: "CIO material, every bit of it, is written for the 'milkman in Omaha' and his family and friends. There is a minimum of economics, few statistics, very little history and a maximum appeal to emotion rather than reason. Every piece is an 'eye-catcher,' with a minimum of text and a profusion of clever 'art' to hammer home the points made. The whole emphasis is on effective content and [the] result is highly effective but relatively inexpensive material. The most impressive of the CIO booklets probably cost a fraction of the cost of [NIIC's] 'You and Industry' booklet."[61]

The report went on to lament that "CIO's program is appealing because it expresses what the people <u>want</u>. To the people it is constructive." For example, a recent ad, "How're We Going to Make Both Ends Meet?," far outshone NIIC's endeavors. "With that appeal to the eye and current experiences of millions of Americans," it offered "a simply stated, highly plausible, argument for the guaranteed annual wage as the answer." Similarly, the CIO's recent film, *Hell Bent for Election*, although "the last word in 'corn' judged from any professional standpoint . . . carried a 'wallop' far greater than any NAM movie." The NIIC's problem, according to the report, was that it felt compelled to "rest its case on what <u>we</u> know the people <u>should</u> want based on practical experience and sound economics. Thus we are compelled to the position of opposing the people's desires. Our insistence that we are for jobs and high wages, etc. must be qualified by 'but . . .' or 'if . . .' At once we are destructive." The dry economic messaging of NIIC, the report concluded, were no match for the CIO, which "writes for the masses." The NIIC, the report recommended, needed to learn from the CIO's tactics if it was to win workers' support.[62]

Among the report's proposals was "an overhauling of our public relations activities and material to broaden the market for our story"; a "complete re-writing" of NIIC's recent campaign materials; and the "production now of 'down-to-earth' popularly written analyses of where jobs and higher wages come from, the fallacy of the guaranteed annual wage proposal and a simple statement of our social security philosophy—all for widest possible distribution."[63] These tactics continued a trend that had been materializing since the 1930s—the appropriation and reworking of labor's populist rhetoric by management and its allies.

With the postwar era on the horizon, NAM and NIIC staffers' discussions about how best to delegitimize the New Deal became even more fervent. Internally, each organization asserted that the New Deal was ushering in "slavery" and that NAM stood virtually alone in the struggle to avert this catastrophe by defending the "freedom" of workers and the broader American citizenry. An internal report on the development of NAM publicity in March 1944 noted, "To convince people that freedom versus slavery is the issue, requires us to convince them that President Roosevelt or the bureaucrats (or any other group of *personalities* with whose ideology we take issue) desire to make people into slaves." The author lamented, however, that while such rhetoric was useful in rallying NAM's existing allies, it "makes few converts . . . from the tremendous number of 'middle-of-the-roaders' who hold the balance of power and should be our primary audience." Dismayed at what it regarded as a myopic public incapable of recognizing the tyranny of FDR and the New Deal, the author noted that unfortunately for NAM, this group "believes that we *are* free men."[64]

The author suggested that NIIC employ in its advertising a slogan along the lines of "Free Men Need Incentives, Not Commands," a creed that he believed was illustrated by the "oft-cited contrast between the initiative of American and German soldiers." Whereas the former adhered to "Incentives" such as "Rewards" and "Encouragement," the latter were subjected to "Directives, Orders, Bureaucratic planning [and] Mandates." The author stressed that likening Roosevelt and his "bureaucrats" to the oppressions associated with such German incentives would be highly beneficial to NIIC.[65] This thinking informed NAM advertisements like "The American Way Is to the Right" (figure 4.11).[66] Such cartoons conflated the New Deal (symbolized by "government investment") with Nazism and communism at the same time. Even before the war was over, then, NAM was grouping one of the United States' allies—the Soviet Union—with fascists in its efforts to delegitimize the New Deal. Such rhetoric also infused the materials circulated by other pro-business bodies like the Citizenship Educational Services Inc. The organization's articles and cartoons compared the Nazis' takeover of industry with the New Deal's regulation of business, suggesting that the totalitarianism imposed on German workers was poised to spread to America due to the New Deal, leading to the "enslavement of labor."[67]

Such self-serving sentiments underscore the extent to which business's most ardent champions were prepared to go to in using the war to advance

FIGURE 4.11. An advertisement circulated by NAM toward the end of World War II. In correlating "government investment" (a euphemism for the New Deal in NAM's schema) with totalitarianism and defining "private investment" as the route to "jobs," "freedom," and "opportunity," the ad offered its viewers a clear rationale for the need to replace the New Deal with a business-led economy. National Association of Manufacturers Collection (Acc. 1411), Hagley Museum and Library, Wilmington, DE.

their private ambitions. At a time when Americans were dying on the front lines, NAM and its allies were training their weapons not on Hitler and the Axis powers but on what they claimed were more grave threats to American democracy—the nation's president, the New Deal, and labor unions. In casting the American government as an agent of "slavery" and dismissing the public as deluded "middle-of-the-roaders" who obstructed business's self-evident right to control the economy, NAM established blueprints for the ideology that management deployed in the workplace in the years ahead. The dichotomy at the core of this ideology—between the tyranny of government and labor unions and the freedom-granting effects of business—provided cannon fodder in motivational campaigns that would be unleashed in the factory by management at large industrial corporations throughout the postwar period. The sentiments invoked by NAM were also to become hallmarks of the free market ideology invoked by conservative think tanks after the war and later became hallmarks of the New Right.[68]

Rationalizing Motivation: NAM's "Soldiers of Production" Rallies

In 1943 NIIC launched a new motivational initiative (derived from its campaigns of the 1930s)—its "Soldiers of Production" rallies. The rallies were led by a roster of pro-business speakers whom NIIC dispatched around the country giving speeches to large groups of workers in the factory at no cost to employers, who typically arranged for the rallies to be broadcast on local radio stations and reported on in local newspapers. For employers, the events offered an appealing way to communicate motivational messages to workers and to promote cooperation and loyalty. The rallies allowed NAM to bring new energy to its motivational crusade. Between mid-1943 and late 1944, over three hundred companies across the country staged rallies.[69] As estimated by NIIC, over half a million workers attended rallies between July 1943 and January 1945, and 5.3 million listeners had heard radio broadcasts of them.[70]

Speakers from NAM included high-profile advocates of business leadership and celebrated servicemen. Its roster featured such businessmen as Dr. Allen Stockdale, a Christian minister and free-enterprise evangelist from Oklahoma, and Dr. Neal Bowman, a former marketing professor at Temple University. It also included Captain Edgar J. Wynn, a Canadian pilot, and Colin McKenzie, a former merchant marine revered for having survived three torpedo attacks in one day. Each of these speakers gave around twenty-five speeches per month in 1943 and 1944, and sometimes more.[71]

The speakers were aided by NIIC staff, who supplied them with quotes from pro–free enterprise literature to integrate into their speeches. In December 1944, it sent its speakers a compilation of "sharp epigrams" from Friedrich Hayek's *The Road to Serfdom* (cribbed not from the book itself but a review of the book in the *Atlantic Monthly*), as well as some choice quotes from writings by Alexis de Tocqueville, Peter Drucker, Walter Lippmann, and the former socialist-turned-free-enterprise-advocate Max Eastman. The quotes from Hayek consisted of warnings against monopoly that, in the context of NAM's schema, served as barbs against the excesses of the New Deal. These included, "Our freedom of choice in a competitive society rests on the fact that if one person refuses to satisfy our wishes, we can turn to another. But if we face a monopolist, we are at his mercy. And an authority directing the whole economic system would be the most powerful monopolist conceivable." A passage from de Tocqueville stated, "Democracy extends the sphere of individual freedom; socialism restricts it. Democracy attaches all possible value to each man; socialism makes each man a mere agent, a mere number." From Lippmann, NIIC provided a quotation lambasting "coercive organization" of the individual's "affairs" and the "uniformity" that it produced and, from Drucker, the assertion that "the complete collapse of the belief in the attainability of freedom and equality through Marxism has forced Russia to travel the same road toward totalitarianism."[72]

Peppered into their speeches, these and similar quotes offered NAM's speakers some pithy condemnations of the New Deal and tributes to the moral sanctity of free enterprise. Like "The American Way is to the Right" and other advertisements, the speeches contradict the deeply held myth that everyone put aside their interests and political differences during the war in the name of national victory. While millions of Americans were being called on to do their part by working longer hours, enduring rationing, growing victory gardens, and putting private ambitions on hold, NAM was busy using the war to advance its private interests by disseminating propaganda that likened the New Deal to a totalitarian regime and impugned the Soviet Union, an American ally.

As was the case before the war, the rallies were highly rationalized and orchestrated affairs organized around NAM's free enterprise messaging and

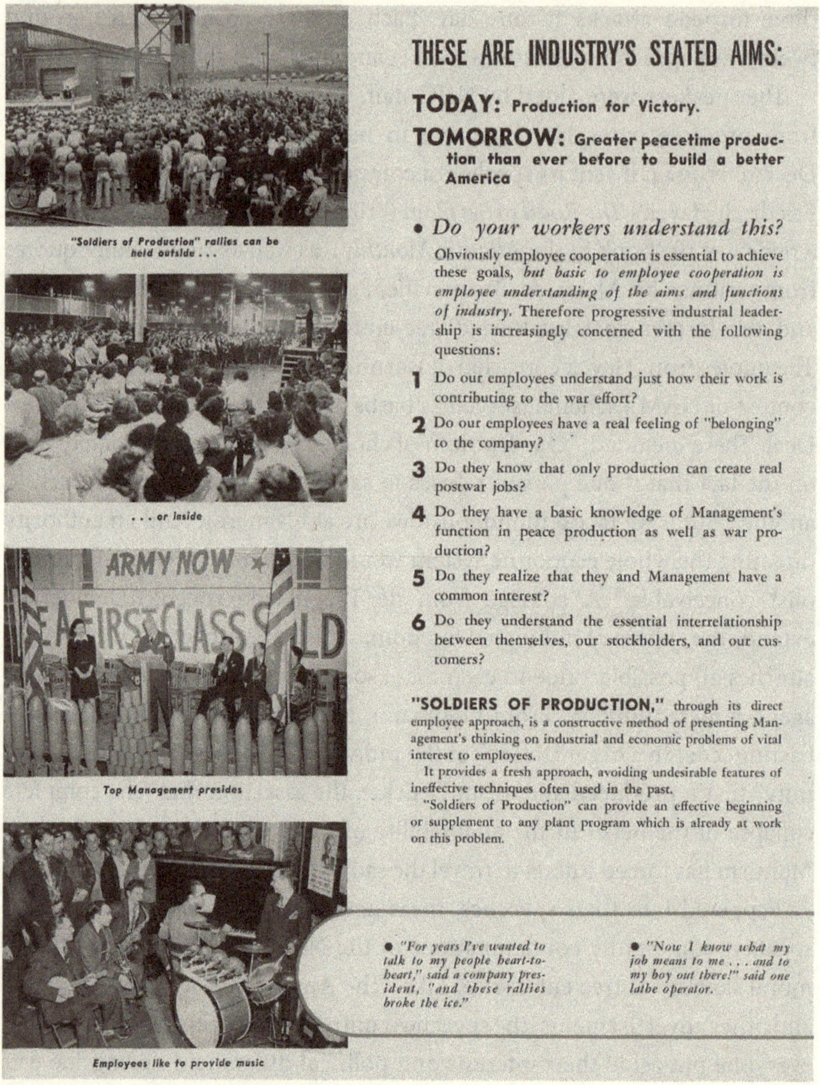

THESE ARE INDUSTRY'S STATED AIMS:

TODAY: Production for Victory.

TOMORROW: Greater peacetime production than ever before to build a better America

• *Do your workers understand this?*

Obviously employee cooperation is essential to achieve these goals, *but basic to employee cooperation is employee understanding of the aims and functions of industry.* Therefore progressive industrial leadership is increasingly concerned with the following questions:

1 Do our employees understand just how their work is contributing to the war effort?

2 Do our employees have a real feeling of "belonging" to the company?

3 Do they know that only production can create real postwar jobs?

4 Do they have a basic knowledge of Management's function in peace production as well as war production?

5 Do they realize that they and Management have a common interest?

6 Do they understand the essential interrelationship between themselves, our stockholders, and our customers?

"SOLDIERS OF PRODUCTION," through its direct employee approach, is a constructive method of presenting Management's thinking on industrial and economic problems of vital interest to employees.

It provides a fresh approach, avoiding undesirable features of ineffective techniques often used in the past.

"Soldiers of Production" can provide an effective beginning or supplement to any plant program which is already at work on this problem.

• *"For years I've wanted to talk to my people heart-to-heart," said a company president, "and these rallies broke the ice."*

• *"Now I know what my job means to me . . . and to my boy out there!" said one lathe operator.*

"Soldiers of Production" rallies can be held outside . . .

. . . or inside

Top Management presides

Employees like to provide music

FIGURE 4.12. As illustrated in this page from its "Soldiers of Production" booklet, NAM's efforts to advance business's authority drew on wartime theories of motivation that encouraged managers to exploit the "social side" of the factory in order to promote feelings of unity and instill employee discipline. National Association of Manufacturers Collection (Acc. 1411), Hagley Museum and Library, Wilmington, DE.

steeped in spectacle. The main promotional booklet by NIIC outlined each stage of its thirty-minute rally. As the booklet explained, each event began with records being played while employees assembled. Second, the "Star Spangled Banner" was sung by all, led by a company "song leader." With the audience warmed up, a company representative would introduce the NAM speaker. With this, the rally entered its fourth and main stage: the twenty-minute speech wherein the speaker called on workers to do their patriotic duty by supporting the company and the war effort. With the main event concluded, the company president took the stage to reiterate the importance of the speaker's sentiments and emphasize the need for workers to join the firm and NAM in the war effort. Next, workers were asked to sing a patriotic song led once more by the company song leader before the seventh and final stage of the event, employees returning to work accompanied by recorded music.[73]

As NIIC reminded employers, the rally itself was but one part of a larger motivational campaign strategy. The company would, it claimed, continue to reap the rewards of the rally through subsequent broadcasts of the event on local radio stations. A series of "follow-up" activities included the display of photographs of and reports about the rally on plant bulletin boards; the monthly distribution to workers of five-minute recordings by the speaker containing an "inspiring message"; the display of cartoon-based posters around the factory; and the circulation of NIIC messages via house organs or NAM literature. By offering employers these motivational services, NIIC claimed that its campaign could be "tailor-made" to suit the needs of each company.[74]

National Industrial Information Council staff members accompanied NAM speakers during the rallies to document the reactions of the workers in attendance. Staff gathered quotes from workers and management, took photographs for use in promotional copy, and conducted head counts of attendees, then submitted reports to NIIC's head office. The reports provided a wealth of information for the NIIC propaganda apparatus. In a typical two-week period, a speaker would give between nine and twelve speeches to crowds of between 5,000 and 13,000 workers. The audience was boosted significantly by the radio broadcasts that typically followed each rally. For example, an estimated audience of over 100,000 listeners in Baltimore heard broadcasts of rallies that were attended by around 13,000 workers in July 1943.[75] This pattern was repeated throughout the country during the war. In less than a week in late September 1943, nearly 5,500 workers in Williamsport, Pennsylvania, attended fifteen rallies, but the recordings of the rallies were heard by an estimated 225,000.[76]

In letters to their superiors, NIIC staffers reported enthusiastic reactions to the rallies. In a 1945 letter describing a speech by Dr. Allen Stockdale to a shift of African American women at a tobacco plant in Winston-Salem, North Carolina, one staffer reported excitedly, "Oh, what a scene. 800 present—750 of whom were colored women in their various colored costumes and bandana head gear—right in the middle of big piles of leaf tobacco . . . Can you picture 750 negro women singing 'Remember Me' and 'Swing Low, Sweet Chariot.' (I guess we had better bring the show to Broadway)."[77]

As staffers' reports about the rallies indicate, NIIC's objective had far less to do with increasing employee motivation and productivity than with maximizing the audience for NAM's anti–New Deal and antiunion messaging. Daily, and over the long term, NIIC was focused on a finely tuned numbers game. Selling the product—pro-business ideology—was the goal. Increasing workers' productivity and advancing the war effort barely registered in the minds of NIIC's staff. Whether trying to enlist businessmen or to sell workers on the virtues of free enterprise, NIIC was focused first and foremost on expanding its audience.

At its core, the crusade by NIIC to indoctrinate workers through NAM's ideology amounted to an exercise in spectacle that, beneath staffers' self-assured pronouncements about the economic theories informing its vision for America, was a slick salesmanship enterprise wrapped in a veneer of intellectualism. In marshaling these methods, NAM and NIIC helped lay the foundations for motivational specialists after the war. Similar methods, as corporate motivational specialists would soon find, could supply powerful ammunition in their efforts to sell workers and the broader public on the need for business and management leadership of the economy.[78]

Despite widespread wartime assertions about work's rewards, the war entailed ambivalent outcomes for workers. On the one hand, workers broadly identified with the need to defeat the Axis powers, and in the wake of the attack on Pearl Harbor and the nation's formal entry to the war, millions took war jobs and experienced economic gains. However, despite romanticized images of camaraderie in the wartime factory, there was little unanimity about what workers were fighting for. Most workers were motivated more by personal aspirations than by the lofty values embodied by the Four Freedoms. Although a discussion of the attitudes of those in the theater of war toward their work is beyond my scope, we should note that they, too, were workers, and their motivations as workers were diverse. As Michael Adams argues, popular assumptions that military members were universally motivated by patriotism do not stand up to scrutiny. Interviews and oral histories illustrate that those who served during the war were compelled more by a commitment to their fellow troops than by idealism.[79] Additionally, although the factory became more racially diverse, African American and other workers of color were often funneled into lower-paying jobs as employers found ways around New Deal labor laws. Women, meanwhile, were often treated as second-class workers by men who bristled at them taking jobs traditionally worked by men.[80] For their part, union leaders acquiesced under the pressure of war's demands to managerial calls for cooperation and unity. This development led union leaders to abandon the militant stance that had proven so effective in advancing the cause of industrial democracy in the 1930s.

World War II marked one of the most intense periods of development of motivational discourse in the United States to date. Two main changes stand out in particular. First are innovations on the design front, namely, the rapid refinement of emotionally stimulating visual communications and the rise of slick, streamlined campaigns. While these innovations were not entirely new, they occurred at unprecedented speed as specialists like the War Advertising Council, Sheldon-Claire, and NAM/NIIC became instrumental in shaping motivational propaganda for use in the factory. The second development was the adoption by motivational propagandists in the latter stages of the war of a far more strategic approach to their messaging than in the past. Most notable, with the postwar era on the horizon, they began to infuse their messages with emotive visions of work's *long-term* rewards. In doing so, propagandists paved the way for the rise of a wide-ranging apparatus for promoting the tenets of the emerging postwar order. Those tenets—the ideologies of classlessness, consumption, and obligatory labor-management cooperation—would soon form the foundations of the most powerful motivational apparatus that managers and their allies had ever deployed in the workplace.

CHAPTER 5

Selling Workers on Their Jobs

CONSUMPTION-BASED MOTIVATION AND MANAGEMENT DOMINION IN THE POSTWAR ERA

> A really free people can live well materially and spiritually where there is the incentive to work, create, compete, save, invest, and profit. But there must be either force to *drive* men to work. Or there must be incentive to make men *want* to work.
>
> —Lemuel Boulware, General Electric's vice president of employee and community relations, 1949

> As in all propaganda, the point is to make man endure, with the help of psychological narcotics, what he could not endure naturally, or to give him, artificially, reasons to continue his work and to do it well.
>
> —Jacques Ellul, *Propaganda: The Formation of Men's Attitudes*, 1965

Although World War II expanded motivation's role in managerial quests for control, widespread industrial instability in the war's aftermath quashed any hopes among managers and their allies that motivational messaging would help them advance their ideological goals on a longer-term basis. With mass layoffs of war workers across the country and fears of a return of depression circulating in the press, workers had little to feel motivated about and were hardly disposed to viewing management positively. Between 1945 and 1947, industry became a battleground in the struggle over the nation's political and economic future. Mobilized by their unions, millions of workers went on strike, demanding wage increases to offset earnings lost due to wartime wage freezes. While the strikes stoked workers hopes for industrial democracy, for management they served as a stark reminder that enlisting workers' spontaneous cooperation would be far from easy.

However, developments from the late 1940s onward gave managers new reasons for optimism that motivational techniques could yield benefits. Especially influential was the "consensus ideology" that dominated the political and economic arena after the war. Consensus ideology rested on two main precepts, each of which had a direct influence on employers' motivational efforts throughout the postwar period. First, it asserted the belief that mass consumption, fueled by the superior virtues of the "American way of life," would lead to a rising standard of living for workers and their families. In turn, consumption would end the class conflict that had simmered for decades and give rise to a classless society. Second, it maintained that American capitalism was morally superior to communism and antithetical to socialism. This view underpinned American efforts to contain communism globally and supplied the foundations for domestic politics. Together, these two precepts became articles of faith among politicians, businessmen, and civic leaders, reaching deeply into institutions.[1]

While the influence of consensus ideology is well known, its role in management's efforts to advance its goals in the workplace has been less noted. Following the war, the motivational apparatus—the communication forms, techniques, rhetoric, and imagery through which managers and their allies integrated motivation in the workplace—fully absorbed the edicts of consensus. In the process, management integrated the legitimizing ideals of mainstream political doctrine into its claims and advanced larger goals: to weaken the visions of work upheld by the labor movement and the New Deal. By realizing these goals, managers believed, they could extend their authority beyond the sphere of industry, achieving dominion over the prevailing economic ideas that governed the postwar order.[2]

Motivation gained further influence due to changes in large organizations. In the highly bureaucratic corporations that dominated industry, staffed by a growing army of white-collar workers, effective communications techniques were considered essential to employees' integration into the firm and to organizational efficiency. The concept of communications was attractive to managers also because it lacked the negative connotations associated with propaganda, a term that came to be associated after the war with misinformation and manipulation.[3] These developments obscured the fact that motivational campaigns now became even more concerned with a strategic manipulation of the worker's mind. As sociologist C. Wright Mills observed in 1951, the period witnessed the rise of a new management technique for instilling discipline that relied not on control but *self*-control. The aim of "the latest psychological equipment," Mills observed, was "to have men internalize what the managerial cadres would have them do, without their knowing their own motives." This approach was "more insidious than coercion precisely because it is hidden; one cannot locate the enemy and declare war upon him."[4] The motivational apparatus deployed by management after the war operated partly in this way.

This chapter traces management's use of motivational propaganda in the postwar period. After charting some of the broader developments in motivation, I examine motivational techniques deployed by two of the era's largest industrial corporations—General Motors and General Electric. As Elizabeth Fones-Wolf and Kim Phillips-Fein have argued, business leaders waged a relentless crusade to weaken the New Deal and labor unions through pro–free enterprise and antiunion campaigns after the war.[5] Motivational propaganda, I argue, played an influential role in this crusade by helping management to define cooperation and company mindedness as obligatory in their employee communications. But the increasingly sophisticated character of the campaigns offered management something further: the ability to refashion the prevailing definitions of work and its rewards and to tie them to new political and economic ideals. Although industrial work became even more arduous owing to management's speedup of production and class grievances remained rife, management grew increasingly effective at honing motivational ideology and "selling" workers on their jobs. After several decades of experimentation, the motivational project emerged as a coherent ideology. Its heyday had arrived.

POSTWAR MANAGEMENT AND MOTIVATION

Management's efforts to exploit motivation were boosted significantly by the dramatic developments in labor-management relations that followed the war's end. Particularly significant was the 1947 Taft-Hartley Act. Passed by a Republican Congress in an attempt to weaken unions' power and influence, the act outlawed the closed shop (which many managers denounced as a form of "compulsory unionism"); banned unions from engaging in sympathy strikes and secondary boycotts; required them to expel members of the Communist Party and other radical organizations; and barred supervisors from joining the same unions as rank-and-file workers. No less consequential was the act's "employer free speech" provision. This measure ended New Deal regulations that prevented employers from criticizing unions in their publicity.[6] A further boon for management was that, in the atmosphere of obligatory compromise that followed the act's passage, labor leaders abandoned the commitment to industrial democracy that had galvanized workers hopes in the 1930s and focused instead on winning wage increases. In the aftermath of the labor-management settlements of the late 1940s, union leaders became increasingly supportive of prevailing consensus ideals and thus were less inclined to challenge management messaging than they were in the past.[7] With labor unions compromised amid these changes, management at large corporations felt increasingly emboldened in deploying motivational techniques.

Motivation's stock among managers also grew because it was now enshrined in the empirical arguments of social science. The field of human relations rapidly gained acceptance throughout management after the war. Until the war's end, its influence was mainly linked to the research of Elton Mayo and his Harvard Business School colleagues. But now the field's theories worked their way into workplace policies. Human relations allowed managers unprecedented stealth in their efforts to indoctrinate and discipline workers. As Howell Harris points out, through human relations, many managers sought to trade "crude authoritarianism" for "smooth manipulation and persuasion."[8] The antiunion goals of human relations found cover amid rhetoric about the freedom-granting properties of consensus and Cold War discourse about the individual's autonomy (which was habitually contrasted with the oppressive conditions under which workers toiled under communism). Human relations specialists cast management as an agent of liberal democracy and a friend of the worker, tactics used in different ways for decades but now anchored in dominant national ideologies.[9]

Central in shaping management's motivational apparatus was a branch of human relations known as "employee relations," or ER. After the war, ER departments became familiar fixtures at industrial corporations, dealing with all aspects of the employer-employee relationship, including employee hiring, training, and education, as well as orchestration of motivational communications devices, including posters, films, literature, employee contests, and radio spots. Following the lead of Mayo and other human relations theorists, ER specialists sought to ease conflict arising from dissatisfaction with Taylorism. At less than eighty dollars a year per worker, ER programs were a cheap way to infuse the factory with motivational sentiment and encourage "cooperative" attitudes.[10] Between 1949 and 1950 alone, companies that had ER departments grew from around a dozen to about fifty.[11] Under the umbrella of human and employee relations, managers used motivational communications in far more rationalized ways than in the past. For managers and the growing cadre of motivational specialists in industry, such techniques became indispensable in the mission to instill discipline in the factory. Moreover, from the late 1940s onward, workers across industries were subject to increasingly homogenous motivational sentiment as corporate ER specialists began to network with one another. Spurred by conversations at the 1950 American Management Association Conference, ER specialists from large corporations began to meet annually to share research findings on employee motivation under the name "Dearborn Group." The group's thirteen members included representatives of General Motors, Ford, AT&T, DuPont, Inland Steel, Esso, Standard Oil, and U.S. Rubber, collectively employing around 1.6 million workers.[12]

Distinct in the era's motivational research was its extensive integration into university-led research initiatives and private consulting. The former included the University of Chicago's Committee on Human Relations in Industry and its Industrial Relations Center, each of which conducted large studies into motivation in conjunction with major industrial employers.[13] No less influential in the rise of motivation were private consulting firms. Among the motivational services taken up by employers were employee attitude surveys, counseling and interviews, films and literature, and employee education courses.[14] Whether in the form of formal research studies or employee communications, human relations helped management to integrate motivational techniques into the firm's culture. By the early 1950s, motivation was cited increasingly by management specialists as an important priority for organizations. In a sign of this shift, the first section of one of the major management textbooks of the period, Morris

Viteles's *Motivation and Morale in Industry*, published in 1953, was entitled "Mobilizing the Will-to-Work" and included chapter-length discussions of morale building, teamwork, and the integration of workers into the organization.[15]

Amid the mood of consensus that infused industry and the culture at large, management invariably couched work's rewards in individual terms. This tactic took its cues from the prosperity motivation that proliferated during the war. In the minds of many businessmen, the state had stimulated class consciousness through the New Deal. They believed that appeals for a spirit of collective support for the war effort, though necessary, had also encouraged communitarian-based ideals of work that invoked the specter of class consciousness and thus now needed to be reined in. Like earlier devotees of motivation, management experts believed that industrial stability would occur only if workers abandoned their "maladjusted" collective class sympathies. Motivational messaging paid tribute to the "average family man" who strove to give himself and his family a life of consumer abundance made possible by a rising standard of living.[16] Such sentiment modified the Depression-era ideal of communitarian striving, swapping its class idioms for promises that workers could reap material and psychological rewards by embracing consumer capitalism. By integrating such rhetorical language into the workplace and other spaces where workers were exposed to mass publicity, management hoped to banish communitarian-based motivation, along with its class-based intonations, to history.

Behind the sanguine messages about workers' consumption-based rewards were some less favorable realities. Although wages increased and a rising standard of living did occur for many workers, as journalist Godfrey Hodgson argues, the much-touted gains made by ordinary Americans were modest when considered alongside those better off. Moreover, the rising standard of living was far from a cure-all for class inequity. This ideal's most notable effect, Hodgson argues, was to institute the illusory impression that a "universal middle class" had arrived, making class an irrelevancy and pushing class to the margins of national discourse.[17] Moreover, although wartime ideals of racial pluralism continued to flourish and workers of color made gains as many corporations implemented racial desegregation and antidiscrimination policies, when it came to motivation, most specialists lagged behind, depicting white and usually male workers as the default symbols of motivated labor in posters, films, and other media, as if following scripts written in the 1920s.[18]

Some observers doubted the effectiveness of corporate attempts to influence workers' minds in the 1950s. Among the most noted critiques was William H. Whyte's 1952 book *Is Anybody Listening?* His answer to this question was clear: "The evidence is frighteningly strong that they aren't. The employee, surveys indicate, is as misinformed about business as ever." Corporations' campaign to sell workers on the merits of free enterprise, he argued, was "not worth a damn." Much of the publicity produced in the "Great Free Enterprise Campaign," for workers' edification, he observed, reflected the obsessions of businessmen and public relations (PR) specialists more than it influenced workers.[19] Whyte was correct that such propaganda was largely an expression of business's own preoccupations. Yet what he failed to recognize was that the point of such efforts was not to "convince" workers but to recast the prevailing definitions of work and its rewards within the organization and in the culture at large in the case of PR campaigns. By doing so, communications specialists believed, workers and the public could be habituated to the idea that labor-management cooperation, free enterprise ideals, consumption-based values, and other familiar postwar precepts were "official." If individual workers identified with specific assertions, well and good, but molding the official values of the organizations in which people worked and lived was the major goal of such campaigns.[20]

The motivational project gained momentum because its sentiments aligned closely with the era's political and economic orthodoxies. The Keynesian faith in cooperation and consensus, as well as its claim that class inequities were receding amid the postwar boom, reached deeply into American life even as class grievances remained as rife as ever. Assertions about the arrival of a classless social order spread through advertising and PR, each of which echoed the prosperity-fueled rhetoric espoused by the field of motivational research (MR), which flourished after the war. Rooted in Freudian theories originating in prewar Vienna, MR emphasized the happiness that Americans would attain if they embraced consumer-based desires. The field's most prolific devotee, Ernest Dichter, achieved fame and fortune advising leading corporations on the hidden desires that compelled people to buy products. An Austrian-born Jew who fled Europe amid the rise of

Nazism in 1938, Dichter founded the Institute for Motivational Research in 1946 and conducted numerous studies on consumer motivation. He advised his corporate clients that products were "symbols of personal growth and creative self-expression" that could help alleviate and offset class-based disenchantment if presented effectively through advertising.[21]

While management remained focused on assuaging class grievances by touting the rewards available to workers if they embraced consensus ideals, on its lower frequencies, workplace motivation began to adapt MR's rhetoric about personal fulfillment. In an era when work itself became increasingly punishing on the mind and body due to speed-ups of production, and when automation further eroded workers' autonomy on the line, employers instead proclaimed the extrinsic rewards that work supplied through competitive wages and access to consumption. This tactic echoed some of Peter Drucker's postwar writings. Drucker argued that the corporation, as "the representative social institution of our time," was the most important mechanism for integrating the individual into society. Only by harmonizing the interests of management and workers, he argued, could management achieve this goal.[22] For many employers, promoting consumer-based rewards and the familial bonds available to employees at large industrial corporations presented a means to achieve such ends. Much like the advertisements for consumer goods created by Dichter and other MR specialists that saturated the culture at large, the goal of the motivational techniques they deployed was to mitigate the class-based disenchantments arising from lost autonomy in an industrial society by exposing workers to continual reminders of the value of work.

The quest for authority in industry was hardly a one-sided affair. Throughout the postwar era, labor unions waged their own campaigns to maintain workers' allegiances and win over younger employees, few of whom had a strong affinity with the hard-fought union struggles of the past. To these ends, unions promoted "social unionism" by using newspapers, magazines, radio, posters, and films, as well as sport and entertainment. As robust as unions' efforts were, however, they struggled to match the scale and sophistication of management's communications apparatus. Often underfunded, unions' endeavors to secure workers' loyalties failed to match those of business. No less problematic was that the central message of union publicity—the need for economic security and a rising standard of living for workers and their families—was often the same as that espoused by management. Faced with powerful organizations like the National Association of Manufacturers and well-funded corporate campaigns, labor unions consistently found themselves at a disadvantage.[23]

Throughout the era, American motivational specialists and managers continually contrasted the "voluntary" nature of cooperation in the factory with the forced coercion imposed on workers in the Soviet Union. Yet despite its democratizing lingo, the aim of motivational propaganda in America was the same as that used under the aegis of communism: to instill morale and discipline among workers and render them more productive and easier to control.[24] American-style motivation resembled the forms of soft coercion endemic to the postwar era.[25] Although Americans liked to think of their relationship to work in democratic terms, the motivational propaganda they were exposed to was no less manipulative than that used elsewhere. Such conclusions are evident in the techniques deployed by the nation's industrial giants.

MOTIVATION AS SOCIAL SCIENCE AT GENERAL MOTORS

Nowhere did the management quest to exploit motivation flourish more than at the nation's largest industrial corporation, General Motors (GM). The company's interest in employee motivation was prompted in large part by a desire to establish managerial authority over the United Automobile Workers (UAW). One of the most militant unions in the Congress of Industrial Organizations (CIO), the UAW had been in a long struggle for influence over industrial planning. At the end of the war, the UAW staged widespread strikes in efforts to recoup wages lost due to wartime wage freezes and to force management to accede to the union's demands. The ensuing labor-management conflict led to the most acrimonious strikes in the country since those of 1919, culminating in a 113-day stoppage in 1945–46 involving over 200,000 workers.[26] The strikes eventually ended in a historic compromise in which the UAW won significant wage increases for workers while abandoning its more radical aspirations amid the pressures imposed by the new bargaining environment of the late 1940s.[27] But for management, the strikes prompted renewed efforts to advance the firm's motivational apparatus.

In the face of looming postwar conversion of industry back to peacetime production and the threat of expanded union power, GM embarked on a wide-ranging campaign to generate employee goodwill toward the company. This campaign was largely concerned with employee motivation, a goal that it approached by attempting to focus workers' minds on the "positive" aspects of their jobs. Specialists at the firm's Employee Research Section, which it founded in 1945, coordinated this task. Steeped in social science techniques and human relations rhetoric, the section mounted one of the era's most extensive projects to integrate motivational communications in the factory. Into the mid-1950s, the section's employee relations specialists produced an array of communication forms, including employee contests, literature racks, films, posters, and suggestion schemes. Espousing the superior rewards enjoyed by workers at GM relative to other employers, the firm's competitive wages, and the sense of community in the "GM family," the firm's motivation-infused campaigns sought to sell management's ideas directly to employees.[28]

The firm's motivational initiatives also spoke to the broader quest to produce a more integrated organization in which workers equated their interests with those of the company and management, ideas reflected in the influential writings of management theorist Peter Drucker. In his 1946 book, *Concept of the Corporation*, Drucker encouraged managers to understand that their efforts to establish legitimacy were dependent on recognizing the corporation as a "social institution." Among the corporation's main social functions were to instill a sense "dignity" and "status" and to encourage workers to believe that they could advance in society. The challenges, he argued, were rife in the auto industry, especially GM, where he conducted much of his research for the book during the war. The worker, he wrote, "often . . . has no idea what he is doing or why. There is no meaning in his work, only a pay check." Thus, it was vital to provide him with a feeling of control over his work and a feeling of being a "partner" with management.[29] For decades, Drucker's arguments have been cited in management textbooks as evidence of the rise of a more humane and democratic form of management. Yet, Drucker's theories did not depart from Frederick Taylor's view that management should control all aspects of production.[30]

Although GM's top brass rebuffed many of Drucker's proposals (he encouraged management to cultivate a more worker-centered production ethos to aid long-term economic viability), the firm was more receptive to his ideas about creating a "responsible worker" who had a "managerial aptitude."[31] C. E. Wilson, the executive who founded the Employee Research Section, was especially supportive of these ideas; for him, Drucker's thoughts embodied a useful strategy of motivation, given that the UAW expanded its own efforts to win workers' allegiances after the war. These initiatives included educational programs, numerous newspapers and other literature, its own stores, radio shows, as well as recreational activities that spanned sports, musical groups, and hobby exhibitions.[32] Over the next few years, GM found that its ER campaigns were an expedient tool for undercutting the UAW's community-building strategy.

Motivation through Positive Thinking: The "My Job and Why I Like It Contest"

General Motors' most prominent motivational campaign, its 1947 "My Job and Why I Like It Contest" (MJC), invited all hourly paid workers to submit letters explaining why they "liked" their jobs, and offered as incentives over five thousand prizes (all of which were GM products), including cars for the forty letters that its panel of judges deemed the best. For at least two reasons, labor historians have generally not dwelled on the MJC. First, thousands of the submissions were from salaried, white-collar, and nonunion employees (who were more likely than blue-collar workers to adopt the affirming rhetoric that GM wished to elicit). Second, workers expressed positive regard in hopes of winning a prize, and therefore, the letters did not reflect their real attitudes. However, the fact that the contest was a deceptive effort to generate employee goodwill toward the firm is precisely what makes it a useful case study into motivational ideology. Not only did it embody management's larger strategic effort to undermine unions in the Taft-Hartley era, but it was also one of the first major postwar motivational initiatives to apply social science techniques. An examination of the contest thus allows us to grasp both GM's adept honing of motivation and the rationale that informed the postwar motivational project more generally.[33]

The MJC was publicized with great fanfare for several months prior to the entry deadline and generated a participation rate of over 58 percent, with nearly 175,000 workers in forty-nine states submitting letters.[34]

General Motors' employee-relations specialists, Chester Evans and La Verne Laseau, the contest's principal organizers, described its objectives in a 1950 research monograph: "To encourage more constructive attitudes in the minds of employes [*sic*] by directing their attention to the positive aspects of their jobs . . . To place certain educational bulletins in the hands of employes that would indicate some of the benefits derived from employment with General Motors . . . To collect material for the enlightenment of supervisory and management groups [and] To obtain a body of data for the analysis of employe-attitudes."[35] The firm also hoped that the contest would aid its mission to redefine foremen as members of management and linchpins of cooperation. To give workers "a natural reason for talking with employes," the organizers assigned supervisors the task of distributing entry forms and publicity to workers in the months prior to the contest deadline.[36]

As indicated by its title and its goals, the contest was a deeply ideological exercise in engineering positive regard for GM among workers and in crafting the image of a harmonious "GM community." The firm viewed these objectives as highly desirable given that workers and management were engaged in another contest during this period—a highly acrimonious one—over wages and labor's role in industrial planning. The MJC publicity made clear to workers that only "positive" comments about their job and GM were appropriate, effectively precluding critical responses from winning entries. The organizers' claims that the contest offered a window into the "true feelings" of the rank and file prompted skepticism among many workers, as well as from the UAW, not least because thousands of the entries were submitted by white-collar workers, a fact that was obscured by GM's characterization of the letters as the collective expression of "GM employees." In response to the artful stratagem behind the contest, Walter Reuther lambasted it as a "one-sided opinion poll" aimed at eliciting favorable statements about GM from employers that could "later be used in so-called goodwill advertising." He suggested that it should have been called "What I Like or *What I Don't Like* about My Job."[37] At least one union publication, Flint Local 659's *The Searchlight*, included letters from workers satirizing the contest in the form of mock entries that poured scorn on GM's history of union-busting tactics and emphasized the CIO's pivotal role in forcing the company to improve working standards.[38]

In the weeks prior to the contest, supervisors throughout the company were briefed on its "background, mechanics, and overall objectives" and received a "Plan Book" explaining how to administer promotional activities.[39] Managers received posters, banners, streamers, and other materials for installment during a "teaser campaign" to "arouse curiosity and stimulate interest" among workers for two weeks prior to the contest.[40] The firm encouraged managers to supplement this campaign with their own publicity and to print workers' guesses about the meaning of the teaser slogans in plant newspapers. It also instructed managers to ask local radio stations to cover the MJC and supplied a "sample script" that modeled a typical exchange between the radio interviewer and a worker. Before the contest, some plants organized floats and paraded them through the town, while others held open house events (to "acquaint 'homefolks' with the employe's job"). Many such events drew audiences ranging between twenty thousand and forty thousand.[41] As illustrated below, promotional materials encouraged workers to approach their letter as a "family affair," portraying a male worker writing his letter at the dining table aided by his wife and children (figure 5.1).[42] Materials like this helped organizers tap the emotionally powerful ideology of "containment," which, as Elaine Tyler May argues, designated the home-centered family as a "psychological fortress" against class rhetoric and Cold War threats.[43] General Motors also tried to boost participation by emphasizing that workers could win regardless of writing ability. A postcard mailed to employees' homes depicted a bust of a frowning William Shakespeare next to that an "average" worker. Its caption stated, "You don't have to be a GENIUS . . . So, you're not so hot as a writer? So what? You don't have to be a good writer to enter—or even to win—the big 'My Job' contest."[44]

Contest publicity drew on the ideas of positive-thinking author Norman Vincent Peale, who advised GM during the design stage.[45] This publicity made clear to participants that expressing a "positive" disposition in the letter would be advantageous. At the outset of the promotional stage, workers received three "Thought Starter" booklets whose sentiments resembled the "Thought Conditioners" in Peale's books. The first, "Getting Started," invoked the tone of a heart-to-heart talk, using "we" and "our" to define the worker as a member of a community united in moving beyond negativity: "Few things in life are perfect. Our daily contacts and associations all

FIGURE 5.1. "Poster no. 6," "Plan Book for General Motors Employes." Kheel Center for Industrial Relations, Cornell University, Ithaca, NY. License supplied by the General Motors Media Archive, GM Heritage Center, Sterling Heights, MI.

leave certain things to be desired. In fact, it's easy to concentrate so much on what's wrong that we entirely lose sight of the good things we have. For example, there are things many of us criticize about our government, but not one of us would want to trade the American way of life for any other. The same holds true of our jobs. No job is perfect. But whatever your job may be, there are many good things about it."[46] The booklet thus proscribed narrow limits on the commentaries that workers should offer regarding their employer and job. Similarly, the design of the entry form discouraged workers from expressing "gripes." The form also instructed workers to include any critical comments in the "P.S." section on the back of the form (subtly categorizing such comments as afterthoughts that should be expressed separately from the letter).[47] Workers evidently took the hint that critical comments would not help their chances of winning: just over 7 percent of entrants used this section.[48]

General Motors described the judging process with the same lingo used in contest publicity, informing workers that their letter would be assessed based on "sincerity, originality, and subject matter, without consideration of writing ability."[49] In reality, judging was a highly orchestrated exercise in codifying "positive" employee attitudes. In turn, the project's coordinators aimed to establish the firm's transparency in the eyes of employees and the public and, as Reuther and many other critics claimed, generate a body of data through which to uphold management's legitimacy. To categorize workers' responses, the adjudicators (GM appointed the Statistical Analysts Company of Detroit to conduct this work) developed a list of seventy-nine recurring themes present in a sample of one thousand letters and produced a coding manual based on them. The analysts later condensed the themes to a list of eighteen. Next, a team of around forty "coding readers" coded all 174,854 letters, scoring how closely each articulated the themes listed in the manual on an International Business Machines card.[50]

Of the letters submitted, reproductions of a mere seventy-one survive (the forty first-place winners, which were reproduced in a GM booklet titled "The Worker Speaks," and thirty-one nonwinning letters, which Evans and Laseau included in their book). General Motors has declared neither its reasons for discarding the bulk of the letters nor when it took place. Whatever the case, this occurrence illustrates the calculating nature of the firm's use of a mere fraction of the entries to support its claim that workers held a positive outlook on their jobs and the company.[51] Two main themes appear in all the winning letters, as well as most of the available nonwinners. First, they laud GM's democratic values and humane management. Second, authors extol the "GM community" and the "American way of life" (and variants of these terms). The extant letters reveal that many participating workers adopted the rhetoric espoused in the contest literature (expressing, for example, a belief in the possibility of personal advancement at the firm and identification with the GM "family"). Many also tied their personal or family histories, and often their journey toward citizenship, to their employment at GM. Accolades to GM products and pride in being a GM employee appear often, as do expressions of patriotism and denouncements of America's enemies (fascism during World War II and communism amid the current Cold War). While the specific themes of the surviving letters vary, one trait is quite consistent: many of the authors invoke the style and tone common in much of the era's canned advertising and PR speech and the sponsored radio soaps of the era that included plugs for manufacturers. This tendency is hardly surprising given that the advice offered to participants in promotional materials was itself steeped in such language. Many employees evidently took the hint, resulting in letters that could have passed for advertisements for General Motors.

A brief discussion of three letters, chosen for their typicality of the extant entries, illustrates how employees adopted the language modeled in the promotional materials. Betty Kraft, a secretary to the head of GM's patent office, couched her appreciation of her job within an account of a recent interaction with her son Carl. Declining Carl's request that she stay home from work to spend time with him, she segued into an homage to the firm. "From the time I was a little girl going to school," she explained, "I have heard the remark, 'If it's made by General Motors it must be good!' and General Motors has maintained that reputation for honesty, dependability and fairness toward employees and customers alike all through the years." After this syrupy opening, she told Carl about the "spirit of good fellowship enjoyed by G.M. folks" and the company magazine of the same name, which helped "bring us closer to our fellow workers and acquaint us with the many activities engaged in by those employees." She added that "in a few years" he could participate the "Annual Soap-box Derby sponsored by Chevrolet Division of General Motors (you know, Chevrolet, the kind of car we hope to have some day). It's a wonderful thing for growing boys, develops sportsmanship, ingenuity and ability to think for themselves." After telling Carl that "Future" at GM "means not only years of steady and fruitful employment with an established and respected firm" but also "the GM Retirement Plan," which will "help me to be independent in the later years of my life," Carl said his prayers and, with a sentiment that must have thrilled the judges, "asked the Lord to 'God bless General Motors!'"[52] Indeed, Kraft's approach impressed them: she was one of the forty first-place winners. She got her Chevrolet in the end.

It remains entirely possible that many authors of such letters, even though adopting an overly sentimentalized parlance, did hold a highly positive regard for their jobs and the firm. However, more important than ascertaining how participants "really" felt is to grasp the contest designers' success in coaching them to adopt sentiments and phrasings that helped GM to amass "evidence" of workers' goodwill toward the firm and, in turn, management's legitimacy from workers' perspectives. Whether such letters reflect authors' strategic efforts to win a prize or genuine positive regard for GM, the exercise helped GM to get workers to define themselves as contented, loyal, and motivated employees. For the contest's orchestrators, workers' true feelings were irrelevant. The payoff for the firm was the letters, which could be reproduced for years in company publicity—the "so-called goodwill advertising" that Walter Reuther predicted.[53]

The next two examples were not winners, but they typify tactics used by many authors. The first writer structured his letter around his family's journey toward American citizenship. He explained that after emigrating from Italy in 1920, he had encountered hardships as a non-English speaker with six children and no steady job. The turning point came, he wrote, when he joined GM's Chevrolet division in 1934. There he experienced the "team spirit and loyalty" of his new workmates, as well as "security" and "comfort in peace of mind." World War II, he wrote, brought home the full significance of his job by teaching him that "my job was more than a job . . . It was an INSTRUMENT—maybe you'll call it a Gun . . . A Tank . . . A well trained army . . . But to me it was an INSTRUMENT with which to fight for the Freedom of our country . . . an INSTRUMENT with which to insure us of a free press, Free Religion, and a chance to work side by side with our fellow men and enjoy life as only a free American can." These realizations, he concluded, "OPENED A NEW WORLD FOR ME . . . one that has enabled me to raise a good American family . . . that is more than proud to be associated with the General Motor Industry."[54]

The final example, written by a machinist, underscores how some entrants adopted rhetoric modeled in contest publicity about the virtues of capitalism and the problems caused by "griping" (a management euphemism for union agitation). The author included nineteen short paragraphs, each of which offered a reason for his job satisfaction. Dismissing the need for unions, he declared, "I have never felt any necessity for having anyone (or any committee) speak for me when I considered that I had a 'grievance'—I have been courteously heard (even when *I* was not necessarily courteous in my complaint) and fairly treated." He was equally dismissive of complaints about poor working conditions, explaining, "I have yet to meet the 'Simon Legree' type of foreman I had thought to find." The "average factory worker," meanwhile, was not "slaving his life away for a mere pittance."[55]

The author's reference to Simon Legree, the brutal overseer in Harriet Beecher Stowe's novel *Uncle Tom's Cabin*, echoed statements in the contest guidelines. Adopting this terminology once more, he scoffed that "factory workers do most of their 'griping' about their jobs because it has long been the popular thing to do—and that they do not realize the bad light in which it places them in the eyes of people who do not know the actual conditions." To conclude, he lauded the virtues of "free Private Enterprise," adding that he had "a large and healthy fear of Communism, Socialism, or any other form of government control of industry." He concluded, "Private Enterprise is such an integral part of Democracy that I cannot conceive of the one without the other. The attempts of the 'little minds' to shackle the 'great minds' of the nation is a real threat to our progress, freedom, economy, and to our very system of government."[56]

In deploying the rhetoric of advertising, American exceptionalism, and free enterprise, these three letters typify some of the most common tactics used in the extant letters (and, Evans and Laseau's report of the contest claimed, the entries more generally). Given GM's extensive coaching, it is hardly surprising that workers adopted these tactics. The firm succeeded in prompting workers to submit letters that confirmed the image that it set out to create—one of a content workforce that identified with the firm. Thus, the contest demonstrated a recurrent principle of motivational ideology: In order to be effective—to shape workers' dispositions, values, and behaviors in ways favored by management—genuine identification was unnecessary. Training workers to adopt positive sentiment was enough.[57] As Seth Seiders and his associates had recognized two decades earlier, what workers actually thought of motivational messages was secondary to controlling the prevailing definitions of work and its rewards. Moreover, the contest was far from a "one-shot" event. The publicity that it generated proved helpful for years to come as GM reproduced quotes from the letters and photographs of the lavish awards ceremony in its employee communications and PR materials and annual reports.

Motivation through "Mental and Spiritual Nourishment" and "Two-Way Communications"

The Information Rack Service, a second project conducted by GM's Employee-Relations Section, allowed a subtler and no less manipulative use of motivation. Launched in 1948 and used widely through the 1950s, the service involved the placement of racks carrying company literature in cafeterias, clocking-in/out areas, and other high-traffic spaces in all GM plants. A key objective according to its architect, ER specialist Harry Coen, was to undercut workers' view of company publicity as "propaganda" by "let[ting] the employe help himself" to the literature, a scenario depicted endlessly in promotional publicity (figure 5.2). The racks should "feed" workers' hunger for information, Coen advised, "without overfeeding it, to give the employee what he wanted without appearing to cram down his throat more than he wanted."[58] As another staffer put it, the goal of the racks was to provide "mental and spiritual nourishment to our employes."[59] Such language, steeped in euphemistic language about providing "nourishment" for workers illustrate the calculated approach to manipulating workers common to ER and human relations in industry during this time.

The project began with an initial pilot run of twelve racks in five GM plants before expanding rapidly over the next few years to over thirteen hundred racks in its U.S. and Canadian locations and an additional fifty beyond GM in educational and civic institutions by the end of 1952.[60] During this four-year period, GM circulated 47 million copies of 280 different booklets, with a distribution of over 1.3 million per month to its 300,000 employees. The largest category represented (at 35 percent) was "economic and social" themes (which consisted primarily of pro–free enterprise sentiment). However, Coen's staff believed that, as one of them put it, they should be "careful not to overdo the economic information," which "would be a quick way to kill off interest in the racks."[61] In an effort to avert potential accusations

FIGURE 5.2. Workers "help themselves" to booklets in GM's Information Rack Service. General Motors Annual Report to Employees, 1949. Kheel Center for Industrial Relations, Cornell University, Ithaca, NY. License supplied by the General Motors Media Archive, GM Heritage Center, Sterling Heights, MI.

that the firm was propagandizing, Coen and his team made sure to include plenty of "material of natural and spontaneous interest to employes," such as gardening, fishing, and sports.[62]

Among the economics-themed booklets were two main genres, each of which served not only as economic indoctrination but also as a form of motivational sentiment. The first genre deployed narratives about GM's role in shaping national progress. This tactic is typified by "The Story of General Motors," a 1948 eighty-page history of the company replete with illustrations resembling those used in children's storybooks, and "American Battle for Abundance," produced in the early 1950s (figure 5.3).[63] The former began with the 1892 invention of the horseless carriage, continued with GM's founding in 1908, and culminated in the "pioneering period" of the mid-twentieth century, all of which were aided by GM's ingenuity, the booklet claimed. Amid the uncertainty of World War I, the firm brought Chevrolet into the "General Motors family" and expanded into Canada.

FIGURE 5.3. "American Battle for Abundance," undated GM booklet, circa early 1950s. Kheel Center for Industrial Relations, Cornell University, Ithaca, NY. License supplied by the General Motors Media Archive, GM Heritage Center, Sterling Heights, MI.

In the 1920s, as women's suffrage and prohibition went into effect, GM advanced its own forms of liberation, initiating employee insurance plans and health initiatives and expanding educational opportunities at its Institute of Technology. The firm's public service continued in World War II, when it made good on the government's calls for "500 tanks a day," developed military technology, and trained military personnel to use weaponry. With the war over, GM was now helping to build "the highest standard of living in the world."[64]

While such booklets offered sanguine and often exaggerated accounts of GM's role in national progress, a second genre of economics-themed booklets took a more forceful approach by lambasting the corrosive effects of socialism and Marxism on the individual's sense of motivation. One such booklet reproduced a 1947 speech by GM's president C. E. Wilson, the founder of its Employee Research Section, entitled "The Great Delusion: Where Marx Went Wrong." While allowing that Marx "reported accurately" about class inequality in nineteenth-century Europe, he asserted that his "diagnosis was wrong." Taking a cue from Hayek's *Road to Serfdom*, a tactic used by many managerial devotees of free enterprise, Wilson pointed to "statism" as the root of class inequality. Hitler and Mussolini had, he argued, tried to "make statism work once they had committed themselves to [Marxist] philosophy." Importantly, he added, "A communistic or socialistic government . . . must replace the positive incentives of a free society with the negative incentives of fear and coercion." Luckily, in Wilson's view, such problems had been averted in America because of the rapid pace of ingenuity in American industry, which offered a "standard of living . . . nine times as high as that of the people of the rest of the world."[65]

Workers could also pick up booklets that included transcripts of radio addresses by anticommunist crusader Henry J. Taylor, who was introduced, grandiosely, as a "world traveler, author, [and] seeker of facts." In a 1952 address entitled "The Truth about Moscow," Taylor emphasized the powerful incentives of cheap, abundant consumer goods that GM workers enjoyed in contrast with their counterparts in the Soviet Union, for whom "hot water piping . . . is practically unknown" and whose kitchens "consist of two or three pots." Roasters and broilers were nonexistent "because there are so few ovens," and "the city's only lawn mower is on the lawn of the American Embassy." Women, according to Taylor, suffered especially.

Invoking habitual assertions by male Cold War authorities about the supposedly liberating effects of domestic abundance, he declared that, whereas American women experienced a lightened workload due to domestic convenience, women did "the burden of the work in Moscow."[66]

General Motors' Information Rack System, like its "My Job Contest," embodied instinct theorist Ordway Tead's call for management to regulate "the content of [workers'] mental life and the impulses by which they are moved."[67] While the effects of motivational practices on workers were indeterminate, they nonetheless proved invaluable in the firm's efforts to cast the worker's cooperation with management as obligatory and to construe itself as an agent of workers' well-being. The larger ideological framework within which these ideals were promoted—the era's marriage of social science, consumer capitalism, and Cold War consensus—provided a strong foundation on which the company honed its motivational apparatus.

The firm's Suggestion Plan Scheme, to note a final piece of its motivational arsenal, illustrates the deft use of democratizing rhetoric that characterized the firm's assertions about workers' satisfaction. A familiar fixture in the factory since the nineteenth century, suggestion plans had long helped employers to promote company mindedness among employees. They were also inherently manipulative because they operated from the assumption that workers were content to help management in its quest to extract more productivity from them. In the decade following the firm's 1942 revamping of its suggestion plan, workers submitted around 450,000 suggestions, over 100,000 of which were adopted.[68] By 1949 alone, GM had paid over $4.5 million in awards for suggestions, all of which went to rank-and-file workers, as technical and supervisory employees were ineligible for prizes.[69] Participation in the scheme rose significantly into the early 1950s. In 1947, nearly 20 percent of GM workers submitted suggestions; by 1951 nearly 40 percent had done so.[70]

The scheme's value, according to its chief designer, Donald Morse, lay in embroiling workers in "two-way communications" with management. Morse told ER specialists from other companies that "in the very process of making a suggestion, [the worker] just about has to adopt a positive, constructive, let's say, a helpful attitude, and at that point, his thinking and the company's become one." This dialogue typically involved discussions between the worker and his or her supervisor, aided perhaps by some initial sketches or calculations; management's acknowledgment of the suggestion; discussions between management personnel and the worker about the proposed idea; and updates on management's investigation into its practicality. These exchanges, Morse noted, brought the worker into a protracted conversation with management and "add materially to his feeling of satisfaction and importance."[71]

General Motors' specialists believed that the scenario of the worker submitting a suggestion provided a powerful motivational metaphor. Photographs of workers posing while submitting a suggestion became a familiar genre piece in publications disseminated through the information racks and home mailings. Such images asserted the existence of a motivated attitude among workers and shored up perceptions of company mindedness throughout the "GM family." Like images of workers "help[ing] themselves" to literature from the information racks, photographs of them posing while submitting suggestions implied that they were autonomous and their cooperation voluntary. The factory, according to these images, was a space of what Drucker called "human effort."[72]

The refining of motivational techniques by GM presented valuable research opportunities. In the five years following the war, GM had not only instituted streamlined motivational communications in its plants but had also helped create a flourishing field of research on employee motivation. By 1950, it had established fifteen research collaborations on motivation with universities. A report circulated among members of the Dearborn Group listed a doctoral study on the use of facial expressions in the testing of employee attitudes, a study by Paul Lazarsfeld at Columbia University into reactions to the UAW strike at Flint, a University of Michigan study of "communications channels in first-line supervision," and several studies of the "My Job Contest."[73]

The company's quest to perfect its motivational apparatus reflected a deepening awareness among industrial leaders that motivational techniques and discourse could be indispensable in managerial efforts to discipline workers. In an era when workers continued to struggle for autonomy and control in the factory, GM's motivational initiatives helped the firm to recast the prevailing definitions of work and its rewards in ways that characterized workers' cooperation with management as obligatory. At the heart of the banal messages about the rewards of working at GM was a sophisticated apparatus of human engineering that drew on the most sophisticated forms of manipulative inducement of the day. As the firm's ER specialists saw it, for motivational discourse to do its work, it was not necessary to achieve a genuine transformation of workers' attitudes about the firm or their jobs. Habituating them to management's desired ideals was enough.

BOULWARISM: MOTIVATION AND ANTIUNION STRATEGY AT GENERAL ELECTRIC

Another industrial giant, General Electric (GE), deployed motivation in an even more systematized, long-term campaign to advance managerial dominion. Like GM's, GE's attempt to hone motivation was prompted by the postwar strike waves. The third largest employer in the nation during the 1950s, with nearly two hundred thousand workers, many of whom were unionized in the United Electrical Workers (UE), GE became an epicenter of the labor conflict that engulfed the industrial scene at the end of the war. In 1946, UE struck, demanding a wage increase of two dollars per day as a catch-up following wartime wage controls. Thousands of workers joined picket lines and, in some cases, effectively shut the factory down. The intensity of the strike caught GE off guard, but it was even more surprised that local communities were overwhelmingly supportive of the strikers. In the end, GE had little choice but to give in, conceding to a wage increase of around $1.50 per day. While the strike's outcome was a painful lesson in labor and community relations for GE, it also prompted it to develop a more sophisticated strategy for eliciting employee goodwill.[74] The central pillar of this strategy was a job marketing program aimed at selling workers and local communities on the idea that GE, not unions or government, was the true defender of their interests. In the decade and a half following the war, GE implemented this program forcefully, a tactic that placed it on the front lines of management's quest to stifle labor opposition and redefine work's rewards in individual terms.

At the helm of GE's job marketing program was one of the most devoted figures in the crusade for management authority in postwar America, who would become a tireless evangelist for employee motivation: Lemuel Ricketts Boulware (figure 5.4).[75] In choosing Boulware to orchestrate the program, GE brought into the fold not only an adept manager but also

FIGURE 5.4. Lemuel Ricketts Boulware hamming it up during an undated photo shoot (circa 1950s) at a lecture podium in front of boards displaying motivational tactics. The slogan atop the board on the left states, "Build an Employee Awareness Politically—Economically—Spiritually." With his finger aloft, Boulware strikes the pose of a wise and judicious conciliator, embodying physically one of the ideological claims of Boulwarism. Lemuel R. Boulware Papers, Kislak Center for Special Collections, Rare Books and Manuscripts, University of Pennsylvania, Philadelphia, PA.

a sales expert with a wealth of experience in marketing ideas. Boulware's route to the front lines of the motivational project came via salesmanship. After graduating as a business major from the University of Wisconsin in 1916, he spent twenty years learning the core strands of business in a variety of managerial positions, winding up in 1935 as vice president of Carrier Air Conditioners in New Jersey. It was in his work in sales and marketing, however, that Boulware found his niche. As vice president of the Easy Washing Machine Company from 1925 to 1935, he developed techniques that he would later adapt in his "job marketing" work at GE.[76] Like many sales experts, Boulware believed that the essence of successful selling was emotional appeal. Yet his approach to motivation was influenced less by a Freudian massaging of desires as proposed by Ernest Dichter than by the rationalized techniques based on repetition of messages familiar to salesmanship since the early twentieth century.

Boulware's beliefs were rooted in an intense distaste for the state's "interference" in business. These views had ripened during World War II. In early 1939, he took a break from his career and embarked on a six-month world tour with his wife. After visiting the Orient and Africa, the Boulwares wound up in Europe in the summer, staying in Berlin two weeks before Hitler invaded Poland. After returning to America the day before the war began, Boulware enjoyed several months of relaxation at his cabin in the Laurentian Mountains before reentering business in 1940 as a general manager at the Colotex Corporation. In spring 1942, he accepted an invitation to serve as Operations Vice Chairman of the U.S. government's War Production Board.[77]

Like other government officials, Boulware condemned the Nazis in his wartime speeches. Yet many of his strongest criticisms centered on their use of state power, a theme that would later become prominent in his work at GE. Typical was a March 1942 speech to military leaders, in which he condemned Germany's imposition of a forty-hour workweek and its requirement that employers relinquish overtime pay to the government "as a contribution by the citizens." By seizing almost half of industrial production and imposing extensive taxation, he argued, the German state kept workers in a "subsistence or bare existence standard of living." He scoffed that the state managed to sustain workers' morale by doling out "weak beer, propaganda movies [and] Sunday picnics on foot." If the German state's control of business offended his free market ideals, however, Boulware "reluctantly confess[ed]" that Germans were "strong and healthy, and the morale good," a situation due largely to the state's "complete control of all channels of information."[78] Although aghast at the German *state*'s control of the nation's communications apparatus, he would soon pursue similarly strategic goals for the more virtuous task of *corporate* control.

Boulware's beliefs placed him in good stead for his work at GE, which became a pioneer in the crusade to weaken state involvement in business and union power after the war. He joined GE in January 1945 as vice president of its affiliated companies, but after the June 1946 strike, he was appointed to oversee the firm's employee and community relations programs. One of Boulware's innovations concerned the firm's labor negotiation strategy. Previously, negotiations at GE, as at many firms, had followed a predictable pattern. When presented with the union's demands, management responded with a "lowball" offer that the union countered with a modified demand. Further offers and counterdemands followed until a settlement was reached. In the wake of the 1946 strike, GE concluded that its use of this negotiation strategy had encouraged workers' perception that management, by always holding back in its offers, was disingenuous and self-serving. In contrast, workers regarded the union as a staunch ally because it forced management to "come clean" with a genuine offer. GE also feared that the 1946 wage increases, which UE justified by the rising cost of living, established a dangerous precedent whereby UE could use further increases in the cost of living as justification for more wage increases. This situation, GE argued, undermined the firm's competitiveness, fueled inflation, and destroyed jobs.[79] Boulware developed a new strategy to combat the union. In the future, management would listen to its demands, study the issues, and come back with an offer that it believed fair, which it would not amend unless new information arose. "Boulwarism," as this strategy came to be known pejoratively, was widely regarded by GE's unionized workforce as a form of management demagoguery. Yet to union leaders' dismay, it proved a highly effective weapon in the firm's mission to undercut union power.[80] Boulware's tactics gained further traction owing to internal union friction. In 1949, the UE left the CIO when its leaders refused to testify that they were not Communists. The CIO subsequently approved membership of a new anticommunist union, the International Union of Electrical Workers (IUE), a situation that, as Kim Phillips-Fein argues, led to "a divided labor force—an ideal testing ground for Boulware's propaganda campaigns."[81]

"Indoctrination and Reindoctrination": Crafting Motivational Communications

Boulwarism was distinct not only in its approach to labor negotiations but also in its highly orchestrated use of motivational communications techniques. Boulware deemed employee communications as a means of "economic education" and "moral enlightenment."[82] The materials that Boulware developed to advance these goals channeled his distaste for "centrally planned" socialist economies, which he believed suppressed "incentive, competition and risk." As he argued in one of his most noted speeches, Salvation Is Not Free, "A really free people can live well materially and spiritually where there is the incentive to work, create, compete, save, invest, and profit." Only capitalism could accomplish this goal, he claimed. Socialism, on the other hand, used "force to drive men to work," a method that was incompatible with American work ideals and should thus be eradicated. As he told his audiences, "We have simply got to learn, and preach, and practice what's the good alternative to socialism. And we have to . . . interpret this to a majority of adults in a way that is understandable and credible and attractive."[83]

The communications apparatus that Boulware built was more extensive than at any other industrial corporation. It included an array of literature disseminated to workers and throughout the communities where GE operated. These publications included the *Commentator* (which included a didactic four-page treatment of a specific theme weekly) and *Monogram* (a more text-based monthly magazine). Another publication, *Employee Relations News Letter*, was issued to twenty thousand managerial staff, half of whom were foremen and other supervisors.[84] Print media included pamphlets and booklets containing speeches by Boulware and other businessmen and free market advocates. Boulware's staff disseminated these publications not just to GE workers and communities but also to GE's "friends and competitors who have contracts with the same unions or who face the same problems."[85] In addition, the company's motivational apparatus included films (often screened in the workplace or local theaters), suggestion schemes, and radio ads.[86]

While GE's publicity made no secret that the firm's aim was to "sell" workers on the merits of its economic arguments, its rhetoric of transparency elided larger ideological ambitions. For Boulware and his colleagues, GE's communications apparatus was a weapon through which to define the federal government and unions as a hindrance to the interests of business and workers alike. The firm's top brass described their goals in even more unambiguous terms in internal documentation. In a June 1947 letter to Boulware summarizing the responsibilities of his job, GE's president, Charles E. Wilson (no relation to his namesake at GM), stated that the goal of the firm's Employee-Relations Department was the "indoctrination and reindoctrination" of workers and the public so that they would internalize a "managerial" view.[87] Yet the sense of pragmatism associated with "economic education" allowed GE latitude in its efforts to depict union wage demands as a front for furthering the self-interest of conflict-prone union leaders.[88] General Electric maintained that its own vision of a "business system" based on the interdependent needs of employees, customers, shareholders, and management offered a more realistic and commonsense approach to labor relations.[89] Boulware regarded employee communications not simply as a convenient tool for spreading messages but also as the engine of a moral crusade, believing that the "advertising media" and "public relations men" had an "obligation . . . to promote economic education, moral re-awakening and political sophistication"—sentiments that he expressed frequently in his correspondence to businessmen, journalists, and civic leaders throughout his tenure at GE.[90]

Boulware's vision of economic education was principally concerned with adjusting—or *correcting*, as he and his colleagues saw it—the motives that shaped workers' attitudes about their job and their disposition toward management. Among his first actions on joining GE was to initiate a study of workers' "motives and beliefs." The study concluded that workers were motivated by nine main factors: "Good pay"; "Good working conditions"; "Good bosses"; "Steady work"; "A chance to get ahead"; "To be treated with respect"; "To get the facts about what's going on"; "To be doing something worth while"; and "To have other reasons for really liking their jobs, such as finding them interesting and deeply satisfying."[91] From 1947 through the 1950s, GE espoused these nine motives, or "Elements of Job Improvement," as it called them jointly, as a mantra in its employee communications channels.[92] In espousing its commitment to fulfilling these motives, GE portrayed itself as a devotee of workers' economic progress and job satisfaction, an image that proved advantageous in its mission to discredit unions. The firm also invoked motivational rhetoric in its training and educational initiatives, adapting techniques developed elsewhere, including DuPont's How Our Business System Operates course, which seventy thousand GE workers had taken by January 1952.[93]

While Boulware sought to link job security to the firm's competitiveness in workers' minds, he also endeavored to separate workers' collective toil from the firm's profits. Any suggestion of this link, he believed, could arouse union agitation for wage increases and profit sharing, a situation that the firm was anxious to avoid. He emphasized this point in a June 1952 letter to a manager at Trumbell Electric, a GE subsidiary, who had recently erred in making this connection in a loudspeaker announcement in the factory. He wrote to the manager, "We have had to learn not to attribute profits to the efforts of individual employees, or to the sum total of the efforts of individual employees below the top supervisory level." The individual worker, he explained, "does not . . . produce a profit because the fellow next to him, or at the other end of the shop, may be doing so poor a job as to offset the good one." Besides, he added, profits were "determined by those upper executives who have not single responsibilities, but multiple responsibilities of the profit planning and making era."[94] If Boulware recoiled at the thought of workers' wages being indexed to profits, however, the firm showed no such qualms in adopting this practice as a tool for incentivizing managers, who, as part of GE's "restructuring" measures in the 1950s, received bonuses that were based on their plant's profitability.[95]

Boulware's efforts to disassociate workers' productivity from the firm's profits helped GE challenge the viability of wage agreements won by unions in the auto industry that were taken up by other unions throughout industry. In its employee literature, GE informed workers that linking wages to company profits was not in workers' interests because profits could just as easily fall. Typical was a December 1947 issue of the *Commentator* entitled "Should Pay Be Equal Everywhere?" This question was answered in the bylines, which asked, "Would it create ghost towns? Would you have to move?" Having invoked the specter of the insecurity that would result from pay equalization, it stated, "The worker . . . cannot in fairness be penalized for poor selling, reckless finance, poor judgment as to what product to make, unwise risks, lack of research, or even plain bad luck on the part of management. Likewise, he cannot in fairness lay claim to any of the profits that arise from the sounder handling of those matters by one management as compared with another." Besides, it continued, the "experiment in setting wages nationally [had] failed" because it did not account for local-level factors that determined the overall competitiveness of a factory or a company.[96] The claim that profit volatility could lead to wage decreases grossly overstated the likelihood of declining profits. Yet such messaging served to couch incentive in the language of individual self-interest rather than the collective terms emphasized by union leaders.

The *Commentator*'s motivational rhetoric placed heavy emphasis on the importance of "competitiveness." Specific issues of the publication challenged the efficacy of universal wage increases; encouraged workers to help maximize production and eliminate waste (the latter "won't make him any more tired when he goes home at night"); and condemned union negotiation tactics while asserting that management acted in good faith.[97] Others challenged union criticisms of management "speed-ups" of production (a term that GE argued was misleading). A May 1949 issue entitled "What Is a Speed-up? And What Is Just an Honest Day's Work?" made the firm's position clear. It noted that although "in the pick and shovel days—and in the early days of crude factory operation—there was all too frequently some justification for increased output per worker to be described" as a "speed-up," the term mischaracterized the present situation. Now, it explained, "the buyer is back in the driver's seat, and serving notice on us that he will not buy unless we really take an interest in our work." It concluded, "If making better products at lower prices to sell more customers and create more jobs can be called a speed-up, then we have all got to recognize that there is now—instead of the old bad kind of speed-up—a new kind of good speed-up."[98]

Print-based media, with its didactic visual lessons about virtues of capitalism, allowed GE to sermonize workers through slick, repetitive messaging. The company deployed four claims in particular—that "excessive" wage increases would lead to crippling inflation; that its positions on wages were fair; that wage negotiations must be based on local-level dynamics; and that union positions on wages were unrealistic. The visual culture of Boulwarism stripped away the complexity of economic issues and presented them as simple dichotomies and choices for the worker. This tactic was typified in a February 1948 cartoon in the *Commentator* that asked, "Are we better off . . . grumbling and griping about everything—sort of wearing blinders because we don't want to see any of the good things about our job and the company we work for . . . or teaming up?" (a scenario that depicted workers as a baseball team that was pitted against "inflation," represented by a stubborn-looking giant). Photo-textual ads, on the other hand, helped infuse messaging with an aura of realism. Photographs of employees at work or at home with their families echoed claims in the accompanying text that workers were satisfied with their jobs and were company-minded "shareowners" in GE.[99]

Illustrated ads used charts, graphs, and other visual imagery to symbolize the economic "facts" according to GE, as typified in the 1960 ad below (figure 5.5). The visual trope used here—the depiction of a wage gradient represented by illustrations of a worker who grows in tandem with rising wages—was deployed in a number of variations in GE propaganda. The firm circulated similar comparison images showing GE workers as giants alongside workers in England, Japan, Germany, and elsewhere. Other copy used the image of the escalator (which, predictably, the GE worker climbed rapidly) to convey that the company's wages kept parity with the cost of living—a claim that elided its strategic efforts to reduce wage costs by expanding, throughout the 1950s, into the nonunionized south where workers had little or no bargaining power.[100] In its variety of forms, visual motivational propaganda helped GE construe its positions on wages and other economic matters as reasonable while subtly condemning the "antagonists" of industrial progress—unions, the state, and the collectivist ideals associated with New Deal liberalism.

The IUE deployed its own communications apparatus throughout this time, including newspapers, booklets, and magazines, the content of which assailed management's positions and Boulwarism. The IUE's strategy is illustrated in a 1962 article authored by its president, James B. Carey, and distributed to the union's members in booklet form, entitled "The Intent of GE Propaganda." Carey argued that Boulwarism's "take it or leave it" policy did not amount to "genuine collective bargaining" and was illegal, and the purpose of the company's propaganda was to "undermine the union and destroy its bargaining power."[101] Yet IUE's defiance was no match against GE's powerful messaging arsenal, which hit workers with a continual barrage of publicity vilifying union leaders as perpetual gripers who failed to grasp the reality of market forces. Not only did the union lack the abundant resources available to Boulware, but the company's transfer of production to the nonunionized south, coupled with a relentless campaign to sow divisiveness among workers and turn them against union leaders, placed IUE

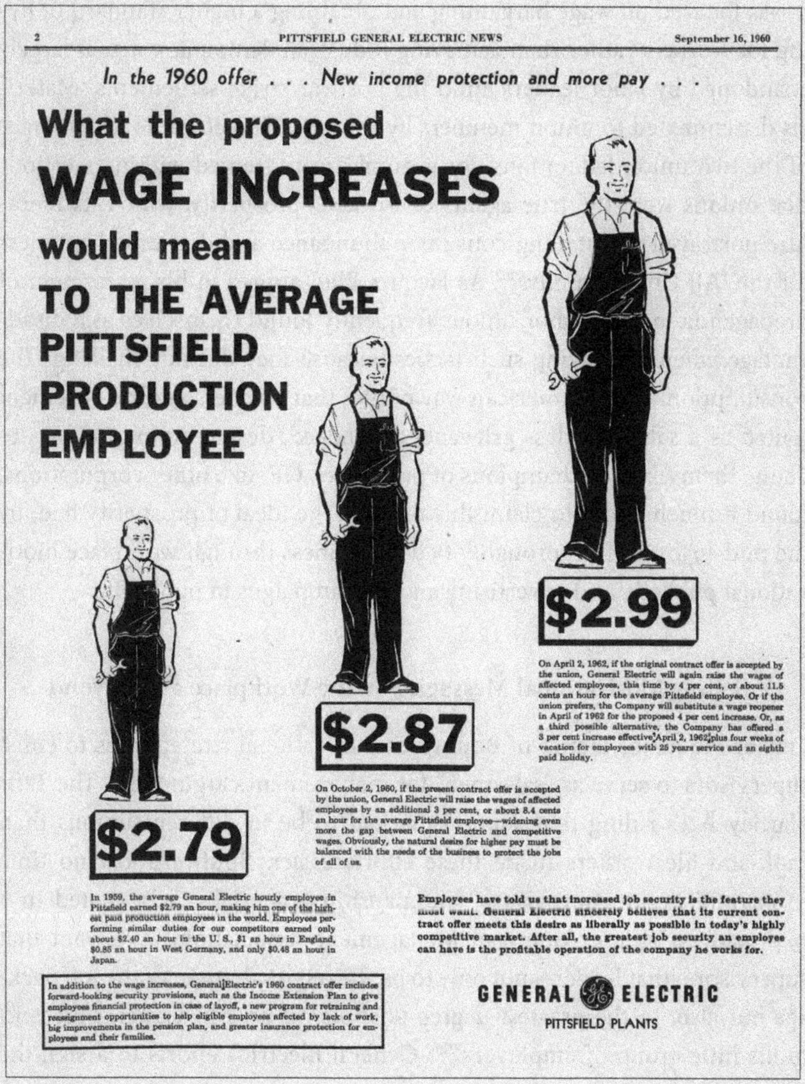

FIGURE 5.5. *General Electric News*, September 14, 1960. Lemuel R. Boulware Papers, Kislak Center for Special Collections, Rare Books and Manuscripts, University of Pennsylvania, Philadelphia, PA.

on the back foot, attacking Boulwarism but unable to impede its growing dominance.

As was the case for other unions throughout the postwar era, IUE posed a less formidable challenge to management than had its predecessors because it was focused on wage bargaining and obtaining a higher standard of living for workers rather than achieving industrial democracy, a goal largely abandoned by labor leaders amid the postwar strike settlements. Materials disseminated to union members by the AFL-CIO after the 1955 merger of the two union federations, for example, were framed within assertions that unions were the true agents of workers' prosperity, which its literature portrayed as entailing consumer abundance and domestic happiness for the "All Union Family."[102] As Jacques Ellul argued in his assessment of propaganda in 1965, labor unions frequently found themselves at a disadvantage when employing such tactics because they did not challenge the consumption-based "American way of life" that business and management touted as a salve for class grievances.[103] Indeed, despite unions' efforts to define themselves as champions of prosperity, GE, like other corporations, found it much easier to claim this mantle. The ideal of prosperity had, by the mid-1950s, been thoroughly tied to business through workplace motivational publicity and advertising and PR campaigns in public life.

Selling Motivational Messaging in the Workplace and Beyond

One of the major tactics of Boulware's motivational strategy was to enlist supervisors to serve as "salesmen" for management's arguments. The Taft-Hartley Act's ruling that supervisors had to be in different unions than rank-and-file workers made these efforts easier. Boulware lost no time in exploiting the supervisor's salesmanship potential. As he stated in a 1948 address to the American Management Association, "We want that supervisor—that leader—not only to be the retail salesman of the job package but also, to the greatest degree possible, to be 'Mr. General Electric' to his little group of employees."[104] General Electric's efforts to assign the supervisor as a member of management were not an immediate success. Yet they proved effective over the long term as the firm integrated managerial responsibilities into supervisor training methods and subjected supervisors to a constant flow of messaging in the form of company newspapers, booklets, and films.[105]

General Electric also utilized its employee communications channels creatively when enlisting supervisors as "ambassadors" for its arguments, sometimes scoffing at unions in the process. This tactic is illustrated in the photograph below, which appeared in the *Commentator* in July 1949 along with the text (figure 5.6). The photograph depicts E. C. Peterson, a GE warehouse superintendent, with his wife, daughters, and grandson, who sits on top of him. The scenario, along with the phrase underneath—"I Don't Want to Be Agitated"—offers a not-so-subtle denouncement of unions. The implication of the phrase, taken from a letter that Peterson had recently submitted to the *Commentator*, is clear: he has no time for labor strife, an attitude that other "responsible" workers should adopt. In the letter, which appeared below the image, Peterson laid tribute to the firm and the "assets" of his job at GE over nearly three decades. These assets included his "job," which was "a better one" than he began with; a "five room house . . . automobile . . . modest bank account . . . a few war bonds under the mattress . . . electric refrigerator . . . radio . . . ironer [and] home work shop." These rewards, he continued, were due to GE, not unions. One of the benefits of his job, he wrote was the "company pension . . . which was started about 1912 . . . long before the agitators 'thunk' it up. Free insurance—additional insurance—Hospitalization insurance—annual vacation—steady pay—a feeling of security. The greatest asset of all."[106]

In 1953, GE added another strand to its array of motivational techniques by hiring Hollywood actor Ronald Reagan as a public and employee relations ambassador for the firm. Reagan hosted *GE Theater*, a weekly half-hour television show that sometimes included didactic talks about the virtues of free enterprise. Reagan also traveled the country touring GE's plants as part of the company's mission to encourage employee goodwill toward the firm and management. Although Reagan's role was not to promote Boulwarism specifically, he eventually took on a more active role in selling GE's free market and antiunion idealism to workers.[107]

To achieve GE's goal of "indoctrination and reindoctrination" Boulware devised a stealth strategy for enlisting "opinion leaders"—clergy, schoolteachers, social workers, hairdressers, bartenders, and others—to disseminate the firm's messaging throughout the community.[108] In a frequently given presentation to managers and civic leaders entitled "How to Transmit Ideas to Community Groups," Boulware emphasized the need to control the "flow" of ideas between three groups—"Idea Starters" (businessmen); "Idea Spreaders" (influential individuals and groups in the community); and "Idea Users" (citizens and workers). One of the challenges facing

The message entitled *"I Don't Want to Be Agitated,"* reproduced below, was forwarded on May 12, 1949, by W. A. Mann, Manager of General Electric's Apparatus Office in Milwaukee, with this note:

"Your message 'Jobs Depend on Faith' *made a profound impression on E. C. Peterson, Superintendent of our Warehouse. He sat up last night and reduced his thoughts to writing. I have had a copy made and attach it, as I feel sure you will be interested in knowing what reaction some of these articles produce."*

Neither the title, nor a word, nor a comma, nor a capital letter has been changed. It's just as written by Mr. Peterson, who is shown in the accompanying photograph with Mrs. Peterson, their daughters, and granddaughter.

"I Don't Want to Be Agitated"

"THOSE who unfairly attack General Electric — or seek to damage the good name it tries so hard to *deserve* — may shake the faith of the customer in the Company and its products and, by so doing, rob men of their jobs and futures.

"Those who rise to the Company's defense — who seek to help the Company *deserve* its good reputation — make jobs better and steadier not just at General Electric, but in every community where the Company buys, or makes, or sells products."

(The above are excerpts from the G. E. Commentator of May 6, 1949.)

Two closing paragraphs which can be read in twenty-two seconds. The second time, I gave it forty-seven seconds. The part which reads — "and, by so doing, rob men of their jobs and futures" — fascinated me.

My memories went back to the close of World War I. A returning hero, so they called me, but I had no job. Just a sixty buck "bonus" and not much hope. An odd job here, another there. Was still paying dues as an electrician, but no electricity wandering around waiting to be harnessed.

Was 24 years old when we were married. A war bride, you might say. From London she was.

1921 — Assets: A war bride, couple of furnished rooms, temporary job, and lots of uncertainty.

1922 — Started with General Electric Company. Was told that job would be steady. A ray of hope. Wife and I celebrated by "eating out."

1949 — (or 27 years later) Assets: Still have my job, only it's a better one. Still have my war bride, plus — two married daughters — a granddaughter — five room house — automobile — modest bank account — a few war bonds under the mattress — electric refrigerator — radio — ironer, etc., — home work shop — Company pension in the offing (which was started about 1912, or long before the agitators 'thunk' it up.) — Free insurance — Additional insurance — Hospitalization insurance — annual vacation — steady pay — a feeling of security. The greatest asset of all.

These are the things which I have received from the Company in exchange for my humble efforts. These are the things which I have received through the continued faith of our customers in our Company's products and in the integrity of its Management and employees.

The Company has faith in me and I have faith in the Company. I am not yet dumb enough to believe that we can receive something for nothing. If we do, it can only be at the expense of someone else. And that someone else may be me.

I have no time or sympathy for "those who unfairly attack General Electric — or seek to damage the good name it tries so hard to deserve — and, by so doing, rob men of their jobs and futures."

I asked for a job and it was given to me. If I am dissatisfied, I am free to leave at any time. I am not working in a slave camp.

I believe that "Those who rise to the Company's defense — who seek to help the Company *deserve* its good reputation — make jobs better and steadier not just at General Electric, but in every community where the Company buys, or makes, or sells products."

By preserving the Company's future, I am merely preserving my own. Just simple arithmetic.

E. C. Peterson

E. C. PETERSON
WAREHOUSE SUP'T.

P.S. I had no rich uncle or a college degree.
Milwaukee 5/12/49

GENERAL ELECTRIC

FIGURE 5.6. "I Don't Want to Be Agitated" was the title of a letter written by E. C. Peterson, a GE warehouse superintendent in Milwaukee in 1949. *Commentator*, July 8, 1949. Lemuel R. Boulware Papers, Kislak Center for Special Collections, Rare Books and Manuscripts, University of Pennsylvania, Philadelphia, PA.

business, he asserted, was the influence of left-wing "intellectuals" on the opinions of average Americans. He cited the view of William Schlamm, conservative author and coeditor of the *National Review*, that "totalitarianism (and especially Bolshevism) are not expressions of economically distressed underdogs, but rather diseases prevalent among rather well-fed intellectuals." He repeated Schlamm's claim that the "editorial staffs of metropolitan newspapers" contained "fifty times more collective lunacy (particularly of the Stalinist type) than among the poverty-stricken Okies, the needle workers or unemployed miners." Only by enlisting "opinion leaders" to direct the "transmission of ideas" could businessmen counter this messaging, he claimed.[109]

Boulware never tired of enlisting other leaders to the cause. He developed a large mailing list of businessmen, managers, and civic leaders, encouraging them to join business's "battle of survival" by implementing the kind of "incentives" campaigns that he had pioneered at GE.[110] In his speeches and correspondence, he declared that European countries with "planned economies" were in crisis because their governments snuffed out workers' incentives by imposing "collectivist" ideals, which businessmen failed to counter. "Free citizens," he wrote to a colleague, should be "free to work and spend or save and risk" and ignore "the false god of security."[111] To these ends, he urged fellow businessmen to circulate articles from the *Freeman* and other conservative journals to their employees. These articles included "Free Men vs. the Union Closed Shop" by Donald Richberg, former executive director of Roosevelt's National Recovery Administration who now opposed the closed shop, nearly half a million copies of which had been reprinted by business leaders since publication. He also encouraged the dissemination of "Will Freedom Be Sold Out in the Name of Its Defense?" a February 1952 article published in the *Freeman* by former Minnesota senator Joseph H. Ball. General Electric reprinted the piece as a double-page spread in 200,000 copies of one of its employee publications, a measure that Boulware encouraged railroad companies to adopt.[112]

Boulware was no less evangelistic when offering input on motivational campaigns produced by other employers and advertising agencies, which sometimes sought his advice. Among his most frequent criticisms was that designers were not aggressive enough in countering socialism. Replying to an executive at a New York agency in February 1952 who had sent some of his firm's recent copy, Boulware objected that it "suffer[ed] from . . . the typical pleasant, non-controversial public-relations approach." Specifically, it espoused rhetoric about "freedom" without emphasizing that the Left was bent on recasting freedom in "collectivist" terms. He continued, "A communist or other socialist or collectivist can hide under the banner of your ad just as well as a free enterpriser can." It was imperative, he noted, to explain to workers that they were being led astray by "unintelligent or dishonest" political leaders. These leaders, he argued, were "leading us step by step into the bad [collectivist] arithmetic of freedom" that destroyed the individual's autonomy under totalitarianism abroad. What was needed, Boulware concluded, was "to get our ablest people in the communications field to . . . contest our enemies rather than furnishing a pleasant umbrella for them to get away with more murder."[113]

Boulware's devotion to individualistic motivation placed him at odds with President Harry Truman's support for union demands for "catch-up" wage increases. Boulware regarded Truman's stance as tantamount to socialism. He called on businessmen to stand up to Truman by disseminating to their workers and the public editorials by critics of unions. As he put it in an October 1949 speech to the Economic Club of Detroit, businessmen needed to preserve America's "system of freedoms, incentives, and competition" from the effects of "collectivism," which would amount to a "police state of poverty, slavery, and hopelessness."[114] Although Boulware was heartened by Eisenhower's 1952 election, he remained highly critical of the new administration's labor policies, which he believed far too accommodating of "collectivist" models of incentive.[115] In the face of mainstream conservatism's failure to promote individual-based incentives, he argued, business had to act. As he told an audience at the Phoenix Chamber of Commerce in 1958, "The businessmen's prompt attainment and immediate sound use of political effectiveness," was "the most urgent task facing our free country today for our own self-preservation."[116]

Boulware's efforts to promote individualistic motivation received a boost from GE's decentralization strategy in the mid-1950s. President Ralph Cordiner replaced GE's fifteen-component structure with a sleeker one consisting of over a hundred departments, each led by its own management team, allowing more agile local-level control over operations.[117] While decentralization was aimed at making management more efficient, it was also integral to what Cordiner and Boulware called GE's war on "bigness"—the company's mission to neutralize the power of labor unions and government involvement in business's affairs. Like many corporations, GE's decentralization push involved shifting many operations to the southern states where labor laws were weak or absent and, Boulware scoffed, workers "had not yet been taught by unions to loaf on the job or stretch out the work in the false effort to protect the jobs."[118]

In 1956, GE merged its public relations and employee relations programs and placed Boulware in charge, further expanding his control over its communications apparatus. With Boulware's help, the firm began to decentralize its methods for awarding financial incentives to workers. Over the next few years, it stopped basing employee bonuses on company-wide performance and allowed managers at plant level to base them on workers' *individual* performance, a practice that replicated the firm's method for incentivizing managers.[119] General Electric's quest to individualize motivation was aided by its founding of the Hopf Institute of Management in the late 1950s. Situated in Ossining in the Hudson Valley in rural New York, the institute hosted management courses, seminars, and training, each of which served as channels for the firm's efforts to hone individualistic motivation. The Hopf's location had long been a hub for the development of motivation. Ernest Dichter's Institute for Motivational Research was less than four miles away in Croton-on-Hudson.[120] Roycroft, the artisan factory where Elbert Hubbard had penned "A Message to Garcia," was also across the state in rural East Aurora. The founding of the Hopf reflected the state's position as an epicenter of motivational ideology, second only to Chicago.

At the end of his tenure, Boulware was no less insistent that a strategic deployment of motivational ideology was vital to the exercise of management power. In a speech shortly before his 1960 retirement, he reminded the audience that the "essence of good fortune" in America was "the productiveness of that combination of the liberty and incentive of the individual to work, save, risk, compete—and strive to excel—with the incentive to compete." However, he believed, even as the 1960s loomed, the specter of the New Deal still continued to derail the "free market kind of incentive." The "government's thirty-year interference with incentive," he lamented, had led to "constantly mounting damage to values, progress, and . . . well-being for the whole public as well as for the very citizens the program was intended most to help."[121]

The communications apparatus that Boulware built helped GE's motivational and antilabor efforts well beyond his retirement. In fall 1960, GE won a swift victory over the IUE after it initiated a strike concerning the firm's rollback of employe benefits. With union opposition largely neutralized, GE turned its attention to countering workers' negative views of company "profits"—which, it lamented, was deemed a "dirty word" by "critics of 'big business.'" Workers' dissatisfaction at GE's profits was hardly surprising given that its net earnings more than doubled to over $470 million between 1964 and 1971. To counter union calls for wage increases, GE supplied plant managers with "Idea Starter" packs that espoused the "economic fact of life" that profits were integral to job security. The first pack announced that workers who believe "profits are too high are quite apt to lack the motivation needed to make [GE's profitability] program successful."[122]

Although the architect of GE's motivational apparatus had officially retired, his distinctive brand of motivational ideology lived on at the company for years to come. By the early 1970s, GE had developed a more personal model of motivational messaging that used individual workers as advocates of company profits in employee newsletters (figure 5.7).[123] Much like GM's "My Job and Why I Like It Contest" over two decades earlier, these materials included workers' answers to questions that all but required them to adopt company rhetoric. In using workers as mouthpieces for company ideologies, such items also replicated Boulware's earlier tactic of using supervisors to sell workers on their jobs.[124]

Motivational discourse had powerful and congealing effects on managerial quests for control and dominion in the postwar era. From advertising to positive-thinking literature, and from public relations to the sophisticated techniques honed by ER and communications experts, this discourse helped motivation's devotees to wage war on the New Deal and the labor movement and to stifle the simmering class grievances that threatened to erupt throughout the era. Channeling the period's increasingly sophisticated communications techniques and consensus orthodoxies, motivation became a quasi-official language through which management and its allies undermined the class- and communitarian-based definitions of work associated with the New Deal and labor.

PLANT PANEL

QUESTION: *Based on your observations, do you think that employees' jobs are more secure when a company's profits are high or low? Why?*

LUCILE DAY, Comp. 128, printed circuit board assembler

"I think our jobs are more secure when profits are high. It stands to reason that we are going to have jobs as long as the company makes a good profit. If we don't do neat, good work people won't want to buy the product. Good work will help bring customers and will also help make good profit and good jobs. For example, these printed circuit boards have to be perfect before I let them go so that the customer won't get a bad product."

BOB SHIFLEY, print services, 2nd shift repro-technician

"The answer is kind of obvious. The employee is more secure when the company's profits are high. As long as the company is making sales, sales will lead to higher production which leads to more job security. Higher profits mean more sales. A basic part the employee can play is in the quality of the product. Regardless of your individual job, you can help put out a better product by showing interest in your job. That will help the company put out a better product and will make it easier to sell. It gives the company an advantage over competition, especially in an area like controls, where several companies offer similar products. One of GPC's basic selling points has to be quality."

PAT LOMASCOLO, Comp. 163, Parcel Post packer

"Jobs would be more secure if profits are high because there would be good business and more orders. If the work that we put out is good, this will help toward creating higher profits and it will insure that we have good jobs. If we make good material and products it would assure us of good jobs. The only way to keep good jobs is to put out work that will bring the company good profits."

You can't be sure of anything these days. Just think of all the mothers who, 20 years ago, had their daughters vaccinated in places they thought wouldn't show.

THE NEW TELEPHONE NUMBER FOR THE GEEC CLUBHOUSE IS 662-3713.

Prepared for the men and women of General Electric Company

- 39 -

FIGURE 5.7. As we see in this "Plant Panel" page from a February 1971 GE newsletter for workers at a factory in Bloomington, Illinois, by the early 1970s the company's motivational messaging often centered on using statements solicited from workers by management to validate company profits. Such practices continued, in different form, General Motors' tactic of using statements from workers to substantiate larger managerial objectives. Lemuel R. Boulware Papers, Kislak Center for Special Collections, Rare Books and Manuscripts, University of Pennsylvania, Philadelphia, PA.

The architects of motivational communications at GM and GE also helped pave the way for the promotion of neoliberal economic theories in the workplace. The core principles of neoliberal economic thought, which had been gaining traction in political economy since the end of the war—a devotion to the free market and individual responsibility; a belief that government involvement in the economy was an unnecessary intrusion akin to socialism; and the thought that unfettered capitalism would make class an irrelevancy—echoed much of the motivational sentiment designed for use in the postwar factory.[125] Indeed, the ideals espoused in GE's motivational apparatus were later enshrined in the neoliberal policies implemented by its former motivational speaker, Ronald Reagan, who remained friends with Boulware throughout his presidency.[126]

Sophisticated motivational propaganda was not limited to such large corporations as GM and GE, however. Throughout the postwar era, many smaller employers that were not equipped to produce their own communications systems relied on the services of independent vendors. These vendors provided managers with posters and literature that took their cue from the sophisticated motivational materials used by industrial giants like GM and GE. Managers at such firms, it turned out, found them no less useful in placating class tensions and shoring up their control and authority than those at large corporations.

CHAPTER 6

The New Hucksters of Cooperation

COLD WAR CONSENSUS CAMPAIGNS AND THE AMERICAN WAY OF WORK

> I think we're definitely selling religion—a religion that's the American way of life.
>
> —Ralph Rogers, Sheldon-Claire salesman, 1949

> Immediate problems are not solved by remote control. 'Getting along with people' cannot be legislated . . . [workers] must learn these facts, not alone intellectually, but emotionally, and every message and contact we make with them must echo in their brain and also tingle in their nerves.
>
> —Ben Schenker, Sheldon-Claire campaign designer, 1949

Although motivational ideology proliferated throughout the postwar era, its spread did not happen mechanically or universally. Although such large corporations as General Motors and General Electric had ample resources for streamlined motivational campaigns, this was not usually the case for smaller companies. For many managers at small and midsize firms, running a factory left little time for developing motivational campaigns. However, if they were absorbed in the immediacies of production, when they read management journals and heard about techniques used by other firms, they could not but conclude that motivational communications could provide useful ammunition for eliciting workers' cooperation.[1]

Many managers also learned about motivational communications through visits by salesmen who worked for independent suppliers of posters and other motivational publicity. The most successful of these organizations was the Sheldon-Claire Company, the firm that attained wartime success with its emotion-laden campaign, *This is America*. After the war, the company tailored its campaigns to the economic and social ideals associated with the era's consensus ideology, a design strategy that held much appeal for the factory managers that it sold to. With government support no longer available after the war, Sheldon-Claire's owner, Lew Shalett, focused on honing his sales apparatus. The firm's annual sales hovered at around $800,000 but reached $1 million in 1953, boosted by its renewals—sales to clients who continued to buy the campaigns over a multiyear period, which, by the early 1950s, accounted for around 70 percent of its business.[2] Although these sales did not match those of the Seth Seiders Syndicate in the 1920s, Sheldon-Claire achieved them with a smaller sales team and remained in business far longer.[3]

The company's success was made easier by several factors. First, as witnessed at GM and GE, workers' cooperation with management was increasingly obligatory in industry after the war, especially after the wage settlements of the late 1940s went into effect. Until that time, some employers declined to buy the campaigns based on concerns that workers would object to them as propaganda. By the early 1950s, however, as labor-management bargaining increasingly eclipsed class conflict, managers' apprehensions about purchasing the campaigns receded. Second, as the firm's salesmen explain, the campaigns received few objections from union officials. Most unionized workers at the small manufacturing firms that Sheldon-Claire supplied were represented by American Federation of Labor (AFL) unions, which were generally less militant and more accepting of the era's dominant ideal of labor-management cooperation than were the CIO unions that represented workers in larger industries.[4] The era's prevailing mood of labor-management bargaining meant that Sheldon-Claire and its clients faced a far smoother path when integrating the campaigns in the factory than did large industrial corporations. The irony was that the campaigns were premised on the same idea as were those at large corporations—to advance managerial definitions of work's meaning and rewards and shore up management's authority and control.

The firm's sales were boosted by its slick self-marketing as an "impartial" outsider, a claim belied by its campaigns, which were designed to help management to instill its own perspectives among workers.[5] Rhetorically, the campaigns mirrored those produced at GE by Lemuel Boulware, whose commitment to weakening union opposition to management Shalett shared. Shalett's ideological likeness to Boulware's was evident to his associates. According to Jerry Johnson, an accountant from Golman, Brookstone & Co. who worked closely with Shalett on the firm's taxes throughout the late 1950s, Shalett was "just another Lemuel Boulware"—an "Ayn Rand type" who knew that the "antilabor" thrust of the campaigns was "a key value to his biggest customers." To Johnson and his colleagues at Golman, Brookstone, Sheldon-Claire's campaigns were "Apple Pie American Exceptionalism applied to Soviet and Nazi heroic art . . . Top grade huckstering as motivation."[6] Although the campaigns were designed to help management shore up its control and authority, however, these goals were masked by their sanguine assertions about the consumer-based rewards that workers stood to receive if they helped their employer to remain competitive by practicing company mindedness.

Shalett also exploited Cold War contestation to the hilt. In the mid-1950s, the firm began to expand into Europe, capitalizing on the United States' efforts to sell European managers on American productivity models and work ideologies through the Marshall Plan. Shalett believed that Sheldon-Claire could do a brisk business given that employers across Europe were seeking to reign in labor union powers and win authority and legitimacy for management. A skilled self-promoter, Shalett also used the firm's international expansion to cast himself as a leader in the quest to advance the moral supremacy of "management in the free world" over the Soviet Union's state-run industrial system. These ambitions ultimately led to a 1958 mission to Moscow, where he toured factories, and then a media crusade warning Americans that the Soviets' "fanatical zeal to overtake the U.S.A." was succeeding by selling workers on "the promise of a better tomorrow" once the Soviet Union had surpassed American productivity.[7]

This chapter explores Sheldon-Claire's influence on motivational ideology in the postwar period. I begin by detailing the firm's campaign design rationale and its salesmen's role in selling the campaigns and smoothing their integration into the workplace. A full assessment of how the campaigns influenced management's broader labor relations efforts at Sheldon-Claire's client companies is not possible because the firm's archived papers do not include extensive business records.[8] However, transcripts of meetings at which salesmen discussed their work selling the campaigns offer illuminating insights about managerial interest in motivation. The chapter's second half traces the company's European expansion and Shalett's crusade to make motivation a pillar of the U.S. Cold War struggle. While Sheldon-Claire's European sales did not match its domestic business, its forays into Europe and Shalett's grandstanding illustrate the deepening influence of motivational ideology during the Cold War and demonstrate how the expanding management crusade to sell workers on their jobs that began at corporations such as GM and GE paved the way for a broader proliferation of motivational ideology in industry. In turn, Sheldon-Claire's dissemination of campaigns touting the rewards of labor-management cooperation and work's individual, consumer-based rewards illustrates how neoliberal values became integrated into the communications apparatuses used by many firms throughout the postwar period.[9]

MOTIVATIONAL CAMPAIGNS AND CONSENSUS IDEOLOGY

Sheldon-Claire's success was encouraged by several developments in the postwar era: First, consensus ideology was invoked favorably, not only by industrial leaders but also by labor leaders, politicians, and civic leaders. Second, "employee communications"—a term that Sheldon-Claire used to describe its campaigns in marketing materials—was deemed by social scientists and management specialists an essential tool for aiding the integration of the individual worker into the organization, a development seen at General Motors and General Electric.. Third, the era saw rising esteem for management consultants. Although Sheldon-Claire was more strictly a sales operation, Lew Shalett and his associates did an effective job in marketing the firm as a consultant to management.

Ever since the early days of the motivational business, designers had struggled over how to create messaging that served management's goals while also speaking credibly to workers. Shalett had an indispensable ally in developing Sheldon-Claire's campaigns: his chief of design, Ben Schenker. An experienced employee communications consultant, Schenker brought to the firm a sophisticated design sensibility based on streamlined, emotionally resonant messaging. Schenker's expertise allowed for continuity of messaging over the course of each campaign's thirty posters and, for renewal clients, over a multi-year period, mirroring the strategies of consumer advertising.[10] The core of campaign methodology, Schenker acknowledged, was the translation of the theories of economic and political consensus espoused by its foremost exponent, Eric Johnston, the president of the U.S. Chamber of Commerce. Channeling Johnston's calls for labor and management to find "areas of agreement," Schenker declared that the route to industrial cooperation lay in "reasonableness and emotional maturity" (which, in management parlance of the day, implied that labor had the most maturing to do).[11] The key to the campaigns, Schenker believed, was to blend economics-based messages and arresting images. As he told his colleagues, "Immediate problems are not solved by remote control. 'Getting along with people' cannot be legislated . . . [workers] must learn these facts, not alone intellectually, but emotionally, and every message and contact we make with them must echo in their brain and also tingle in their nerves."[12]

Schenker also invoked the term *economic literacy*, a concept that mimicked rhetoric used by GE to rebuff union arguments for higher wages, to encourage workers to perceive their economic interests as dependent on their employer's competitiveness. As illustrated in four posters from the firm's 1946 campaign *We Depend on Each Other*, Schenker made creative use of visual metaphors to advance this goal (figures 6.1–6.4). The first three posters inform workers that by embracing a company-minded approach to production (figure 6.1); "co-operation" and teamwork (figure 6.2); and a commitment to competitiveness and customer satisfaction (figure 6.3), they will enjoy economic rewards and security. In figure 6.4 (actually the final poster in the series), the worker joins a manager, a salesman, and a customer in showcasing the product that they have "planned," "produced," and will "sell" and "buy." The cooperation of these four groups, the campaign asserts, is vital to competitiveness and job security.[13] Collectively, these and other posters in the campaign presented workers with a condensed representation of the consensus ideal of cooperation and a vision of a highly unified organization in which the satisfied worker performs an integral role.

The themes distilled in *We Depend on Each Other* established a formula that Sheldon-Claire reprised in its campaigns for the rest of the decade, including *It's Up to All of Us* (1947); *Produce Better, Live Better* (1948); *We Can't Have Unless We Give* (1949); and *It Makes a Difference to You!* (1950). Regardless of specific theme, each campaign, as these titles suggest, was

FIGURES 6.1 (LEFT) AND 6.2 (RIGHT). Sheldon-Claire Company Records, 1946. Archives Center, National Museum of American History, Smithsonian Institution, Washington, D.C.

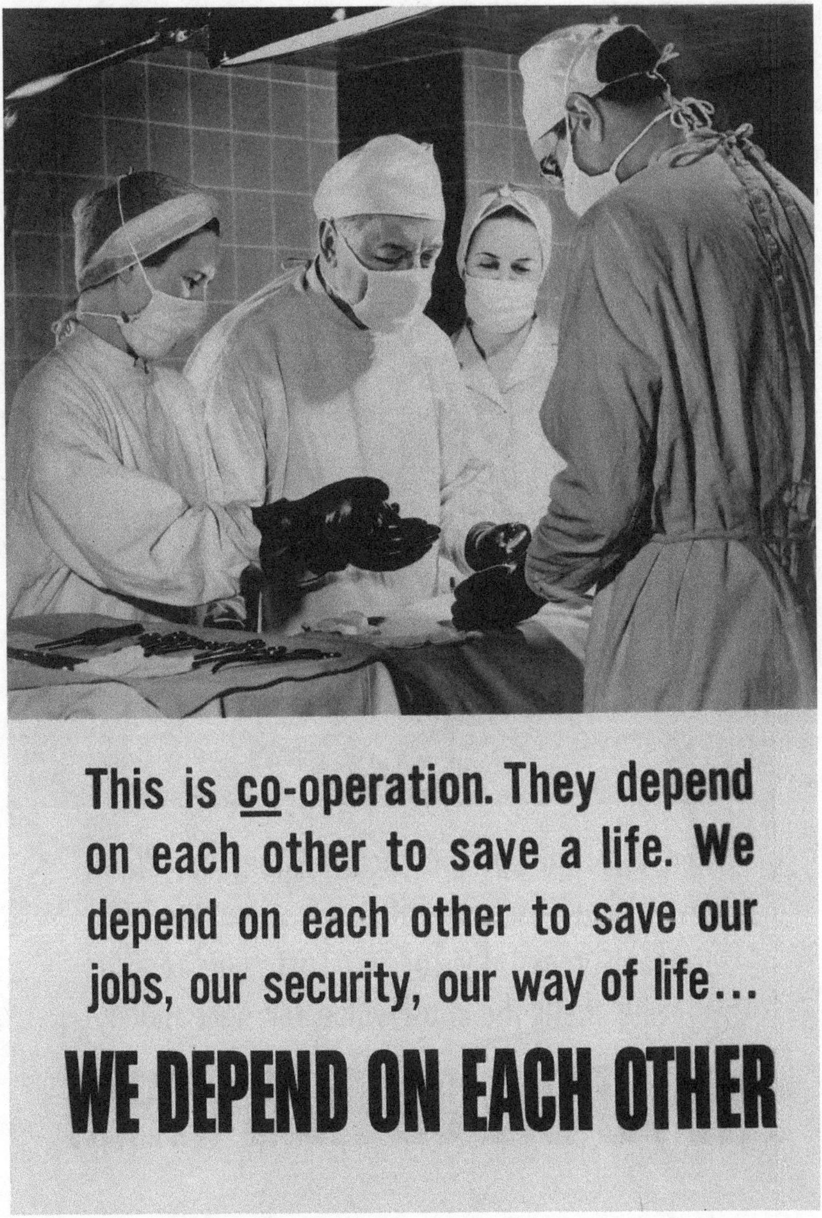
This is co-operation. They depend on each other to save a life. We depend on each other to save our jobs, our security, our way of life...
WE DEPEND ON EACH OTHER

FIGURES 6.3 (LEFT) AND 6.4 (RIGHT). Sheldon-Claire Company Records, 1946. Archives Center, National Museum of American History, Smithsonian Institution, Washington, D.C.

"We planned it well"-- says management
"We produced it well"--- says the worker
"That's why I can sell it"-- says the salesman
"That's why I'll buy it"-- says the customer
WE DEPEND ON EACH OTHER

anchored in the same core principle: that workers' economic and job security depended on their acceptance of managerial ideals. Whether promoting cooperation, pride of workmanship, or the need for sacrifice (refraining from costly wage increases, for example), the campaigns linked workers' livelihoods to the success of the firm and, by extension, the virtues of business leadership. In turn, the posters provided managers with tools through which to promote the individual worker's integration into the organization. This goal became central for management after the war because, for more and more workers, work itself became less rewarding. In an era when workers felt increasingly removed from the final product due to the rationalization and speedup of production, appeals to teamwork in the name of job security became dominant in motivation.[14] By supplying managers with slick motivational communications materials that resembled those used by leading industrial corporations, Sheldon-Claire arrived at a winning product. In helping its client managers to integrate messages touting market-based values and the virtues of management business leadership (while subtly sidelining unions), the campaigns also channeled the emerging creeds of neoliberal economic policy into the factory.

Indoctrinating the "Merchandisers" of Motivation: Supervisors

Following the lead of motivational strategies used by GE and other large corporations, Sheldon-Claire built its campaigns largely around an effort to enlist supervisors as campaign "merchandisers." This feature formed a major selling point, given management's long-standing efforts to use supervisors to elicit workers' goodwill toward their employer. After the war, the campaigns increasingly abandoned the word *foreman* in favor of the more managerial-sounding *supervisor*, a designation that reflected the Taft-Hartley Act's ratification of the foreman's/supervisor's managerial status. Through booklets, flyers, and other materials and via training sessions coordinated by its salesmen, Sheldon-Claire supplied managers with a powerful weapon for enlisting supervisors as allies when promoting cooperation, teamwork, and other motivational ideals. Although some managers opted to buy only one part of a campaign (usually the posters), salesmen persuaded most prospects to buy the entire package by stressing that the supervisor's role in merchandising the campaign was crucial to its overall effectiveness.[15]

Sheldon-Claire's efforts to enlist supervisors as campaign merchandisers were couched in decidedly masculine terms. Ignoring the fact that some supervisors in industry were women, Lew Shalett and his associates only depicted male supervisors and assumed a male reader in supervisors' literature. The firm's deliberations over campaign design contain no discussion about tailoring materials for female supervisors, and at no point did anyone ponder how such male-oriented materials might be received by women supervisors. Such assumptions, along with the posters' depiction of workers exclusively as men (and women only as homemakers or consumers) continued a practice dominant in management's motivational efforts for decades, with some exception during World War II, when images with women war production workers were circulated widely.[16]

The firm's 1948 campaign *Produce Better, Live Better* marked significant advancements on the design front. Sheldon-Claire added a variety of booklets and memos (many of which were titled "Confidential," strategically bestowing a sense of magnitude on the supervisor's role) that detailed how to administer the campaigns and maximize their impact. One "Confidential Memo to Supervisors" explained the meaning of four forthcoming posters in the campaign (figure 6.5). Using the metaphor of the social body to represent the free enterprise system, the four posters collectively portray an "interdependent . . . industrial system" founded on the cooperation of capital, management, employees, and customers. In this schema, capital is the "heart" (poster 5); management the "head" (poster 6); employees the "hands" (poster 7); and customers "supply the life blood" (poster 8) of business. Within this four-part ensemble, workers have two main functions. They build the capital—the "heart" that pumps the system and creates jobs—and they provide the "hands" that convert capital into products and services. The side text informed supervisors that workers' livelihoods depended on them recognizing the interdependence of the system and doing their part to satisfy the customers who are its "lifeblood."[17] Such communiqués provided management with a tool for depicting industry and the firm in harmonious terms and for enlisting supervisors to promote such visions to workers.

The campaign's installation booklet for managers underscores the six-step process that managers, aided by supervisors, should undertake to administer and merchandise the campaigns. The illustration below details the first two steps (figure 6.6). During this stage, the supervisor receives preliminary information about the campaign and proceeds with the strategic

FIGURE 6.5. "Confidential Memo to Supervisors," from *Produce Better, Live Better*, 1948. Sheldon-Claire Company Records, 1948. Archives Center, National Museum of American History, Smithsonian Institution, Washington, D.C.

installation of posters in places of high visibility (at eye level and near doorways). Each poster was displayed in a special frame for the "Poster of the Week," and though not depicted here, the frame was equipped with three spotlights to showcase the poster. Subsequent illustrations in the

A COMPLETELY PLANNED AND SCHEDULED CAMPAIGN FOR IMPROVING EMPLOYEE COOPERATION IN YOUR PLANT

Step No. 1 ***Telling the Supervisor***

Before introducing any employee relations program, it is wise to present it completely to foremen and supervisors. The best way to do this is at a meeting. Whether you hold a meeting or not, the booklet "A Guide to Supervisors" should be distributed at least one week before the opening announcement appears in the plant. If a meeting is not held, the booklet should be transmitted to supervisors along with a letter from a major executive.

Step No. 2 ***Plant Circulation***

Select the proper locations for displaying posters to assure adequate circulation within the plant.

One: Survey locations reaching maximum number of employees. (In addition to working areas, washrooms, toolrooms, elevators, cafeterias, rest rooms, reception rooms, entrances and exits are usually effective locations.)

Two: Posters should never be placed on company bulletin boards which contain notices and announcements as these compete for attention. Frames specially provided for posters should be used.

Three: Posters should be displayed in direct line of vision of reader. Center of poster should not be more than five feet from floor.

FIGURE 6.6. This booklet explained to managers and supervisors the process for administering its 1948 campaign *Produce Better, Live Better*. Comprising "confidential" memos and supervisor opinion polls, the campaign embodied the streamlined formula that Sheldon-Claire pioneered throughout the postwar era. Sheldon-Claire Company Records, 1948. Archives Center, National Museum of American History, Smithsonian Institution, Washington, D.C.

booklet explain that each Sunday, the supervisor should place an "opening announcement" in a special frame to inform workers of the theme of the next poster. Next, the supervisor received a series of "confidential memos" signed by a "major executive" at the company. Finally, he received "opinion polls," which he used to survey workers' responses and record his own appraisal of the campaign. The systematized nature of this and other campaigns offered employers ways to promote the individual worker's integration into a smooth-running organization.[18]

The "supervisor opinion polls" provided managers with additional ammunition for involving supervisors in the administration of the campaigns. They required supervisors to record their impressions of workers' perceptions of posters at each stage of the campaign. The completed forms were then submitted to managers, some of whom subsequently returned them to the salesman who serviced the firm's contract. The forms also asked supervisors to indicate what they believed to be the "most effective poster," the "most effective illustration," and the "most effective copy" and provided a space for additional comments. In the few extant responses to this campaign, supervisors adopted a company-minded tone, assuming their ascribed role of campaign merchandisers. A foreman at the National Lock Company stated, "I think these posters have generated a lot of thought among the people working in this plant and makes them wonder if their friends in a competitive plant are doing better work and putting out a better product." A foreman at Stockman Brothers surmised, "Although these posters do not induce conversation concerning them, doubtless their value lies more or less in the subconscious impressions created by seeing them repetitiously." Other foremen offered accolades to specific posters, sometimes echoing the language of the campaigns in their comments. Thus the polls served a dual purpose, helping employers to involve foremen in the administration of the campaigns while obliging them to adopt a managerial disposition.[19]

After several years of increasing sales, in 1950 Schenker and Shalett nonetheless concluded that the campaigns' focus on "economic literacy" had become "repetitious" and prone to "preachiness," and they thus initiated an overhaul in design.[20] Their efforts to distill economic ideas into posters had, they agreed, led to overly wordy captions that impeded the immediacy of messaging that posters were best suited to. Moreover, the verbose and didactic captions risked prompting the accusation that the campaigns were antagonistic toward unions (one that was well founded given that their purpose was, in part, to help managers temper workers' interest in unions). A better way to make the worker "more cooperative," they agreed, was to mimic consumer advertising. They therefore enlisted the help of Magill-Weinsheimer, a leading Chicago advertising agency. After Schenker

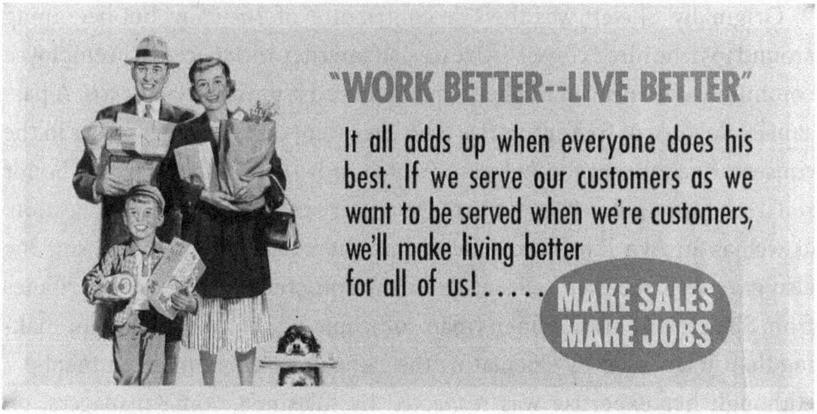

FIGURE 6.7. Throughout the 1950s Sheldon-Claire's campaigns increasingly resembled mainstream consumer advertising. The poster above, included in its 1955 campaign, *Make Sales, Make Jobs*, conveys the claim that work's rewards lie in consumption and that they are possible only if workers perceive work and its rewards through market-based ideals. The poster's title embodies the essence of twentieth-century motivational ideology, asserting that by adhering to the work ethic and identifying with capitalism's individual model of striving and reward, one can attain happiness and security. Sheldon-Claire Company, 1955, emovieposter.com.

died later that year, Shalett worked increasingly with Magill-Weinsheimer, which developed a new "billboard" format (figure 6.7). From here on, the campaigns included fifty-two posters per year, an increase over the previous thirty, providing managers with a poster for every week of the year.[21]

The posters mostly avoided explicit condemnations of socialism and communism, a measure aimed at averting worker criticisms that the campaigns were antiunion propaganda. However, the supporting materials supplied to managers made clear that the campaigns were designed to combat both. Such statements were common in a serialized bulletin entitled *They Say*, which Sheldon-Claire sent to managers throughout the 1950s. This bulletin consisted of seven to eight pages of material that blended warnings about the need for business to defend free enterprise from "Socialists," "Communists," and "Statists" with sales pitches for Sheldon-Claire's services, and it situated employee motivation as a vital weapon in capitalism's struggle against communism. It also included quotes from management authorities, such as Lemuel Boulware, that espoused management's moral authority and condemned labor unions and government intrusion in business.

Originally, Shalett was the sole contributor of *They Say*, but beginning around 1951, he hired conservative freelance writer and specialist in employee communications Helen Bugbee, who authored it until the late 1950s. A passionate devotee of free enterprise who later went on to author articles in the conservative journal the *Freeman* (which today still lists her in its "honor roll"), she brought a free market, antiunion sensibility to the publication, as well as an Ayn Rand–like assertion of the virtues of individualism. She also gave well-received talks at the firm's conferences and earned tributes from Shalett and his salesmen (many of whom wrote to thank her for making their jobs easier by elucidating the campaigns' economic arguments).[22] Although her expertise was respected by salesmen, some managers, on seeing a woman's name listed as the author of *They Say* during salesmen's presentations, responded negatively to the publication. In response, Shalett asked her to obscure her gender by signing it "H. Bugbee," an arrangement that lasted until around 1956, when her full name was reinstated.[23] Although Bugbee's influence beyond authoring *They Say* is not detailed in the firm's extant documents, she likely played a more central role in developing the campaigns than is acknowledged in its records. One salesman later went so far as to describe her as the "intellectual brains" behind the campaigns throughout the 1950s.[24] Some of her articles in conservative magazines during the 1950s, such as "Good Sense Makes Good Business" and "We Can't Protect Prosperity," present arguments that echo the sentiments of Sheldon-Claire's campaigns.[25] Whatever the reasons behind her obscured role at the firm, like Shalett's masking of her authorship of *They Say*, it underscores the ways in which the firm maintained an exclusively masculine vision of motivation.

BUILDING THE SALES APPARATUS

Shalett understood that slick designs would only take the firm so far. Its success required an effective sales apparatus. Help was at hand in the form of Charles Rosenfeld, the mastermind behind the Seth Seiders Syndicate's sales organization two decades earlier. In appointing Rosenfeld as his director of sales strategy and salesman training, Shalett found a right-hand man who, more than anyone else, possessed the knowledge and expertise on which the motivational poster business had been based since its early days.

Between them, Rosenfeld and Shalett knew most of the salesmen who had worked in the business since that time. Gathering these experienced hands together, along with many younger salesmen, they assembled a small but capable sales force of twenty-five full-time salesmen in 1947, a number that grew to around fifty in the mid-1950s.[26] Taking the campaigns from town to town, factory to factory, these salesmen supplied managers and supervisors with know-how for implementing motivational communications in the workplace. Given their pivotal role in disseminating the campaigns and maintaining face-to-face relationships with the firm's clients, a discussion of their work is vital here.[27]

Salesmen were paid on a commission-only basis (at a rate of 25 percent) and "volume bonuses," meaning that the more they sold, the more they earned. Sheldon-Claire therefore sought men who, as its job ads stated, were "aggressive, seasoned, and successful," had "a personality that commands attention," and were "in the habit of earning from $15,000 to $20,000 a year consistently on a commission basis."[28] More seasoned salesmen received "pyramid overrides" on the sales of those who worked under them and thus made considerable earnings.[29] However, according to salesman David Bernstein (who was also Shalett's nephew), Shalett found ways to manipulate sales in efforts to avoid paying bonuses.[30]

Salesmen's belief in the products that they sell, or at least an ability to project that belief, has long been understood to be essential to successful selling.[31] This dynamic applied no less to Sheldon-Claire's salesmen. Their contributions to conversations at sales meetings and the recollections of former salesmen underscore that they believed in the virtues of the product. In each case, salesmen expressed the view that the campaigns were a useful "educational" tool that aided mutual understanding between workers and managers. However, as former salesmen David Bernstein recalls, he and his colleagues had little interest in Lew Shalett's speeches about the campaigns' value in advancing management's ideological goals, being far more interested in making sales.[32] They paid little heed to the popular motivational literature of the day, and, after a day of selling, they were more inclined to reach for a magazine and a drink than a book by one of the era's sales experts. As Bernstein explains, "We knew more about it than they did because we knew the structure of a sale, what made a sale . . . If the guy had the mouth and the balls and the street smarts, this is what you needed—nothing more."[33]

If salesmen's attention was focused on the size of their commission checks, Shalett nonetheless endeavored to instruct them about the firm's larger political mission at Sheldon-Claire's annual sales meeting. Although by available accounts salesmen experienced the meetings selectively, tolerating the antiunion and pro-management speeches but listening up when it came to advice about selling, a brief discussion of Shalett's efforts to infuse them with his own ideals helps illustrate the larger ideological goals that informed the campaigns and the firm's mission according to its owner. For two or three days every year, Shalett gathered the sales force, along with Rosenfeld, Schenker, and guest speakers from the management world, usually at the Waldorf Astoria in New York. Among the regular speakers were Alvin Dodd, president of the National Management Association; Larry Appley, president of the American Management Association; and Russell J. Greenly, head of the successful Greenly Foremanship Training Service. With assistance from these management luminaries, Shalett instructed salesmen at length about the larger stakes of management's quest to instill cooperation and win workers' hearts and minds.[34] Rosenfeld and senior salesmen gave talks about tactics for overcoming sales resistance, and until his death in 1950, Ben Schenker provided a walk-though of the new campaign that the salesmen would sell over the next year.[35] The guest speakers edified salesmen on the need to help management win the war of ideas against labor unions through motivational messaging and advised them on how to win managers over when pitching the campaigns to them.

At the sales meetings, Shalett and his associates made clear that they regarded the campaigns as a powerful weapon with which managers could advance antiunion goals.[36] In 1947, Dodd claimed that unions had prejudiced workers against management via "psychological appeals to emotion, impressions, innuendos."[37] If designed well, he added, Sheldon-Claire's messages could be effective in countering this problem because they were produced by an independent entity and were thus "above suspicion."[38] At the firm's 1956 conference, labor lawyer Louis Waldman encouraged salesmen to exploit anticommunist rhetoric when selling the campaigns. A former socialist, Waldman became a devotee of anti-communism and a staunch advocate of management leadership after the war. He used his speech to warn Sheldon-Claire's salesmen about "the class struggle doctrinaires" for whom "every step toward cooperation means the destruction of the

FIGURE 6.8. Sheldon-Claire salesmen, some accompanied by their wives, at a dinner during one of the firm's sales meetings in the mid-1950s. Sheldon Shalett (Rosenfeld's assistant and Lew Shalett's son) stands second from right, next to his cousin and fellow salesman David Bernstein at far right. Lew Shalett sits at the far end of the table. Courtesy of David Bernstein.

militancy of the working class." By informing themselves about the "communist philosophy," he explained, salesmen would boost their sales. Managers, he assured them, "will look up to you [as] the man who [is] talking the language that will spell out the destiny of that business."[39]

Although salesmen were far more interested in selling than in advancing management power, the conferences nonetheless allowed Shalett and his associates to expose them to the larger goals that informed the campaigns that they had to sell to factory managers. In the discussions that followed the guest talks, many salesmen picked up on the speakers' ideas. As one salesman put it in 1947, by teaching workers "what their share of the consumer dollar had to do with the profits," the campaigns could clear up "a lot of misunderstanding and fusses between management and labor . . . over night."[40] Speaking in 1950, veteran salesman Ralph Rogers enthused that, with its new campaign, *We Can't Have Unless We Give*, Sheldon-Claire was "selling religion—a religion that's the American way of life. It's the finest educational program that has ever been produced in this country by anybody." Yet salesmen's deployment of such rhetoric was more tactical than sincere. As Bernstein recalls, salesmen learned to echo Shalett's rhetoric back to him "because he was signing their checks. They'll say God is dead if it'll make a buck for them."[41] Yet regardless of how sincere was their regard for the campaigns, through their adoption of such sentiments they became influential boosters of the motivational project. Moreover, their exposure to the ideologically laden arguments of management luminaries and their boss proved useful when they pitched the campaigns to managers in the factory.

SELLING AND IMPLEMENTING CAMPAIGNS IN THE FACTORY

In the atmosphere of obligatory cooperation that flourished in industry throughout the postwar era, salesmen found it increasingly easier to get a foot in the door when calling on factory managers, and they faced fewer barriers to making sales than in the past.[42] It didn't hurt matters that Charles Rosenfeld, the architect of the Seth Seiders Syndicate's sales apparatus, brought to Sheldon-Claire decades of knowledge about selling motivational publicity, not least the scripted sales talks that blended rationalized and personality-driven selling. As Bernstein explains, salesmen played the role of "Pinocchios" who mouthed the words of their "ventriloquists," Shalett and Rosenfeld.[43] This dynamic reflects sociologist C. Wright Mills's observation during this time that "the last autonomous feature of selling, the art of persuasion and sales personality," was "expropriated from the individual salesman."[44] If they worked from organized scripts, however, salesmen were hardly automatons. While they were expected to adhere to Rosenfeld's methods, they did not deliver his sales talks mechanically, and they deployed improvisation as needed to make a sale.[45]

If the postwar environment was a welcoming one for motivation, there was no guarantee that a manager would sign on the dotted line when the time came to renew a contract or when he listened to a campaign pitch. Salesmen therefore used their V.P.S.s—the verbal proof stories—when attempting to convince the manager to buy a campaign. The V.P.S., as will be recalled, was a story or anecdote that, if used correctly by the salesman, persuaded the prospect of the value of the campaign. Salesmen were expected to learn their V.P.S.s by heart and to integrate them into their closers to nullify the prospect's hesitancy. Thus, each salesman left his training with full command of the firm's "organized sales talk," which, if delivered capably, established in the prospect's mind the certainties of "problem," "cure," and "proof."[46]

In his sales talks, Ralph Rogers, who sold the campaigns on the northwest coast and in Canada, expounded on the value of campaigns in "selling [the worker] more pride in your products" and gaining workers' help in boosting the firm's competitiveness and customer satisfaction. Among the benefits of campaigns, he insisted to managers, were "increasing production," "cutting down turnover," and "building morale." If the prospect resisted, Rogers often deployed a more creative tactic whereby he pointed to respected figures who, he claimed, had endorsed the campaigns. Frequently, he summoned the legitimizing voice of management authority Paul Hoffman, president of the Studebaker Corporation and director of the distribution of Marshall Plan aid in Europe. Holding aloft a photograph of Hoffman being sworn in at the Oval Office and reminding the wavering prospect that the Marshall Plan was a "human relations plan," Rogers would state that Hoffman was an ardent admirer of Sheldon-Claire's campaigns: "When I called Mr. Hoffman last September . . . [h]e not only has bought [the campaign], but he says today it has made him more money and given his workers more happiness on the job than anything else they have ever had . . . As he walks through that plant, he puts his hands behind his back, and he stands and looks at those posters, and he reads the panel message, and he hears the workers behind him say, 'Gee, even the boss reads this. It must be good stuff.' He has instructed all his works managers, his supervisors, his foremen, his straw bosses, right on up, to do the same thing."[47] Whether Rogers met or spoke with Hoffman is unclear. Yet using sales tactics of this sort—as they did week in, week out in the late 1940s and 1950s—Rogers and his fellow salesmen smoothed integration of the campaigns into factories across the country.

When encountering resistance from a manager, a salesman might deploy a different kind of V.P.S.: testimonial letters from satisfied clients or business associations that attested to the campaign's value. Whether extolling the poster messages or designs or the campaign's positive effects on employee attitudes, authors of testimonials often noted that workers were more accepting of them because they were not created by their employer. Typical was a letter from a manager of McIntosh Inc., a Detroit heavy-metal parts company, who wrote that the campaigns had been "helpful in teaching its employees the facts of life—business life" and that "their fortunes, their welfare are dependent upon the company's position and continued success." He added, "They will believe you when they won't believe us—you are an impartial outsider to them whereas we are prejudiced in their eyes. From day to day all this helps in getting the work out and keeping the quality up, but we feel the effects most at bargaining time when all the committeemen take a more serious view of company position—when our statements of conditions and position don't get retorts like "baloney"—and when we even hear a few admissions like: "Oh, I agree if there's no profit, there's no jobs" and "We can see your side of it, what with competition and all." Such letters illustrate the subtle power of Sheldon-Claire's campaigns. By enlisting the services of a supposedly "impartial" outsider, employers could gain a layer of insulation against workers' criticisms that they were subjecting them to "company propaganda."[48]

A potential hurdle for salesmen was that some managers tried to rebuff them, citing possible union objections to the campaigns. This challenge was rare when making renewal sales because any union concerns had generally been addressed when management purchased its first campaign at an earlier time. Such objections to the campaigns did sometimes occur when salesmen presented them to new prospects. Even then, however, it was limited because the predominantly AFL unions at the firms that Sheldon-Claire supplied were generally accommodating toward labor-management cooperation. Sheldon Shalett and David Bernstein explain that union resistance to the campaigns was a nonissue. In a sign of how normalized consensus ideology had become in the industrial arena in the mid-1950s, Shalett recalled, the unions "believed that cooperation was . . . good, the unions weren't antagonistic to that . . . everyone was interested in the same result, and besides, it didn't cost the union anything."[49]

Until the early 1950s, salesmen sometimes spoke with union representatives to try to sell them on the merits of the campaigns, either at the behest of managers, who were concerned about potential union criticisms, or at the suggestion of the salesman. At these confabs, salesman would make the case that the campaigns were aids for promoting "understanding" between labor and management. As salesman Ralph Rogers advised managers, "Present your picture right. Don't hide it. The workers want you to come out in the open and explain it to them." If management failed to be up front, he argued, the union rep would "wonder, 'why isn't he showing this to me?'" Rogers told his colleagues that such meetings usually resulted in his gaining the representative's agreement.[50]

Some union locals even wrote letters to their members encouraging them to get behind the campaigns. Letters sent to union members in the Pacific Northwest in 1954 and 1955 are a case in point. All expressed praise for the campaigns, noting their mutual benefits for workers and management alike, and encouraged workers to support them.[51] In July 1954 the Cannery Warehousemen, Food Processors, Drivers and Helpers Local 656 in Eugene, Oregon, received a letter from the union's secretary-treasurer extolling the forthcoming campaign, *Make Sales, Make Jobs*. Echoing the language of the campaigns' posters, it reminded workers that "close cooperation between employer and employee must prevail" and that workers must "do our part in a program of selling."[52] The two thousand members of Local 670 of the Cannery Workers Union in Salem, Oregon, received a similarly enthusiastic letter stating, "As you pass through the plant you will observe posters calling your attention to the fact that we are all working for the Customer. Our plant, and I mean our plant, since we all depend upon its productivity for a living, must receive, pack, store and ship products as economically and as attractively as is possible in order to Make Sales Make Jobs."[53] Parroting the campaign's esteem for the "customer," its use of "we," "us," and "our/ours," along with its main slogan, such letters underscore the growing adoption of management's motivational language among union leaders in the mid-1950s. The authors of the above letters supplied copies to salesmen, who subsequently used them as V.P.S.s when encountering prospects who were concerned about potential union objections to the campaigns.[54]

In an era when business and civic leaders beyond the factory became influential advocates of cooperation, salesmen were able to capitalize on local networks when attempting to increase sales. As seen in Lemuel Boulware's use of "opinion leaders," networks were indispensable to the spread of motivational ideology and the ascendance of the motivational project in the postwar era. Networks proved no less useful for Sheldon-Claire's salesmen, especially in small towns.

The experiences of George Lubin, who sold in the upper Midwest in the late 1940s, illustrate both how networking could boost sales and how salesmen aided the integration of the campaigns beyond the factory and throughout local communities. Lubin concentrated on businesses that employed between 50 and 250 workers, regarding this strategy as more fruitful than trying to sell to large urban factories. Lubin's sales in Ottawa, Illinois, exemplify this tactic. Of the twenty companies in the town, he sold the campaign to seven. Lubin found that after buying a campaign, some managers would call relatives or friends who ran other factories to recommend that they meet with Lubin. These developments often led to multiple sales and meant that he could pitch to one person instead of "selling six or eight guys in one company." In such communities, he added, "the fathers and wives, the sisters and brothers working in different plants . . . receive the message simultaneously, and . . . discuss it among themselves." Stressing this point to prospects, he noted, helped boost sales.[55]

Louis Eley, a salesman in the New York region, was one of many who discovered that small-town networks could yield sales beyond the factory. In 1948, Eley sold three sets of *It's Up to All of Us* to the vice president of the Delta Ford Company in Rockland County. On a follow-up visit, Eley met with the company's president, who purchased copies of the campaign booklet for each of the plant's 350 workers, for the 80 students in the local high school, another 25 for the company's directors, and copies for the town's 200 "leading citizens." The president also purchased three extra frames in which to display posters in the local bank (which he also owned). He also arranged for Eley to present the campaign to the manager of a factory in neighboring Orangeberg County, which resulted in a further sale. By exploiting competition between the two counties, Eley was invited to present the campaign to various business and industrial associations and received the Chamber of Commerce's blessing in the form of an enthusiastic testimonial letter. Eventually, *It's Up to All of Us* was displayed widely in businesses throughout both counties.[56]

In an era when the ideals of consensus reached ever deeper into institutional life, Sheldon-Claire's motivational campaigns found an increasingly warm embrace by managers and business leaders after the war. By presenting themselves as representatives of an impartial service provider whose products were designed to advance understanding between labor and management, salesmen extended motivational messaging into the public sphere, harmonizing it with business's quest for authority. Embedding themselves in local business communities, they were able to elevate the status of the campaigns, casting them as visual embodiments of the consensus ideology that permeated the culture at large.

Getting Foremen in the "Right Frame of Mind"

Because of the emphasis that Sheldon-Claire placed on the role of the supervisor in merchandising the campaigns, salesmen frequently offered to provide instruction to groups of foremen. Transcripts of Sheldon-Claire's sales meetings contain numerous discussions between salesmen about how they went about this work. These accounts provide illuminating insights into how salesmen integrated motivational ideology into the factory through a use of personality-driven coaching and persuasion.

Salesmen usually gave talks to supervisors at the beginning of a campaign but often returned to give additional talks throughout the year. Milton Prager, a veteran of the 1920s, believed that the key to selling the campaigns to a supervisor was to realize that he was essentially a "decent person" who "feels that somehow he is not doing the right kind of job. He doesn't feel himself competent or smooth enough to get the proper enthusiasm and . . . understanding of his people to accomplish the particular objective that is his." To win their support for the campaigns, Prager would give talks to groups of supervisors in the factory, detailing motivational techniques used by management in the past, such as coercion and attempts to "bribe" employees with "parties" and "picnics." Both approaches, he told them, had "failed because in each case supervisors failed to understand that every worker, even the least informed worker is . . . sophisticated . . . So how are you going to get your objectives, gentlemen . . . unless you get the wholehearted support and cooperation of each of your workers[?]" The answer, he informed supervisors, was that they were "salesmen."

As "salesmen," he told them, "each and every one of you have a God given quality, which you have not developed, for doing a much better job in supervising, in indoctrinating, in enthusing, in inspiring, in gaining the confidence of the people you come into contact with."[57] To succeed, he added, they must realize that a poster was not just "a picture on the wall." Conversely, "if you make it live, and understand its objectives and purposes, and use it as your tool, as your aid, and back it up, you will find it not only helps you individually and your department, but it will help the entire company as a whole. It will also help in getting you more respect from the people you are trying to teach and supervise." Prager found that such talks eased managers' concerns about foremen's reluctance to back the campaigns and made them feel more accepting of their role as campaign merchandisers.[58]

Many salesmen got supervisors involved during the presentations. Salesman William Jackson told his colleagues, "If I was a teacher of gymnastics . . . my class here certainly couldn't put an inch on their muscle if I stood up here and took the exercise." Instead, "the trick" was to get supervisors to "take the exercise" themselves. With this goal in mind, Jackson gathered supervisors and as many managers as possible, distributed the campaign's introductory booklet, and asked supervisors to read aloud a line or a paragraph to prompt discussion of the campaign and its objectives. By using these tactics, Jackson explained, salesmen could resolve supervisors' "misunderstandings" and "cynicisms" and help them rehearse answers to potential questions or objections from workers before the campaign began.[59]

Salesman Nick Mihailoff frequently gave presentations to groups of supervisors. An immigrant from the Soviet Union who had earned a master's degree in engineering at Massachusetts Institute of Technology before working as a supervisor trainer for Pan American Airlines, Mihailoff had an atypical journey to Sheldon-Claire. As a "convert" to American free enterprise, he proved effective in getting supervisors behind the campaigns. Like many salesmen, he also sometimes found himself offering reassurance to managers who expressed concerns that the campaigns might stoke foremen's opposition to management. After one of his presentations to a group of unionized foremen in 1949, a manager fretted to Mihailoff that one foreman, who had initially expressed skepticism toward the campaign, would not come on board. Mihailoff replied that the foreman was "a borderline case," and despite "leftish inclinations," he mainly "wants to have the satisfaction of accomplishment by displaying his initiative." He told the manager

Sheldon-Claire Reps. are never through learning. Here, a group reviews new developments in motivational programing during an annual company-wide seminar.

Field Representatives

Since supervisors are the direct link between employees and management, representatives are especially trained to conduct dramatic meetings to teach them basic motivational principles.

FIGURE 6.9. A page from a 1959 Sheldon-Claire booklet showing Sheldon-Claire salesmen receiving training (above) and a salesman telling a group of supervisors about "developments in motivational programming" (below). Sheldon-Claire Company Records, 1959. Archives Center, National Museum of American History, Smithsonian Institution, Washington, D.C.

that "if the management is smart, if they can swing him on their side, he may become the best salesman they have for the management." These tactics paid off, Mihailoff reported. Revisiting the factory the next week, he learned that the foreman in question had been promoted to floor manager.[60]

Managers sometimes praised salesmen and their talks to foremen in testimonial letters. Typical is a letter from a plant manager of a metal stamping company in Tucker, Georgia, who wrote that in a recent presentation, a salesman "gave a real moving one hour talk on what leadership really means to us . . . He was able to get all of our supervisors in the proper frame of mind to accept this 12-week program. Each week thereafter, we used your leadership pamphlets and posters throughout the plant as a short introduction to each session, before moving onto other topics such as economic environment, organizations, etc. Your program gave us a real basis to build our entire training program around."[61] At the heart of this letter is a recognition that salesmen offered two things that management was often unable to provide: an emotionally resonant rationale for supervisors to participate in the campaigns, and a template from which to develop its training.

By the mid-1950s, as foremen were brought increasingly under the umbrella of management, salesmen continued to meet with them during visits to make renewal contracts. Through these confabs, salesmen gave foremen ongoing direction about how to "sell" the campaigns' messages to workers. David Bernstein frequently met with supervisors at Honeywell in Minneapolis, his largest contract. A photograph taken during one of his visits there in 1956 depicts him (left) with four supervisors and a manager gathered around a display board that he used to demonstrate the goals of that year's campaign, *It Makes a Difference to You!*, which asserted that job security was dependent on labor-management cooperation (figure 6.10). Bernstein's demonstration, as illustrated in the headings atop the board, revolved around "communicate" and "motivate," two core concerns for management throughout the era.

For Honeywell and other companies served by Sheldon-Claire, salesmen's coaching of foremen served as a subtle form of indoctrination in managerial ideals. Even as many foremen surely recognized the campaigns' ideological objectives, they had little incentive to oppose them given that their tributes to teamwork, cooperation, and company mindedness echoed foremen's ascribed responsibilities.[62] As representatives of a supposedly

FIGURE 6.10. Sheldon-Claire salesman David Bernstein (left) posing with four supervisors and a manager at Honeywell in Minneapolis in 1956. Salesmen such as Bernstein played a powerful role in the proliferation of motivational campaigns in the postwar workplace and in enlisting supervisors as "merchandisers" of the campaigns. Courtesy of David Bernstein.

impartial organization dedicated to helping supervisors accomplish their goals as "team leaders," salesmen faced few impediments when presenting the campaigns to supervisors. Their accounts of their work illustrate that they played an influential role in management's efforts to enlist supervisors as merchandisers of motivational messaging and, in turn, in smoothing the proliferation of motivation in the workplace.

THE COLD WAR MOTIVATION WAR

Buoyed by its success, during the 1950s Shalett endeavored to build Sheldon-Claire's international presence. Accompanied by his wife and office manager, Wanda, he made several trips to Europe to establish new branches of Sheldon-Claire. The firm's international expansion was made possible by

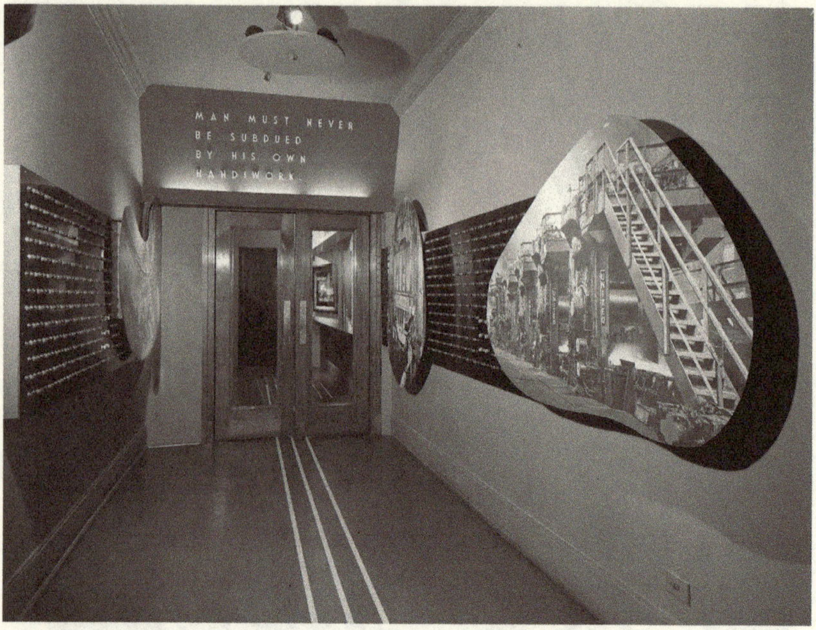

FIGURE 6.11. In 1950 Sheldon-Claire moved to lavish 7,500-square-foot offices on the top floor of 540 Lake Shore Drive, overlooking Lake Superior, close to Michigan Avenue's advertising district. Designed by leading Chicago architect Bertrand Goldberg, the offices embodied the modernist sensibilities of the firm's campaigns. Stepping out of the elevator, visitors encountered an industrial-themed mechanical animation wall complete with moving gears and mobiles. The corridor was lined with industrial images, and atop the double doors was the slogan, "Man must never be subdued by his own handiwork." The reception area, visible beyond the doors, included a front desk designed like a factory pay window, framed by several of the firm's motivational posters. HB-13036-D, Chicago History Museum, Hedrich-Blessing Collection, Chicago, IL.

its decade of success since World War II and by low operating costs. Owing to its large inventory of campaign materials and poster art, the firm only needed to put around 20 percent of its income into production costs and 30 percent toward marketing and sales, leaving Shalett with the rest, much of which he sank into the company. Living in one of the penthouse suites on North Lake Shore Drive in the prestigious Gold Coast neighborhood of Chicago, Shalett and his wife were, as one associate put it, "typical American small business Babbit's [*sic*] of their time."[63]

The firm's international expansion took time to implement, and most of its new beachheads were modest at first. In 1950, Canadian salesman

Allan East commanded a small team of around five salesmen in Canada; Jack Aptaker, the salesman hired by Shalett to develop the British market, initially covered the United Kingdom alone, eventually hiring three other salesmen; and French salesman Nick Tatarinov oversaw a small sales team that sold in France, Belgium, and Switzerland. The firm marketed its campaigns as an "industrial education" program, a tactic that allowed it to receive payment from clients in the form of United Nations Educational, Scientific and Cultural Organization (UNESCO) coupons.[64] Figures on the firm's international sales are not available, but its combined international and domestic sales grew to an estimated $1.5 million per year throughout the second half of the decade.[65] Regardless of how much of this business consisted of nondomestic sales, Shalett used the firm's international presence to boost his own image as an important ally in management's struggle to outmotivate and outproduce the Soviet Union.[66]

The role of workplace motivation in Cold War contestation has largely been overlooked by historians, so a brief contextual detour is in order before we detail Sheldon-Claire's efforts to profit from Cold War tensions.

From the end of World War II, the overarching objectives of U.S. economic planners were to contain the spread of communism and establish a Western economic order under the auspices of American-led consensus ideology.[67] The Marshall Plan, which supplied aid and investment to European nations from 1948 to 1952, was a major vehicle for these goals.[68] A less noted aspect of the Marshall Plan is its efforts to export American-style models of productivity, labor-management consensus, and work values. The major developments in American management ideology after World War II—the growing influence of human relations, the reverence of labor-management cooperation, and the promotion of neoliberal ideals of work—began to establish roots in Western Europe where management efforts to weaken labor unions were accelerating.[69]

The plan's approach to industry in Europe revolved around two main ideas: First, rising productivity, aided by a loosening of regulations, was defined as the route to social progress. The plan would raise the standard of living in European nations by increasing wages and access to material goods. The second idea was more understated in the plan's publicity but no less important to its success: its administrators sought to make European labor unions more receptive to labor-management consensus. Mirroring efforts in the United States, they encouraged unions to adopt the role of "partners in prosperity," helping management to boost productivity in return for higher wages for their members (and abandoning their class-conscious and often antimanagement stances in the process).[70]

The quest to export American ideas about productivity and work involved a massive motivational propaganda campaign that was coordinated by the body responsible for administering the plan in Europe: the European Cooperation Agency (ECA). Led by Paul Hoffman, former president of the Studebaker Company, the ECA disseminated posters, pamphlets, films, and radio broadcasts to businesses across Europe and organized exchange programs and exhibits—"the largest international propaganda operation ever seen in peacetime."[71] The ECA sponsored the production of between 200 and 250 films between 1949 and 1953, including documentary-style and drama-based productions as well as cartoons. Screened in movie theaters, public venues, and the workplace, these films were seen by an estimated forty million Europeans.[72] These films sought to destabilize "old world" conceptions of work, but given the attachment that many European workers had toward traditional craft labor, filmmakers implied that "modern" productivity could be achieved without compromising craft and tried to limit heavy-handed exaltations of American work values.[73]

As Victoria de Grazia, among others, argues, the ECA's efforts to sell American-style consensus to workers in Europe faced significant obstacles. American industrial production, with its ceaseless acceleration of the production line and alienating effects on workers—"Fordism," as it came to be known—was anathema given the profound threats that it posed to craft and autonomous labor that European workers had long valued. Further undermining the ECA's crusade was the fact that many labor unions in Europe were communist-led or significantly influenced by communism and thus far less accommodating to calls for labor-management consensus.[74] However, although the ECA did not prompt a sudden adoption of American-style productivity, it gave managers leverage to define cooperation as the guiding principle in labor-management relations, to normalize the purging of radicals from unions, and to advance management power.[75] While it was not adopted universally, by the mid-1960s, American-style productivity was making discernible inroads in Europe.[76] As Anthony Carew details, the Marshall Plan had significant effects on the balance of power between workers and management, which became apparent only after the plan ended. The "psychological boost" that European managers received due to U.S. support, he illustrates, emboldened many of them to exploit "divisions and weakness in the ranks of the labor movement to restructure industry to their own advantage."[77]

For Sheldon-Claire, the crusade to export American production and work ideals presented rich opportunities to exploit foreign markets. In communicating visually and rhetorically the precepts of labor-management cooperation and the claim that jobs and wages were dependent on such neoliberal ideals as business competitiveness and company mindedness, these campaigns brought the sensibilities then emphasized through the ECA's propaganda into workplace motivation. The core sentiments of campaigns such as *Make Sales, Make Jobs* (1954), *Our Work Guarantees Our Wages* (1956), and *Help Your Company, Help Yourself* (1958), for example, were entirely in line with the principles that the ECA promoted. Moreover, Sheldon-Claire needed only to modify American spelling in its publicity in order to market it to employers in the United Kingdom and much of Canada. For clients in Western Europe and Francophone regions of Canada, it translated the text to French, Belgian, or Swiss as the situation required (figure 6.12).[78]

Director of sales in France, Nick Tatarinov, noted that early efforts to market the campaigns in 1954 had proven difficult because some French employers "dislike the American character of the posters." Sheldon-Claire responded by modifying some posters, but the problem remained because employers were equally negative toward the "American copyright." As Tatarinov saw it, "This continues to be a real handicap to our expansion there because of the Commies: They are against everything that is American." By 1956, however, he had built up strong sales. The success of the campaigns, he believed, was because employers in France, Belgium, and Switzerland had "to solve exactly the same problems" as their American counterparts, including "the problem of communication, the problem of production costs and the problem of being in good terms with their personnel." Emphasizing these issues during his sales pitches to European managers had a positive effect on sales, he reported. Smaller firms employing 100 or so workers generally purchased six to eight sets of the campaigns, while midsize firms employing 300 to 400 workers often bought 20 sets, and those with 750 or

FIGURE 6.12. An image from a 1959 Sheldon-Claire promotional booklet entitled, "Employee Motivation Comes of Age," which touted its international business. The closing slogan in this French poster reads, "Satisfied customers mean a successful business." Sheldon-Claire Company Records, 1959. Archives Center, National Museum of American History, Smithsonian Institution, Washington, D.C.

more workers typically requested up to 45 sets. Like his colleagues in the United States, Tatarinov found that offering to give instruction to groups of foremen could secure a sale. European managers and foremen found these talks appealing, he noted, "because they don't know how to display" the campaigns and were self-conscious about presenting them to workers.[79]

Breaking into the British market proved more difficult than doing so in mainland Europe. The experiences of Jack Aptaker, the firm's first director of sales in the United Kingdom, underscore the combination of economic and cultural factors that thwarted Sheldon-Claire's attempts to export

American-style motivation to British workplaces. At Sheldon-Claire's 1956 sales meeting in Chicago, Aptaker recounted his efforts to build the firm's U.K. sales. Those efforts had been stymied by numerous "stalls," a situation that was compounded by the "stigma attached to the salesman in England." Another challenge was the skepticism of many unionized British workers who were quick to equate the campaign's references to the importance of "profit" with management "exploitation." The British market was also harder to crack than that of the United States, he added, because industrial problems in Britain were even "tougher" than those in the United States. Compounding matters, he observed, was the "ignorance" of British managers about the benefits of motivation. He read his fellow salesmen an article from *Personnel Management* that lamented that British workers were "skeptical of management exhortation" because of their radical unions, many of which were "communist dominated." Only over the last year, with the aid of three additional salesmen, he noted, had sales increased. Managers, he explained, were warming to "effective and unpatronizing communication media," while "the British worker" was starting to "realize that his own prosperity is tied up with how well and how fast he works."[80]

Testimonial letters from international clients reveal that they, like their U.S. counterparts, found the campaigns to be useful in boosting productivity and mitigating labor-management tensions.[81] In April 1957, A. Nurton, the personnel officer at Bristol Aircraft, informed Sheldon-Claire that prior to using its posters, the company had been experiencing widespread lateness and absenteeism, but after one month using the campaign, each had declined significantly. The reduction in lost hours, he noted, was caused not solely by the campaign but also by the additional pretext that it offered for management to caution workers who it deemed to be remiss. During the inception of the campaign, Nurton added, "certain people were interviewed and warned regarding their timekeeping." While the "individual action" taken with workers had been effective in reducing lost hours, he concluded, "the poster campaign assisted to a large measure."[82] The integration of the campaigns did not always go unchallenged. In 1956, when the management of a brassware company in Barking, Essex, installed its first Sheldon-Claire poster, some workers expressed their opposition by fixing a whip to the frame. Their manager laughed off the gesture in a letter to Sheldon-Claire's salesman, stating, "Obviously they have taken interest . . . whoever fixed the whip is at least one of the persons who we hope to convince that we are all in the same boat."[83]

Like salesmen in the United States, those in Europe attempted to smooth the campaigns' integration in the factory by giving talks to foremen. In 1959, the director of a latex company in Haslingden, Lancashire, wrote to Sheldon-Claire praising a lecture by one of its salesmen to over forty of its foremen. He noted that the foremen had "previously only been interested in the Trade Union propaganda, and it was very interesting indeed to listen to the questions after the lecture and to note that the material in your posters is at least being absorbed and understood by a good percentage of the people."[84] Many clients in Europe praised the talks that salesman Nick Tatarinov gave to their foremen and managers. Some larger companies, such as Société Anonyme de l'Union des Papeteries, a paper mill in Belgium, bought twenty-five sets and enlisted Tatarinov to give talks to workers and supervisors to help the campaign's integration. A chocolate company in Brussels wrote that "a campaign of this kind widens the horizon of the labor and management of the shop" and that its "success" was "real." The director of a spark plug company in Paris wrote to compliment Sheldon-Claire's maxim that "Customer Is King," noting that its posters had achieved "maximum effectiveness" in influencing workers and supervisors. In June 1954, the assistant manager of an electrical company in Paris wrote that since implementing Sheldon-Claire's campaign three months earlier, its workers, who were "being solicited with all kinds of social economic theories," were beginning to understand that they worked for the "community of customers rather than a boss."[85]

Although Sheldon-Claire's European success was slow to develop, its international expansion allowed Shalett to boost the firm's image as an ally in managers' motivational efforts. A 1959 booklet for clients announced that Sheldon-Claire's international "expansion has been rapid, because management throughout the free world realizes that employee motivation programs play an important role in helping them effectively compete with the captive Communist bloc in the struggle for free markets."[86] If such triumphal rhetoric was overblown, it underscored the increasingly central role of motivational ideology in management quests for authority during the Cold War.

A MISSION TO MOSCOW: "WHAT MAKES IVAN RUN?"

Throughout the 1950s, Shalett harbored a desire to visit the Soviet Union to observe Soviet motivational methods. Soviet officials, he declared, discouraged him by claiming that the visit would be a "waste of time" because "we don't have any need for the type of persuasive techniques or the incentives that are used in the capitalistic system."[87] Shalett's hopes were also frustrated by Cold War travel restrictions. Any American who wished to visit the Soviet Union had to gain permission from American and Soviet authorities, making such trips difficult or even impossible. The situation altered following Stalin's death in 1953, which prompted a thawing of exchanges between Soviet and American specialists. Over the next several years, the U.S. and Soviet governments engaged in an increasingly robust program of exchanges, involving specialists from industry, science, and the arts. Far from fueling isolation owing to an East-West schism as scholars once believed, the Cold War spurred cross-pollination of culture and ideas.[88]

This new era of openness ultimately opened the door for Shalett to realize his ambition. In fall 1958 toward the end of a European trip, Shalett and his wife, Wanda, were granted a three-week travel visa to Moscow. Shalett had no plan in place for accessing Soviet factories, but in a stroke of luck, on the plane they met *Life* magazine photographer Howard Sochurek, who was traveling to Moscow to work on a photo assignment for the Soviet government. Sochurek provided Shalett with contact information for Ivan Ilyachev, the director of the Soviet Agitational Propaganda Bureau, a connection that proved fruitful when Ilyachev agreed to arrange several factory tours for him and his wife.[89]

During the factory tours, Shalett, accompanied by a member of Ilyachev's staff and an interpreter, asked workers and managers about their attitudes toward their work, the Soviet Union, and the United States. Wanda, a Polish immigrant who spoke some Russian, subtly informed her husband that the bureau interpreter was "sugarcoating" some of the responses by the workers and managers whom they talked with.[90] With his characteristic bluster, Shalett later wrote to Sheldon-Claire's American clients that despite the criticisms that some Russian workers expressed, they were "so enthused over the prospect of becoming the masters of the world—leaders not only in the field of heavy industries but in consumer goods—that they take it upon themselves to convert the slackers who have not bought the concept."[91] Workers often pursued this goal, he explained, through the workers' committees, which were "organized for the purpose of checking and double checking their fellow workers to make sure that no one is lying down on the job."[92]

Shalett later underscored these claims by reproducing in Sheldon-Claire's literature images of posters created by Soviet workers (which he gathered during his tours of Soviet factories) that espoused the need to outproduce the United States (figure 6.13).[93] This practice of workers creating their own posters had long been common in the United States, where employers had encouraged it, sometimes during factory poster contests. Even so, Shalett's image of legions of Soviet workers eagerly motivating each other was a powerful one at a time when Americans were bombarded with warnings about the threat of communism. In comparing Soviet and American motivational posters, Shalett observed far more similarities than differences, later recalling, "It was a revelation to me because I thought I was back in the United States except that the communiqués were in Russian."[94]

The contradictory feelings expressed among workers as described by Shalett—on the one hand, expressions of criticism of fellow workers who were deemed to be "slacking" and, on the other, affirmations of commitment to Soviet mastery of the world—were reflected too among managers, he claimed. Shalett recalled a tour of the Moscow Ordzhonikidze Machine Tool Factory, which employed "4,000 people working two shifts of 48 hours each." Shalett talked for two hours with its managing director, "Mr. Kozichev," who explained "the whole organizational set-up" and "all that was being done to stimulate and motivate his workers to help him make his quota of 2,000 lathes a year." Kozichev, like managers throughout the Soviet Union, Shalett stated, was in a precarious position because trade unions and workers' committees had the power to replace him if they were dissatisfied with his performance. He and other managers were thus "always in a squeeze between the trade union on one side and the workers on the other side, watching his every move." On asking Kozichev how it felt "to be the whipping boy of the trade union and the workers' committees," he replied through the interpreter, "How does the general manager of a factory operating under your system feel when he is caught between the squeeze of union demands and stockholders' demands?" The situation that Kozichev described, Shalett concluded, reflected the fact that Soviet "management is

FIGURE 6.13. In its marketing publicity, Sheldon-Claire reproduced several of the worker-produced posters that Shalett brought back from Moscow. In the annotation at the bottom, the firm emphasized the success of the Soviet Union's propaganda campaign, informing its clients that Soviet workers made posters "at their own expense!" Sheldon-Claire Company Records, 1958. Archives Center, National Museum of American History, Smithsonian Institution, Washington, D.C.

more or less in the same spot, compelled to do the same thing that management must do in a competitive society to command the will of the worker—to secure their willing cooperation for increased productivity."[95]

Shalett's Moscow trip revealed that, despite his assertions about a Cold War clash of ideals about work, the purpose of Sheldon-Claire's campaigns was the same as those deployed by Soviet propagandists. Although couching their motivational messages through differing ideologies—capitalism and communism—the purpose of motivational propaganda was in both cases the same. Each sought to help managers discipline workers by invoking emotion-laden promises about work's rewards and to stoke workers' fears that their jobs were dependent on teamwork and labor-management cooperation.

SELLING THE MOTIVATIONAL WAR

After returning to Chicago in November, Shalett embarked on a media campaign in which he warned Americans about the success of the Soviet Union's workplace propaganda initiative. In speeches and in interviews, Shalett painted himself as a dutiful hero who had ventured into the belly of the beast and returned with knowledge that would help managers in the United States and the West best their Soviet counterparts in the motivational war. At business luncheons and in radio and television interviews, he paraded Soviet posters gathered during his Moscow trip, using them to warn audiences that because of its superior propaganda machinery, the Soviet Union was doing a far better job of motivating workers than were American managers. The result, he warned, was that the United States was in danger of losing the Cold War production battle and—most devastating—the struggle for global dominance, a possibility that he illustrated with graphs comparing the two nations' productivity.

A November television interview on *World Spotlight*, a half-hour news program on public television station WTTW, Chicago, is a case in point (figure 6.14). In his introduction to the program, host Carter Davidson, director of the Chicago Council on Foreign Relations, an organization dedicated to boosting the influence of Chicago's business community in the Cold War crusade, echoed Shalett's rhetoric in his opening monologue, apparently drawing on information supplied by Shalett. Davidson announced, for example that "the Russians have approximately 325,000

FIGURE 6.14. Shalett (right) pointing to Soviet posters during his TV interview with Carter Davidson, director of the Chicago Council on Foreign Relations on Chicago's public television station, WTTW, November 1958. Sheldon-Claire Company Records, 1958. Archives Center, National Museum of American History, Smithsonian Institution, Washington, D.C.

zealous propagandists assigned to the job of getting the most out of Russian workers and proving that a communist economy can beat American free enterprise," phrasing used by Shalett in his speeches. In the face of this state-sponsored motivational campaign stood the comparatively tiny Sheldon-Claire, whose owner, Lew Shalett, commanded "about 135 sales executives who sell his ideas for higher production and increased efficiency to business management in the United States and other free countries of the west."[96] During this and other interviews, Shalett showed some of the seventy-plus posters that he had brought back from the Soviet Union and noted that Sheldon-Claire, in a spirit of reciprocity, had since sent some of its own campaign materials to Soviet industrial leaders.[97]

Shalett proclaimed to an audience of over 150 management and labor representatives at the first Partners in Prosperity luncheon in Chicago (an event cosponsored by Sheldon-Claire) that "employee motivation has become a world-wide economic problem," and it was therefore necessary to "build a fire inside, not under the worker in order to secure their vital cooperation." The need for motivation, he added, was pressing given Soviet premier Nikita Khrushchev's frequent claims that the Soviet Union's superior production power would "crush" the United States. Moreover, Shalett argued, the "barbaric" Soviet "propaganda machine," which was coordinated by over a third of a million agents under the leadership of Agitational Propaganda director Ivan Ilyachev, assaulted Soviet workers with a constant stream of lies. The main objective of their propaganda, he claimed, was to "dramatise the future, because they know it is difficult to reconcile the drab, dismal present economic conditions to future promises." He warned the audience, "Yes, my friends, we can say what we please about the Soviet system—the viciousness of their propaganda, the ruthlessness of their propagandists. We can criticize them, ridicule them, we can point to the crudeness of their work, the poor quality of their products, we can decry their Godlessness, their political philosophy and lack of integrity, and their almost inhuman treatment of the masses. But in one department they are doing a brilliant, masterful job—in one department they are supreme. In one department they have done more with words then many countries have done with bullets. They have the most efficiently organized, the most intelligently operated, and the most effective propaganda machinery ever devised to communicate and motivate their people to do what must be done and what they believe can only be done—their way."[98]

Shalett's puffed-up rhetoric typified the Cold War bellicosity of the Chicago business community at this time. During the 1950s, the city became a hub of pro–free enterprise sentiment as its business and civic leaders strived to define themselves as vital players in the larger national anticommunist struggle. These efforts were also boosted significantly by Chicago's prominent role in the nation's Cold War military defense system. Beginning in 1953, the U.S. military installed Ajax missile sites along Lake Shore Drive and in the city's surrounding areas as part of its antiballistic missile program. In June 1958, just a few months before Shalett's Moscow trip and ensuing media crusade, the military replaced the Ajax missiles with the more powerful Nike missile system, whose warheads were twice as powerful as the bombs dropped on Hiroshima and Nagasaki. In all, twenty-two firing sites were installed in upstate Illinois and Indiana, making the Chicago area one of the most heavily fortified in the nation. In the wake of the concern that followed the Soviet's successful launch of Sputnik the previous year, the Nike program was hailed as a vital bulwark in the nation's defenses against Soviet attack. Looking out from the balcony of his lavish pension on Lake Shore Drive, not far from several Nike batteries, Shalett must have felt elated at his newfound status as a prominent champion of motivation.[99]

To advance his agenda, Shalett developed a relationship with prominent anticommunist and antilabor politician Senator Carl T. Curtis of Nebraska, an influential member of the McCellan Select Committee on labor-management rackets. In Curtis, Shalett found an ally who could lend authority to his warnings about the need for employers to embrace motivational campaigns. At the Partners in Prosperity luncheon, Curtis gave a keynote speech that union "racketeering" was threatening to destroy the very foundations of American democracy and that industry and workers needed to pull together to get rid of the "thieves, hoodlums, crooks, the Marxists, those leaders who use violence to gain their end, the corrupt and those union leaders who engage in unlawful political activities."[100] To top off the event, Mayor Daley of Chicago presented an award to the Magnaflux Corporation, a firm that Shalett and his cronies deemed to be an exemplar of labor-management cooperation (figure 6.15).

Shalett's performances during his post-Moscow media crusade bring to mind the infamous "kitchen" debate between then Vice President Nixon and Soviet premier Nikita Khrushchev the following year at the American Exhibition in Moscow. During their tour of the exhibits, the two men stopped at a display showcasing a modern, American-style kitchen and engaged in a debate over the relative merits of American and Soviet lifestyles. Nixon seized the moment to expound upon the virtues of the United States' consumer-based economy over a Soviet system that failed to provide modern consumer goods for its people.[101] Like Nixon, Shalett extolled the moral supremacy of American economic and social values over communism but also warned that American management was in danger of losing out to their Soviet counterparts in the Cold War production battle.

Shalett repeated these assertions to anyone in earshot in the wake of his Moscow trip. In an article in the *Chicago Daily Tribune* early in 1959, he warned that when Ilyachev, the head of Soviet Agitational Propaganda "wants to distribute a message to stir up the workers, he has only to press a button and the walls of plants and factories are covered with posters."[102] Sheldon-Claire repeated Shalett's pronouncements in an array of literature

FIGURE 6.15. Lew Shalett (left) and Senator Carl T. Curtis of Nebraska (right), at the 1958 Partners in Prosperity Award Luncheon following Mayor Richard J. Daley's presentation of the award to the Magnaflux Corporation. Steve Bailey, business agent for Local 130 of the Chicago Journeymen Plumbers Union, is at center. Sheldon-Claire Company Records, 1958. Archives Center, National Museum of American History, Smithsonian Institution, Washington, D.C.

for its clients. One major forum for this rhetoric was *They Say*, the monthly booklet produced by the firm's in-house specialist in free market economics, Helen Bugbee, and supplied to its clients. *They Say* was billed as "a review of current labor-management problems," which, unsurprisingly, entailed a constant stream of stories about the virtues of labor-management cooperation and the importance of effective communications in the workplace. Mostly, though, *They Say* was a means for promoting Sheldon-Claire's product. Shalett's Moscow trip and his reinvigorated mission to advance motivation provided an abundance of material for the booklet. Its December 1958 issue consisted of a report on Soviet motivational propaganda techniques, replete with reproductions of some of the posters that Shalett gathered in

Soviet factories. The report warned, "As a result of [its] all-out drive, backed by unlimited resources, the Soviets appear to be ahead of the U.S. in the vital field of employee motivation." Meanwhile, "fewer than 1% of all American businesses and industries have an organized, integrated program for motivating employees," which was "ironic because the Soviets are using visual communications techniques which were pioneered and developed in America to achieve their objectives."[103]

The Shaletts' Moscow trip served Sheldon-Claire's interests in another way: it provided Lew Shalett with an abundance of material with which to motivate his salesmen. In the months and years following the trip, he transmitted newsletters to his salesmen in the United States, Canada, and Europe at a rate of two to three times per week, directing them to tell their prospects that Soviet workers were more fired up to win the production battle than were American workers. To bring the point home, Shalett often included reproductions of posters made by Soviet workers on the newsletters' covers. In the first newsletter after his return from Moscow, he warned that the Soviet Union was succeeding in motivating "Ivan and Boris and Anya and the millions of their comrades upon whom [it] is counting," not because they were better than their American counterparts but "because of their shrewd appraisal of the human mind." Moreover, Ilyachev's army of "salesmen" were working constantly "in all the fifteen Republics—inspiring the worker to get on with it—to get crackin'—to do what must be done to beat the West—with the same communicating and motivating methods created, designed and produced by the Sheldon-Claire Company!" The company's salesmen were, he added, "not only in the right business, but at the right time! . . . there is no better method for mobilizing people's minds and controlling their actions than the products and services rendered by Sheldon-Claire."[104]

In a subsequent newsletter, Shalett scoffed at a recent visit to the United States by Anastas Mikoyan, Khrushchev's chief emissary. He announced to salesmen, "Mikoyan Came! Mikoyan Saw! But Mikoyan Didn't Fool Anybody!" before agreeing with one business leader that the trip was little more than a "burlesque show" and lambasting Mikoyan as an "arch propagandist." Shalett added, "Mikoyan . . . represents in everybody's mind—including your prospect—the symbol of the vicious and ruthless type of propaganda that the Soviets are using to motivate their workers to cooperate, to produce more—to beat the West." Mikoyan's visit, he told his salesmen, provided a valuable sales opportunity: "By injecting the Russian story into the interview you not only add color and excitement to the pitch—but you arouse certain fears, certain emotional values in your prospect's mind that motivate HIM to buy a Sheldon-Claire campaign to help HIM achieve HIS objectives!" This, he concluded, was "the most powerful ammunition you can use to destroy the smugness, the complacency, the indifference of those wise guys who know all the answers—but have not yet been aroused to the problems—the threats that endanger not only our way of life—but their jobs!"[105]

Despite Shalett's claims about the freedom-granting nature of motivation in the United States and the West, the firm's campaigns revolved around the very same mechanism that Shalett condemned when used by the Soviet Union: *fear*. The script of the firm's training program in the late 1950s informed inductee salesmen that "by and large, the underlying impetus, in virtually every program has been a threat . . . to engender fear—not fear of physical or economic reprisal, to be sure, but the threat of loss of security." It continued: "No, we haven't said to the man or woman whom we address our motivational messages—'Work hard or you will be beaten' or 'Work hard or you will be fired'—but we have repeatedly said, 'Work hard or the company will go out of business—and you will be out of a job.' A sugar-coated capsule, but still the same bitter medicine inside. So no matter how you slice it—we're threatening—we're selling <u>fear</u>."[106]

This statement underscores a central contradiction in the firm's mission, and one that characterized the ECA's campaign to promote American models of productivity in Europe. Each claimed that, through work, one gained autonomy and freedom, a transaction that was contrasted against the situation of workers subject to coercive propaganda under communism. In reality, workers in the United States and the West were exposed to a similar motivational regimen as their counterparts in the Soviet Union, albeit one anchored in a different political ideology. Although motivation in the West emphasized "humanistic" ideals—voluntary labor-management cooperation, a rising standard of living, and individual prosperity—it comprised its own brand of manipulation and obscured the fact that cooperation was more obligatory than voluntary.

For employers in the United States, Sheldon-Claire's campaigns served an array of goals. Not only did they help indoctrinate rank-and-file workers and supervisors in the firm's official ideals regarding subjects such as labor-management cooperation, wages, business competitiveness, and political ideology, but they also integrated employees into the organization, both through exposure to campaign sentiments and by enlisting foremen as "merchandisers." The campaigns also lent credence to the claim that the "American way of work," so to speak, was freer than work was elsewhere. However, if many American workers experienced expanded rewards in the form of competitive wages and access to consumption, work itself was another story. As the factory worker and novelist Harvey Swados observed in a 1957 article in the *Nation*, "The Myth of the Happy Worker," workers of the era felt little of the freedom extolled by devotees of motivation. Rubbing against the grain of the era's orthodoxy that class distinctions were disappearing amid the postwar boom, Swados observed, "The plain truth is that factory work is degrading. It is degrading to any man who ever dreams of doing something worthwhile with his life." Whereas "for the immigrant worker, even the one who did not dream of socialism, his long hours were going to buy him freedom. For the factory worker of the Fifties, his long hours are going to buy him commodities . . . and maybe reduce a few of his debts . . . Almost without exception, the men with whom I worked on the assembly line last year felt like trapped animals."[107]

Swados's observations reflected an increasingly common reality for workers, both men and women, from the late 1950s onward. Wages and access to consumption offered little consolation to workers in an era when automation and speedups on the line were eroding their craft traditions and autonomy. Concerned that workers' resentments to these new demands were compromising productivity and fearing revived class hostility, management began to develop a different approach to motivation. The messaging emphasizing consumption and Cold War consensus used since the end of World War II by corporations and specialists such as Sheldon-Claire would soon fade. However, once again, the strategy deployed in the new techniques would rely no less on attempts to manipulate the worker's mind.

EPILOGUE

Motivation in an Age of Diminishing Rewards

> Now imagine if you could take all the fun and addicting, motivating elements in a game and combine that with actually productive activities in the real world!
>
> —Yu-kai Chou, "The Beginner's Guide to Gamification," 2012

If Cold War motivational rhetoric served industrial corporations and independent campaign suppliers like Sheldon-Claire well, it rapidly lost relevance as the postwar boom began to slow in the mid-1960s and the postwar consensus, with its emphasis on labor-management bargaining, started to erode in the face of a new cycle of class conflict toward the end of the decade. In collective memory, the era's class tensions have been largely overshadowed by its more visible events, including the civil rights movement, the war in Vietnam, the antiwar movement, second wave feminism, and the counterculture. Yet events in industry—not least surging strikes toward the end of the decade—were no less dramatic and consequential. Workers' responses to automation and speedups on the production line, moreover, were to prompt a wide-ranging shift in managers' approaches to motivation.

Industrial tensions exploded into full view in the early 1970s in a wave of widely reported strikes involving millions of workers in the auto, mining, trucking, and steel industries. To the frustration of many labor leaders, younger workers, fueled by the rebellious stance of young people in other arenas, rejected the fealty of older workers toward consensus-era union-management bargaining. Operating independent of unions, they engaged in unofficial strikes and informal action on the line, leading to the most widespread industrial strike waves since the end of World War II.[1] The strike by workers at General Motors' Lordstown, Ohio, plant in 1971–72 came to symbolize the widening discontent among workers as well as management's inability to maintain control. In efforts to compete with foreign automakers then supplying the American market with cheap cars, the General Motors Assembly Division implemented new production technologies that it hoped would create the world's fastest assembly line. Instead of turning out sixty cars per hour as had been the case with previous models, workers would be expected to complete one hundred of its new Vega. Many operations previously performed by workers were automated, a change that managers cast as a job improvement measure that would also boost morale. The firm asserted that, "by giving [the worker] less to do he will do it better." As it turned out, however, the workforce, whose average age was under twenty-five, felt very differently. The new production regimen was physically brutalizing, compounded the erosion of craft, and made clear that management regarded employees as little more than machine parts. In protest, workers let cars leave the line unfinished, waged informal slowdowns and sabotage, and engaged in mass absence. After management responded with a zero-tolerance policy toward dissent, workers finally staged a strike that lasted three weeks. Management ultimately lost little in the strike, conceding only to reinstate the 1970s contract and to abandon disciplinary layoffs. Workers' biggest goal—to gain a say in the organization of production—was unsuccessful.[2] Yet the strike also portended trouble for management. With its competitive wages and other compensations, as well as promises of improved working conditions, Lordstown had been heralded as the acme of industrial progress. Such measures, it seemed, could not be relied on to assuage the frustrations of a younger industrial workforce who had little firsthand memory of the golden age of labor-management bargaining.

Assessing the era's industrial conflicts, journalists and academics concluded that the worker was "alienated" and that the American work ethic was corroding. This view was captured in a widely reported 1973 study commissioned by the Nixon administration, entitled *Work in America*. On its first page, the authors warned, "Significant numbers of American workers are dissatisfied with the quality of their working lives. Dull, repetitive, seemingly meaningless tasks, offering little challenge or autonomy, are causing discontent among workers at all occupational levels." The consequences, they noted, included not just declining productivity, strikes, and absenteeism but also poor-quality work, damaged physical and mental health, and family instability.[3]

In efforts to increase productivity and curb industrial unrest, managers turned to a different approach to motivation: "work enrichment." Although talk about "enriching" work had formed a core strand of motivational ideology since the nineteenth century, it gained new prominence after 1970. Some of the era's most influential management theorists had already rejected the view that workers were motivated solely by extrinsic rewards (such as pay and access to consumer goods). Because motivation resided *inside* the worker, they reasoned, enriching work was a more effective means of boosting productivity than the carrot and stick of monetary or material incentives. Peter Drucker argued that managers should promote workers' participation in the planning of tasks and individualize motivation by rewarding them based on their personal performance.[4] Douglas McGregor, drawing on Abraham Maslow's hierarchy of needs, proposed in 1960 that managers focus more on helping employees reach their full "potential," a tactic that he argued, was integral to integrating the worker into the organization and achieving greater efficiency. "Man," as his famous "Theory Y" stated, "will exercise self-direction and self-control in the service of objectives to which he is committed."[5] Motivation theorist Frederick Herzberg argued that the route to effective motivation lay in identifying the causes of work satisfaction and dissatisfaction and then modifying jobs so that they offered workers a feeling of achievement, recognition, and growth. When management enriched jobs in these ways, he posited, workers experienced "self-actualization" and thus became more amenable to management's objectives.[6]

Work enrichment rhetoric helped management obscure the extent of the crisis affecting work in two ways. First, the era's industrial tensions were due not just to workplace monotony but also to the erosion of workers' long-term economic security amid the decline of the postwar economy. As David Harvey has detailed, beginning in the late 1960s, the Keynesian economic model that had led to stable national growth and economic security for millions of workers and their families since the end of World War II began to unravel. This unraveling was fueled not only by the deskilling and decline of higher-paying jobs caused by automation but also by growing international competition and spiraling inflation fueled by the war in Vietnam. Workers' economic well-being deteriorated as business leaders embraced neoliberal economic policies based on aggressive antiunion tactics that frequently entailed downsizing and outsourcing.[7] The ideas proffered by devotees of work enrichment focused on neutralizing workers' opposition to these neoliberal nostrums. Herzberg, for example, touted job enrichment as a means to wean workers off their "addiction" to wage increases. These increases, he argued, operated much like "heroin," whereby as workers became conditioned to them, they needed "more and more to produce less effect."[8]

Second, although work enrichment seemed to promise greater autonomy for workers, it was principally a means to shore up managerial control. As labor economist Harry Braverman argued in his highly influential 1974 book *Labor and Monopoly Capital*, work enrichment rhetoric masked the root cause of alienation—workers' loss of ownership of and control over their work—by equating it to a mere "feeling of distress, a malaise, a bellyache about his or her work." Work enrichment, he noted, was "a style of management rather than a genuine change in the position of the worker," and its objective was to contain the effects of worker discontent arising from the destruction of craftsmanship.[9] Labor scholars had emphasized the effects of alienation for years. Two decades earlier, Daniel Bell had warned that automation was creating the army of "interchangeable factory 'hands'" that Marx had predicted, as well as a widening gulf of opportunity between the skilled and the semiskilled.[10] Only in the late 1960s, when productivity slowed and industrial conflict proliferated, did alienation and its problems become a cause célèbre for managers—and for politicians like Nixon, whose appeals to white working-class discontent proved indispensable when courting the "silent majority."[11]

Ultimately, work enrichment did little to stir employees' feelings of goodwill toward management or optimism about work's rewards. Even at firms where managers implemented it comprehensively, it did little to quell the class antagonisms arising from automation, the constricting economy, and management's increasing adherence to neoliberal economic theories.[12] And yet, if work enrichment schemes failed to allay the discontent sweeping industry, they planted seeds that would bear fruit in the years ahead. The core developments soon to unfold—the hyperindividualism of the Reagan era, the rise of the New Economy based on service and informational labor, and the advent of the internet—would provide management with ample opportunities to exploit work enrichment rhetoric. Moreover, motivational sentiment would soon spread into the culture at large as self-improvement gurus began to espouse the personal rewards of a motivated life to a mainstream audience.

Today, a century after its advent, the motivational project remains a powerful arm of management ideology. It has, however, undergone two major changes in recent decades. First, management has couched its rhetoric increasingly in the language of employee empowerment and has become extraordinarily adept at infusing it into the workplace. As a walk around many workplaces today confirms, managerial jargon espousing the personal fulfillment and self-discovery offered through work has become ubiquitous. This rhetoric circulates via such traditional mediums as posters, films, and literature but also through play- and game-based techniques, "employee wellness" programs, and wearable self-tracking devices. These techniques invoke language about employee empowerment while masking their true objectives—to discipline workers, extract more labor from them at less cost, and instill managerial values in the workplace.[13]

Second, motivational discourse now infuses the culture at large far more broadly than it used to. Its wide circulation is fueled by the self-improvement industry, which is projected to grow to over $14 billion per year by 2023. The industry's products include not just employee motivation tools marketed to employers but also self-help books, videos, apps, seminars, and life coaching services. Through these and other channels, motivational sentiment has suffused the workplace and a large portion of public and private life.[14]

While on its surface today's rhetoric appears very different from that of the past, its goal remain unchanged—to advance management's hegemony. In the workplace and in the culture at large, such discourse helps shore up neoliberal assaults on wages and economic security by reinforcing the idea that we should regard work principally as a route to personal well-being, not economic security. As countless studies have illustrated, economic gains for workers have receded dramatically since the 1970s as work has become less secure.[15] Given this state of affairs, understanding the power of our era's motivational ideology is vital.

NEOLIBERAL MOTIVATION: ILLUSIONS OF EMPOWERMENT, FANTASIES OF SUCCESS

The type of motivational rhetoric that infuses the workplace and the culture at large today hardly came from nowhere. Its roots lie in the 1980s and 1990s, when self-help books took the best-seller lists by storm and management specialists began proclaiming that the "flexible" jobs of the New Economy were liberating everyone from the harsh demands of the industrial age.[16] This rhetoric fused traditional management oratories about the rewards of hard work with a New Agey reverence for the marketplace. During the second half of the 1990s—"management's summer of love," as Nigel Thrift aptly calls this period—management gurus argued that flexible work arrangements and the new emotionally attuned dotcom managers of the day were rapidly remaking the workplace into a space of emotional support and gratification.[17] Such claims gained esteem through books like Jack Canfield's *Chicken Soup for the Soul* and Spencer Johnson's *Who Moved My Cheese?*, which imparted managerial values to millions of readers, including many white-collar workers who received copies from their managers.[18]

In reality, workers experienced deepening losses throughout the eighties and nineties. As Arlie Hochschild shows in *The Time Bind*, flexible work was the latest in a long line of management tactics aimed at honing Taylorist quests to extract more labor from workers at less cost. The flexibility emphasized by the era's "work enrichment" schemes promised workers greater control over their work flow but extended the demands of work into the home, compounding alienation.[19] The era also witnessed the rise of an even more intense regimen of managerial control than existed in the past, as management doubled down on neoliberal cost-cutting measures. At a time when the stock market was supposedly yielding untold wealth to ordinary Americans and work was becoming more rewarding, workers lost security even as many of them began incorporating motivational ideals in their cubicles and embracing them through CDs and books.[20]

Despite its illusory claims, the neoliberal motivational ideals that management promulgated in the eighties and nineties established a formula that managers have deployed into our own day. Whether we look at manufacturing, the service industry, or higher education, neoliberal motivation is central to management's efforts to infuse a belief in work's promises among workers. This strategy is even more evident in "creative" work settings, where managers emphasize the personal esteem derived from "meaningful" work while minimizing pay and benefits, a practice seen in the proliferation of unpaid internships in such "prestigious" work spaces as museums and academe. This tendency has given rise to what Miya Tokumitsu calls "do what you love" ideology. The "ideal worker," according to this belief, "is not the anonymous shift worker but the enlightened genius who never stops working . . . The passion-driven worker has work on the brain all the time (much to the delight of his or her boss) and hence eagerly incorporates this work into his or her identity."[21] Today's managerial assertions about fulfilling and meaningful work are, like the claims about the liberating effects of flexible work since the 1980s, just a means to keep workers buying into the same old promises while extracting more labor from them at less cost.

Over the last decade, neoliberal motivation has proliferated in the culture at large, both in the United States and around the world. A case in point is the massively successful franchise *The Secret*, which includes a book (with sales of over twenty million copies) and a film. Produced by Rhonda Byrne, an Australian TV producer-turned-self-help-guru, *The Secret* offers an innovative spin on the age-old notion that anyone can realize their dreams by deploying the "law of attraction" and "visualizing" their goals. Weaving mystical, *Da Vinci Code*–like imagery, adrenalizing music, and commentaries from self-improvement luminaries, the film tells viewers that through a combination of positive mental energy and visualization, anyone can actualize their desires. As author Lisa Nichols tells viewers, "What you think about, you bring about. Your life is a physical manifestation of the thoughts that go in your head." For sympathetic viewers, *The Secret*'s claims about the power of self-motivation and visualization are boosted by the assertions of its parade of commentators, most of whom are prominent figures in the New Thought movement. Those featured include "inspirational" minister Michael Beckwith (author of *Life Visioning: A Transformative Process for Activating Your Unique Gifts and Highest Potential*); visualization proponent Marci Shimoff (*Happy for No Reason: 7 Steps to Being Happy from the Inside Out*); and Jack Canfield (the *Chicken Soup for the Soul* series). Beyond its main claims, *The Secret* asserts that the Law of Attraction has long been known to successful individuals, including everyone from Plato to Einstein and Beethoven to Lincoln, but has been hidden from the masses by the powerful. This conspiratorial theme is accompanied by scenes of a scribe during ancient times hurriedly trying to smuggle the scroll that contains the secret, accompanied by heart-pounding music.[22]

Among the most influential of the motivational gurus to appear in *The Secret* is the inspirational speaker Esther Hicks (whose ideas about visualization partly inspired Byrne to make the film but who was cut from a later version owing to a legal dispute).[23] Along with her late husband, Jerry, a former Amway salesman and circus acrobat, Hicks has made a fortune offering seminars ($225 a ticket) that advance the belief that people can make up their own reality and achieve whatever they wish through the power of "thought vibrations." At her seminars, Hicks summons—she has her followers believe—otherworldly spirits that she collectively calls "Abraham," who "responds" to the audience's questions through Hicks. Regardless of the manifestly bogus and exploitative nature of the whole enterprise, Hicks has millions of followers. According to her, what happens to people is solely a result of their own choices. This principle holds true, she informs followers, not only for everyday events like the outcome of a job application but also serious ones like child abuse and murder and world-historical events like the Holocaust. The victims of these last examples, while deserving of sympathy, nonetheless played a role in their own fate through their prior thoughts and actions, Hicks claims. When asked how six million Jews "attracted" their deaths in the Holocaust, she replied in part, "When you hang around with one another and you talk about things in the way that you do, and you talk about victimhood and you talk about injustice and you beat the drum of unfairness, how could anything other than someone to fulfill that vibrational escrow happen?"[24] It's no coincidence that a film like *The Secret* would spur such interest in the 2000s and 2010s. Not only was this the era when the motivational industry went into overdrive via rocketing sales of books, CDs, and seminars but it was also a period when neoliberal ideology eroded faith in the idea that one could achieve economic security through work. In a time when work offers less security and when many people find economics opaque, the neoliberal mysticism espoused in *The Secret* and its ilk have no small appeal.[25]

The Secret's brand of motivational rhetoric has been promoted widely on the national and world stage by talk show hosts such as Oprah Winfrey. Winfrey's gushing tributes to self-improvement have exposed millions of viewers around the globe to a steady diet of motivational ideas. A long-time devotee of self-empowerment who explains her own success in terms of bootstrap individualism, Winfrey has hosted motivational specialists on her show on multiple occasions. In a special episode devoted to *The Secret* in 2007, featuring Michael Beckwith and fellow "expert" James Arthur Ray, Winfrey stated that the film embodied her show's main message: "Taking responsibility for your life. Knowing that every choice that you've made has led you to where you are right now." This and other episodes feature testimonies from viewers who offer fawning praise for *The Secret*, attesting to how it saved their troubled marriages and careers and resolved their financial problems, stories that predictably elicit ecstatic responses from the audience. Winfrey's enthusiasm knows no bounds when giving motivation's disciples a platform. When hosting Byrne, Winfrey went into full-on evangelizing mode, telling her viewers, "Watch it with your children."[26]

While motivational rhetoric has always conjured far-fetched visions of the rewards of individual striving, it has increasingly taken on the form of money-making schemes. Nothing demonstrates this reality more than the stadium-packing "business seminar" known as Get Motivated! Founded in the 1990s by noted Republican Party donors Peter and Tamara Lowe, Get Motivated! has drawn hundreds of thousands of Americans to hear its rotating roster of high-profile conservatives from the worlds of politics, business, sport, and entertainment espouse the creed that a motivated attitude can lead to personal success. Billed as a means to help attendees hone their business skills and attain personal and career advancement, Get Motivated! is, in reality, a profit venture that works by selling its captive audience additional products. The eleven-hour seminar includes several breaks during which attendees are encouraged to visit adjacent rooms to sign up for workshops that promise to help participants improve their job prospects and, for managers, boost teamwork in their organizations. This formula is rooted in the sales training workshops developed by the Christian-conservative sales specialist Zig Ziglar in the 1980s. A long-time presenter at Get Motivated! before his 2012 death, Ziglar's brand of evangelistic success rhetoric set the stage for the capitalism-on-steroids sentiment touted by the event's speakers to this day, some of whom are Ziglar's protégés.

On March 14, 2011, I joined over twenty thousand attendees when Get Motivated! visited the Moda Center in downtown Portland, Oregon.

Among the speakers were regulars Colin Powell, Laura Bush, Rudi Giuliani, Terry Bradshaw, and Bill Cosby. Each extolled the power of a motivated attitude, attesting to how it had helped them and others achieve success. Powell regaled the crowd with stories about how a motivated attitude to leadership had brought success in his military career; Giuliani used his time to praise his own "motivated" performance in the aftermath of the 9/11 attacks on the World Trade Center; Laura Bush delivered a sentimentalized account of "my George," who, "during recount after recount" in Florida on election night in 2000, kept his resolve (which she deemed a lesson in the importance of motivational thinking); and Bradshaw waxed about how a motivated attitude on the field made all the difference between losing and winning. To cap it off, Bill Cosby affirmed the virtues of motivation by satirizing those who, he explained, could use it the most—*un*motivated teenagers and welfare dependents—much to the crowd's delight.

As if to preempt such doubts, many speakers warned of the dangers of losing faith in motivation. This theme was hammered home by self-improvement devotee Krish Dhanam, an entrepreneur who emigrated to the United States from India in the 1980s before becoming one of Zig Ziglar's most beloved students. Dhanam recalled how, after arriving in New York City "with nine dollars my pocket and a vision of promise in my heart," he came to "epitomize the American Dream" by embracing American individualism. The rags-to-riches story that Dhanam served up is the sort that conservative audiences have long liked to point to as evidence that anyone can succeed in America if they work hard enough, and predictably, the crowd lapped it up. Among the most elated responses of the day occurred when Dhanam turned his ire on those who cast doubt on the possibility of upward mobility. For Dhanam, such doubts are the work of "elites" who undermined the individual's success by "telling you that you don't belong." The rapturous applause that Dhanam received for this and other zingers illustrates a central tenet of neoliberal motivation: it's not a rigged system that stands in the way of anyone's success but a lack of determination, along with the corrupting influence of nonbelievers.

Despite the enthusiastic responses from the audience that day, not everyone was sold. Many attendees, it turned out, had been required to attend by their employers (to whom Get Motivated! provides tickets for free). Judging by the bored-looking groups of coworkers clustered in the concession area, it was clear that few would return to work feeling motivated. A group of young women employed at a nursing home killed time by texting and chatting, appearing underwhelmed at the talks. One dismissed the event aptly as "an advertisement for the Republican Party," a conclusion shared by her coworkers, who nodded in agreement. Still, neither the skepticism of many attendees nor the midafternoon thinning of the crowd undermined the event's success. Whenever the sign-up tables appeared throughout the day, hundreds flocked to enroll for workshops. And when TV news stations dropped by to get some reactions, attendees—at least those included in the evening reports—enthused that the speakers' wisdom would help them fine-tune their career prospects, hone their business skills, and enhance teamwork in their organizations.[27] Regardless of how truly motivated they may have felt, attendees, by cheering the speakers, signing up for another workshop, or expressing their enthusiasm to the TV cameras, helped grease the wheels of the motivational machine for another day.

One hardly needs to buy into money-making schemes like *The Secret* or Get Motivated! to be exposed to neoliberal motivation today. The discourse circulates widely in daily life. Its proliferation is seen in the output of organizations like the Foundation for a Better Life (FFBL). For over fifteen years, FFBL has installed billboards and aired TV ads carrying inspirational messages along the nation's highways and on TV about individuals whose actions it believes should be emulated, an ideal captured in the slogan that concludes each message: "Pass It On." Owned by billionaire businessman Philip Anschutz, its messages are steeped in tributes to individual success and character, including many historical figures.[28] The actions of Abraham Lincoln, Mahatma Gandhi, and Nelson Mandela, to name a few, are framed as poignant anecdotes about inspiring individuals disconnected from larger political events. This practice employs the visual and rhetorical simplification that has always been a hallmark of motivational messaging. As the designers of twentieth-century workplace communications understood, images of virtuous-looking individual strivers, coupled with pithy captions, are integral to emotionally appealing messaging. Whereas in the past, these design tactics encouraged faster production in the name of such tangible goals as victory over fascism and economic security, today FFBL and other devotees of inspirational messaging use them to promote a belief in the virtuousness of individual striving, whose reward is an ethereal sense of fulfillment.

This strategy is evident in FFBL's billboards featuring "everyday heroes" who have prevailed over difficult challenges to achieve distinction. Typifying the genre is a billboard featuring Liz Murray, who grew up in a drug-filled home and became homeless before going on to Harvard, authoring a popular memoir, and becoming a motivational speaker. Pictured in a lecture hall embracing a psychology textbook, Murray embodies the familiar claim that anyone can achieve success regardless of the circumstances into which they are born if they work hard enough. Other billboards, like one depicting a good-hearted mechanic, lay tribute to those who have acted with generosity or good character without thought of personal gain (figure 7.1).

According to FFBL's website, when its creative director dropped into a garage to get his car fixed, the mechanic, Mike—"the 'Mother Teresa' of the automotive world"—worked on it for three hours before concluding that the problem could not be fixed, graciously refusing payment. The foundation used the incident as a touching parable about the importance of cultivating character in one's work.[29] Like Elbert Hubbard's "A Message to Garcia" and many other motivational texts, FFBL's billboard uses a real-life incident as the basis of a moving story to remind its audience that a good work ethic is a principled goal. The irony is that for many who view such billboards along highways during their commutes or who view similar messages in the workplace, cultivating good work ideals provides little comfort amid an increasingly precarious labor market that is less and less likely to offer the economic security that work did in the past.[30]

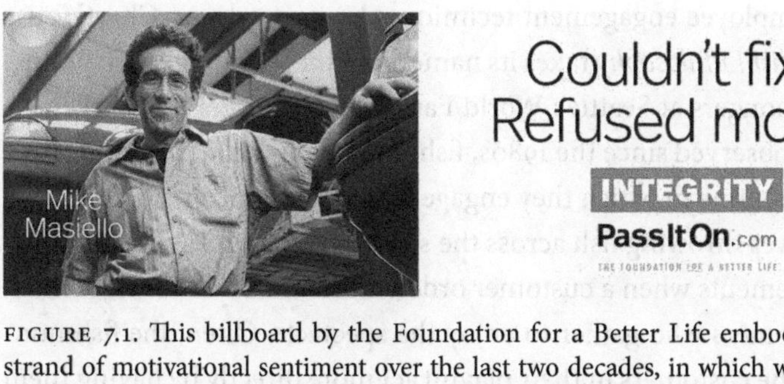

FIGURE 7.1. This billboard by the Foundation for a Better Life embodies a common strand of motivational sentiment over the last two decades, in which work's meanings are defined as personal rather than economic. Such publicity echoes techniques used by managers in the workplace during the same period. Image courtesy of The Foundation for a Better Life.

NEW FRONTIERS IN WORKPLACE MOTIVATION: PLAY, GAMIFICATION, AND SELF-TRACKING

In the early twenty-first century, managers have turned increasingly to motivational techniques based on *play*. Managerial uses of play vary, but typically they involve infusing work with elements of fun, games, and worker self-expression to facilitate team building (and, less ostensibly, to encourage workers to adopt a managerial attitude). As workers in office and nonoffice settings alike know, types of play-based motivation common at work today include training days structured around "fun" themes, role-playing and game-based exercises, and employee presentations in which workers and managers are expected to engage in elements of performance. From the now-cliché Hawaiian shirt Friday to more recent innovations like manager-employee role reversal exercises, outings to escape rooms, and even workplace murder parties, play-based motivation holds appeal for managers because its emphasis on enjoyment infuses their techniques with a nonideological facade. This tactic is invaluable to management in concealing its true objectives: to define a positive attitude as a de facto requirement in the workplace and render workers more accepting of managerial goals. Ultimately, play-based motivation is a means for managers to collapse the distinction between work and leisure and to conceal the inherent power hierarchies between themselves and workers.[31]

Among the most noted examples of play-based motivation is the employee "morale-building" book *Fish! Philosophy* (which, since its 1998 publication, has sold over five million copies and been adapted into a larger package of employee engagement techniques by its producer, ChartHouse Learning).[32] *Fish! Philosophy* takes its name from the infamous work philosophy of fishmongers at Seattle's World Famous Pike Place Fish Market. As visitors have observed since the 1980s, fishmongers at the market perform a high-energy routine in which they engage customers in playful banter. This routine involves throwing fish across the shopping area and yelling humorous announcements when a customer orders a fish, much to the enjoyment of other customers who gather to enjoy the spectacle. Often, the fishmongers involve the customers in their playful act more directly by having them catch a fish or by holding up a fish and manipulating its mouth so that it appears to be talking to the customer. According to ChartHouse's website, its owner, John Christensen, was inspired to write the book after he witnessed the fishmongers' performance during a chance visit to the market. In video footage shot by him, the fishmongers explained that the idea behind their routine boiled down to one idea: "choose your attitude." By "choosing" their attitude, the fishmonger explained, they could bring a sense of "fun" to their work and "make the customer's day," a situation that was good for workers and for business.[33]

In *Fish! Philosophy*, Christensen and his coauthors assert that when workers choose to adopt a positive and playful attitude—the ideals exemplified at Pike Market—the workplace will become a happier and more productive environment. The book, which takes the form of an inspirational story, is a fictionalized retelling of Christensen's visit to the market that modifies his experience to heighten the story's effect on the reader. Christensen has been replaced by a woman, Mary Jane, who, after taking a position at a bank in Seattle, is tasked with improving its dysfunctional third-floor department known by other workers as the "toxic energy dump" because of its unhappy and abrasive staff. A few weeks into her quest, Mary Jane takes a lunchtime walk to mull over her vexed efforts and happens on a group of fishmongers at Pike Place Fish Market performing the playful act described above. One of the fishmongers, Lonnie, befriends Mary Jane, and a heart-to-heart ensues in which she tells him about her struggle to improve work conditions; Lonnie offers to help her bring the "energy" that she had witnessed to the bank. Upon Mary Jane's second visit to the market, Lonnie explains the secret to the fishmongers' energized approach to their work. The idea developed, he explains, after they made an "amazing" discovery: "There is always a choice about the way you do your work, even if there is not a choice about the work itself . . . We can choose the attitude we bring to work."[34]

For Mary Jane, this insight is a revelation, and she soon begins giving presentations to the bank's employees that apply the "choose your attitude" ideal. After her efforts receive a positive reception from the staff, she consults further with Lonnie, who tells her about three other core principles that make for a positive workplace and good customer relations at the fish market: "play," "make their day," and "be there." Inspired by these conversations and by motivational CDs and books, Mary Jane adapts the fishmongers' four-part work ethos into an employee-engagement program at the bank. Via heartfelt inspirational talks, she encourages her colleagues to "choose your attitude," embrace a sense of "play" in their work, "make their day," and "be there" for each other, all of which, she explains, will make their jobs more rewarding and the workplace more positive. Eventually (and predictably, given the didactic goals of the book's authors), the employees come on board. By the end, they are putting up their own motivational posters and giving enthused presentations about how to change the bank to be more "fun" and "rewarding." Aided by the now motivated employees, the "toxic energy dump" transforms into a positive and energetic working environment where employees feel empowered.[35]

Despite its veneer of innocuous self-help, *Fish! Philosophy* is very much in the same manipulative tradition as GM's "My Job and Why I Like It" contest and many of the other motivational devices discussed in this book. Sold to human resources departments, which, in turn, present it to workers as a fun-based team-building program, the book is a tool for accommodating workers to managerial objectives. The "choose your attitude" ideal that it extols masks workers' increasing inability to control their labor. It appeals to managers because it casts workers not as what they truly are—performers of labor—but as contented team members in a workplace supposedly devoid of power hierarchies. The fishmongers' approach to work, far from embodying a devotion to managerial ideals, can be more realistically understood as a way to cope with the demands of cold, demanding labor and make the day go faster, a tactic used by workers for centuries. The book's interpretation of the fishmongers' behavior has been challenged by the workers themselves. As one of the fishmongers stated in a now deleted YouTube video entitled "Pike Place Hates Fish! Philosophy," "The guys that work here don't actually like the FISH! videos" and just "put on a show" for Christensen during the three days that he visited to shoot the footage.[36]

Since the book's 1998 publication, ChartHouse has developed additional tie-in products whose goals include "improving teamwork and trust among employees," boosting "engagement and morale," and "build[ing] a culture Millennials love." These products span an array of workbooks, e-learning videos, study kits, and employee and manager training programs. The last of these products brings to life the principles laid out in the *Fish! Philosophy* book via workshop facilitator Deena Ebbert. As seen in ChartHouse's videos, Ebbert gives high-energy interactive talks that involve throwing toy fish to participants, a practice that adapts the fishmongers' routine at

Pike Market (figure 7.2).[37] As Kevin Carson argues, employers' distribution of *Fish! Philosophy* and their utilization of Fish! training programs is often a prelude to restructuring initiatives in which management demands increased productivity from workers, compounding burnout while giving no additional compensation. Using Fish! Philosophy programs, "management attempts to deal with burnout entirely through cheerleading and slogans . . . without having to increase staffing levels or pay, or otherwise alter its own contribution to the problem."[38] Although management typically buries such goals in soothsaying about the happy and rewarding workplace, they are occasionally made more explicit. A case in point is South African management organization Goldfish Consulting. On its website, the firm explains that its name was inspired by Fish! Philosophy and that it "specializes in interventions that can assist organisations through the difficult economic climate of the country . . . This often requires restructuring and sometimes downsizing in order to find and unlock the value the strategic initiative anticipated."[39]

The *Fish! Philosophy* book and its array of tie-in programs and products embody many of the motivational techniques used by management since the publication of "A Message to Garcia." Much like Hubbard's essay and a number of the techniques discussed in this book, the goal remains

FIGURE 7.2. Deena Ebbert and an audience during a high-energy Fish! Philosophy workshop. Promoted as a means to boost teamwork, engagement, and morale, the workshops also help smooth management efforts to instill company mindedness and accommodate employees to restructuring and other management initiatives. YouTube/ChartHouse Learning.

the same: to help employers accommodate workers to managerial priorities. Those priorities have always fluctuated in response to historical circumstances and organizational needs. The products and services sold by ChartHouse and other consultants today are just the latest iteration of over a century of techniques used by management and its allies to encourage workers to view managerial goals like cost cutting and boosting productivity as imperative, even if these objectives work against employees' interests.

Play-based approaches to motivation have become even bigger business in recent years, especially in the form of *gamification*—the integration of game mechanics into organizations and work to increase employee engagement. Gamification takes place principally, though not wholly, online. Games such as FarmVille and Angry Birds, introduced in 2009 and 2010, respectively, were soon taken up by numerous businesses as tools to motivate employees. Typically, the player-worker collects points and "badges" for completion of tasks that are designed around the organization's core ideals (teamwork, customer service, and so on). Gamification is now a big business. Around 70 percent of the employers globally use "gamified applications for employee performance, marketing, and training."[40] The global gamification market was over a $7 billion in 2019 and is projected to increase by nearly a third by 2025 according to more recent projections.[41] Gamification's popularity has prompted bold claims by its devotees, many of who have authored widely read books and are regular speakers in Silicon Valley. As gamification author Gabe Zichermann writes, for example, "smart companies" can increase employee productivity by 40 percent by using gamification. "The Revolution," he asserts, "Will Be Gamified."[42]

Gamification's devotees tout it as a tool of democratization, but its goal is to subtly instill discipline through the distraction of games. This goal is evident when considering the ideas of gamification specialist Yu-kai Chou. One of the wave of gamification innovators who emerged early in the first decade of the twenty-first century, Chou is today known for Octalysis, an eight-component model of motivation that uses "human-focused design" and recent ideas about left brain/right brain processes. As Chou explained in a 2016 presentation at Google, Octalysis works by manipulating workers' emotions, a process that he likens to "a theme park." As he puts it, in a "factory, you're paying these people to sit there and do relatively mundane things. But in the case of a theme park, they're paying [them] to stand in line for hours and hours 'cause they want to enjoy that experience so much."[43] As he adds in the first of ninety Beginner's Guide videos about gamification on YouTube, "Now imagine if you could take all the fun and addicting, motivating elements in a game and combine that with actually productive activities in the real world!"[44]

Despite the excited claims of the high priests of the "gamified revolution," gamification is just another attempt to maximize discipline and productivity while masking the power differentials between workers and managers. This dynamic, we have seen, gained traction during the 1930s when managers tried to bring the motivational properties of Coney Island–type amusements into the factory. Now as then, by tapping humans' predilection for playing games, management seeks to collapse the distinction between work and play and thus render workers more amenable to its goals. As a number of ludic or game theorists have argued, by engaging workers in a perpetual state of amusement, gamification embodies a far more embedded form of employee discipline than was possible in the past.[45] As Mathias Fuchs argues, like neoliberalism, gamification "enhances performance for the ruling system," and its "unconscious motivational processes" are more effective than those that use "persuasion" or "brute force."[46] Although some recent studies emphasize that gamification fuels alienation by eliciting inauthentic expressions of happiness among workers, this poses little concern to management, for whom, we have witnessed, greasing the wheels of employee discipline has overwhelmingly been more important than achieving authentic feelings of motivation among workers.[47]

Not all motivation revolves around play and games. Another device used widely by management today—*employee self-tracking*—marks a supercharged version of the Taylorist approach to work incentivization whereby the worker's body is calibrated to the machinery of production. As many people who work at corporations and universities today know, self-tracking devices are widely used in conjunction with "employee wellness" programs, often as a means to monitor health, and sometimes in conjunction with productivity tools whose function is ostensibly to help workers alleviate stress by helping organize tasks and workflow. In the white-collar workplaces where wellness programs mainly proliferate, self-tracking is thus associated with employee empowerment, a fact that helps management mask its true objectives: instilling discipline and increasing its control over the worker.[48]

Self-tracking in the name of employee wellness takes on a variety of forms. Many employers have begun deploying wearable devices and other sensory technologies to surveil workers. "Mindful" devices and "digital health coaches," for example, log workers' daily physical exercise or productivity. Far from a form of liberation for workers, wellness devices signal the rise of a more prosthetic form of Taylorism. In 2013, 90 percent of employers offered wellness programs to employees, and by 2016, a third of employers provided wearable devices to workers whose stated uses ranged from tracking activity, saving money, and improving employees' health and happiness.[49] In 2015, nearly 600,000 American employers implemented wellness programs that involved having employees use wearable fitness tracking devices, a development that allows an ever-invisible management to monitor workers' behaviors and emotions and to gather an immense body of data on them. As Phoebe Moore observes, "Before too long, it will be possible for employers to literally track our blood, sweat and tears."[50] Moreover, while wellness programs present self-tracking as a choice, many workers participate in them because of an implicit expectation that they conform to organizational norms and because doing so will "auger well with their supervisors." By adhering to these expectations, workers "become implicated in a panoptic mode of surveillance."[51]

In recent years, Amazon has explored the potential of self-tracking devices in order to streamline work and thus increase efficiency in its fulfillment warehouses. In 2018, for example, the corporation submitted a patent for its self-tracking wristband that would follow the worker's every move while working (figure 7.3).[52] According to the proposed patent, the device would track the position of the employee's hand vis-à-vis inventory bins via ultrasonic sound pulses and radio transmissions and vibrate if they engage in "undesirable" movements.[53] Conceived ostensibly to make production and workflow more efficient, the proposed device would allow managers to implement supercharged forms of Taylorism that come closer than ever to rendering workers into robots. Although Amazon has not implemented the device in its warehouses as of spring 2020, its interest in such technologies reveals how far one of the world's most stringent managements is going in developing ideas that may be used in the future to incentivize employees to work more efficiently. Amazon's incentivization techniques are not limited to blue-collar workers. As the *New York Times* reported in a 2015

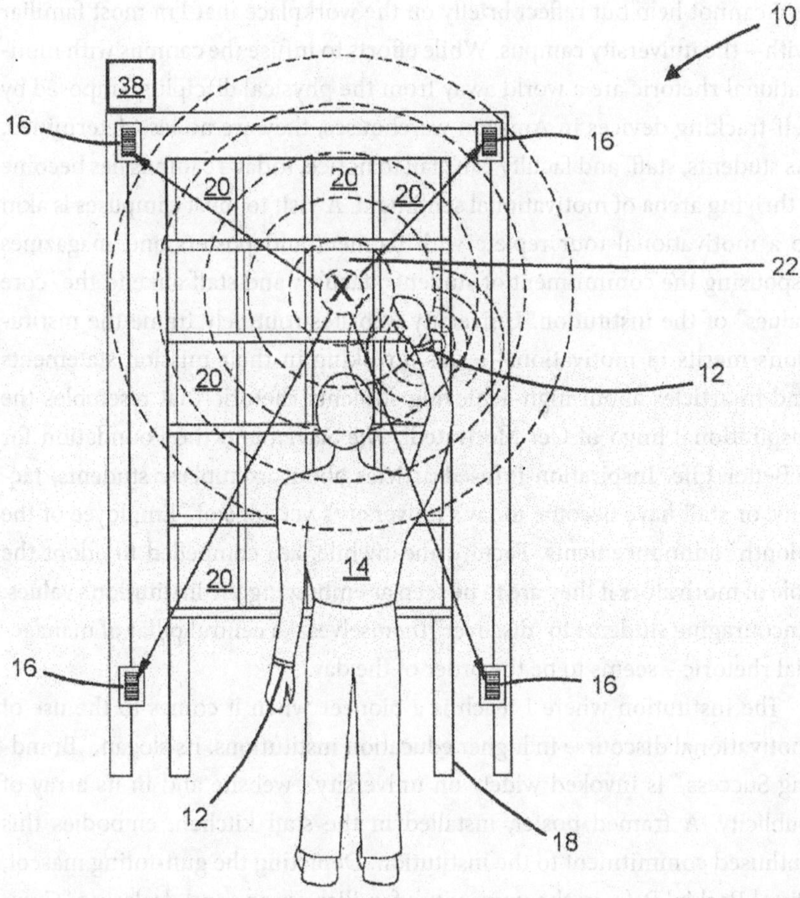

FIGURE 7.3 Taylorism on steroids: an illustration from Amazon's 2018 patent for a wearable self-tracking device for its warehouse workers. The proposed device would track the worker's hand movements and send haptic feedback in the form of an ultrasonic buzz to the worker's wrist if they placed an item in the wrong bay. Amazon Technologies, Inc./United States Patent and Trademark Office, Patent US009881276, January 30, 2018.

exposé, the company's approach to motivation involves "running a continual performance improvement algorithm on its staff" and instilling a culture of intense competition among them. Amazon's "genius," some veterans observe, is "the way it drives them to drive themselves." As one employee stated, "If you're a good Amazonian, you become an Ambot," a name that "means you have become at one with the system."[54]

I cannot help but reflect briefly on the workplace that I'm most familiar with—the university campus. While efforts to infuse the campus with motivational rhetoric are a world away from the physical discipline imposed by self-tracking devices in Amazon warehouses, they are no less determined. As students, staff, and faculty can't fail to notice, today's campus has become a thriving arena of motivational sentiment. A visit to most campuses is akin to a motivational tour replete with banners and posters and magazines espousing the commitment of students, faculty, and staff alike to the "core values" of the institution. University websites routinely frame the institution's merits in motivational terms, invoking in their mission statements and in articles about high-achieving students rhetoric that resembles the inspirational lingo of Get Motivated!, *The Secret*, and the Foundation for a Better Life. Inspiration-infused articles about exemplary students, faculty, or staff have become today's university's versions of "Employee of the Month" announcements. Faculty, meanwhile, are compelled to adopt the role of motivators if they are to be seen as embracing the institution's values. Encouraging students to "discover" themselves—a central pillar of managerial rhetoric—seems to be the order of the day.

The institution where I teach is a pioneer when it comes to the use of motivational discourse in higher education institutions. Its slogan, "Branding Success," is invoked widely on university's website and in its array of publicity. A framed poster, installed in the staff kitchen, embodies this enthused commitment to the institution. Depicting the gun-toting mascot, Pistol Packin' Pete, in the university's familiar orange and declaring "Cowboy Pride Works!," the poster reminds staff and faculty that they are integral players in the institution's mission. I cannot help but notice its similarities with the publicity used by management to instill company mindedness among workers in the twentieth-century factory. Its ebullient slogan echoes the one in the baseball-themed poster from Sheldon-Claire's 1941 workplace campaign, *This is America*, that opens this book (figure 0.1). "Cowboy Pride Works!" is a similarly incontrovertible slogan, one that it would seem inappropriate to question.

However they are packaged—as play, games, wellness, or organizational efficiency—the techniques and sentiment deployed by management today reflect the goals that managers have pursued since the dawn of the motivational project: control over the worker and authority in the workplace.

Today's workplace is increasingly a realm of emotion and bodily management that presents engagement, drive, and the like as integral to work. Although management always wants workers to identify with its messages and adopt its techniques willingly, as I have argued throughout this book, the success of motivational ideology does not hinge on whether workers "believe the message." For management, controlling the official definitions of work and its rewards remains the goal. Even a surface-level acceptance of the inherent value of the ideals espoused by management is enough to keep motivational ideology working.

CONCLUSION

We live today in the shadow of the motivational project. In our workplaces and educational institutions, in public spaces and on the internet, we are exposed regularly to motivational sentiments that can be traced to those first forged by allies of management in the factory in the early decades of the twentieth century. Motivational discourse is no longer confined to the workplace or, indeed, the subject of work. We encounter messages urging us to cultivate determination, ambition, and other motivational ideals just about everywhere. Much of this output bears echoes of the ideas first articulated by businessmen, industrial social scientists, and motivational poster suppliers and later developed by champions of free market capitalism and influential managers. Take a closer look at the posters, banners, and social media circulated by your employer, university, or local businesses today, and you are likely to notice the resemblance. Motivation has, it seems, became the soup in which we swim.

If motivation has grown more multifarious in recent times, its core assertions have nonetheless remained the same: a commitment to industriousness, whether in our work or our personal lives, will make us happier and more successful. Such claims are belied by the fact that even the most sanguine motivational messaging used by employers today says little if anything about work's economic rewards. Aside from the get-rich-quick rhetoric espoused by many success gurus, today's motivational lingo mostly asserts that work will deliver personal fulfillment and self-discovery. This shift reflects work's declining ability to offer economic security.[55] Even so, motivational sentiment continues to exert a powerful hold, urging us to stay or get motivated and to believe in capitalism whatever our job may be.

The illusory nature of motivational rhetoric is evident no more clearly than in our day's most ubiquitous motivational ideologue: Donald Trump. At the core of the image that Trump projects to the world (and a central part of the sales pitch that he made when running for president) is the claim that he is a "self-made" billionaire whose success came from hard work and determination. In a 1990 interview with *Playboy* magazine, he declared, "Rich men are less likely to like me, but the working man likes me because he knows I worked hard and didn't inherit what I've built."[56] Trump reiterated his claim of being self-made during his presidential campaign, asserting that his father had given him a "small loan of a million dollars" and that he "had to pay him back with interest."[57] Yet, for anyone who cares to check, Trump is far from the self-made man he claims to be. His wealth comes mostly from inheritance, tax evasion, money laundering with oligarchs, and marketing his own persona. According to the most in-depth study of how he acquired his wealth, from the time he was a toddler to the present, Trump received from his father the 2018 equivalent of at least $413 million and was a millionaire by the time he was eight. Bailed out by his father during spiraling failures in the 1980s and 1990s, he cultivated the image of a self-made billionaire while dodging millions of dollars in taxes.[58]

While his own wealth was handed to him on a plate, Trump has excelled at selling others on how to achieve success. Trump is not known for espousing the "bootstrap" rhetoric long upheld by Republicans, being more prone to touting his own work ethic. Yet even his claims about success were first crafted by hired hands. One of his highest-selling books, *The Art of the Deal* (1987), was written by somebody else, it turns out. In 2016, its coauthor (more accurately, its ghostwriter), Tony Schwartz, revealed that he wrote every word of it and that all Trump contributed were a few marks on the manuscript in a red felt-tipped marker to indicate passages he wanted to be cut.[59] Trump's penchant for peddling motivational scams is further embodied in Trump University, a venture that amounted to a "multilevel marketing scheme."[60] Like Get Motivated!, Trump University offered a free ninety-minute seminar that served as a hook for getting attendees to sign on for incrementally larger seminars, including the Trump Gold Elite, a package that touted "persona mentorship" by instructors "handpicked by

Trump." As enrollees discovered, Trump University did not offer a degree, and its curriculum consisted of sales and investment materials provided by an unnamed third party that supplies motivational speakers and time-share rental companies.[61] Despite the fraudulent nature of such enterprises, Trump's election revealed that motivational ideologues who promise us the world but give us nothing in return remain as powerful as ever.

In many ways, our era feels like an eerie echo of the motivational crusade of the middle decades of the twentieth century—only worse. Intangible assurances of self-discovery and personal fulfillment seem to be the horizon of what many workers can hope to achieve through work today. However, the motivational bandwagon trundles along unabated, prompting little critical response. The idea that Americans must be perpetually motivated if they are to be successful workers and citizens remains utterly uncontroversial, questioned by a mere handful of critical voices who are almost totally drowned out in the cavalcade of motivational cheerleading that dominates public discourse. To question the motivational mantra, it seems, is an affront to American values and, therefore, outside the realm of polite conversation.

Given that the power of the motivational project shows no signs of subsiding, it is incumbent on us to expose motivational discourse for what it is: a sham promise. In tracing the architecture of the motivational project—its discourse, communications techniques, and ideology—this book takes a step in that direction. Only by asking where the motivational project comes from and why it continues to hold such influence over our lives might we begin to see it for what it is: an apparatus for shoring up managerial hegemony and embedding capitalist values ever more deeply within our consciousness.

NOTES

ABBREVIATIONS

AOF	Archives Organization File, Kheel Center for Labor-Management Documentation and Archives, Cornell University, Ithaca, NY
CHRC	Charles H. Rosenfeld Collection, University of Chicago Special Collections Research Center, Chicago, IL
DGR	Dearborn Group Records, Kheel Center for Labor-Management Documentation and Archives, Cornell University, Ithaca, NY
FMM	*Factory Management and Maintenance*
HRNC	Herbert R. Northrup Collection of Boulwarism Research Materials, Kislak Center, University of Pennsylvania, Philadelphia, PA
LBP	Lemuel Boulware Papers, Kislak Center for Special Collections, Rare Books and Manuscripts, University of Pennsylvania, Philadelphia, PA
NAM	National Association of Manufacturers Collection, Hagley Museum and Library, Wilmington, DE
OWI	Office of War Information Collection, National Archives, College Park, MD
PFEB	Francis Edwin Brennan Papers, Library of Congress, Washington, D.C.
PHFP	Henry F. Pringle Papers, Library of Congress, Washington, D.C.
RSCC, NMAH	Records of the Sheldon-Claire Company, National Museum of American History, Smithsonian Institution, Washington, D.C.
SCSC	Sheldon-Claire Company sales conference
WWE	"World-Wide Endorsements and Acknowledgements of Sheldon-Claire Services"

INTRODUCTION

1. The motivational or self-improvement industry was valued at nearly $11 billion a year as of 2018 and is projected to grow to almost $14 billion by 2023. See John LaRosa, "$11 Billion Self-Improvement Market Is Growing," October 16, 2019, https://www.marketdataenterprises.com/11-billion-self-improvement-market-is-growing-by-john-larosa/. See also Barbara Ehrenreich, *Bright-Sided: How Positive Thinking Is Undermining America* (New York: Picador, 2009), chap. 4, and Jonathan Black, *Yes You Can! Behind the Hype and Hustle of the Motivation Biz* (New York: Bloomsbury Publishing, 2006).

2. Assertions of the superior virtues of American ideals of work and productivity formed a central pillar of U.S. quests for ideological dominance in Europe after World War II. See Victoria de Grazia, *Irresistible Empire: America's Advance through Twentieth-Century Europe* (Cambridge, MA: Belknap Press of Harvard University Press, 2005), chap. 7. See also Anthony Carew, *Labour under the Marshall Plan: The Politics of Productivity and the Marketing of Management Science* (Manchester, U.K.: Manchester University Press, 1987).

3. On the long quest to promote the work ethic and work ideology, see Reinhold Bendix, *Work and Authority in Industry: Ideologies of Management in the Course of Industrialization* (New York: Harper, 1956), 281–340, and Sharon Beder, *Selling the Work Ethic: From Puritan Pulpit to Corporate PR* (New York: Zed Books, 2000).

4. Exemplars of this work include Hugo Münsterberg, *Psychology and Industrial Efficiency* (Boston: Houghton Mifflin, 1913); Walter Dill Scott, *Increasing Human Efficiency in Business: A Contribution to the Psychology of Business* (New York: Macmillan, 1912); and Ordway Tead, *Instincts in Industry: A Study of Working-Class Psychology* (Boston: Houghton Mifflin, 1918).

5. On businessmen's quests for power and assaults on labor, see Elizabeth Fones-Wolf, *Selling Free Enterprise: The Business Assault on Labor and Liberalism, 1945–1960* (Urbana: University of Illinois Press, 1994), and Kim Phillips-Fein, *Invisible Hands: The Businessman's Crusade against the New Deal* (New York: W. W. Norton, 2009). On neoliberalism and industry, see David Harvey, *The Condition of Postmodernity: An Enquiry into the Origins of Cultural Change* (Cambridge, MA: Blackwell Publishers, 1990), chaps. 8 and 9.

6. As several scholars gave shown, managers' interest in emotions (or, more accurately, their efforts to use workers' emotional needs and desires to advance managerial prerogatives), has a long and complex history. As relevant studies are cited in the notes for the forthcoming chapters, I shall not list them here to avoid repetition. The shift from the body to the mind in managerial efforts to discipline and control workers is

examined at length in Gerard Hanlon, *The Dark Side of Management: A Secret History of Management Theory* (New York: Routledge, 2016), esp. chap. 6.

7. Businessmen's gradual embrace of images is detailed in T. J. Jackson Lears, *No Place of Grace: Antimodernism and the Transformation of American Culture, 1880–1920* (Chicago: University of Chicago Press, 1981). The adoption of images by managers and employers is examined in Stuart Ewen, *PR! A Social History of Spin* (New York: Basic Books, 1996); Roland Marchand, *Creating the Corporate Soul: The Rise of Public Relations and Corporate Imagery in American Big Business* (Berkeley: University of California Press, 1998); and David Nye, *Image Worlds: Corporate Identities at General Electric, 1890–1930* (Cambridge: MIT Press, 1985). On management communication techniques before this embrace of images, see JoAnne Yates, *Control through Communication: The Rise of System in American Management* (Baltimore: Johns Hopkins University Press, 1989).

8. Godfrey Hodgson, *America in Our Time: From World War II to Nixon, What Happened and Why* (New York: Vintage, 1978), 81–82.

9. On the racial roots of industrial social science, see Mark Pittenger, *Class Unknown: Undercover Investigations of American Work and Poverty from the Progressive Era to the Present* (New York: New York University Press, 2012). The effects of Anglo-Saxonism and whiteness on discourse about labor are detailed in Matthew Frye Jacobson, *Barbarian Virtues: The United States Encounters Foreign Peoples at Home and Abroad, 1876–1917* (New York: Hill and Wang, 2001), chap. 2.

10. The most influential critique of this sort from the era is Smedley D. Butler, *War Is a Racket: The Antiwar Classic by America's Most Decorated Soldier* (Los Angeles: Feral House, 2003 [1935]).

11. Marchand, *Creating the Corporate Soul*; Fones-Wolf, *Selling Free Enterprise*; Phillips-Fein, *Invisible Hands*. See also William L. Bird, *A Better Living: Advertising, Media, and the New Vocabulary of Business Leadership, 1935–1955* (Evanston, IL: Northwestern University Press, 1999). Television also played a powerful role in the efforts of free enterprise proponents to undermine New Deal liberalism. See Anna McCarthy, *The Citizen Machine: Governing by Television in 1950s America* (New York: New Press, 2010), esp. 10–23.

12. Miya Tokumitsu, *Do What You Love: And Other Lies about Success and Happiness* (New York: Regan Arts, 2015).

13. Michel Foucault, "Truth and Power," in *Power/Knowledge: Selected Interviews and Other Writings, 1972–1977*, ed. Colin Gordon (New York: Pantheon Books, 1980), 109–33; Sverre Raffnsøe, Andrea Mennicken, and Peter Miller, "The Foucault Effect in Organization Studies," *Organization Studies* 40, no. 2 (December 2019): 155–82; Nikolas Rose, *Inventing Our Selves: Psychology, Power, and Personhood* (Cambridge,

U.K.: Cambridge University Press, 1996). For an account of management governance of workers at corporations, see Megan Brown, *The Cultural Work of Corporations* (New York: Palgrave Macmillan, 2009), esp. chap. 4.

14. For insights into this important history and, in turn, my arguments about motivation in this book, see Teresa Brennan, *The Transmission of Affect* (Ithaca, NY: Cornell University Press, 2004), chap. 1; Eva Illouz, *Cold Intimacies: The Making of Emotional Capitalism* (Cambridge, U.K.: Polity Press, 2007); Simon Williams, *Emotion and Social Theory: Corporeal Reflections on the (Ir)Rational* (London: Sage Publications, 2001); William Davies, *The Happiness Industry: How the Government and Big Business Sold Us Well-Being* (New York: Verso, 2017); Frank Biess and Daniel M. Gross, eds., *Science and Emotions after 1945: A Transatlantic Perspective* (Chicago: University of Chicago Press, 2014); and Samantha Warren, "'Show Me How It Feels to Work Here': Using Photography to Research Organizational Aesthetics," *Ephemera: Critical Dialogues on Organization* 2, no. 3 (2002): 226.

15. See Walton Rawls, *Wake Up America! World War I and the American Poster* (New York: Abbeville, 2001); James Aulich, *War Posters: Weapons of Mass Communication* (London: Thames and Hudson, 2011); and Pearl James, ed., *Picture This: World War I Posters and Visual Culture* (Lincoln: University of Nebraska Press, 2009).

16. Jacques Ellul, *Propaganda: The Formation of Men's Attitudes* (New York: Vintage Books, 1973 [1962]). On "political propaganda," see 62–70. On behavior, see 20–25. On Ellul's persuasive debunking of the assumption that propaganda must convince its audience of its claims in order to be effective, as well as on how sociological propaganda operates through unconscious processes, see the appendix to "Effectiveness of Propaganda," 259–302. On social conditioning, see 33–43.

17. Jackson Lears and Roland Marchand show that advertising had a profound effect on modernity in America, regardless of the fact that specialists had only a weak understanding of how advertisements influenced individuals. T. J. Jackson Lears, *Fables of Abundance: A Cultural History of Advertising in America* (New York: Basic Books, 1994), and Marchand, *Creating the Corporate Soul*. On visual education and visualization in industry, see Elizabeth Wiatr, "Between Word, Image, and the Motion Picture: Visual Education and Films of Industrial Process," *Historical Journal of Film, Radio and Television* 22, no. 3 (2002): 333–51, and Lee Grieveson, "Visualizing Industrial Citizenship," in *Learning with the Lights Off: Educational Film in the United States*, ed. Devin Orgeron, Marsha Orgeron, and Dan Streible (Oxford: Oxford University Press, 2019), 107–23.

18. Helena Flam, "The Transatlantic Element in the Sociology of Emotions," in Biess and Gross, *Science and Emotions after 1945*, 18.

19. During the 1960s and 1970s, labor historians who worked on gender encountered resistance when arguing that discourse analysis should be given greater attention

in labor history, largely due to the field's traditional commitments to empiricism. This tendency continued into the 1990s. See Leonard Berlanstein, ed., *Rethinking Labor History: Essays on Discourse and Class Analysis* (Urbana: University of Chicago Press, 1993), esp. Berlanstein's introduction (1–14). Later scholarship suggests that labor history is becoming more accommodating of discourse analysis. See Donna T. Haverty and Daniel J. Walkowitz, eds., *Rethinking Labor History: Essays on the Working-Class Experience, 1756–2009* (New York: Continuum, 2010), esp. the introduction. For a discussion of the tensions between social/labor history and discourse that also seeks to reconcile these tensions, see Geoff Eley and Keith Nield, *The Future of Class in History: What's Left of the Social?* (Ann Arbor: University of Michigan Press, 2007). See also *American Capitalism: Social Thought and Political Economy in the Twentieth Century*, ed. Nelson Lichtenstein (Philadelphia: University of Pennsylvania Press), 2006. This volume includes several articles that examine management and business ideologies in relation to work.

20. Arlie Hochschild, *The Managed Heart: Commercialization of Human Feeling* (Berkeley: University of California Press, 2003 [1983]).

21. Analysis of the role of visual images and aesthetics in influencing emotions and behavior in the workplace has now become a major field in the study of work. See, for example, Emma Bell, Samantha Warren, and Jonathan Schroeder, eds., *The Routledge Companion to Visual Organization* (New York: Routledge, 2014). Importantly, as Tim Strangleman argues in the same volume, the "sociology of work" has long emphasized the ways that images influence work and perceptions of work, but this legacy has often been overlooked. Tim Strangleman, "Visual Sociology and Work Organization: An Historical Approach," 243–58. On game-based "employee-motivation" tools, see Rajat Paharia, *Loyalty 3.0: How to Revolutionize Customer and Employee Engagement with Big Data and Gamification* (New York: McGraw-Hill, 2013).

22. Williams, *Emotion and Social Theory*, 3. Studies of the history of motivation by management scholars, no less than labor and cultural historians, have largely ignored the kind of motivational rhetoric and ideology examined in this book. Management school scholars have focused mainly on the history of formal research studies of motivation. See, for example, Gary P. Latham, *Work Motivation: History, Theory, Research, and Practice* (Thousand Oaks, CA: Sage Publications, 2007).

23. For persuasive accounts of the ways in which the behaviors of individuals in organizations are influenced unconsciously, see John A. Bargh, introduction to *Social Psychology and the Unconscious: The Automaticity of Higher Mental Processes*, ed. John A. Bargh (New York: Psychology Press, 2007), 1–9, and James S. Uleman, "Introduction: Becoming Aware of the New Unconscious," in *The New Unconscious*, ed. Ran R. Hassin, James S. Uleman, and John A. Bargh (Oxford: Oxford University Press, 2005), 3–18.

24. Ellul, *Propaganda*, xvi.

CHAPTER 1: MOTIVATION, MANAGEMENT, AND INDUSTRIAL MODERNITY

1. Elbert Hubbard, *A Message to Garcia* (1899; repr., East Aurora, NY: Roycroft, 1916), 164. Hubbard omitted the accent in García in the essay's title and its text. I have retained this style when quoting from both.

2. Jules Zanger, "'A Message to Garcia': The Subsidized Hero," *American Studies* 20, no. 1 (Spring 1979): 99–108.

3. The influence of "A Message to Garcia" and other writings by Hubbard on publicity disseminated to workers by employers is discussed in a biography by his former general manager and friend, Felix Shay. Felix Shay, *Elbert Hubbard of East Aurora* (New York: Wise, 1926), esp. 110–11 and 159–63. On Hubbard's influence on businessmen, see T. J. Jackson Lears, *No Place of Grace: Antimodernism and the Transformation of American Culture, 1880–1920* (Chicago: University of Chicago Press, 1981), chap. 2.

4. My insights into the history of managerial efforts to exploit communication tools are informed by several studies, including Stuart Ewen, *PR! A Social History of Spin* (New York: Basic Books, 1996); Roland Marchand, *Creating the Corporate Soul: The Rise of Public Relations and Corporate Imagery in American Big Business* (Berkeley: University of California Press, 1998); and David Nye, *Image Worlds: Corporate Identities at General Electric, 1890–1930* (Cambridge, MA: MIT Press, 1985).

5. Alfred J. Chandler, *The Visible Hand: The Managerial Revolution in American Business* (Cambridge, MA: Belknap Press of Harvard University Press, 1977).

6. See Elspeth Brown, *The Corporate Eye: Photography and the Rationalization of American Commercial Culture, 1884–1929* (Baltimore, MD: Johns Hopkins University Press, 2005), chap. 1.

7. On workers' use of strikes and employers responses to them in the late nineteenth and early twentieth centuries, see David Montgomery, *The Fall of the House of Labor: The Workplace, the State, and American Labor Activism, 1865–1925* (Cambridge: Cambridge University Press, 1987), and Jeremy Brecher, *Strike!*, revised, expanded, and updated ed. (Oakland, CA: PM Press, 2014 [1972]), chaps. 1–4.

8. Marchand, *Creating the Corporate Soul.*

9. Progressives' concerns over and critiques of industry's effects on workers are detailed in Daniel T. Rodgers, *The Work Ethic in Industrial America, 1850–1920* (Chicago: University of Chicago Press, 1974), chap. 2.

10. Rodgers, *Work Ethic in Industrial America*, chap. 4. On the accommodating stance of progressives toward industrialization, see Robert H. Wiebe, *The Search for Order, 1877–1920* (New York: Hill and Wang, 1967), chap. 6, and Lears, *No Place of Grace*, chap. 6.

11. Rodgers, *Work Ethic in Industrial America*, 83.

12. Joel M. Winkelman, "A Working Democracy: Progressivism and the Politics of Work" (PhD diss., University of North Carolina, 2012), 93, 86.

13. Reinhold Bendix, *Work and Authority in Industry: Ideologies of Management in the Course of Industrialization* (New York: Harper, 1956), 263–65. On success literature in the late nineteenth and early twentieth centuries, see Judy Hilkey, *Character Is Capital: Success Manuals and Manhood in Gilded Age America* (Chapel Hill: University of North Carolina Press, 1997).

14. The roots, development, and consequences of the "human factor" in industry are detailed extensively in Bruce E. Kaufman, *Managing the Human Factor: The Early Years of Human Resource Management in American Industry* (Ithaca, NY: ILR Press of Cornell University Press, 2008). On personnel management, which couched the management of the labor force in humanistic discourse, see Sanford Jacoby, *Employing Bureaucracy: Managers, Unions, and the Transformation of Work in American Industry, 1900–1945* (New York: Columbia University Press, 1985).

15. For Taylor's most influential work on the subject, see Frederick Winslow Taylor, *The Principles of Scientific Management* (New York: Harper & Brothers Publishers, 1911).

16. See Richard Gillespie, *Manufacturing Knowledge: A History of the Hawthorne Experiments* (Cambridge: Cambridge University Press, 1993), 11–12. On the development and influence of scientific management, see Daniel Nelson, *Managers and Workers: Origins of the Twentieth-Century Factory System in the United States, 1880–1920* (Madison: University of Wisconsin Press, 1995), chap. 4, and Gerard Hanlon, *The Dark Side of Management: A Secret History of Management Theory* (New York: Routledge, 2016), 102–17.

17. See Carl Cederström and Andre Spicer, *The Wellness Syndrome* (Malden, MA: Polity, 2015).

18. See Daniel A. Wren and Arthur G. Bedeian, *The Evolution of Management Thought*, 6th ed. (Hoboken, NJ: John Wiley & Sons, 2009), chap. 9; Sanford Jacoby, *Modern Manors: Welfare Capitalism since the New Deal* (Princeton, NJ: Princeton University Press, 1997), chap. 1; and Kaufman, *Managing the Human Factor*, 75–86.

19. Jacoby, *Modern Manors*, 15.

20. Terry Smith, *Making the Modern: Industry, Art, and Design in America* (Chicago: University of Chicago Press, 1993), 47–55. Quote from page 53.

21. See T. J. Jackson Lears, *Fables of Abundance: A Cultural History of Advertising in America* (New York: Basic, 1994), 261–98.

22. See Nikki Mandell, *The Corporation as Family: The Gendering of Corporate Welfare, 1890–1930* (Chapel Hill: University of North Carolina Press, 2002), and Nye, *Image Worlds*, 85.

23. Andrea Tone, *The Business of Benevolence: Industrial Paternalism in Progressive America* (Ithaca, NY: Cornell University Press, 1997), 105.

24. As David Nye points out in a case study of General Electric during this time, industrial photographs included many kinds of images and did not amount to a single or coherent ideology; instead, they allowed the corporation to craft and present its image to different audiences, including engineers, workers, managers, and consumers. Nye, *Image Worlds*, introduction.

25. Larry Peterson, "Producing Visual Traditions among Pullman Workers: The Uses of Photography at Pullman," Special Issue: Tradition and the Working Class, *International Labor and Working-Class History*, no. 42 (Fall 1992): 40.

26. For insights into the *Pittsburgh Survey* and the rise of "visual education," see Yann Giraud and Loïc Charles, "Economics for the Masses: The Visual Display of Economic Knowledge in the United States (1910–1945)," *History of Political Economy* 45, no. 4 (Winter 2013): 567–610.

27. See, for example, Frederick Sanger, "The Making of Right-Hand Men: VII Developing an Office Manager," *System, the Magazine of Business*, July 1915, 46–53.

28. *System, the Magazine of Business*, September 1915, 226.

29. At this juncture, some industrial psychologists, working from nineteenth-century phrenology, claimed that there was little point in trying to condition workers because their aptitudes were biologically fixed. See Brown, *Corporate Eye*, chap. 1, for an extensive and illuminating discussion.

30. See Kaufman, *Managing the Human Factor*, 110–35, and Wren and Bedeian, *Evolution of Management Thought*, 192–200.

31. Taylor, *Principles of Scientific Management*, 119, 131; Wren and Bedeian, *Evolution of Management Thought*, chap. 9.

32. Walter Dill Scott, *Increasing Human Efficiency in Business: A Contribution to the Psychology of Business* (New York: Macmillan, 1911). On "competition," "concentration," and "wages," see 48–74, 104–31, and 132–64, respectively. The quotes are from 186 and 234.

33. On Scott's influence in industrial psychology, see Edmund C. Lynch, "Walter Dill Scott: Pioneer Industrial Psychologist," *Business History Review* 42, no. 2 (Summer 1968): 149–70.

34. Brown, *Corporate Eye*, 47–51.

35. Hugo Münsterberg, *Psychology and Industrial Efficiency* (Boston: Houghton Mifflin, 1913), 190.

36. Münsterberg, *Psychology*, 234.

37. See, for example, Gary P. Latham, *Work Motivation: History, Theory, Research, and Practice* (Thousand Oaks, CA: Sage Publications, 2007), 9–11.

38. On the rise of personnel departments in the 1910s, see Kaufman, *Managing the Human Factor*, chap. 4, and Jacoby, *Employing Bureaucracy*, 102–4, 142, and 164–65.

39. See Nelson, *Managers and Workers*, chap. 3. From the middle of the decade onward, management magazines began to pay more attention to the psychological dimensions of the foreman's work. See, for example, the two-part series in *American Machinist*: C. B. Lord, "Personality in the Shop—Psychology of the Foreman I," *American Machinist*, February 25, 1915, 315–16, and C. B. Lord, "Personality in the Shop—Psychology of the Foreman II," *American Machinist*, March 11, 1915, 421–22.

40. On the "new foremanship" and its limits, see Kaufman, *Managing the Human Factor*, 129, and Jacoby, *Modern Manors*, 22.

41. Image from *Industrial Management*, November 1918, 67. On the foreman's responsibilities, including "diplomacy," "tact," and similar skills, see Fred H. Colvin, "The Foreman and His Job," *American Machinist*, January 20, 1921, 81–82.

42. The Wilson administration's broadly supportive stance toward labor and Wilson's pursuit of labor-friendly legislation is discussed in Joseph McCartin, *Labor's Great War: The Struggle for Industrial Democracy and the Origins of Modern American Labor Relations, 1912–1921* (Chapel Hill: University of North Carolina Press, 1997). As McCartin notes (34), the most consequential of the labor laws passed by Wilson were the La Follette Seamen's Act, the Keating-Owens Child Labor Act, the Kern-McGillicuddy Federal Employees' Compensation Act, and the Adamson Act.

43. See James Robert Mock and Cedric Larson, *Words That Won the War: The Story of the Committee on Public Information* (Princeton, NJ: Princeton University Press, 1939), chap. 8.

44. Creel quoted in Alan Axelrod, *Selling the Great War: The Making of American Propaganda* (New York: Palgrave Macmillan, 2009), xi. The figures and CPI usage of "people's war" and "capital's war" are quoted from Mock and Larson, *Words That Won the War*, 162, 169.

45. Mock and Larson, *Words That Won the War*, 187–89.

46. Axelrod, *Selling the Great War*, 142–43. Reference to "people's war" from Mock and Larson, 162, 169. On the CPI's approach to posters, see also Mock and Larson, *Words That Won the War*, chaps. 4 and 8; Walton Rawls, *Wake Up, America! World War I and the American Poster* (New York: Abbeville Press, 1988), chap. 6; and Stewart Halsey Ross, *Propaganda for War: How the United States Was Conditioned to Fight in the Great War of 1914–1918* (Jefferson, NC: McFarland, 1996), chap. 5.

47. Quoted in Kaufman, *Managing the Human Factor*, 59.

48. Joseph A. McCartin, "'An American Feeling': Workers, Managers, and the Struggle over Industrial Democracy in the World War I Era," in *Industrial Democracy in America: The Ambiguous Promise, ed.* Nelson Lichtenstein and Howell John Harris (New York: Cambridge University Press, 1996), 76.

49. Mock and Larson, *Words That Won the War*, 191, 197–98.

50. McCartin, *Labor's Great War*, 67–68.

51. "Selling the War to the Working Man," *Printers' Ink*, February 14, 1918, 69–82.

52. Michael J. Hickey, "What the Industrial Conservation Move Is Doing," *Michigan Manufacturer and Financial Record*, February 2, 1918, 4. See also George Weiss, "Bridging the Chasm between Capital and Labor," *Forum*, November 1916, 633–40.

53. Lynch, "Walter Dill Scott," quoted in Nelson, *Managers and Workers*, 164.

54. See Kaufman, *Managing the Human Factor*, 164–74, and Jacoby, *Employing Bureaucracy*, chap. 5.

55. The YMCA's *Among Industrial Workers (1916)* listed around fifty large companies currently using "industry" films. It also listed numerous organizations that loaned films and portable motion picture machines, lantern slides, and visual exhibits focused on health and safety, saving, thrift, and other aspects of industrial education. *Among Industrial Workers (Ways and Means): A Hand Book for Associations in Industrial Fields* (New York: Industrial Department, International Committee Young Man's Christian Associations, 1916), 70–97. On the educational film industry and industrial films, see Anthony Slide, *Before Video: A History of the Non-Theatrical Film* (New York: Greenwood Press, 1992), esp. chaps. 1 and 2.

56. See Lee Grieveson, "Visualizing Industrial Citizenship," in *Learning with the Lights Off: Educational Film in the United States*, ed. Devin Orgeron, Marsha Orgeron, and Dan Streible (Oxford: Oxford University Press, 2019), 107–23. On the use of industrial films in schools and factories, see Elizabeth Wiatr, "Between Word, Image, and the Machine: Visual Education and Films of Industrial Process," *Historical Journal of Film, Radio and Television* 22, no. 3 (2002): 333–51. On visualization in the films of Frank B. Gilbreth, see Scott Curtis, "Images of Efficiency: The Films of Frank B. Gilbreth," in *Films That Work: Industrial Film and the Productivity of Media*, ed. Vinzenz Hediger and Patrick Vonderau (Amsterdam: Amsterdam University Press, 2009), 85–99.

57. *Reel and Slide*, January 1919, 19; DeVry ad on p. 48.

58. "Free Factory Movie Exhibitions," *Furniture Manufacturer and Artisan*, November 19, 1919, 243.

59. "Free Factory Movie Exhibitions." The word *employe* (with one *e*) was used widely in management circles well into the 1950s, when *employee* became more prevalent. I have retained original spellings in quotations here and throughout the book.

60. Heide Solbrig, "Film and Function: A History of Industrial Motivation Film" (PhD diss., University of California, 2004), esp. chaps. 1–2. See also Wiatr, "Between Word, Image, and the Machine."

61. H. L. Clarke, "Visual Education as a Constructive Force in Industry," *Visual Education*, September–October 1920, 12–13.

62. Slide, *Before Video*, chap. 2.

63. Chicago was also home to the Society of Visual Education and the National School of Visual Education. See Orgeron, Orgeron, and Streible, "A History of Learning with the Lights Off," in their edited volume, *Learning with the Lights Off*,

48. Beginning in the 1910s, organizations that sold salesman training literature and correspondence course materials considered visualization an important sales technique. See Arthur F. Sheldon, *The Art of Selling* (Chicago: Sheldon School, 1911), 112, 120, 142–43; Walter H. Cottingham, "Selling—the Lifeblood of Business," *Personal Salesmanship: Students' Business Book Series* (Chicago: A. W. Shaw, 1909), 10; and Thomas Herbert Russell, *Salesmanship Theory and Practice* (Chicago: Washington Institute, 1910), 239. On Chicago's dominant role in industrial sociology, see Andrew Abbott, "Organizations and the Chicago School," in *The Oxford Handbook of Sociology and Organizational Studies*, ed. Paul Adler (Oxford: Oxford University Press, 2009), 399–420. On the proliferation of the field of industrial psychology in Chicago, see Morris Viteles, *Industrial Psychology* (New York: Norton, 1932), 44.

64. George J. Zehrung, "Taking the Cinema to Mill and Shop," *Reel and Slide*, January 1919, 19 (my emphasis).

65. William J. Banning quoted in Ewen, *PR!*, 195–96.

66. E. P. Corbett, "Selling Goods by Illustrated Lectures," *Reel and Slide*, February 1919, 9, quoted in Sean Savage, "The Eye Beholds: Silent Era Industrial Film and the Bureau of Commercial Economics" (master's thesis, New York University, 2006), 8.

CHAPTER 2: QUESTS TO SHAPE THE WORKER'S MIND

1. See, for example, Carleton H. Parker, "Motives in Economic Life," *American Economic Review* 8, no. 1 (March 1918): 212–14; Carleton H. Parker, *The Casual Laborer, and Other Essays* (New York: Harcourt, Brace and Howe, 1920); and Daniel Bloomfield, ed., *Employment Management* (New York: H. W. Wilson, 1919).

2. Exemplars include Ordway Tead, *Instincts in Industry: A Study of Working-Class Psychology* (Boston: Houghton Mifflin, 1918), and Lionel D. Edie, *Principles of the New Economics* (New York: Thomas Y. Cromwell, 1922). On the development and influence of instinct theory, see Malcolm Rutherford, *The Institutionalist Movement in American Economics, 1918–1947: Science and Social Control* (Cambridge: Cambridge University Press), chap. 1, and Christian Cordes, "The Role of 'Instincts' in the Development of Corporate Cultures," *Journal of Economic Issues* 41, no. 3 (September 2007): 747–64. On Veblen's theory, see Thorstein Veblen, *The Instinct of Workmanship and the State of the Industrial Arts* (New York: Macmillan, 1914).

3. Edward L. Bernays, *Propaganda* (New York: Liveright Publishing, 1928), 9. On Bernays and the influence of his work, see Stuart Ewen, *PR! A Social History of Spin* (New York: Basic Books, 1996).

4. On management's shift from bodily discipline to mental manipulation, see Gerard Hanlon, *The Dark Side of Management: A Secret History of Management Theory* (New York: Routledge, 2016).

5. See Frederick Lewis Allen, *Only Yesterday: An Informal History of the 1920s* (New York: Harper Perennial, 2010 [1931]), and T. J. Jackson Lears, "From Salvation to Self-Realization: Advertising and the Roots of the Consumer Culture, 1880–1930," in *The Culture of Consumption: Critical Essays in American History, 1880–1980*, ed. Richard Wightman Fox and T. J. Jackson Lears (New York: Pantheon, 1983), 1–38. Interest in the restorative effects of motivation was influenced partly by the veteran rehabilitation movement. Throughout the interwar period, the state and civic organizations embarked on a wide-ranging campaign to rehabilitate disabled World War I veterans that echoed aspects of industrial motivation, not least the use of emotion-based propaganda. On the rehabilitation movement, see John M. Kinder, *Paying with Their Bodies: American War and the Problem of the Disabled Veteran* (Chicago: University of Chicago Press, 2015), esp. chap. 4. Many specialists whose work influenced theories about motivation in industry first researched morale and motives in studies of injured soldiers, not least, Walter Dill Scott. See Edmund C. Lynch, "Walter Dill Scott: Pioneer Industrial Psychologist," *Business History Review* 42, no. 2 (Summer 1968): 149–70.

6. For a detailed discussion of management efforts to resolve the "labor problem" in the 1920s, see Bruce Kaufman, *Managing the Human Factor: The Early Years of Human Resource Management in American Industry* (Ithaca, NY: ILR Press of Cornell University Press, 2008), chap. 5.

7. For further insights into management's enlistment of psychology and use of psychological discourse during this time, see Loren Baritz, *The Servants of Power: A History of the Use of Social Science in American Industry* (Middletown, CT: Wesleyan University Press, 1960), chap. 4, and Reinhold Bendix, *Work and Authority in Industry: Ideologies of Management in the Course of Industrialization* (New York: Harper, 1956), 281–97.

8. For an excellent account of the development of instinct theory, see Pier Francesco Asso and Luca Fiorito, "Human Nature and Economic Institutions: Instinct Psychology, Behaviorism, and the Development of American Institutionalism," *Journal of the History of Economic Thought* 26, no. 4 (December 2004): 445–77.

9. Parker, "Motives in Economic Life," 212, 14.

10. Parker, "Motives in Economic Life," 220, 227. An illustration of Parker's elite-minded distaste for labor unions (and one that typifies instinct theorists' stance on unions and workers more generally) is provided by Don Mitchell, who examines Parker's work heading the California State Immigration and Housing Commission's investigation of the Wheatland Riot of August 1913. While allowing that the employer, E. C. Durst, fueled the riot by engaging in wage suppression and failing to provide sanitary toilets and drinking water for workers, Parker described workers as "maladjusted," concluding that the strike occurred largely because of the "abnormal"

psychology and "pugnacious instincts" of workers and the Industrial Workers of the World. See Don Mitchell, *The Lie of the Land: Migrant Workers and the California Landscape* (Minneapolis: University of Minnesota Press, 1996), 46–51.

11. Tead, *Instincts in Industry*, 148.

12. Tead, x, xiv, 30–31, 67–85, 94–95, 113–14.

13. For a detailed analysis of Williams's book, see Mark Pittenger, *Class Unknown: Undercover Investigations of American Work and Poverty from the Progressive Era to the Present* (New York: New York University Press, 2012), chap. 2.

14. Whiting Williams, *What's on the Worker's Mind: By One Who Put on Overalls to Find Out* (New York: Charles Scribner's Sons, 1921), 294.

15. Exemplars of the criticism of instinct theory include Knight Dunlap, "Are There Any Instincts?" *Journal of Abnormal Psychology* 14, no. 5, (December 1919): 307–11, and A. J. Snow, "Psychology in Economic Theory," *Journal of Political Economy* 32, no. 4 (August 1924): 487–96. These authors did not dispute the claim that psychology was important in workers' emotions, however.

16. Rutherford, *Institutionalist Movement*, 125. On Chicago's role in the institutionalist movement, see chap. 5. See also Geoffrey M. Hodgson, "Instinct and Habit before Reason: Comparing the Views of John Dewey, Friedrich Hayek and Thorstein Veblen," in *Cognition and Economics*, ed. Elisabeth Krecké, Carine Krecké, and Roger G. Koppl, vol. 9 of *Advances in Austrian Economics* (Bingley, U.K.: Emerald, 2007), 109–43.

17. On welfare capitalism, see Roland Marchand, *Creating the Corporate Soul: The Rise of Public Relations and Corporate Imagery in American Big Business* (Berkeley: University of California Press, 1998); Lizabeth Cohen, *Making a New Deal: Industrial Workers in Chicago, 1919–1939* (Cambridge: Cambridge University Press, 1990); and Gerald Zahavi, *Workers, Managers, and Welfare Capitalism: The Shoeworkers and Tanners of Endicott Johnson, 1890–1950* (Urbana: University of Illinois Press, 1988).

18. See Richard Gillespie, *Manufacturing Knowledge: A History of the Hawthorne Experiments* (Cambridge: Cambridge University Press, 1993), and Baritz, *The Servants of Power*, chaps. 5 and 6.

19. Many historians have challenged the view that researchers "discovered" the influence of emotion in the workplace during the Hawthorne Studies. See Gillespie, *Manufacturing Knowledge*, and John. S. Hassard, "Rethinking the Hawthorne Studies: The Western Electric Research in Its Social, Political and Historical Context," *Human Relations* 65, no. 11 (November 2012): 1431–61. As Kyle Bruce argues, human relations was, in many ways, more exploitative of workers than scientific management. The Taylor Society, he points out, included a strong progressive wing, whereas human relations was largely aligned with conservative managerial goals. Kyle Bruce, "Democracy or Seduction? The Demonization of Scientific Management and the

Deification of Human Relations," in *The Right and Labor in America: Politics, Ideology, and Imagination*, ed. Nelson Lichtenstein (Philadelphia: University of Pennsylvania Press, 2012), 42–76.

20. Robert H. Zieger, "Herbert Hoover, the Wage-Earner, and the 'New Economic System,' 1919–1929," *Business History Review* 51, no. 2 (Summer 1977): 165; Robert H. Zieger, "Solving the Labor Problem: Herbert Hoover and the American Worker in the 1920s," in *Herbert Hoover Reassessed: Essays Commemorating the Fiftieth Anniversary of the Inauguration of Our Thirty-First President*, comp. Arthur Link (Washington, D.C.: United States Government Printing Office, 1981), 177–87; David M. Hart, "Herbert Hoover's Last Laugh: The Enduring Significance of the 'Associative State' in the United States," *Journal of Policy History* 10, no. 4 (October 1998): 419–44.

21. David Brody, *Labor Embattled: History, Power, Rights* (Urbana and Chicago: University of Illinois Press, 2005, chap. 5.

22. Irving Bernstein, *The Lean Years: A History of the American Worker, 1920–1933*, Sentry ed. (Boston: Houghton Mifflin, 1972), 146. Employers' ambivalence to workers and unions was reflected in the decline of the number of personnel departments in the 1920s. See Sanford Jacoby, *Employing Bureaucracy: Managers, Unions, and the Transformation of Work in American Industry, 1900–1945* (New York: Columbia University Press, 1985), chap. 6.

23. Martin J. Sklar, *The United States as a Developing Country: Studies in U.S. History in the Progressive Era and the 1920s* (Cambridge: Cambridge University Press, 1992), 165–66.

24. My discussion of Seiders's career and the syndicate's formation is drawn from documentation in the Charles H. Rosenfeld Collection at the University of Chicago Special Collections Research Center (hereafter CHRC), and Neil McCullough Clark, "Seth Seiders" (unpublished article, 1926), box 5, folder 5, Neil McCullough Clark Collection, Center for Southwest Research, University of New Mexico, Albuquerque. The Charles H. Rosenfeld Collection has been reorganized since the research was conducted. I have endeavored to identify new archival locations for all materials cited, but some items may have been relocated.

25. Seth Seiders Syndicate photograph album, box 6, folder: "Photographs," CHRC.

26. See "Big Order Report," October 10, 1927, Mather and Co., black binder: "Letters: Leroy Fox," box 4, CHRC.

27. Felix Shay, *Elbert Hubbard of East Aurora* (New York: Wise, 1926), 111.

28. Art S. to Charles Rosenfeld, January 11, 1928, black file, 1-3, box 1, CHRC.

29. See Stuart Ewen, *Captains of Consciousness: Advertising and the Social Roots of the Consumer Culture*, 25th anniversary ed. (New York: Basic Books, 2001).

30. Lippmann argued that the masses had become incapable of rational thought and called for the creation of a corps of experts who could disseminate information to the public, thus helping them understand the complex issues of the day. See Walter Lippmann, *Public Opinion* (New York: Free Press, 1922), and Walter Lippmann, *The Phantom Public* (New York: Harcourt, Brace, 1925). Dewey advanced a more democratic vision, countering that the solution to the challenges of mass society was for public institutions to harness the power of modern communications. Used properly, he posited, radio, newspapers, and other new media could help build the "Great Community" and deepen Americans' sense of connectedness. See John Dewey, *The Public and Its Problems: An Essay in Political Inquiry*, edited and with an introduction by Melvin L. Rogers (Athens, OH: Swallow Press, 2016 [1927]), 170. On the influence of Lippmann's and Dewey's theories about communication, see Brett Gary, *The Nervous Liberals: Propaganda Anxieties from World War I to the Cold War* (New York: Columbia University Press, 1999), chaps. 1 and 2, and Daniel Czitrom, *Media and the American Mind from Morse to McLuhan* (Chapel Hill: University of North Carolina Press, 1982), chap. 4. On the influence of mass communications in the 1920s, see Warren Susman, *Culture as History: The Transformation of American Society in the Twentieth Century* (New York: Pantheon Books, 1984), chaps. 7 and 13.

31. Hoover quoted in "Herbert Hoover Said—Notes from His Address of Welcome to the Delegates to the Houston Convention, A.A.C. of W.," *Advertising and Selling Fortnightly*, May 20, 1925, 21. Seiders quoted in Seth Seiders, "Billions of Dollars Annually Wasted," *Banker and Manufacturer* 18, no. 12 (December 1924): 12, 13.

32. Seth Seiders, "Getting the Best Out of Your Help," *Banker and Manufacturer* 19, no. 1 (January 1925): 32, 49. Similar articles that he published during this period include Seth Seiders, "Selling the Employee His Job," *Pacific Factory*, November 1924, and Seth Seiders, "How to Cut Waste—Methods That Have Succeeded," *Pacific Factory*, January 1925.

33. For a more detailed discussion of Mather's designs, see David A. Gray, "Managing Motivation: The Seth Seiders Syndicate and the Motivational Publicity Business in the 1920s," *Winterthur Portfolio* 44, no. 1 (Spring 2010): 77–122.

34. Mather & Co. Poster Catalog, 1924, box 34, folder 1, CHRC.

35. "What Are Loafers Paid?," Mather Poster Collection, Hagley Museum and Library, https://digital.hagley.org/posterexhibit_078.

36. Looking back at the poster business of the 1920s two decades later, the most successful supplier of motivational posters of the day estimated that 75 percent of the messages in Mather's posters were generated by its sales specialists and salesmen. Lew Shalett, "Our Heritage," proceedings of the Sheldon-Claire Company sales conference, January 31–February 1, 1947, 5, box 29, folder 7, CHRC.

37. On elites' belief in the virtues of white labor in the early twentieth century, see Matthew Frye Jacobson, *Barbarian Virtues: The United States Encounters Foreign Peoples at Home and Abroad, 1876–1917* (New York: Hill and Wang, 2001), chap. 2.

38. The first poster may be viewed here: https://sova.si.edu/details/NMAH.AC.0877#ref24. The second one is viewable here: https://www.internationalposter.com/product/one-man-is-due-for-promotion-mather-work-incentive/.

39. Sinclair Lewis, *Babbitt*, with a new introduction by Sally E. Parry (New York: Signet Classics, 2007), 75.

40. Many of Mather's posters can be viewed in various online archives. See, for example, the Smithsonian Institution National Museum of American History's Guide to the Emanuel Gerard Collection of Mather and Company Employee Motivation Posters, https://sova.si.edu/details/NMAH.AC.0877.

41. See Howard M. Weiss and Arthur P. Brief, "Affect at Work: A Historical Perspective," in *Emotions at Work: Theory, Research, and Applications for Management*, ed. Roy Payne and Cary Cooper (New York: John Wiley, 2001), 133–71. On the use of floral and decorative borders in the middle-class home after the turn of the century, see Karen Zukowski, *Creating the Artful Home: The Aesthetic Movement* (Salt Lake City, UT: Gibbs Smith, 2006), 62–69.

42. See Gray, "Managing Motivation," for more extensive analyses of this and several other Mather posters.

43. Seth Seiders, "Introductory," in binder entitled "Sales Talk," 3, box 1, CHRC.

44. On the indebtedness of Mather artists to the *Plakatstil* or *sach Plakats* style, see John Heller, "Mather Work Incentive Posters," in *Posters: Identification and Price Guide*, ed. Tony Fusco, 2nd ed. (New York: Avon, 1994), 204. Heller draws parallels between Mather's posters and the designs of the German poster artist Ludwig Hohlwein.

45. For examples of Mather's animal-themed posters (as well as others), see https://sova.si.edu/details/NMAH.AC.0877.

46. Seiders, "Getting the Best Out of Your Help," 34.

47. On management efforts to infuse managerial values among foremen, see Daniel Nelson, *Managers and Workers: Origins of the Twentieth-Century Factory System in the United States, 1880–1920*, 2nd ed. (Madison: University of Wisconsin Press, 1995).

48. "Monthly Digest of Current Books, Newspapers and Magazines in Relation to the Human Element in Business," box 4, binder: "Survey Copies," Seth Seiders Syndicate, CHRC.

49. *Constructive Letters to Pivot Men*, W. C. Mitchell and Company, box 6, folder: "W. C. Mitchell and Co.," CHRC.

50. "Yourself, Incorporated," Constructive Talk to Pivot Men, no. 54, Seth Seiders Inc., *Constructive Talks to Pivot Men*, 1927, author's collection.

51. Seth Seiders Inc., *Secretary's Record Book: For Use in Prompt, Easy, Sure Distribution of the Seth Seiders "Constructive Talks to Pivot Men,"* box 7, folder 5, CHRC.

52. Ronald F. Dixon, "The Value of Hitching the Plant to a Slogan," *Industrial Psychology Monthly* 2, no. 9 (September 1927): 465.

53. However, Charles Rosenfeld, western division manager of Mather, had only sixty-one salesmen in March 1924. Felix Shay to Rosenfeld, March 7, 1924, 1, box 1, binder: "Mostly letters encouraging salesmen to make more sales," CHRC.

54. A field manager earned 15 percent commission when his salesman sold $5,000 or less a month, 20 percent if the salesman sold between $5,000 and $6,000 a month, and 25 percent if his sales were over $6,000 a month. "District Manager Plan on Seth Seiders Inc.," November 15, 1929, box 1, binder: "Recharging Weak Salesmen, Seth Seiders, Mather & Co.," CHRC.

55. Seth Seiders to Felix Shay, April 10, 1924, box 5, binder: "Sales Talks to–by Salesmen Various SS Services," CHRC.

56. "Dear Mrs. _________," 1924, box 6, binder: "1929: Seiders-Mather-Howard," CHRC.

57. "Mather Poster Training Schedule," box 1, unlabeled file, and Seth Seiders to S. J. Glazel, October 6, 1924, box 1, binder: "Recharging Weak Salesmen, Seth Seiders, Mather & Co.," CHRC.

58. "No apparent benefit," box 5, binder: "Customer Complaints," CHRC. Howard's V.P.S.s are collected in box 1, "Howard Sales Bulletin Binder Code L," CHRC. The syndicate's index to over three hundred V.P.S.s is in "Explanation of House Policy on Sales Territory," box 1, CHRC.

59. See "Are Verbal Proof Stories Ethical?," box 2, binder: "National Research Bureau," CHRC.

60. Felix Shay to Seth Seiders, May 27, 1924, and Seiders to Shay, May 28, 1924, box 5, binder: "Sales Talks to–by Salesmen Various SS Services," CHRC.

61. "A Few Expressions from Concerns Using Mather Pictorial Poster Service," box 5, binder: "Customer Complaints," CHRC.

62. Leroy Fox to salesmen, August 17, 1929, box 4, binder: "Letters: Leroy Fox," CHRC.

63. Leroy Fox, "What do you do when Pivot Men can't read English?," August 17, 1929, box 4, binder: "Letters: Leroy Fox," CHRC.

64. Leroy Fox to salesmen, August 19, 1929, box 4, binder: "Letters: Leroy Fox," CHRC.

65. Leroy Fox to salesmen, August 19, 1929. As Timothy Spears and Walter Friedman illustrate, scientific salesmanship drew from prevailing notions of intelligence based on the claims of phrenology. See Timothy Spears, *100 Years on the Road: The Traveling Salesman in American Culture* (New Haven, CT: Yale University Press, 1995),

217–19, and Walter A. Friedman, *Birth of a Salesman: The Transformation of Selling in America* (Cambridge, MA: Harvard University Press, 2004), chap. 3.

66. A small handful of Mather's posters depicted subjects of color, though never as workers. These posters centered on common racial stereotypes, including an African tribesman, a black "pearl diver," and a Native-American hunter, some of which are viewable here: https://sova.si.edu/details/NMAH.AC.0877.

67. "A Study in Contrasts," box 5, binder: "Sales Talks to–by Salesmen Various SS Services," CHRC.

68. Seiders's legal troubles are detailed in a court case transcript in an untitled manila folder, box 6, CHRC.

69. Leroy Fox to Headmasters, n.d., Brown binder, box 5, folder 3, CHRC.

70. Mike Smith, "Al Capone's Jemez Hideout," *New Mexico Magazine*, July 2007.

CHAPTER 3: VISIONS OF STRIVING

1. On work and communal bonds in the 1930s, see Robert S. McElvaine, *The Great Depression: America, 1929–1941* (New York: Times Books, 1993), 199–202; Warren Susman, *Culture as History: The Transformation of American Society in the Twentieth Century* (New York: Pantheon Books, 1984), 154; Morris Dickstein, *Dancing in the Dark: A Cultural History of the Great Depression* (New York: W. W. Norton, 2009); and Lary May, *The Big Tomorrow: Hollywood and the Politics of the American Way* (Chicago: University of Chicago Press, 2000).

2. Michael Denning, *The Cultural Front: The Laboring of American Culture in the Twentieth Century* (New York: Verso, 1997).

3. Richard Gillespie, *Manufacturing Knowledge: A History of the Hawthorne Experiments* (New York: Cambridge University Press, 1991), 103 (for a fuller account of Mayo's career, see chap. 4); James Hoopes, *False Prophets: The Gurus Who Created Modern Management and Why Their Ideas Are Bad for Business Today* (Cambridge, MA: Perseus, 2003), chap. 5.

4. Gillespie, *Manufacturing Knowledge*, 242–43; Hoopes, *False Prophets*, 143.

5. Gillespie, *Manufacturing Knowledge*, 120.

6. This account of Mayo's background and career is informed by Hoopes, *False Prophets*, 133–35.

7. Mayo's meeting with Malinowski is documented by Hoopes, 97–98.

8. Gillespie, *Manufacturing Knowledge*, 97–100; Hoopes, 132–36.

9. Quoted in O'Connor, "The Politics of Management Thought: A Case Study of the Harvard Human Relations School and the Human Relations School," *Academy of Management Review* 24, no. 1 (1999): 126.

10. Hoopes, *False Prophets*, 141–46.

11. Hoopes, 142–43.

12. Elton Mayo, *The Human Problems of an Industrial Civilization*, with an introduction by F. J. Roethlisberger (New York: Viking, 1933), 116, 149. For critical analyses of Mayo's theories during this time, see Reinhard Bendix and Lloyd Fisher, "The Perspectives of Elton Mayo," *Review of Economics and Statistics* 31, no. 4 (November 1949): 312–19; Loren Baritz, *Servants of Power: A History of the Use of Social Science in Industry* (New York: John Wiley and Sons, 1960), chaps. 5–6; and Gerard Hanlon, *The Dark Side of Management: A Secret History of Management Theory* (New York: Routledge, 2016), chap. 4.

13. My argument here draws on Hanlon's discussion of Mayo's theories. See Hanlon, *Dark Side of Management*, 169–77. On Mayo's emphasis on the mind as opposed to Taylor's focus on the body, see Hanlon, 14.

14. Gillespie, *Manufacturing Knowledge*, 100.

15. Reinhold Bendix, *Work and Authority in Industry: Ideologies of Management in the Course of Industrialization* (New York: Harper, 1956), 307–40; Nikolas Rose, *Inventing Our Selves: Psychology, Power, and Personhood* (Cambridge: Cambridge University Press, 1998), 137–40.

16. Baritz, *Servants of Power*, 118, 119–20.

17. See, for example, Sanford Jacoby's case studies of Eastman Kodak, Sears Roebuck, and Thompson Products. Sanford Jacoby, *Modern Manors: Welfare Capitalism since the New Deal* (Princeton, NJ: Princeton University Press, 1997), chaps. 3–5, and Bruce Kaufman, *Managing the Human Factor: The Early Years of Human Resource Management in America* (Ithaca, NY: ILR Press of Cornell University Press, 2008), 263–79.

18. Irving Bernstein, *The Lean Years: A History of the American Worker, 1920–1933*, Sentry ed. (Boston: Houghton Mifflin, 1972), 460.

19. Quoted in Lawrence F. Hanley, "Popular Culture and Crisis: King Kong Meets Edmund Wilson," *Radical Revisions: Rereading 1930s Culture*, ed. Bill Mullen and Sherry Lee Linkon (Urbana: University of Chicago Press, 1996), 246. On Hoover's response to the Depression, see Bernstein, *Lean Years*, 460–62, 465–73; Caroline Bird, *The Invisible Scar: The Great Depression, and What It Did to American Life, from Then until Now* (New York: David McKay, 1969), chap. 4; and McElvaine, *Great Depression*, chaps. 3–4.

20. McElvaine, *Great Depression*, 66.

21. Brian Farmer, *American Conservatism: History, Theory and Practice* (Newcastle, U.K.: Cambridge Scholars Press, 2005), 227.

22. William E. Leuchtenburg, *Herbert Hoover*, American Presidents Series: The 31st President, 1929–1933, ed. Arthur M. Schlesinger Jr. and Sean Wilentz (New York: Henry Holt, 2009), 130–31; Bird, *Invisible Scar*, 71.

23. Bird, *Invisible Scar*, 59.

24. Bernstein, *Lean Years*, 252–53.

25. Bird, *Invisible Scar*, 71.

26. Herbert Hoover, "Radio Address to the Nation on Unemployment Relief. October 18, 1931," in *Herbert Hoover: Containing the Public Messages, Speeches, and Statements of the President*, January 1 to December 31, 1931, 487–91. Quotes on 490.

27. *Good Housekeeping*, January 1, 1932, 124.

28. *Literary Digest*, November 21, 1931, 45.

29. *Literary Digest*, November 21, 1931, 45.

30. Bernstein, *Lean Years*, 460; McElvaine, *Great Depression*, 59.

31. Bernstein, *Lean Years*, 460–62.

32. On Hoover's faith in advertising, see Bernstein, *Lean Years*, 301–2, 460–62; on his enlistment of advertising experts during his 1932 reelection campaign, see Dennis W. Johnson, *Democracy for Hire: A History of American Political Consulting* (Oxford: Oxford University Press, 2017), 17–18.

33. Indeed, Raymond Moley and Rexford Tugwell, two of the New Deal's architects, later credited Hoover with establishing the foundations of the New Deal. According to Moley, "Herbert Hoover originated the New Deal." Tugwell stated, "We didn't admit it at the time, but practically the whole New Deal was extrapolated from programs that Hoover started." McElvaine, *Great Depression*, 70.

34. On the continuance of individualism in modified form during the New Deal, see Dickstein, *Dancing in the Dark*, chap 7.

35. McElvaine, *Great Depression*, 258–59.

36. William E. Leuchtenburg, *Franklin D. Roosevelt and the New Deal, 1932–1940* (New York: Harper), 41.

37. See Jason Loviglio, *Radio's Intimate Public: Network Broadcasting and Mass-Mediated Democracy* (Minneapolis: University of Minnesota Press, 2005), chap. 1. On FDR's "Forgotten Man" radio speech in 1932, see McElvaine, *Great Depression*, 125. On FDR's tactics and his appeal, see McElvaine, 118–41.

38. Steinbeck's interest in "group-man theory" and, specifically, his indebtedness to philosopher John Elof Boodin is discussed in Jeffrey Wayne Yeager, "The Social Mind: Elof Boodin's Influence on John Steinbeck's Phalanx Writings, 1935–1942," *Steinbeck Review* 10, no. 1 (2013): 31–46.

39. See May, *Big Tomorrow*, and Dickstein, *Dancing in the Dark*, 233.

40. Denning, *Cultural Front*, 266, 268.

41. Denning, 266–68.

42. My argument here is informed by Fredric Jameson's discussion of "class and allegory" in film. Jameson posits that film allows viewers to indulge their grievances

but ultimately resolves them in favor of the status quo. See Fredric Jameson, *Signatures of the Visible* (New York: Routledge, 1992), chap. 2.

43. On the Historical Section's history, see F. Jack Hurley, *Portrait of a Decade: Roy Stryker and the Development of Documentary Photography in the Thirties* (n.p.: Louisiana State University Press, 1972); Carl Fleischhauer and Beverly W. Brennan, eds., *Documenting America, 1935–1943* (Berkeley: University of California Press, 1988); and Cara A. Finnegan, *Picturing Poverty: Print Culture and FSA Photographs* (Washington, D.C.: Smithsonian Books, 2003).

44. Rexford Guy Tugwell, Thomas Munro, and Roy Stryker, *American Economic Life and the Means of Its Improvement* (New York: Harcourt, Brace, 1925).

45. Roy Emerson Stryker and Nancy Wood, *In This Proud Land: America 1935–1943 as Seen in the FSA Photographs* (Boston: New York Graphic Society, 1973), 14.

46. This esteem for white agrarian virtues was echoed in other "official images" of the era, including those created under the auspices of the Civilian Conservation Corps (CCC). As Maren Stange argues, CCC photos celebrated Anglo-Saxon agrarianism while ignoring the racial complexity of agricultural labor. See Maren Stange, "The Record Itself: Farm Security Photography and the Transformation of Rural Life," in *Official Images: New Deal Photography*, ed. Pete Daniel, Merry A. Foresta, Maren Stange, and Sally Stein (Washington, D.C.: Smithsonian Institution Press, 1987), 66–70. As Cara Finnegan details, magazine articles about the southern farm tenancy system and rural poverty used FSA photographs in ways that downplayed the racial dynamics of each and that served mainly to emphasize the white Depression experience; see Finnegan, *Picturing* Poverty, esp. 78–94 and chap. 4. Framing the experiences of struggling farmers in terms that middle-class viewers could empathize with was fundamental to the section's strategy. Images of honest-looking Americans who appeared predisposed to hard work but were hindered by circumstances beyond their control were deemed a necessary tactic for motivating middle-class viewers to support New Deal programs. Similarly, images and captions that seemed to invoke dependency on government handouts were to be avoided. See Curtis, *Mind's Eye, Mind's Truth: FSA Photography Reconsidered* (Philadelphia: Temple University Press, 1989), viii–ix, 6.

47. See Roy Stryker, "The FSA Collection of Photographs," in Stryker and Wood, *In This Proud Land*.

48. *Migrant Mother* has received extensive discussion and analysis in histories of FSA photography, and rather than rehashing this well-trodden ground, I will refer the reader to some important works. See Wendy Kozol, "Madonnas of the Fields: Photography, Gender, and 1930s Farm Relief," *Genders*, no. 2 (Summer 1988): 1–23; Finnegan, *Picturing Poverty*, chap. 2; and James Curtis, *Mind's Eye, Mind's Truth*,

chap. 3. The photograph may be viewed at https://www.loc.gov/pictures/resource/fsa.8b29516/?co=fsa.

49. See, for instance, Lisa Helene Kaplan, *"Introducing America to Americans": FSA Photography and the Construction of Racialized and Gendered Citizens* (PhD diss., Bowling Green State University, Bowling Green, 2015), esp. 126–29; Stange, "The Record Itself"; Sharon Musher, *Democratic Art: The New Deal's Influence on American Culture* (Chicago: University of Chicago Press, 2015), 130–44; and Finnegan, *Picturing Poverty*, chap. 5.

50. Several studies have addressed the section's shift to a more optimistic portrayal of American life from the late 1930s onward and the ways in which this new direction advanced more conservative ideals than the section emphasized previously. See, for example, Paula Rabinowitz, *They Must be Represented: The Politics of Documentary* (New York: Verso, 1994), chap. 4. Myles Orvell discusses the nostalgic portrayals of small-town life in FSA photographs in *The Death and Life of Main Street: Small Towns in American Memory, Space, and Community* (Chapel Hill: University of North Carolina, 2012), esp. 104–15. John Raeburn explores how the section's emphasis on Depression-era exigencies such as poverty and distress were largely erased when art museums used FSA photographs in exhibits during the war, in *A Staggering Revolution: A Cultural History of Thirties Photography* (Urbana: University of Illinois Press, 2006), 183–93.

51. Stryker, shooting script entitled "Suggestions recently made by Robert Lynd (co-author of *Middletown*) for things which should be photographed as American Background," 1936, in Stryker and Wood, *In This Proud Land*, 187.

52. Quoted in Lawrence W. Levine, *The Unpredictable Past: Explorations in American Cultural History* (New York: Oxford University Press, 1993), 287.

53. Russell Lee, "Life on the American Frontier—1941 Version," *U.S. Camera*, October 1941, 52.

54. Quoted in Levine, *Unpredictable Past*, 287.

55. *Factory* had already consolidated eight other titles by this time, and *Industrial Maintenance* had absorbed nine. A full list of the publications folded into these two magazines appears in *Factory Management and Maintenance* (henceforth *FMM*) 95, no. 1 (January 1937): 108.

56. John Richelsen, "Plants Are Like People," *FMM* 95, no. 9 (September 1937): 66.

57. Ellis Rosenthal, "Employees 'Go on the Air' on Public Address System," *FMM* 95, no. 7 (July 1937): 134. In 1933 *FMM* reported that a company in New Jersey had a pianist play every afternoon to inspire faster production. "Management Shorts," *FMM* 91, no. 5 (May 1933): 179.

58. Allan H. Mogensen, "Every Worker Has Ideas," *FMM* 93, no. 4 (April 1935): 148 and advertising section, 83–84.

59. Frank Voelkl, "Slogan Contest Teaches: 'Do It for the Customer,'" *FMM* 98, no. 9 (September 1940): 160, 162.

60. Tom A. Burke, "Safety: Seventeenth in the Series of *Factory Management and Maintenance* Plant Operation Library," *FMM* 94, no. 7 (July 1936): S-284.

61. Burke, "Safety," S-283.

62. Dr. Mathew Luckiesh, "Workers Are Human Seeing-Machines," *FMM* 92, no. 3 (March 1934): 93–96.

63. J. F. Andrews, "Swapping Ideas Betters Safety Programs," *FMM* 97, no. 8 (August 1939): 38–39, 110–16. Image from p. 38.

64. Burke, "Safety," S-281–82.

65. The first quote is from T. J. Maloney, "Color Increases Shop Efficiency," *Factory and Industrial Management* 83, no. 4 (April 1932): 139; the second is from Burke, S-279.

66. As Jennifer Klein argues, economic security became a powerful symbol of progress during the middle decades of the twentieth century. See Jennifer Klein, *For All These Rights: Business, Labor, and the Shaping of America's Public-Private Welfare State* (Princeton, NJ: Princeton University Press, 2003).

67. For analysis of the episode, see "Diego Rivera at Rockefeller Center: Fresco Painting and Rhetoric," *Western Journal of Speech Communication* 41, no. 2 (Spring 1977): 70–82.

68. James Guimond develops this line of discussion, exploring FSA photographs that depict NAM billboards. James Guimond, *American Photography and the American Dream* (Chapel Hill: University of North Carolina Press, 1991), chap. 4.

69. The first four figures are stated in Sharon Beder, *Free Market Missionaries: The Corporate Manipulation of Community Values* (New York: Earthscan, 2006), 17. The figure for billboard poster installations is from "Experts All: Who's Behind Industry's Public Relations Program," folder: "Miscellaneous NIIC Material, 1938–1940," box 848, series 1, National Association of Manufacturers Collection, Hagley Museum and Library, Delaware (hereafter NAM). The figure of billboard viewings is from William L. Bird, *A Better Living: Advertising, Media, and the New Vocabulary of Business Leadership, 1935–1955* (Evanston, IL: Northwestern University Press, 1999), 222. The figure for film viewings is quoted in "Report of Motion Pictures Theatrical and Non-Theatrical Showings," April 27, 1938, box 113, folder: "Public Relations-Motion Slide Films Rep. of Motion Picture Showings," series 1, NAM.

70. "Service for Plant Publications," June 1936, no. 10, box 111, folder: "Public Relations: Service for Plant Publications," series 1, NAM.

71. "Experts All."

72. "Report of Motion Pictures Theatrical and Non-Theatrical Showings." See also Bird, *A Better Living*, 131–33.

73. "Men and Machines," box 111, folder: Public Relations Posters, series 1, NAM;

"Continuity Outline for 'America Marching On' No. 2 Production in 1938 N.A.M. Series," box 113, loose materials, series 1, NAM.

74. "Men and Machines."

75. "Shooting Continuity, *Your Town—A Story of America*," box 113, loose materials, series 1, NAM.

76. See Rick Prelinger, "Eccentricity, Education and the Evolution of Corporate Speech," in *Films that Work: Industrial Film and the Productivity of Media*, ed. Vinzenz Hediger and Patrick Vonderau (Amsterdam: Amsterdam University Press, 2009). For an illuminating account of the development and influence of motivational films and their relationship to social science, see Heide Solbrig, "Film and Function: A History of Industrial Motivation Film" (PhD diss., University of California, San Diego, 2004).

77. The film can be viewed online at the Internet Archive, https://archive.org/details/0560_From_Dawn_to_Sunset_14_01_40_00.

CHAPTER 4: THE WAR OVER MOTIVATION

1. On American domestic propaganda during the war, see John Morton Blum, *V Was for Victory: Politics and American Culture during World War II* (San Diego: Harcourt Brace, 1976); Allan M. Winkler, *The Politics of Propaganda: The Office of War Information, 1942–1945* (New Haven, CT: Yale University Press, 1976), chaps. 1–2; and William L. Bird Jr. and Harry Rubenstein, *Design for Victory: World War II Posters on the American Home Front* (New York: Princeton Architectural Press, 1998).

2. Studs Terkel, *The Good War: An Oral History of World War II* (New York: New Press, 1984).

3. On narratives about the "good war," see Michael C. C. Adams, *The Best War Ever: America and World War II* (Baltimore, MD: Johns Hopkins University Press, 1994). For an illuminating critique of assumptions about wartime motivation and of discourse about the Greatest Generation, see Kenneth D. Rose, *Myth and the Greatest Generation: A Social History of Americans in World War II* (New York: Routledge, 2008).

4. On efforts by advertisers to exploit the war to bolster their standing in the postwar era, see Frank W. Fox, *Madison Avenue Goes to War: The Strange Military Career of American Advertising, 1941–1945* (Provo, UT: Brigham Young University Press, 1975); Inger L. Stole, *Advertising at War: Business, Consumers, and Government in the 1940s* (Urbana: University of Illinois Press, 2012); Mark Leff, "The Politics of Sacrifice on the American Home Front in World War II," *Journal of American History* 77, no. 4 (March 1991): 1296–1318; Cynthia Lee Henthorn, *From Submarines to Suburbs: Selling a Better America, 1939–1956* (Athens: Ohio University Press, 2006); and Dannagal Goldthwaite Young, "Sacrifice, Consumption, and the American Way

of Life: Advertising and Domestic Propaganda during World War II," *Communication Review* 8, no. 1 (2005): 27–52.

5. Fox, *Madison Avenue Goes to War*, esp. chap. 2, and Stole, *Advertising at War*. On the quest by business to advance free enterprise ideology and secure its power and influence after the war, see Elizabeth Fones-Wolf, *Selling Free Enterprise: The Business Assault on Labor and Liberalism, 1945–1960* (Urbana: University of Illinois Press, 1994).

6. On the war's effects on economics and on relationships between the state and labor, see Alan Brinkley, *The End of Reform: New Deal Liberalism in Recession and War* (New York: Vintage Books, 1995), chaps. 7–9; Steve Fraser, "The Labor Question," in *The Rise and Fall of the New Deal Order, 1930–1980*, ed. Steve Fraser and Gary Gerstle (Princeton, NJ: Princeton University Press, 1989), 55–84; and Alan Brinkley, "World War II and American Liberalism," in *The War in American Culture: Society and Consciousness during World War II*, ed. Lewis Erenberg and Susan E. Hirsch (Chicago: University of Chicago Press, 1996), 319–20.

7. Meg Jacobs, "'How About Some Meat?': The Office of Price Administration, Consumption Politics, and State Building from the Bottom Up, 1941–1946," *Journal of American History* 84, no. 3 (December 1997): 910–41.

8. Liberals' shift from the New Deal's earlier class-based agendas to a wartime consumer-based platform rooted in free market principles is detailed in Brinkley, *End of Reform*, chap. 7, appropriately titled "Liberals Embattled." On full employment, see 250–53.

9. On gains and losses of labor unions, see Nelson Lichtenstein, *Labor's War at Home: The CIO in World War II* (New York: Cambridge University Press, 1982), and George Lipsitz, *Rainbow at Midnight: Labor and Class in the 1940s* (Urbana: University of Illinois Press, 1981).

10. See Lichtenstein, *Labor's War at Home*, 34–36; Brinkley, *End of Reform*, chaps. 8–9; and Lipsitz, *Rainbow at Midnight*.

11. Adams, *Best War Ever*, 71.

12. On the Reuther Plan and resistance to it by industrial leaders, see Nelson Lichtenstein, *Walter Reuther: The Most Dangerous Man in Detroit* (Urbana: University of Illinois Press, 1995), chap. 8.

13. See, for example, Gary P. Latham, *Work Motivation: History, Theory, Research, and Practice* (Thousand Oaks, CA: Sage Publications, 2007), 21.

14. See, for example, Loren Baritz, *Servants of Power: A History of the Use of Social Science in Industry* (New York: John Wiley and Sons, 1960), chap. 8; Howell John Harris, *The Right to Manage: Industrial Relations Policies of American Business in the 1940s* (Madison: University of Wisconsin Press, 1982); and Sanford Jacoby, *Employing Bureaucracy: Managers, Unions, and the Transformation of Work in American Industry, 1900–1945* (New York: Columbia University Press, 1985), 194–204, quote on 201.

15. See F. J. Roethlisberger and William Dickson, *Management and the Worker: An Account of a Research Program Conducted by the Western Electric Company, Hawthorne Works, Chicago* (Cambridge, MA: Harvard University Press, 1939), chap. 25. Quote from 408.

16. Peter F. Drucker, *The Future of Industrial Man* (New Brunswick, NJ: Transaction Publishers, 1995 [1942]), 60.

17. See Nils Gilman, "The Prophet of Post-Fordism: Peter Drucker and the Legitimation of the Corporation," in *American Capitalism: Social Theory and Political Economy in the Twentieth Century*, ed. Nelson Lichtenstein (Philadelphia: University of Pennsylvania Press), 109–31.

18. "Press conference of Archibald MacLeish, Director of the Office of Facts and Figures," January 21, 1942, 3, box 3, subject file: MacLeish, Archibald, 1941–43, Papers of Henry F. Pringle, Library of Congress, Washington, D.C. (hereafter PHFP).

19. "Report to the Nation: The American Preparation for War," 36, box 5, subject file: OEM, Office of Facts and Figures Board Meeting Minutes, PHFP.

20. Leo Rosten, June 10, 1942, "Movies and War Information," box 3, entry 6-A, folder: Bureau—Motion Pictures, Records of the Office of War Information, Records of the Historian Relating to the Domestic Branch, RG-208, Records of the Office of War Information, National Archives, College Park, MD (hereafter OWI). For further insights into Americans' ambivalence about the war, see John W. Jeffries, *Wartime America: The World War II Home Front* (Chicago: Ivan R. Dee, 1996), 171–72, and Rose, *Myth and the Greatest Generation*, 70–71.

21. "The Labor Front," Sam Lubell to Marty Sommers, January 21, 1942, box 6, subject file: OEM Office of Facts and Figures Ideas, memo attachment and pp. 1–2, PHFP.

22. The struggle over propaganda policy at the OWI has been discussed by many historians. For informative analyses, see Blum, *V Was for Victory*, chap. 1; Winkler, *Politics of Propaganda*, chap. 2; and Bird and Rubenstein, *Design for Victory*, chaps. 1–3.

23. "Note to American Artists," August 1942, 3, box 14, folder: World War II—Office of War Information Domestic Operations Correspondence 1942–44, n.d., Papers of Francis E. Brennan, Library of Congress (hereafter PFEB).

24. George A. Barnes to Archibald MacLeish, December 20, 1941, box 42 E-7, folder: Posters, OWI-OFF 1941–42, alpha subject file, OWI.

25. Stole, *Advertising at War*, 12.

26. Stole, 68.

27. Julia A. English to Myrtle A. Weese, March 29, 1945, box 1126, NC-148, entry 236, folder: Poster Ideas—unsolicited, OWI. This file contains numerous rejection letters, and many more are scattered throughout the OWI's papers.

28. Francis Brennan to Elmer Davis, April 6 1943, box 14, folder: World War II—Office of War Information Domestic Operations Correspondence, 1942–44, PFEB.

29. Letter, box 3, entry 6-A: Records of the Historian relating to the Domestic Branch, folder: Bureau of Publications & Graphics Printing Division, OWI.

30. See, for example, "Fifteen Quitting O.W.I. Accuse It of Ballyhoo," *Herald Tribune*, April 16, 1943, box 14, folder: World War II—Office of War Information News Clippings, 1942–44, PFEB.

31. Memo from George H. Lyon, Chief of the OWI News Bureau, August 10, 1943, box 1066, folder: Graphics News Letters, OWI.

32. For further discussion of these developments, see Bird and Rubenstein, *Design for Victory*; Winkler, *Politics of Propaganda*; Blum, *V Was for Victory*; and Stole, *Advertising at War*.

33. See Laura Belmonte, *Selling the American Way: U.S. Propaganda and the Cold War* (Philadelphia: University of Pennsylvania Press, 2008), chap. 4, and Fones-Wolf, *Selling Free Enterprise*.

34. See Maureen Honey, *Creating Rosie the Riveter: Class, Gender, and Propaganda during World War II* (Amherst: University of Massachusetts Press, 1984). The most well known World War II poster depicting a woman worker today—J. Howard Miller's "We Can Do It!"—has for decades been upheld as a symbol of women's empowerment. Although the poster had no connection to the OWI (it was commissioned by Westinghouse Electric), its unique standing in collective memory calls for commentary here. The poster is known popularly as the major image portraying "Rosie the Riveter" and is often assumed to have been used for recruitment purposes or as an affirmation of women's important role in the war effort. Yet the poster has long been misunderstood. It was produced, rather, to motivate women (and perhaps men) already employed in Westinghouse's factories and was, more accurately, part of the firm's efforts to urge increased productivity and instill discipline. Its audience was also far more limited than is often assumed, as it was displayed for only two weeks in February 1943, and only inside Westinghouse's plants. On these points and for a more extensive discussion, see James J. Kimble and Lester C. Olson, "Visual Rhetoric Representing Rosie the Riveter: Myth and Misconception in J. Howard Miller's 'We Can Do It!' Poster," *Rhetoric & Public Affairs* 9, no. 4 (Winter 2006): 533–69.

35. *United We Win* has been widely reproduced in World War II poster books and may be viewed, along with the posters depicting Joe Louis and Dorie Miller, on the National Archives' "Powers of Persuasion" online exhibit, https://www.archives.gov/exhibits/powers_of_persuasion/united_we_win/united_we_win.html. The poster depicting Obie Bartlett may be viewed at http://findit.library.yale.edu/bookreader/BookReaderDemo/index.html?oid=16047887#page/1/mode/1up.

36. On the OWI's liaison with Hollywood film studios and use of films in efforts to represent African Americans and boost support for the war effort among blacks, see Clayton R. Koppes and Gregory D. Black, "Blacks, Loyalty, and Motion-Picture Propaganda in World War II," *Journal of American History* 73, no. 2 (September 1986): 383–406.

37. The entire booklet is available for viewing on the National Museum of African American History website at https://edan.si.edu/transcription/pdf_files/10156.pdf.

38. William H. Hastie to Chandler Owen, May 1, 1942, box 3, folder: General Correspondence 1942–1943, PHFP.

39. On southern congressional members' criticism of *Negroes and the War*, the subsequent loss of funding of the OWI Domestic Branch, and its vexed efforts to develop propaganda aimed exclusively at blacks, see Michele Hilmes, *Radio Voices: American Broadcasting, 1922–1952* (Minneapolis: University of Minnesota Press, 1997), 246–50, quote from 132. As Hilmes argues, the OWI developed a number of radio programs and films that addressed racial issues, but its efforts were often held back by critics who deemed them divisive. See Hilmes, chap. 8.

40. On wartime racial discrimination in industry, see Eileen Boris, "The Racialized Gendered State: Constructions of Citizenship in the United States," *Social Politics* 2, no. 2 (Summer 1995): 160–80, and Boris, "'You Wouldn't Want One of 'Em Dancing with Your Wife': Racialized Bodies on the Job in World War II," *American Quarterly* 50, no. 1 (March 1998): 77–108. For an illuminating study of the racialized and gendered nature of work on the American home front in Montana that also addresses national contexts, see Matthew L. Basso, *Meet Joe Copper: Masculinity and Race on Montana's World War II Home Front* (Chicago: University of Chicago Press, 2013). On race and wartime contests for authority in industry, see Lipsitz, *Rainbow at Midnight*, chap. 3.

41. Jeffries, *Wartime America*; Allan M. Winkler, *Home Front U.S.A.: America during World War II* (Wheeling, IL: Harlan Davidson, 2000 [1986]); and Blum, *V Was for Victory*.

42. Winkler, *Home Front U.S.A.*, 22.

43. Gary Gerstle, "Interpreting the 'American Way': The Working Class Goes to War," in Erenberg and Hirsch, *War in American Culture*, 105–27.

44. Rose, *Myth and the Greatest Generation*, 280.

45. On unions' accommodation of labor-business consensus during and after the war, see Harris, *The Right to Manage*, esp. chaps. 3–5.

46. For a more in-depth discussion of Sheldon-Claire's *This is America*, see David A. Gray, "New Uses for Old Photos: Renovating FSA Photographs in World War II Posters," *American Studies* 47, no. 3/4 (Fall/Winter 2006): 5–34.

47. Sheldon-Claire's archived records do not contain complete order lists or records of annual sales. However, a collage of clients' insignia used for promotional

purposes includes those of around five hundred companies. Untitled collage, subject file: "Our Work Guarantees Our Wages," and "The Competitive Edge: Your Key to Greater Profits" ("Management Manual," 1955), box 2, series 1, Records of the Sheldon-Claire Company, Archives Center, National Museum of American History, Smithsonian Institution, Washington, D.C. (hereafter RSCC, NMAH).

48. More immigrants acquired citizenship during the war than in any previous five-year period, making naturalization a "major social movement" in America. Reed Ueda, "The Changing Path to Citizenship: Ethnicity and Naturalization during World War II," in Erenberg and Hirsch, *War in American Culture*, 202–16.

49. On wartime "wildcat" strikes rooted in white workers' grievances over the gains of black workers, see Lipsitz, *Rainbow at Midnight*, chap. 3.

50. The modification of FSA photographs and their captions has been discussed by several historians. While one might imagine that Lange and her fellow photographers were troubled about such alterations, as John Raeburn points out, "If these journalistic disfigurations discouraged the photographers they have left no record of it." John Raeburn, *A Staggering Revolution: A Cultural History of Thirties Photography* (Urbana: University of Illinois Press, 2006), 164. On captioning, see Maren Stange, *Symbols of Ideal Life: Social Documentary in America, 1890–1950* (Cambridge: Cambridge University Press, 1992), 113–20, and Linda Gordon, "Dorothea Lange: The Photographer as Agricultural Sociologist," *Journal of American History* 93, no. 3 (December 2006): 698–727, esp. 716–19.

51. "Main Street" became a powerful ideal associated with prosperity in the 1930s and 1940s. Indeed, images of American small-town life were encoded with the rewards of the work ethic and consumption. See Myles Orvell, *The Death and Life of Main Street: Small Towns in American Memory, Space, and Community* (Chapel Hill: University of North Carolina Press, 2012); see esp. 104–15. The nostalgic mythos of Main Street formed a core strand of motivational rhetoric about the virtues of individualism throughout the postwar era.

52. Employee Mail-O-Gram no. 4, *This is America*, 1943, box 1, subject file: This is America, series 1, RSCC, NMAH.

53. Employee Mail-O-Gram no. 16, *This is America*, 1943, box 1, subject file: This is America, series 1, RSCC, NMAH.

54. Lew Shalett, "Our Heritage," proceedings of the Sheldon-Claire Company sales conference, January 31–February 1, 1947, 7, box 29, folder 7, Charles H. Rosenfeld Collection, University of Chicago Special Collections Research Center.

55. Herbert Hosking, "The Development of an Advertising Approach," April 27, 1944, 3, box 843, folder: January–May 1944, series III, National Association of Manufacturers Collection, accession number 1411, Hagley Museum and Library, Wilmington, Delaware (hereafter NAM).

56. G. E. Harrison Jr. to "Mr. Sloan" and "Mr. Adams," May 19, 1944, box 843, folder: January–May 1944, series III, NAM.

57. Hosking, "Advertising Approach," 3.

58. Hosking, 3. See also Harrison to "Mr. Sloan" and "Mr. Adams."

59. "Passwords to a Better America," "Reorganization Plans, 1943–1944," 1, box 846, series III, NAM.

60. Efforts by NIIC to hone NAM's language in ways that veiled its antilabor and anti–New Deal agendas are outlined in "Terminology concerning Electric Power and Light," box 847, folder: Semantics, 1943–1944, series III, NAM.

61. "Re: CIO Public Information Program," 1–2, box 845, folder: Misc. Oct. 1944–1945, series III, NAM.

62. "CIO Public Information Program," 2–4.

63. "CIO Public Information Program," 4–5.

64. Letter, March 14, 1944, 2, box 843, folder: January–May 1944, series III, NAM.

65. Letter, March 14, 1944.

66. "The American Way Is to the Right," box 843, folder: "Capital Formation," series I, NAM.

67. "Footprints of the Trojan Horse: Some Methods used by Foreign Agents within the United States" (booklet), 1942, Citizenship Educational Service Inc., New York, box 5, subject file: OEM, Office of Facts and Figures General Memoranda, PHFP.

68. On the expansion of this quest after the war, see Fones-Wolf, *Selling Free Enterprise*; Kim Philips-Fein, *Invisible Hands: The Businessman's Crusade against the New Deal* (New York: W. W. Norton, 2009); and William L. Bird: *A Better Living: Advertising, Media, and the New Vocabulary of Business Leadership, 1935–1955* (Evanston, IL: Northwestern University Press, 1999). For insights into how conservative economists and think tanks advanced free market ideology after the war, see Nancy MacLean, *Democracy in Chains: The Deep History of the Radical Right's Stealth Plan for America* (New York: Viking, 2017).

69. "Companies which have held 'Soldiers of Production' rallies. July 2, 1943–December 1, 1944," box 846, folder: Promotional Material for 1944 NIIC, series III, NAM.

70. "Soldiers of Production Weekly Statistical Report," February 12, 1945, box 842, folder: NIIC Administration Weekly Reports, Jan–Feb 1945, series III, NAM.

71. "Soldiers of Production Advanced Schedule," April 16 1945, box 842, folder: NIIC Administrative Weekly Reports April–May 1945, series III, NAM.

72. "Information Bulletins for NIIC Speakers, December 6 1944," 1–2, box 845, folder: Misc. NIIC Material, series III, NAM.

73. "Your Plant and 'Soldiers of Production,'" 3, box 846, folder: Promotional Material NIIC, 1944, series III, NAM.

74. "Your Plant," 4.

75. "Baltimore Soldiers of Production," 1943, box 847, folder: Soldiers of Production 1943, series III, NAM.

76. "Williamsport, PA. 'Soldiers of Production' Rallies," box 847, folder: Soldiers of Production 1942–1943, series III, NAM.

77. "Employee Programs Division, 'Soldiers of Production' Weekly Report," January 12, 1945, 1–2, box 842, folder: NIIC Administration Weekly Reports, Jan–Feb 1945, series III, NAM.

78. See for example, Sharon Beder, *Free Market Missionaries: The Corporate Manipulation of Community Values* (London: Earthscan, 2006), and Stephen Butterfield, *Amway: The Cult of Free Enterprise* (Boston: South End Press, 1985).

79. Adams, *Best War Ever*, chap. 4.

80. Portrayals of women's expanded opportunities and gains during the war have long been overstated. See Adams, 70.

CHAPTER 5: SELLING WORKERS ON THEIR JOBS

1. On consensus ideology, see Godfrey Hodgson, *America in Our Time: From World War II to Nixon, What Happened and Why* (New York: Vintage, 1976), 67–98.

2. On the larger ambitions that fueled businessmen, including many management figures, see Kim Phillips-Fein, *Invisible Hands: The Businessmen's Crusade against the New Deal* (New York: W. W. Norton, 2009).

3. On the growing influence of "communications" after World War II, see Timothy Glander, *Origins of Mass Communications Research during the American Cold War: Educational Effects and Contemporary Implications* (New York: Routledge, 2009), and J. Michael Sproule, *Propaganda and Democracy: The American Experience of Media and Mass Persuasion* (Cambridge: Cambridge University Press, 1997), chap. 7. As both authors illustrate, propaganda had long been debated by this time, having been criticized by journalists and progressives since the early twentieth century. By the end of World War II, the field of communications research became a powerful force in institutional life as influential organizations enlisted the expertise of social scientists to conduct empirical studies on communications and persuasion. See also Kenneth Cmiel, "On Cynicism, Evil, and the Discovery of Communication in the 1940s," *Journal of Communication* 46, no. 3 (Summer 1996): 88–107.

4. C. Wright Mills, *White Collar: The American Middle Classes* (New York: Oxford University Press, 1951), 110.

5. Phillips-Fein, *Invisible Hands*; Elizabeth Fones-Wolf, *Selling Free Enterprise: The Business Assault on Labor and Liberalism, 1945–1960* (Urbana: University of Illinois Press, 1994).

6. On the Taft-Hartley Act's "employer free speech" provision and its effects on business's approach to communications, see Fones-Wolf, *Selling Free Enterprise*, 78–83, and Howell John Harris, *The Right to Manage: Industrial Relations Policies of American Business in the 1940s* (Madison: University of Wisconsin Press, 1982), 123–25.

7. The literature on labor-management contestation and labor's compromises after the war is vast, but for some illuminating studies, see Nelson Lichtenstein, *Labor's War at Home: The CIO in World War II* (New York: Cambridge University Press, 1982), chaps. 11–12; George Lipsitz, *A Rainbow at Midnight: Labor and Culture in the 1940s* (Urbana: University of Illinois Press, 1994), chap. 7; Alan Brinkley, *The End of Reform: New Deal Liberalism in Recession and War* (New York: Vintage Books, 1995), chaps. 7–9; and Steve Fraser, "The Labor Question," in *The Rise and Fall of the New Deal Order, 1930–1980*, ed. Steve Fraser and Gary Gerstle (Princeton, NJ: Princeton University Press, 1989), 55–84.

8. Harris, *Right to Manage*, 103, 163.

9. On management and Cold War ideology, see Ori Landau, "Cold War Political Culture and the Return of Systems Rationality," *Human Resources* 59, no. 5 (May 2006): 637–63, and Elizabeth S. Kelley, Albert J. Mills, and Bill Cooke, "Management as a Cold War Phenomenon?," *Human Relations* 59, no. 5 (May 2006): 603–10.

10. One 1956 survey of 269 companies calculated that such programs cost employers on average seventy-six dollars a year per employee. Dale Yoder and Roberta J. Nelson, "How Much Should an Employee Relations Program Cost?," *Personnel: The National Journal of Personnel Management* 33, no. 3 (November 1956): 214.

11. "Memorandum, Dearborn Group (Employee Relations Research Section)," May 21, 1951, n.p., box 1, folder 2, Dearborn Group Records, coll. no. 5569, Kheel Center for Labor-Management Documentation and Archives, Cornell University, Ithaca, NY (hereafter DGR).

12. "Memorandum, Dearborn Group."

13. On the postwar rise of employee morale and motivation studies and their effects, see C. Wright Mills, "The Contribution of Sociology to Studies of Industrial Relations," *Berkeley Journal of Sociology* 15 (1970): 11–32; Richard Gillespie, *Manufacturing Knowledge: A History of the Hawthorne Experiments* (New York: Cambridge University Press, 1991), 250–63; Reinhold Bendix, *Work and Authority in Industry: Ideologies of Management in the Course of Industrialization* (New York: Harper, 1956), chap. 5; Loren Baritz, *Servants of Power: A History of the Use of Social Science in Industry* (New York: John Wiley and Sons, 1960), chap. 9; and Sanford Jacoby, *Modern Manors: Welfare Capitalism since the New Deal* (Princeton, NJ: Princeton University Press, 1997), chap. 6. As Jacoby notes, behavioral science research had particular influence at large nonunion firms and helped extend welfare capitalism into the postwar era.

14. Sanford Jacoby, "Employee Attitude Surveys in Historical Perspective," *Industrial Relations* 27, no. 1 (Winter 1988): 74–93.

15. Morris Viteles, *Motivation and Morale in Industry* (New York: Norton, 1953), 1–61.

16. Sarah E. Igo, *The Averaged American: Surveys, Citizens, and the Making of a Mass Public* (Cambridge, MA: Harvard University Press, 2008).

17. Godfrey Hodgson, *America in Our Time*, 86.

18. Jennifer Delton observes that with the help of human relations specialists, corporations made significant strides in integrating the workforce after the war, guided by the view that this policy was "good business." Organizations like the National Association of Manufacturers, she adds, adopted a similar stance. While this may be true, motivational rhetoric and imagery continued to be cast almost exclusively in white terms. See Jennifer Delton, *Racial Integration in Corporate America, 1940–1990* (New York: Cambridge University Press, 2009).

19. William H. Whyte Jr., *Is Anybody Listening? How and Why Business Fumbles When It Talks with Human Beings* (New York: Simon and Schuster, 1952), 2, 7.

20. On this distinction, see Jacques Ellul, *Propaganda: The Formation of Men's Attitudes* (1965; repr., New York: Vintage Books, 1973), 259–302. As Ellul argues persuasively, the assumption that propaganda must convince its audience of its claims in order to be effective is inadequate. Propaganda, as he explains, operates through unconscious processes that habituate audiences to the ideas communicated regardless of the individual's conscious reaction.

21. Dichter quoted in Daniel Horowitz, "The Birth of a Salesman: Ernest Dichter and the Objects of Desire," http://www.hagley.org/library/collections/historicalref/articles/HOROWITZ_DICHTER.pdf, 2. On MR's influence in postwar advertising businesses, see Daniel Horowitz, *The Anxieties of Affluence: Critiques of American Consumer Culture, 1939–1978* (Amherst: University of Massachusetts Press, 2004), 48–64, and Stefan Schwarzkopf and Rainer Gries, *Ernest Dichter and Motivational Research: New Perspectives on the Making of Post-War Consumer Culture* (New York: Palgrave Macmillan, 2010).

22. See Nils Gilman, "The Prophet of Post-Fordism: Peter Drucker and the Legitimation of the Corporation," in *American Capitalism: Social Theory and Political Economy in the Twentieth Century*, ed. Nelson Lichtenstein (Philadelphia: University of Pennsylvania Press), 109–31.

23. On labor's postwar communications campaigns, see Fones-Wolf, *Selling Free Enterprise*, esp. chaps. 4–5, and John Barnard, *American Vanguard: The United Auto Workers during the Reuther Years, 1935–1970* (Detroit, MI: Wayne State University Press, 2004), chap. 8.

24. On the illusory claims by human relations specialists about morale, see Mills, "Contribution of Sociology." On U.S. government efforts to contrast "free" American labor with oppressive working conditions imposed on Soviet workers in its propaganda, see Laura Belmonte, *Selling the American Way: U.S. Propaganda and the Cold War* (Philadelphia: University of Pennsylvania Press, 2008), chap. 4.

25. Brian Holmes argues that the soft coercion proved effective in masking the authoritarian nature of power in postwar capitalism. See Brian Holmes, "The Flexible Personality: For a New Cultural Critique," translate.eipcp.net/transversal/1106/holmes/en.html. On management and Cold War ideology, see Landau, "Cold War Political Culture," and Kelley, Mills, and Cooke, "Management as a Cold War Phenomenon?"

26. See Lipsitz, *Rainbow at Midnight*, chap. 4, and Nelson Lichtenstein, *The Most Dangerous Man in Detroit: Walter Reuther and the Fate of American Labor* (New York: Basic Books, 1995), chaps. 11–12.

27. On the shift in UAW tactics from industrial democracy to economic growth, see Nelson Lichtenstein, "UAW Bargaining Strategy and Shop-Floor Conflict: 1946–1970," *Industrial Relations* 24, no. 3 (Fall 1985): 360–81.

28. Harry B. Coen, "Are Employe-Programs Worth While?": Talk given to the Automotive Parts Manufacturers Association, Detroit, January 30, 1952, 1–2, box 17, loose materials, Archives Organization File, 5583/1, Section 1, Kheel Center for Labor-Management Documentation and Archives, Cornell University, Ithaca, NY (hereafter AOF).

29. Peter Drucker, *Concept of the Corporation* (New Brunswick, NJ: Transaction Books, 1985 [1946]), chap. 3. On "dignity" and "status," see 149–53. Quote from 158.

30. See Stephen P. Waring, "Peter Drucker, MBO, and the Corporatist Critique of Scientific Management," in *A Mental Revolution: Scientific Management since Taylor*, ed. Daniel Nelson (Columbus: Ohio State University Press, 1992), 205–36, and Gerard Hanlon, *The Dark Side of Management: A Secret History of Management Theory* (New York: Routledge, 2016), 6.

31. Drucker, *Concept of the Corporation*, 298–99.

32. Barnard, *American Vanguard*, 266–68.

33. For an exception to labor history's tendency to ignore the contest, see Alan Raucher, "Employee Relations at General Motors: The 'My Job Contest,' 1947," *Labor History* 28, no. 2 (Spring 1987): 221–32. A recent discussion of the MJC, albeit one that relies exclusively on secondary sources, is Rick Wartzman, *The End of Loyalty: The Rise and Fall of Good Jobs in America* (New York: Perseus Books, 2017), 43–52. John Barnard notes that skepticism toward the MJC was due to "the loaded term of the contest and the participation of thousands of white-collar employees." See Barnard, *American Vanguard*, 269.

34. The organizers listed the total number of entries as 174,854. See Chester E. Evans and La Verne N. Laseau, *My Job Contest,* Personnel Monograph No. 1 (Washington, D.C.: Personnel Psychology, Inc., 1950), 10.

35. Evans and Laseau, *My Job Contest,* 4.

36. Coen, "Employe-Programs," 4.

37. Barnard, *American Vanguard,* 269. Emphasis in the original.

38. William L. Bird, *A Better Living: Advertising, Media, and the New Vocabulary of Business Leadership, 1935–1955* (Evanston, IL: Northwestern University Press, 1999), 166. For additional discussion of hostility toward the contest among labor leaders and workers, see Jacoby, *Modern Manors,* 245–46. For a brief discussion of some of the critical letters in *The Searchlight,* see Wartzman, *End of Loyalty,* 50–52. For examples of several of the letters, see Ronda Hauben, "The 'New' Labor Relations and the My Job Contest of 1947–48," http://www.ais.org/~ronda/new.papers/articles/qualitycircles1.txt.

39. Evans and Laseau, *My Job Contest,* 4–5; "Plan Book for General Motors Employes: 'My Job and Why I Like It' Contest," box 61, folder: "General Motors," AOF 5583/1, Section 3.

40. Evans and Laseau, *My Job Contest,* 4–9.

41. Evans and Laseau, 8, 99–101.

42. "Plan Book for General Motors Employes," 4.

43. Elaine Tyler May, *Homeward Bound: American Families in the Cold War Era* (New York: Basic Books, 1988), 11.

44. Postcard Reminder No. 4, "Plan Book for General Motors Employes."

45. Coen, "Employe-Programs," 17.

46. "Getting Started . . . 'My Job and Why I Like It' Contest," 2, box 62, folder: "General Motors Corp," AOF 5583/1, Section 3.

47. Coen, "Employe-Programs," 2.

48. According to Evans and Laseau, 12,589 workers included such comments. Evans and Laseau, *My Job Contest,* 36.

49. The other judges were Edgar A. Guest, prominent poet, reporter, and radio host; James E. McCarthy, business mogul and college dean; and George W. Taylor, former vice chairman of the National War Labor Board and professor of industrial relations at University of Pennsylvania's Wharton School. Evans and Laseau, *My Job Contest,* 11–12.

50. Evans and Laseau, 17–18, 33.

51. The forty top prize-winning letters appear in "The Worker Speaks," General Motors Booklet, 1948, General Motors Business Research Archives, Detroit, Michigan. Twenty-five nonwinning letters appear in Appendix B of Evans and Laseau, *My Job Contest,* and another six letters appear in a discussion of the contest coding structure (20–26).

52. Betty Kraft, "The Worker Speaks," 122–23; General Motors Booklet, 1948, General Motors Business Research Archives, Detroit, MI. The booklet containing the top forty prizewinning letters is available in its entirety at https://www.gmheritagecenter.com/gm-heritage-archive/Events/The_Worker_Speaks.html.

53. Bird, *A Better Living*, 166.

54. Entry no. 74–1702, Evans and Laseau, *My Job Contest*, Appendix B, 25–26.

55. Entry no. 02–0017, Evans and Laseau, Appendix B, 6.

56. Entry no. 02–0017.

57. See Raucher, "Employee Relations at General Motors," 221–32.

58. Coen, "Employe-Programs," 7–8.

59. William H. Lane, "Information Racks: A New Effective Method of Communicating with Employes," 5th Annual Conference Public Relations Society of America, Inc., November 25, 1952, box 63, folder 10, 8–9, AOF 5583/1, Section 3.

60. The racks were located in colleges, universities, YMCAs, and other public and private institutions. Coen, "Employe-Programs," 8–9.

61. Lane, "Information Racks," 2, 6–7.

62. Coen, "Employe-Programs," 7; Lane, "Information Racks," 7–8.

63. "The Story of General Motors," 1960 [1948], box 61, folder 2, AOF 5583/1, Section 3; Charles Franklin Kettering and Allen Orth, "American Battle for Abundance," 1947, box 62, folder 3, AOF 5583/1, Section 3, 20–23, 38–39, 50–73.

64. "The Story of General Motors"; Kettering and Orth, "American Battle for Abundance," 20–23, 38–39, 50–73.

65. C. E. Wilson, "The Great Delusion . . . Where Marx Went Wrong," 1947, 5–8, box 61, folder 2, AOF 5583/1, Section 3.

66. Henry J. Taylor, "The Truth about Moscow . . . ," box 18, folder: "General: General Motors Corp, 1952," AOF 5583/1, Section 1.

67. Ordway Tead, *Instincts in Industry: A Study of Working-Class Psychology* (Boston: Houghton Mifflin, 1918), xiv.

68. Evans and Laseau, *My Job Contest*, 8.

69. Figures quoted in "Conference for College and University Educators, Personnel and Industrial Relations, June 16–28, 1948," 9, box 14, file: "Spaulding Tire Company, Inc.: General Motors Corporation Fourth Conference for College and University Educators, box 63, folder 4, AOF 55831, Section 1. Employees whose duties fell under the category of "creative work," such as engineering, tool design, and production planning, were not eligible for the plan's monetary rewards because submitting ideas was defined as part of their duties. The same rule applied to supervisory employees. See C. E. Wilson, President, Foreword, "General Motors Suggestion Plan," 1947, box 13, untitled file, AOF 5583/1, Section 1.

70. Coen, "Employe-Programs," 13.

71. "Conference for College and University Educators."

72. Drucker, *Concept of the Corporation*, chaps. 1–5.

73. Author's name withheld due to archival restrictions. See "Report on Cooperative Research with Universities by Employee Research Section, General Motors Corporation," n.p., box 2, folder: "Dearborn Conference, General Motors, LIMA, Inland Steel," DGR.

74. On the strike, GE's response to it, and its role in shaping the firm's overhaul of its labor relations strategy, see Phillips-Fein, *Invisible Hands*, chap. 5. Efforts by GE to come to terms with its defeat against the union are detailed throughout its internal memoranda in the years that followed but distilled in *Professional Management in General Electric, Book One: General Electric's Growth*, 75–97, box 81, bound volume, manuscript collection 52, Lemuel Boulware Papers, Kislak Center for Special Collections, Rare Books and Manuscripts, University of Pennsylvania, Philadelphia, PA (hereafter LBP).

75. Box 55, folder 1701, n.d., LBP.

76. This synopsis is drawn from "Lemuel R. Boulware—Management Executive," *Monogram*, June–July 1946, box 6, folder 144, LBP.

77. "Lemuel R. Boulware." See also Herbert R. Northrup, *Boulwarism, the Labor Relations Policies of the General Electric Company: Their Implications for Public Policy and Management Action* (Ann Arbor: Bureau of Industrial Relations, Graduate School of Business Administration, University of Michigan, 1965), chap. 4, and Phillips-Fein, *Invisible Hands*, 97–98.

78. Speech, March 1, 1942, box 15, folder 339, LBP.

79. *Professional Management in General Electric*, 75–97.

80. GE's approach to union negotiations during Boulware's tenure is summarized in a 1955 speech by GE chairman of the board Ralph Cordiner. See "Ralph Cordiner's Notes as Source Material for Remarks at the Duquesne Club Dinner—Pittsburgh, PA. Oct. 6, 1955," box 6, folder 119, LBP. On Boulware's career up until his appointment at GE, see "Lemuel R. Boulware." My discussion of GE's labor negotiations during Boulware's tenure is informed by Phillips-Fein, *Invisible Hands*, chap. 5.

81. Phillips-Fein, *Invisible Hands*, 108.

82. Lemuel Boulware, "How to Transmit Ideas to Community Groups," December 1957, box 14, folder 308, LBP.

83. Lemuel Boulware, "Salvation Is Not Free," in Lemuel R. Boulware, *The Truth about Boulwarism: Trying to Do Right Voluntarily* (Washington, D.C.: Bureau of National Affairs, 1969), 164. Boulware first gave this speech at Harvard University in June 1949 and delivered it many times throughout the 1950s. See Thomas W. Evans, *The Education of Ronald Reagan: The General Electric Years and the Untold Story of His Conversion to Conservatism* (New York: Columbia University Press, 2006), 44, 50.

84. Lemuel Boulware to Roy H. Horton, Humble Oil and Refining Company, March 17, 1952, box 57, General Electric Letterbook, Jan 1952–June 1952 (hereafter Letterbook), LBP.

85. Boulware to Horton. Boulware sent numerous letters of this type to business associates throughout the early 1950s, all of which are collected in this and other letterbooks in his archived papers. For a detailed discussion of GE's array of employee magazines, see Evans, *The Education of Ronald Reagan*, 50–53.

86. While I have chosen not to examine motivational films here, it should be noted that GE, like many other corporations, made extensive use of them after World War II. On GE's use of such films, see Heide Solbrig, "Henry Strauss and the Human Relations Film: Social Science Media and Interactivity in the Workplace," *Moving Image* 7, no. 1 (Spring 2007): 27–50. On the use of films at GE and AT&T, see Heide Solbrig, "Film and Function: A History of Industrial Motivation Film" (PhD diss., University of California, San Diego, 2004), chap. 4. On DuPont's use of films in the 1950s, see Anna McCarthy, *The Citizen Machine: Governing by Television in 1950s America* (New York: New Press, 2010), 51–59. On the Alfred P. Sloan Foundation's use of animated economic education films as "Cold War industrial propaganda," see Caroline Jack, "Fun Facts about American Business: Economic Education and Business Propaganda in an Early Cold War Cartoon Series," *Enterprise and Society* 16, no. 3 (September 2015): 491–520.

87. "Employment Relations Policy and Job Description of Vice President in Charge," attachment to letter from C. E. Wilson to Boulware, June 13, 1947, box 8, folder 155, LBP. For a detailed summation of GE's employee relations strategy, see Boulware's eighteen-page letter to Ralph Cordiner, February 10, 1951, box 8, folder 160, LBP.

88. See "Ralph Cordiner's Notes."

89. V. M. Welsh to Lemuel Boulware, January 21, 1952, box 8, folder 166, LBP. For Boulware's arguments about communications, see *Professional Management in General Electric*.

90. "Rough-out" of speech based on Boulware's suggestions from V. M. Welsh to Lemuel Boulware, January 21, 1952: "The Obligation of Advertising Media and Public Relations Man to Promote Economic Education, Moral Re-awakening and Political Sophistication," box 8, folder 166, LBP. Boulware used variations on this language consistently in his correspondence. See Letterbooks, 1952–1959, series XI, LBP.

91. Lemuel Boulware, "How Big Is Our Job?," Personnel Conference, American Management Association, February 17, 1948, Chicago, 5, box 15, folder 354, LBP.

92. "Employee Communications in Connection with 1960 General Electric-Union Negotiations," 8, manuscript collection 532, box 13, folder 163, Herbert R.

Northrup Collection of Boulwarism Research Materials, Kislak Center, University of Pennsylvania, Philadelphia, PA (hereafter HRNC).

93. Lemuel Boulware to Professor W. Roy Buckwalter, Temple University, January 15, 1952, box 57, Letterbook, LBP.

94. Lemuel Boulware to Elmer T. Carlson, Trumbell Electric Department, Plainville, Connecticut, June 5, 1952, box 57, Letterbook, LBP.

95. See Phillips-Fein, *Invisible Hands*, 103.

96. "Should Pay Be Equal Everywhere?," *Commentator*, December 12, 1947, box 70, file: Oct. 15, 1947–Dec. 23, 1955, LBP.

97. *Commentator*, December 19, 1947, and January 23, 1948, box 70, file: Oct. 15, 1947–Dec. 23, 1955, LBP.

98. *Commentator*, May 27, 1949, box 70, file: Oct. 15, 1947–Dec. 23, 1955, LBP.

99. One piece of copy depicts toolmaker Don Ramsey at work and at home with his family. The piece introduced Ramsey as an "Employee . . . Customer [and] Shareowner." *General Electric News*, April 26, 1957, 8. In *The GE News: The Techniques of Employee Communication*, 39, box: "GE Management Guides," Archives, Museum of Science & Innovation, Schenectady, NY.

100. On GE's relocation of many operations to the south beginning in the 1950s, see Evans, *Education of Ronald Reagan*, 70–72, 102–3, and Phillips-Fein, *Invisible Hands*, 89–90, 104.

101. "Rockefeller Speech Echoes Boulwarism," *IUE News*, November 23, 1959, 6, box 72, folder: "Oversize posters, etc.," LBP. On IUE's efforts to counter Boulware's propaganda, see "Boulware in Tears, Crocodile, That Is," *IUE News*, November 28, 1963, box 7, folder 138, LBP. James B. Carey, "The Intent of GE Propaganda," 2, manuscript collection 532, box 13, folder 178, HRNC.

102. AFL-CIO, "Mr. and Mrs. America, All Union Family," n.d., box 32, folder 715, LBP.

103. Jacques Ellul, *Propaganda: The Formation of Men's Attitudes* (New York: Vintage Books, 1973 [1962]).

104. Lemuel Boulware, "How Big Is Our Job?," 6.

105. As Heide Solbrig illustrates, GE employed film to powerful effect in the early 1950s, not least by enlisting the help of industrial filmmaker Henry Strauss. Employing theories from sociology about small group dynamics and his democratic visions of work, Strauss's 1951 industrial motivation film *The Inner Man Steps Out*, Solbrig argues, presented a more dynamic approach to motivation than often used at GE until this time. For this illuminating discussion, see Heidi Solbrig, "Henry Strauss and the Human Relations Film." Also see Solbrig's equally enlightening 2013 film *Man and the Middle Class: The Work and Vision of Henry Strauss*, https://vimeo.com/71693033. On

Boulware's quest to enlist supervisors as "job salesmen," see Phillips-Fein, *Invisible Hands*, esp. 100–103. On managerial efforts to enlist supervisors' support for management, including at GE, see Fones-Wolf, *Selling Free Enterprise*, chap. 3, and Evans, *Education of Ronald Reagan*, chaps. 3 and 10.

106. *Commentator*, July 8, 1949, box 70, bound volume: "*The Commentator*, Oct. 15, 1947–Dec. 23, 1955," LBP.

107. Although Reagan's work for GE was highly significant in the firm's efforts to instill favorable views of the firm among workers, I do not discuss it here because it is detailed at length elsewhere. See Evans, *Education of Ronald Reagan*, esp. chaps. 5–6, and Phillips-Fein, *Invisible Hands*, 110–14.

108. Boulware's job description listed among his responsibilities the "indoctrination and periodic re-indoctrination, and other selling approaches in both personal interviews and the use of appropriate mass selling materials and methods, all aimed at the individual employee accurately knowing and favorably regarding—and being constantly reminded of—the contents of the job package we sincerely feel he ought to want eagerly to 'buy' every day." Quoted in "Employment Relations Policy and Job Description of Vice President in Charge," 2, box 8, folder 155, LBP. Boulware emphasized the importance of "economic education" frequently. Typical is a memo to Cordiner that states, "We will—in order to get the proper effect upon the morale and productivity of our employees—teach economics to, and make economic teachers of, our management at all levels." Lemuel Boulware to Ralph Cordiner, February 10, 1951, box 8, folder 160, LBP.

109. Lemuel Boulware, "How to Transmit Ideas," 5–10.

110. See, for example, Lemuel Boulware to F. R. Brophy, Vice President in Charge of Sales, R. W. Cramer Company, Inc., June 4, 1952, and Carl M. Jacobs, Frost and Jacobs, June 3, 1952, box 57, Letterbook, LBP. This and other letterbooks in box 57 and neighboring boxes contain numerous similar letters.

111. Lemuel Boulware to R. W. Turnbull, commercial vice president of GE's Apparatus Department, January 19, 1952, 1, box 57, Letterbook, LBP.

112. On incentivizing workers through individual self-interest, see Lemuel Boulware, "Why and How General Electric Is Integrating Public and Employee Relations," address to the American Management Association, July 23, 1956, box 16, folder 410, and Lemuel Boulware, "Wages and Economic Growth," address to the National Association of Manufacturers, December 6, 1956, box 16, folder 414, LBP.

113. Lemuel Boulware to C. J. Renner, Harcon Inc., February 22, 1952, box 57, Letterbook, LBP.

114. Lemuel Boulware, "The Responsibility of Management to Make Known to All, the Economic Facts of Life," address to the Economic Club of Detroit, Michigan, October 10, 1949, 6, box 15, folder 368, LBP.

115. See Lemuel Boulware, "Some Observations on the President's Taft-Hartley Message," box 8, folder 170, LBP. The document is undated, but its folder indicates that Boulware wrote it between July and December 1954, and it responds to Eisenhower's "Special Message to the Congress on Labor-Management Relations" on January 11 that year.

116. Lemuel Boulware, "Politics—The Businessmen's Biggest Job in 1958," address before the Annual Meeting of Phoenix Chamber of Commerce, Phoenix, Arizona, May 21, 1958, in *Vital Speeches of the Day*, July 15, 1958, 591, box 17, folder 429, LBP.

117. See "The Crotonville Story," February 1965, 4, box 6, folder 126, LBP.

118. Lemuel Boulware to Dale W. Gordon, Vice President & Treasurer, the O. A. Sutton Corporation, June 27, 1952, 2, box 57, Letterbook, LBP.

119. The merger was announced in a memo of January 3, 1956, by Keith H. Krandell, box 8, folder 177, LBP. On setting wage incentives at the local level, see "To Members of the Advisory Council" (draft), March 12, 1956, box 8, folder 177, LBP, and "Compensation Meeting Notes," May 7, 1956, box 8, folder 178, LBP.

120. "The Crotonville Story," 6–12.

121. Lemuel Boulware, "A Job of Two Magnitudes," December 8, 1959, 12, box 14, folder 312, LBP.

122. GE Corporate Employee Relations Operation, "Idea Starter Package no. 1: Communicating on Profits," 11, box 6, folder 125, LBP.

123. "Plant Panel," box 6, folder 125, LBP.

124. See "Speeches and publications," boxes 20–22, LBP.

125. As Kim Phillips-Fein argues, businessmen's crusade against the New Deal and labor unions was intimately connected to the rise of neoliberal economic theories after the war. See Phillips-Fein, *Invisible Hands*, chap. 2. On the rising influence of neoliberal thought in human resource management in the 1960s, see Sami Itan, *The Ideological Evolution of Human Resource Management: A Critical Look into HRM Research and Practices* (Bingley, U.K.: Emerald Publishing, 2017), 113–36.

126. For discussions of Boulware's influence on Reagan's political ideals, see Evans, *Education of Ronald Reagan*, chaps. 12–13.

CHAPTER 6: THE NEW HUCKSTERS OF COOPERATION

1. Management literature encouraged managers to deploy motivation and morale-boosting and to sell workers on management ideas during the postwar era. See Patricia Genoe McLaren and Albert J. Mills, "A Product of His Time? Exploring the Construct of the Ideal Manager in the Cold War Era," *Journal of Management History* 14, no. 4 (2008): 386–403; Sanford Jacoby, *Modern Manors: Welfare Capitalism since the New Deal* (Princeton, NY: Princeton University Press, 1997); and Howell

John Harris, *The Right to Manage: Industrial Relations Policies of American Business in the 1940s* (Madison: University of Wisconsin Press, 1982), chap. 6.

2. Lew Shalett, proceedings of the Sheldon-Claire Company sales conference, January 4–5, 1954 (hereafter SCSC, 1954), 9, box 30, folder 3, Charles H. Rosenfeld Collection, University of Chicago Special Collections Research Center, Chicago, IL (hereafter CHRC).

3. For figures on sales, see Lew Shalett, proceedings of the Sheldon-Claire Company sales conference, New York, January 31–February 1, 1947 (hereafter SCSC, 1947), 3, box 29, folder 7, CHRC; Shalett, SCSC, 1954, 9–16. Insights into the firm's sales in the late 1950s are partly informed by Jerry Johnson (former tax assessor for Sheldon-Claire), email to author, March 24, 2011, and Lew Shalett to Alex Bruzas, March 26, 1958, box 9, folder: "Sheldon-Claire," 1, CHRC.

4. Sheldon Shalett, interview with the author, June 10, 2008, Mesa, CO.

5. On the increasing role of outside consultants and service providers in management, see Christopher D. McKenna, *The World's Newest Profession: Management Consulting in the Twentieth Century* (New York: Cambridge University Press, 2006). For a discussion of why Chicago became central to management consulting, see chap. 2 in McKenna's book.

6. Jerry Johnson, email to author, March 20, 2011.

7. "Shalett Says Productivity is Key to Prosperity," "Employee Motivation—Management's Worldwide Headache," November 12, 1958, 5–6, box 7, folder 1, series 9, Records of the Sheldon-Claire Company, Archives Center, National Museum of American History, Smithsonian Institution, Washington, D.C. (hereafter RSCC); *They Say*, December 30, 1958, 2, box 6, folder 4, series 11, RSCC; and Lew Shalett, untitled communiqué to salesmen, October 31, 1958, 4, box 25, folder 9, CHRC.

8. Some of Sheldon-Claire's clients may have left such records, but an examination of the situations at those client companies is beyond my scope.

9. As Gerard Hanlon points out, management has always embodied neoliberal ideas. However, it was only in the post–World War II period that these ideals began to be taken up more explicitly and extensively. See Gerard Hanlon, *The Dark Side of Management: A Secret History of Management Theory* (New York: Routledge, 2016).

10. Shalett frequently acknowledged Schenker's role in the firm's success. See, for example, SCSC, 1954, 7–9.

11. Ben Schenker, SCSC, 1947, 49–51. On Johnston's theorization of liberal consensus, see Eric Johnston, *America Unlimited* (Garden City, NY: Doubleday, 1944).

12. Schenker, SCSC, 1947, 49–51.

13. *We Depend on Each Other*, box 1, folder 7, series 1, RSCC.

14. On the accelerating rationalization of work and its alienating effects after the

war, see C. Wright Mills, *White Collar: The American Middle Classes* (1951; repr., New York: Oxford University Press, 1967), esp. chap. 10.

15. Shalett, SCSC, 1947, 9. On management's campaign to redefine the foreman as a member of management in the 1940s, see Harris, *Right to Manage*, 74–89.

16. Sheldon-Claire's assumptions concerning the gender of supervisors are evident in its campaign materials throughout the 1950s, which frequently use "supervisor" interchangeably with "foreman" and emphasize the need to enlist the supervisor as a "salesman."

17. "Confidential Memo to Supervisors concerning Chapter 1 of the Series, '*Produce Better, Live Better*,'" 2, box 1, folder: "*Produce Better, Live Better* (continued) 1948," series 1, RSCC.

18. *Produce Better, Live Better*, box 1, folder: *Produce Better, Live Better*, 1948, series 1, RSCC.

19. "Foreman Opinion Poll," box 5, folder: chapter II of *It's Up to All of Us*: "Overcoming Competition by the Elimination of Waste," 1947, series 1, loose materials, RSCC. In praising one poster, a foreman at Stefco Steel borrowed the phrasing of a campaign poster, capitalizing and underlining his words to emphasize his point, declaring, "We are inclined to notice prices go up, as in [poster] #2 but seldom think the reason for this as in [poster] #4 which may . . . have a great deal to do with Skyrocketing Prices & Waste." It remains unknown whether any foremen filled out a negative response. If so, these polls were evidently either not returned to Sheldon-Claire or were discarded.

20. Schenker, proceedings of the Sheldon-Claire Company sales conference, Chicago, February 17–18, 1950 (hereafter SCSC, 1950), 208, box 30, folder 1, CHRC; Shalett, SCSC, 1950, 211.

21. Schenker, SCSC, 1950, 210, CHRC.

22. For Bugbee's speeches, see proceedings of the Sheldon-Claire Company sales conference, Chicago, April 4–5, 1952 (hereafter SCSC, 1952), 110–12, box 30, folder 2, CHRC; proceedings of the Sheldon-Claire Company sales conference, Chicago, June 14, 1956 (hereafter SCSC, 1956), 225–30, box 30, folder 5, CHRC.

23. The negative responses to *They Say* among some managers owing to its female author were described by salesman Milton Prager at Sheldon-Claire's 1956 sales conference. Milton Prager, SCSC, 1956, 229.

24. David Bernstein, email to the author, July 22, 2012.

25. Helen Bugbee, "Abundance versus Scarcity," *Freeman*, June 1961, 10–13; "Good Sense Makes Good Business," *Freeman*, November 1969, 692–97; "We Can't Protect Prosperity," *Humanist* (January 1, 1979), 50; and "Industry's Annual Disemployment Factor," *Modern Age*, Fall 1962, 413–16.

26. Shalett, SCSC, 1947, 3; Shalett, SCSC, 1954, 16.

27. As Timothy Spears notes, as foremost agents in a "face-to-face economy," salesmen and the work that they performed shaped business culture and market relations in innumerable ways in the nineteenth and early twentieth centuries. Timothy Spears, *100 Years on the Road: The Traveling Salesman in American Culture* (New Haven, CT: Yale University Press, 1995), xii.

28. *Pittsburgh Press*, July 17, 1955, section 3, 10.

29. Insights on salesmen's backgrounds and the firm's sales bonus practices supplied by David Bernstein, telephone interview with author, April 23, 2011. Further information on sales bonus practices provided by Jerry Johnson, email to author, March 24, 2011.

30. Bernstein, interview.

31. See, for example, Walter A. Friedman, *Birth of a Salesman: The Transformation of Selling in America* (Cambridge, MA: Harvard University Press, 2004).

32. My thanks to David Bernstein and Sheldon Shalett for their helpful insights into how they regarded the campaigns, the company, and Lew Shalett's ideas, as well as their perspectives on how fellow salesmen perceived the same. Shalett, interview; Bernstein, interview.

33. Bernstein, interview.

34. At the 1947 conference Shalett told the sales force that the poster business was "about 30,000 years old. It was then that one of our ancestors—an ape man—designed the first poster. It was a message in hieroglyphics—it was carved in stone." Sheldon-Claire's salesmen, he declared, were the descendants of this ancient communications form. By bringing it to the nation's workplaces, he added, they would advance "civilization." Shalett, SCSC, 1947, 2.

35. Rosenfeld, SCSC, 1950, 84.

36. See SCSC, 1947, 91–120.

37. Alvin Dodd, SCSC, 1947, 95.

38. Dodd, SCSC, 1947, 93.

39. Louis Waldman, "America's Destiny: Labor-Management Cooperation or Class Struggle," SCSC, 1956, 173, 175.

40. Tom Hunt, SCSC, 1947, 59.

41. Ralph Rogers, proceedings of the Sheldon-Claire Company sales conference, January 27–29, 1949 (hereafter SCSC, 1949), 129, box 29, folder 10, CHRC; Bernstein, interview.

42. For an excellent account of changes in the salesman's work in the postwar era, see Jeremy A. Greene, "Attention to 'Details': Etiquette and the Pharmaceutical Salesman in Postwar America," *Social Studies of Science* 34, no. 2 (April 2004): 271–92.

43. Bernstein, interview.

44. Mills, *White Collar*, 181.

45. Bernstein, interview; Shalett, interview.

46. This summary is drawn from Rosenfeld's talks at Sheldon-Claire's annual sales conferences and my interviews with Sheldon Shalett and David Bernstein. Shalett, interview; Bernstein, interview.

47. Rogers, proceedings of the Sheldon-Claire Company sales conference," 1948 (hereafter SCSC, 1948), 133, 161–62, box 29, folder 9, CHRC.

48. Donald J. McIntosh, Vice President, Manufacturing, McIntosh Inc., Detroit, to Shalett, n.d., series 7, box 4, folder 17: "World-Wide Endorsements and Acknowledgements of Sheldon-Claire Services" (hereafter WWE), RSCC.

49. Shalett, interview with author, June 11, 2008, Mesa, CO; Bernstein, interview.

50. Rogers, SCSC, 1948, 177–79.

51. The three letters are J. M. Bennett and J. Frank Jensen, President and Rec. Secretary of the United Brotherhood of Carpenters and Joiners of America to members of Local Union no. 2195, May 27, 1955; E. S. Benjamin, Cannery Warehousemen, Food Processors, Drivers and Helpers, Local Union no. 670, n.d.; and C. F. Burt, Secretary-Treasury, Cannery Warehousemen, Food Processors, Drivers and Helpers, Local Union no. 656, n.d., all WWE, RSCC.

52. C. F. Burt, Secretary-Treasurer, Local Union 656, to Shalett, July 14, 1954, with enclosed letter, both in WWE, RSCC.

53. E. S. Benjamin, Secretary of Cannery Local 670 of the Cannery Workers Union in Salem, Oregon, to the local's two thousand members in an undated letter in 1954, WWE, RSCC.

54. The secretary of Local 656, quoted above, also sent a copy of his letter to Lew Shalett and invited him to use it in Sheldon-Claire's literature. Burt to Shalett, letter.

55. Lubin, SCSC, 1949, 77

56. Eley, SCSC, 1949, 227–28; Fred Germain Jr., Executive Secretary, Middletown Chamber of Commerce, Middletown, New York, to Mr. Myron C. Alting, Miss Swank, Inc., Middletown, New York, February 21, 1949, WWE, RSCC.

57. Prager, "Merchandising through the Supervisor," SCSC, 1949, 190–93.

58. Prager, SCSC, 1952, 53–54.

59. Jackson, SCSC, 1949, 223–26.

60. Mihailoff, SCSC, 1949, 80–91.

61. Joe G. Fleniken, Plant Manager, B & C Metal Stamping Company, to Shalett, n.d., WWE, RSCC.

62. On the proliferation of this discourse, see Harris, *Right to Manage*, chaps. 5–6.

63. Quote and information on operating costs provided in email from Jerry Johnson to author, March 24, 2011. Johnson states that Shalett "milked the profits

down any way he could to avoid double taxation," a practice that was standard for ad agencies of Sheldon-Claire's size at the time. Johnson, email to author, June 12, 2012.

64. Efforts to use UNESCO's humanitarian ambitions as an opportunity to promote Western values during the 1950s is well documented, though mostly with regard to artistic exchanges. See, for example, Michael L. Krenn, *Fall-Out Shelters for the Human Spirit: American Art and the Cold War* (Chapel Hill: University of North Carolina Press, 2005), chaps. 1 and 2.

65. Jerry Johnson, email to author, March 24, 2011.

66. "Employee Motivation Comes of Age," n.p., 1959, box 6, folder: Employee Understanding, series 11, RSCC.

67. Charles S. Maier, "The Politics of Productivity: Foundations of American International Economic Policy after World War II," *International Organization* 31, no. 4 (1977): 607–32.

68. For an overview of literature on the global proliferation of American products and influence in the postwar era, see the introduction to Neil Campbell and Alasdair Kean, *American Cultural Studies: An Introduction to American Culture* (London: Routledge, 2011).

69. For an account of the influence of Cold War ideology and, especially, the Marshall Plan on management's campaign to restrain labor union power in Europe, see Anthony Carew, *Labour under the Marshall Plan: The Politics of Productivity and the Marketing of Management Science* (Manchester, U.K.: Manchester University Press, 1987).

70. David Ellwood, "'You Too Can Be Like Us': Selling the Marshall Plan—American Propaganda during the European Recovery Program," *History Today* 48 (October 1998): 33–39, quoted in *Images of the Marshall Plan in Europe: Films, Photographs, Exhibits, Posters*, ed. Gunter Bischof and Dieter Stifel (Innsbruck, Austria: StudienVerlag, 2009), 9; Carew, *Labour under the Marshall Plan*, chap. 1.

71. David W. Ellwood, *Rebuilding Europe: Western Europe, America and Postwar Reconstruction* (New York: Routledge, 2013), 162.

72. De Grazia places the number of films at approximately two hundred. See Victoria de Grazia, *Irresistible Empire: America's Advance through Twentieth-Century Europe* (Cambridge, MA: Belknap Press of Harvard University Press, 2005), 348. Another study puts the number at 250. See Evan S. Noble, "Marshall Plan Films and Americanization" (master's thesis, Virginia Polytechnic Institute and State University, 2006), ii.

73. De Grazia, *Irresistible Empire*, 348; Noble, "Marshall Plan Films," 33–38.

74. De Grazia, *Irresistible Empire*; Richard Kuisel, *Seducing the French: The Dilemma of Americanization* (Berkeley: University of California Press, 1997). See also Marie-Laure Djelic, *Exporting the American Model: The Postwar Transformation of European Business* (Oxford: Oxford University Press, 2001).

75. On the role of the ECA in advancing management-coordinated anticommunist and antiradical agendas, see Michael J. Hogan, *The Marshall Plan: America, Britain, and the Reconstruction of Western Europe, 1947–1952* (Cambridge: Cambridge University Press, 1987), chaps. 4 and 5, and Carew, *Labour under the Marshall Plan*, chap. 5. On the selective adoption of American management practices, see Jonathan Zeitlin and Gary Herrigel, eds., *Americanization and Its Limits: Reworking US Technology and Management in Post-War Europe and Japan* (Oxford: Oxford University Press, 2000).

76. For an in-depth account of these developments, see Djelic, *Exporting the American Model.*

77. Carew, *Labour under the Marshall Plan*, 223. On the consequences of the "managerial revolution," see chap. 13.

78. "Employee Motivation Comes of Age."

79. Nick Tatarinov, SCSC, 1956, 156–58.

80. Jack Aptaker, SCSC, 1956, 159–61.

81. There are approximately thirty such letters in Sheldon-Claire's documentation from the 1950s. These clients include companies in England, Scotland, Wales, France, Switzerland, Belgium, and Canada. See WWE, RSCC.

82. A. Nurton to Sheldon-Claire, April 2, 1957, WWE, RSCC.

83. N. Alzan, Barking Brassware Co. Limited to J. D. Aptaker, Sheldon-Claire Co., September 11, 1956, WWE, RSCC.

84. F. Hill, Works Director, Durie & Miller Ltd., Haslingden, Rosendale, Lancashire, to Sheldon-Claire (Great Britain) Ltd., January 15, 1959, WWE, RSCC.

85. Société Anonyme de L'union des Papeteries to Canadian Sheldon-Claire Limited, April 18, 1956; R Vecchi, Directeur, ABG (Sociétés Ariès, La Bougie B.G. & S.F.E.D.R. Réunies), to Canadian Sheldon-Claire Ltd., November 28, 1955; Monsieur Boutin, Directeur Adjoint de la Maison Brequet, Compagnie Industrielle des Piles Électroniques, Cipel to Sheldon-Claire, June 4, 1954. All in WWE, RSCC.

86. "Employee Motivation Comes of Age."

87. "Interview—Phil Bowman-Lew Shalett," November 1958, box 7, folder 1, SC Scrapbook, series 9, RSCC.

88. On the increasing openness between the United States and the Soviet Union after Stalin's death, see Walter L. Hixson, *Parting the Curtain: Propaganda, Culture, and the Cold War, 1945–1961* (New York: St. Martin's Griffin, 1998), chaps. 4–6; Yale Richmond, *Cultural Exchange and the Cold War: Raising the Iron Curtain* (University Park: Pennsylvania State University Press, 2003); and Penny M. Von Eschen, *Satchmo Blows Up the World: Jazz Ambassadors Play the Cold War* (Cambridge, MA: Harvard University Press, 2004).

89. For Shalett's account of how the trip materialized, see "Interview—Phil Bowman-Lew Shalett," 2. Wanda Shalett also offered recollections of the trip in my

interview with her. Wanda Shalett, interview with the author, September 9, 2003, Boca Raton, FL.

90. For Shalett's account of his factory tours and his comments about the efforts of Agitational Propaganda guides to misrepresent workers' responses to his questions, see "World Spotlight 1958," box 5, series 14, RSCC. The reference to "sugarcoating" is quoted from my interview with Wanda Shalett.

91. Shalett, "Weekly Bulletin to Sheldon-Claire clients in the U.S., Canada, the UK, and Europe," November 28, 1958, 3–4, 6, box 7, folder 1, series 9, RSCC.

92. Shalett, "Employee Motivation," 5–6, RSCC.

93. *They Say*, December 30, 1958.

94. Interview with Alex Dreier, WNBQ, Chicago, November 7, 1958, box 7, folder 1, series 9, RSCC.

95. Shalett, "Employee Motivation," 5–6.

96. For the transcript of the introduction to the interview, see Attitudes Incorporated, "Introduction to Sheldon-Claire Kinescope," 2, November 1958, box 6, folder: Kinescope Info, series 11, RSCC. For a video of the interview, see World Spotlight, 1958, box 5, series 14, RSCC.

97. "Interview—Phil Bowman-Lew Shalett."

98. Shalett, unpaginated speech given at the Partners in Prosperity Award Luncheon, November 12, 1958, Scrapbook, series 9, box 7, folder 3, RSCC.

99. On the U.S. missile programs of the 1950s and 1960s, see Mark L. Morgan and Mark A. Berhow, *Rings of Super Steel: Air Defenses of the United States Army, 1950–1979* (Bodega Bay, CA: Hole in the Head Press, 2002). My thanks to Jacqueline McGlade for her helpful insights into Chicago's role in the U.S. missile system in the 1950s at the Business History Conference in March 2013.

100. Carl T. Curtis, speech given at the Partners in Prosperity Award Luncheon, November 12, 1958, n.p., series 9, box 7, folder 1, RSCC.

101. Elaine Tyler May, *Homeward Bound: American Families in the Cold War Era* (New York: Basic Books, 1988).

102. *Chicago Daily Tribune*, Monday, February 9, 1959, part 4, 6, Scrapbook, box 6, series 1, RSCC.

103. Sheldon-Claire Co., *They Say*, December 30, 1958. The quotes are from pages 1 and 4.

104. Shalett communiqué vol. 1649, November 5, 1958, 1, 2, and 6, box 25, folder 9, CHRC.

105. Shalett communiqué vol. 1697, January 22, 1959, 1, 6, 7–8, box 25, folder 9, CHRC.

106. "Sales Presentation: How and Why the Business Evolved into Employee Motivation Campaign," 3, box 5, folder: *This is America*, series 10, RSCC.

107. Harvey Swados, "The Myth of the Happy Worker," in Swados, *On the Line, with an Introduction by Nelson Lichtenstein* (Urbana: University of Illinois Press, 1990 [1957]), 243.

EPILOGUE: MOTIVATION IN AN AGE OF DIMINISHING REWARDS

1. On the era's strikes, see Jeremy Brecher, *Strike!*, revised, expanded, and updated ed. (Oakland, CA: PM Press, 2014 [1972]), chap. 7, and Jefferson Cowie, *Stayin' Alive: The 1970s and the Last Days of the Working Class* (New York: New Press, 2010), esp. chap. 1.

2. This account of events at Lordstown is drawn from Cowie, *Stayin' Alive*, 44–49. Quote from 45.

3. Special Task Force to the Secretary of Health, Education and Welfare, *Work in America* (Cambridge, MA: MIT Press, 1973), xv, xvi.

4. Peter F. Drucker, *The Practice of Management* (New York: Collins, 1993 [1954]), see esp. chap. 23, "Motivating to Peak Performance." Drucker's theories were largely in keeping with Taylor's. See Stephen P. Waring, "Peter Drucker, MBO, and the Corporatist Critique of Scientific Management," in *A Mental Revolution: Scientific Management since Taylor*, ed. Daniel Nelson (Columbus: Ohio State University Press, 1992), 205–36.

5. Douglas McGregor, *The Human Side of Enterprise*, annotated ed. updated and with new commentary by Joel Cutcher-Gershenfeld (New York: McGraw-Hill, 2006 [1960]), 65.

6. Frederick Herzberg, Bernard Mausner, and Barbara Bloch Snyderman, *The Motivation to Work* (New Brunswick: Transaction Publishers, 2010 [1959]), and Frederick Herzberg, *Work and the Nature of Man* (New York: Thomas Y. Crowell, 1966), chap. 6.

7. David Harvey, *The Condition of Postmodernity: An Enquiry into the Origins of Cultural Change* (Cambridge, MA: Blackwell Publishers, 1990), chaps. 8 and 9.

8. Frederick Herzberg quoted in Stephen P. Waring, *Taylorism Transformed: Scientific Management since 1945* (Chapel Hill: University of North Carolina Press, 1991), 136. For a discussion of developments in motivational theory during this time, see Waring, chap. 6, and Catherine Casey, *Work, Self and Society: After Industrialism* (New York: Routledge, 1995), 59–61.

9. Harry Braverman, *Labor and Monopoly Capital: The Degradation of Work in the Twentieth Century*, 25th anniversary ed. (New York: Monthly Review Press, 1998 [1974]), app. 2, "The Degradation of Work in the Twentieth Century," 317, 26. On Braverman's anticipation of quality work circles, see the new introduction by John Bellamy Foster, xx.

10. Daniel Bell, "The Study of Man: Adjusting Men to Machines," *Commentary*, January 1947, 2, 86.

11. The literature on Nixon's appeals to working-class alienation is too vast to cite, but for illuminating insight, see Michael Kazin, *The Populist Persuasion: An American History* (New York: Basic, 1995), and Jefferson Cowie, *Stayin' Alive*.

12. See Waring, *Taylorism Transformed*, 142–55. For another noted example of the failure of work enrichment schemes, see Joanne B. Ciulla's discussion of the ill-fated experiment at the Bolivar, Tennessee, plant of Harman Automotive, beginning in the mid-1970s, in *The Working Life: The Promise and Betrayal of Modern Work (New York: Three Rivers Press, 2000)*, 119–22.

13. On recent managerial uses of employee wellness ideology, see Carl Cederström and Andre Spicer, *The Wellness Syndrome* (Malden, MA: Polity Press, 2015), and Davies, *The Happiness Industry: How the Government and Big Business Sold Us Well-Being* (London: Verso 2015). On self-tracking, see Deborah Lupton, *The Quantified Self* (Malden, MA: Polity Press, 2016), and Phoebe V. Moore, *The Quantified Self in Precarity: Work, Technology and What Counts* (New York: Routledge, 2019).

14. See John LaRosa, "$11 Billion Self-Improvement Market is Growing," October 16, 2019, https://www.marketdataenterprises.com/11-billion-self-improvement-market-is-growing-by-john-larosa/.

15. The data illustrating the decline of economic mobility in the United States are too vast to cite, but representative studies include Raj Chetty, David Grusky, Maximilian Hell, Nathaniel Hendren, Robert Manduca, and Jimmy Narang, "The Fading American Dream: Trends in Absolute Income Mobility since 1940," *Science* 356, no. 6336 (April 28, 2017): 198–406, and Michael Hout, "Americans' Occupational Status Reflects the Status of Both of Their Parents," *Proceedings of the National Academy of Sciences of the United States of America* 115, no. 38 (September 18, 2018): 9527–32.

16. See Thomas Frank, *One Market under God: Extreme Capitalism, Market Populism, and the End of Economic Democracy* (New York: Anchor Books, 2001).

17. Nigel Thrift, "Making Sense: An Afterword," in *Magic, Culture and the New Economy*, ed. Orvar Löfgren and Robert Willim (New York: Berg, 2005), 133–34.

18. For an account of the ideological work performed by this literature, see Staffan Furusten, *Popular Management Books: How They Are Made and What They Mean for Organizations* (New York: Routledge, 1999).

19. Arlie Russell Hochschild, *The Time Bind: When Work Becomes Home and Home Becomes Work* (New York: Henry Holt, 2000).

20. See Frank, *One Market under God*, 171.

21. Miya Tokumitsu, *Do What You Love: And Other Lies About Success and Happiness* (New York: Regan Arts, 2015), 42.

22. See https://www.thesecret.tv.

23. Hicks appeared extensively in the original version of the film, along with her coauthor and husband, Jerry Hicks. The pair's contributions were subsequently cut following a legal dispute, but Hicks continues to praise the film. On the success of *The Secret* and insight into how the film draws on success literature of the early twentieth century, see Kelefa Sanneh, "Power Lines: What's Behind Rhonda Byrne's Spiritual Empire?," *New Yorker*, September 13, 2010, and Allen Salkin, "Shaking Riches out of the Cosmos," *New York Times*, February 25, 2007.

24. See "Abraham Hicks the 6 million jews question and Jesus attract that?," August 21, 2011 https://youtube.com/watch?v=Uckk2dbbdEo.

25. See Barbara Ehrenreich, *Bright-Sided: How Positive Thinking Is Undermining America* (New York: Picador, 2009), chapter 4 for further discussion of the rise of the motivational industry.

26. Salkin, "Shaking Riches."

27. For example, see "Big Names Drop in to Portland for 'Get Motivated' Seminar," March 14, 2011, https://www.youtube.com/watch?v=qFN9RbZlE7I.

28. For a critique of Anshutz's support for right-wing cultural causes and of FFBL's billboards, see Alison Kafer, *Feminist, Queer, Crip* (Bloomington: Indiana University Press, 2013), chap. 4.

29. See https://www.passiton.com/inspirational-sayings-billboards/26-integrity.

30. See Chetty et al., "Fading American Dream," and Hout, "Americans' Occupational Status."

31. For insights into how play has been appropriated and put to use to aid productivity, see Emmanuelle Savignac, *The Gamification of Work: Uses of Games in Workplaces* (Hoboken, NJ: John Wiley & Sons, 2017). For analyses of specific types of games, including murder parties, simulation, and role-playing games, and the use of board games and Lego blocks, see chap. 2.

32. Stephen C. Lundin, Harry Paul, and John Christensen, with an introduction by Ken Blanchard, *Fish! Philosophy: A Proven Way to Boost Morale and Improve Results* (London: Hodder, 2014).

33. A preview of the Fish! Philosophy training video can be viewed on YouTube at https://www.youtube.com/watch?v=_AAQT6ifGys&t=23s.

34. Lundin, Paul, and Christensen, *Fish! Philosophy*, 21.

35. Lundin, Paul, and Christensen, 14–84.

36. Fishmonger quoted in N. B. Dubey, *Office Management: Developing Skills for Smooth Functioning* (New Delhi: Global India Publications, 2009), 272.

37. Fish! Philosophy, "Brand Ambassador for The FISH! Philosophy/Keynote Speaker & Facilitator: Deena Ebbert," September 15, 2017, https://www.youtube.com/watch?v=481rRuBXij4.

38. Kevin A. Carson, *Organization Theory: A Libertarian Perspective* (n.p.:

BookSurge, 2008), esp. chap. 8. Carson offers an illuminating discussion of the ways in which *Fish! Philosophy* aids managerial efforts to conceal power relations and define positive attitudes as mandatory. See 269–83.

39. See http://goldfish-consulting.co.za/our-story.

40. Kavitha Desai and Jyothi Magodu Nagaraju, "Gamification—An Innovative HRM Practice @ Workplace," *International Journal of Scientific Research and Review* 7, no. 7 (May 2018): 94.

41. See https://www.mordorintelligence.com/industry-reports/gamification-market.

42. Gabe Zichermann, *The Gamification Revolution: How Leaders Leverage Game Mechanics to Crush the Competition* (New York: McGraw Hill, 2013), 3.

43. Yu-kai Chou, "A Framework on Actionable Gamification," undated talk at Google, uploaded April 20, 2016, https://www.youtube.com/watch?v=u4acIpWrnzo&t=3s.

44. Yu-kai Chou, "The Beginner's Guide to Gamification: Introduction by Yu-kai Chou (1 of 90)," 2012, https://www.youtube.com/watch?v=Cknd7564PVU.

45. See Savignac, *Gamification of Work*; Jennifer Dewinter, Carly A. Kocurek, and Randall Nichols, "Taylorism 2.0: Gamification, Scientific Management and the Capitalist Appropriation of Play," *Journal of Gaming and Virtual Worlds* 6, no. 2 (June 2014): 109–27; and Mathias Fuchs, "Gamification as Twenty-First-Century Ideology," *Journal of Gaming and Virtual Worlds* 6, no. 2 (June 2014): 143–57.

46. Fuchs, "Gamification," 153.

47. On the ways in which managerial exploitation of "fun" in the workplace can be counteractive, see Chris Baldry and Jerry Hallier, "Welcome to the House of Fun: Work Space and Social Identity," *Economic and Industrial Democracy* 31, no. 1 (December 2010): 150–72.

48. See Lupton, *Quantified Self*, and Moore, *Quantified Self in Precarity*.

49. Moore, *Quantified Self in Precarity*, 8–9.

50. Moore, 3. See also Phoebe Moore and Lukasz Piwek, "Regulating Wellbeing in the Brave New Quantified Workplace," *Employee Relations* 39, no. 3 (April 2017): 309.

51. Lupton, *Quantified Self*, 86.

52. Amazon Technologies, Inc. Patent US0099881276, January 30, 2018, https://pdfpiw.uspto.gov/.piw?PageNum=0&docid=09881276&IDKey=&HomeUrl=%2F.

53. See Ceylan Yeginsu, "If Workers Slack Off, the Wristband Will Know (and Amazon Has a Patent for It)," *New York Times*, February 1, 2018, and Olivia Solo, "Amazon Patents Wristband That Tracks Warehouse Workers' Movements," *Guardian*, February 1, 2018.

54. Jodi Kantor and David Streitfeld, "Inside Amazon: Wrestling Big Ideas in a Bruising Workplace," *New York Times*, August 15, 2015.

55. In reality, Americans have less cause to believe in the promises of the motivational ideal than at any time since World War II. See Hugh Gusterson and Catherine Besteman, eds., *The Insecure American: How We Got Here and What We Should Do about It* (Berkeley: University of California Press, 2010), introduction.

56. Glenn Plaskin, "The 1990 *Playboy* Interview with Donald Trump," *Playboy*, March 1, 1990, https://www.playboy.com/read/playboy-interview-donald-trump-1990.

57. Colin Campbell, "Donald Trump: 'My Father Gave Me a Small Loan of a Million Dollars,'" *Business Insider*, October 26, 2015, https://www.businessinsider.com/donald-trump-small-million-dollar-loan. Trump reiterated his claim in 2016. See Glenn Kessler, "Trump's False Claim He Built His Empire with a 'Small Loan' from His Father," *Washington Post*, March 3, 2016, https://www.washingtonpost.com/news/fact-checker/wp/2016/03/03/trumps-false-claim-he-built-his-empire-with-a-small-loan-from-his-father/?utm_term=.161144c51f67.

58. David Barstow, Susanne Craig, and Russ Buettner, "Trump Engaged in Suspect Tax Schemes as He Reaped Riches from His Father," *New York Times*, October 2, 2018.

59. "Donald Trump's Ghostwriter Tells All," Jane Mayer, *New Yorker*, July 25, 2016.

60. Libby Nelson, "Trump University, Explained, *Vox*, February 26, 2016.

61. Nelson, "Trump University." See also John Cassidy, "Trump University: It's Worse Than You Think," *New Yorker*, June 2, 2016. Trump's very name is rooted in the history of duplicitous motivational salesmanship. Earliest uses of the word "trump" were to "fabricate," "deceive," and "dominate"—the tools of the trade for motivational salesmen ever since Seth Seiders established the first nationwide motivational publicity business.

INDEX